D0526315

By the same author

Non-Fiction
Who Dares Wins: The Story of the SAS 1950–1982
This is the SAS: A pictorial history of
  the Special Air Service Regiment
Ten Years of Terrorism
  (co-author with Sir Robert Mark and others)
March or Die: France and the Foreign Legion

Fiction
Freefall Factor

TONY GERAGHTY

The Bullet-Catchers

Bodyguards and the World of Close Protection

GRAFTON BOOKS

A Division of the Collins Publishing Group

LONDON GLASGOW
TORONTO SYDNEY AUCKLAND

Grafton Books
A Division of the Collins Publishing Group
8 Grafton Street, London W1X 3LA

Published in paperback by Grafton Books 1989

First published in Great Britain by
Grafton Books 1988

A CIP catalogue record for this book is
available from the British Library

ISBN 0-586-20622-1

Printed and bound in Great Britain by
Collins, Glasgow

Set in Sabon

Contents

AUTHOR'S PREFACE

This work is an attempt – the first by a professional author – to analyse the craft of the bodyguard as well as to relate his/her history as a recent, modern fact of life. It is a necessary if regrettable sequel to studies of irregular warfare and terrorism such as my earlier book *Who Dares Wins*. The reason for writing it is as grim as it is simple. From being 'out there' in contested areas of the Third World before 1968, threats of sudden death for political reasons are now 'in here' as part of the furniture of Western society.

For the British, who liked to think they could get along without guns, the change has been particularly hard. One member of the royal family (Lord Mountbatten) and three Westminster MPs have been assassinated since 1979 and many more have had lucky escapes. Worse, many other professions have shared that experience. When a UK judge conceals a Derringer pistol in the sleeve of his judicial robe, the bodyguard has truly come into his own.

There are many books devoted to assassins, but none which are primarily concerned, as this is, with those who try to intercept their attacks. They are the men and women who set off for work each day in the conscious knowledge that, if they do their job properly, they might well die violently before it is time to go home. Helen Haarsma, a member of the South Australian counter-terrorist team who dressed prettily for the Queen's tour in 1986 and carried a revolver in her handbag, reflected: 'It's a terrific job. Only when you get home and think about the things that could have gone wrong does it all hit you.'

Usually, the work is boring: either that, or disastrous. In

1984 two US State Department special agents assigned as bodyguards to a visiting Saudi Minister, killed some waiting time in a hamburger bar. As they walked into the place, a gust of wind lifted their coats to reveal that they were heavily armed. A day or so before an armed lunatic had massacred hamburger lovers at a similar establishment. While the agents munched on, other diners scattered and fled. Still puzzled by this, the two moved on to the airport where their leader, a bulky Irish-American, braced himself to greet the Saudi Prince and guarantee his safety on behalf of Uncle Sam.

As the Prince descended the aircraft steps the protection team leader's belt broke under the weight of handcuffs, firearms, spare ammunition, radio, riot gas and hamburger. The Prince watched with interest as the hunched figure of the guard, clutching his trousers, lurched away towards the VIP limousine. At that moment a British officer supplied by the KMS organisation in London* glided discreetly past and took charge. As a Royal Military Police bodyguard told the author after protecting the Prince of Wales in Germany, 'You cannot win in close protection. You "lose your name" if you lose the Man. If you open fire at the wrong moment . . . you also lose your name. If necessary, we will step in front of a bullet. So why do normally sane guys volunteer for a no-hope game like this?'

This book tries to answer the question. It is dedicated to the bodyguards who call themselves 'bullet-catchers' and risk death from an assassination meant for someone else, or from boredom, or the common cold contracted while waiting for the bullet. It is also intended to be more than a study of stoic courage. It inquires into an increasingly political profession. The people who require protection are almost invariably those who exercise great power or

---

* Kini Mini Services is a private company named after the Swahili phrase used to describe a snake moving sinuously through long grass.

influence over other people. Who, then, is to challenge their mystique – and mystique is the central title deed to authority – even in their own interests? Who dares push a head of state to the ground to keep him (or her) out of harm's way? Who would breach the protocol that decrees no commoner should take the initiative in even touching a royal?

As the tactics of terrorism become more refined in the 1980s, moving away from turbulence on the streets or random bombing, towards selective assassination of democracy's leaders, so the bodyguard emerges as a person of political significance himself. No longer is he a mere shadow. If he guards a prime minister for long he will enjoy a unique insight into the manipulation of power and how many beans make five. He will learn that even in democracies, power is increasingly expressed through the barrel of a gun. He might then blossom as a political leader himself, like a former guardian of South Africa's Prime Minister, John Vorster. In 1973 that ex-bodyguard, named Eugene Terre-Blanche, combined with six others to form a fast-growing neo-Nazi organisation known as the Afrikaner Resistance Movement.

Of course, not every bodyguard (nor even a significant minority of the professionals in a self-sacrificing trade) is a putative fascist, but in spite of that the new model bodyguard deserves to be watched because of what he symbolises, in an age of royal prerogatives, as well as what he is. He does not function in isolation from the principal he protects or the potential threat, the bullet that he must catch on behalf of his master. For those reasons, this study begins with an examination of how it is to be the victim of an assassination attempt, from the target's point of view. The target in question is a distinguished one: Queen Victoria, many of whose personal observations are published here for the first time in a war study. The book concludes with an extensive analysis of assassins and their ways, linked to a modern, specially-compiled assassination index. The bodyguard, appropriately, is to be found between the two.

INTRODUCTION

We live in a century in which around a hundred million people have died in over a hundred wars, while another hundred million have been murdered by their own governments: an epoch in which electronic images of personal violence are as common as paintings of the Road to Calvary were, once upon a time. It is as if the new 'religion' of Sartre – that man is bound by a bond of mutual fear – has replaced a Christian theory based upon redemption and mutual love. Rambo has supplanted the figure on the Crucifix, while the Prime Minister switches cars to avoid being murdered on her way to worship with the Queen in a remote Scottish church.

An important part of the change towards a society threatened by amoral and often random violence has been a growth in the demand for bodyguards. The way we run our society (as an alternative to anarchy or despotism) still requires Figures of Authority, some of them elected and some born to power and influence.

Their charisma has always tempted the envious, the deprived and the fearful. Indeed, the sacrifice of the slain god runs deep in human culture – witness the volumes of evidence compiled by Frazer in *The Golden Bough* – while the healing, magical powers of the royal touch still find public expression in the Maundy money distributed by the British monarch. In the contemporary world the sacrificial victim is as likely to be John Lennon as President Kennedy, but who is to say which of them had more personal, popular power?

The age of rationalism in governing human affairs (running from, say, the last English witchcraft trial in 1731 to the first widespread acceptance of mind-blowing psychedelic drugs in the 1960s) would reject human, ritual sacrifice as superstitious nonsense. Culturally speaking, this concept was safely padlocked inside a large toy box and deposited in an unused anthropological nursery.

But as the age of literacy was elbowed aside by the age of electronics, so the box of violent amusements was reopened by a strange alliance combining such revolutionaries as Sartre, Marcuse and Fanon with the entrepreneurs who sell Star Wars fantasies. Unfortunately, not everyone could distinguish between the reality of a car bomb in Beirut, a ticket to the Ayatollah's paradise, and Hollywood.

The instinct to deny that assassination, or its near cousin, abduction, can really happen here is another of the themes of this book, as a counterpoint to the growing importance of the bodyguard. The armed guardian in our society – when we still like to think that human affairs are conducted without violence – is required to be present but not seen. Certainly he must not start to take decisions about the style to be adopted, publicly or privately, by the figure of authority he is protecting. If the guardian is allowed to dictate the style in any situation, at any time, he will surely become a person of political importance in his own right rather than a modern equivalent of the postilion. Better, perhaps, to take refuge in fatalism than suffer the shrinking public identity that goes with total security. Thus, the Prince of Wales in Madrid, 1987: 'If your name is on the bullet there is nothing you can do.'

But there is a point – and it seems to have been reached in Britain – where the risk to the figure of authority is such that government decrees that enhanced protection will be provided whether it is requested or not. Indeed the importance of beating the assassin has now been embodied in preparations (only on a contingency basis, of course) for the Third World War; or, rather, the time known to professional soldiers as Transition To War.

During this period of no-peace/no-war, it is assumed that approximately 1,500 people will be priority targets for assassination. They are the key men and women without whom our complex society would be all but impossible to manage in a time of crisis. Elaborate arrangements to protect them already exist.

Given this drastic change in the way we run things, it seemed right to research and write an all-round study of the bodyguard phenomenon. Strangely enough – although the bodyguard is as old as civilised history – no such work seems to exist elsewhere. True, there are a few slim manuals from mid-America bearing such Chandleresque titles as 'Dead Clients Don't Pay'. There are also a number of individual memoirs. But so far as the author's researches suggest, this is the first serious endeavour to compile evidence for a true history rather than a random selection of anecdotes and reminiscence.

The start point of this history is the attempt by Edward Oxford, when armed with two pistols, to assassinate Queen Victoria in London's Hyde Park on 10 June 1840. It was the first of seven such attempts and the author has been privileged to have access to the intended victim's own, intimate account of how it feels to be a ruler under constant threat in an open society. But why start with Victoria rather than, say, one of the many attempts to kill Napoleon Bonaparte? (These, after all, included the first fairly modern explosive time-bomb.)

While it is true that there had been threats to rulers, and a consequent need of bodyguards, as soon as rulers emerged, potential regicides did not enjoy the special advantage of modern, small firearms until the mid-19th century. Between 1860 and 1890 for instance, the breech-loading rifle was adopted by all the major powers and it remained the standard infantry weapon until after the Second World War. The pistol underwent a series of design revolutions starting with integral percussion cap and bullet first shown at the Great Exhibition in 1851, an innovation promptly copied by Smith & Wesson. High-velocity bullets introduced in 1890 led to military small arms ammunition which has remained basically unchanged.

The other reason for choosing 1840 is political. Until the Reform Act of 1832 there was no point in seeking to bribe or intimidate the common man, since he had no vote. On the contrary, a series of repressive statutes between 1797 and 1829 reflected fears of a revolution in Britain, but the process of enfranchisement which was set in motion in 1832 made power accessible not just to voters but, through the intimidation of voters, to terrorists also. A paradox emerged. This was that in the power-play which followed the simultaneous evolution of modern firearms and contemporary democracy, the figure of authority was more exposed to murder or kidnap than before government by popular consent existed. Government was now seen to be man-made and not ordained by God, and power was up for grabs. A wave of assassinations (often inspired by anarchists) in the late nineteenth and early twentieth centuries demonstrated the point, and the age of the modern close protection officer had arrived.

The research turned up several unexpected conclusions. The first and most important – a sort of First Law of Close Protection – is that a bodyguard is only as effective as he is allowed to be by the person he is protecting, his Principal (also known as 'the Man'). Therefore it became clear that a study of bodyguards would only have coherence if it were also a study of the VIPs concerned. The diplomat under threat of political kidnap in South America is an entirely different type of risk for the protection officer and threat evaluator from that of the president who is about to be assassinated by his own ceremonial guard on public parade in the Middle East, or the under-age heiress in danger from an ardent but unsuitable suitor. (This being the case, the author has written about such groups as kings, politicians and diplomats, villains and theatricals, rather than Bodyguards Through the Ages.)

The second surprise was that the risk facing the bodyguard relates more to the principal's style of doing business than his own. So the Second Law of Bodyguards should read: 'The occupational hazard facing any protection officer reflects the occupation of the principal, not his own.' A popular leader such as Winston Churchill or the Queen (most of the time) needs only one or two regular guardians. They are likely to be at risk more from their own incompetence with firearms than from any external hazard. (Indeed, Inspector W. H. Thompson, Churchill's gun carrier, *did* accidentally shoot himself through both legs with his .32 Webley.) By contrast the teams surrounding Mussolini or Pinochet are exposed to much greater risk by reason of the unpopularity of these dictators. Furthermore, the risk facing all modern bodyguards grows with the proliferation of firearms, explosives and a terrorist culture in the non-Communist world. Relationships between guardian and client are growing brittle as a result. The policy adopted after twenty years' experience by more than a thousand police officers dedicated to personal security in Northern Ireland is that 'our decision must be final. If the Man still insists on going his own way, he must do it without us.'

This history, then, is as much about styles of leadership as protection. The two elements are impossible, in practice, to disentangle. It is also about the use of terrorism and particularly assassination as a political instrument. In general, it is a weapon which seems to enjoy more popularity in the absence of a full-scale war than during such a conflict. More political leaders tend to be assassinated in times, if not of 'peace', then at least when their countries are not fighting for survival in a formal state of war. Some evidence for that assertion will be discovered in the assassination index which forms part of this study.

There is one other element to be identified in the violent dynamic which is now adding a new and sinister dimension to our political, cultural and social behaviour. This is the magnification of the importance, and therefore the potency, attached to assassination (particularly if preceded by a spectacular abduction and show trial, however illegal) when it is projected around the world by television. If the leader's charisma is insufficient to stop the assassin's bullet, where is the power of leadership? Has government any reality, or is the revolver, in Koestler's phrase, 'the great leveller'?

The bodyguard, prepared – in the trade's own jargon – to be 'a bullet-catcher for other people', is also, for a few brief seconds, the only defence left to the open society. He is expressing, as a hard-nosed professional, a Christian precept that runs, 'Greater love hath no man than this, that a man lay down his life for his friends.'

Among many remarkable and hitherto unpublished examples of such courage, this narrative tells the story of a young British corporal who locked 'his' diplomats inside a strong room and then threw the key to them through the bars. They were inside; he was outside, quite alone and beyond help in an African state whose soldiers had just butchered the people next door.

To be truly effective, the bodyguard requires more than strong nerves and skill-at-arms. SAS veterans tell an apocryphal tale about a Middle Eastern ruler who sought absolute safety in a walled garden surrounded by soldiers. Each day he walked round the garden accompanied by a bodyguard who carried every conceivable type of weapon, a fearsome man with so many black belts they caused indigestion. So the ruler thought he was safe until a poisonous snake bit his ankle. The bodyguard had no medical training; not even a first-aid kit. The moral, as they say, is that the fatal threat is usually what the target and his bodyguard had not considered. Unfortunately the search for perfect security can also be the stuff from which madness springs.

In Britain, the bodyguard boom of the 1980s is one of the comparatively unremarked developments of Thatcherism in sharp contrast to the relaxed, even dilettante style of personal security adopted by earlier governments as well as by the monarchy. In some small measure, this might reflect the Prime Minister's appetite for confrontation as well as the unmistakable general growth in the threat to her and to other legitimate politicians. Unlike her predecessors, she had not experienced warfare first hand until the Brighton bomb of 1984. And unlike the Queen, she had not learned at her mother's knee that part of the price of belonging to the ruling élite is that someone out there might be tempted to take a potshot at you, some time.

The bodyguard phenomenon, as the royal family is sharply aware, means more than the presence of a discreet but avuncular guardian. Practised thoroughly, it becomes a lifestyle. At first, it seemed that the only people directly affected by it were such brave but isolated figures as Gerry Fitt, MP (now Lord Fitt). It was not until the autumn of 1987 that the newspapers started to notice how total was the change to the bodyguard society. Under the headline, 'Security screen that must make us all vigilant', the *Mail on Sunday*'s leading article for 13 September observed:

'The Prime Minister will this week begin her crusade to rescue Britain's inner cities from the decay and degradation into which successive governments have allowed them to slump. It is the single most important policy commitment of the Thatcher third term. It should have been one of the highest profile trips of the Thatcher years, but we cannot tell you where her crusade will take her. The names of the four areas, plus timing of her visits, have been withheld. Such details are being kept secret until the last possible moment for fear of a terrorist attack.

'Also during the next month, Mrs Thatcher will visit Berlin to speak at a meeting of Western conservative leaders. Again the timing is secret for security reasons. And from October 6 onwards, the earthy seaside resort of Blackpool will be transformed into an armed camp as Britain's security forces protect her at the Tory conference. If they do their job properly Mrs Thatcher will meet no one who has not been exhaustively screened.

'Make no mistake about it. Mrs Thatcher is a Prime Minister under siege. The terrorist threat is such that Britain's duly elected premier cannot tell people in advance where she may be seen and heard. No one, after Brighton's Grand Hotel bomb attack, could possibly demur at these precautions. But they do mean that public life in this country, indeed democracy itself, is under attack as never before.

'And this sad fact should, surely, redouble the efforts of all right thinking people towards defeating the terrorists and their apologists in our midst. It is not just Mrs Thatcher under threat. It is the fabric of our society.'

Regrettably, the odour of fear which pervades public life in Britain today is not just a British phenomenon. It touches democratic life throughout the world. The armed response symbolised by the bodyguard is the most basic and unhappy change in our political lifestyle since the end of the Second World War. This book is intended to explain, in some measure, how the change happened.

PART I

The Fatalistic
House of Windsor

CHAPTER 1

Assassins' Quarry –
Life as a Right Royal Target

For more than a hundred years, British monarchs have tended to believe that they enjoy protection of a very special kind, the best in fact – that of the Almighty in person – backed up by a loyal, loving people. The style was set by that durable lady Queen Victoria, survivor of at least seven attempts on her life and a series of intrusions into Buckingham Palace by someone known as 'the Boy Jones'.

So perfect was her faith in her sacred bodyguard that on one occasion in 1842 she acted as an assassin's decoy. Her lady-in-waiting, Lady Portman, who was deemed not to share such magic, was removed from the horse-drawn carriage in which the Queen offered herself as a target for the gunman she knew to be waiting under the dark, summer greenery of one of London's royal parks.

Victoria's survival is significant – and still sharply relevant – not only because of the style she set for her successors of the House of Windsor. It also happened that her reign (1837–1901) coincided with a renascence in assassination around the world. The victims of this fashion included an Austrian empress, an Italian king, three presidents of the United States and one of France. Though some of the assailants were deranged, they operated within a climate which lent spurious respectability to political murder. An international deodorant was created to smother the stink of blood. In a telling anarchist phrase it was 'The Propaganda of the Deed'.

As if this were not enough to turn any sensible head of state from ideas of monarchy, the British Queen was also at risk from what was to prove the most unforgiving terrorist movement of all: Irish republicanism. Victoria's reign saw the birth of the Fenian Brotherhood; the first use of dynamite as a political weapon in London; the evolution of the revolver as a more deadly weapon than its predecessors; and the creation of a police Special Branch (initially named the 'Irish Special Branch') to protect her from this new threat.

The Queen's exposure to assassination makes her a highly contemporary figure. Not only was she a target of publicity-seeking madmen and the venom of Irish republicanism, but there was also an international dimension to the growing risk. One student of royal history, Harold Brookes-Baker, publishing director of *Burke's Peerage*, believes that in all there were twenty-eight attempts on the Queen's life, some made while she was travelling in Germany. Certainly when some foreign descendants of Victoria visited her they brought additional problems with them. When Tsar Nicholas II visited Balmoral in 1896, the risk of assassination was such that 'every bush and ditch concealed a detective'. (See *Victoria RI* by Elizabeth Longford.) Nicholas, with his family, was murdered in 1917. It is because Victoria lived, in a sense known to a new generation of royal protection officers, that her experience merits some scrutiny.

The extracts from her personal journal which follow are quoted with the gracious permission of Her Majesty Queen Elizabeth II. They are identified by the bracketed symbol 'RA' (for 'Royal Archives') and, where appropriate, 'QVJ' (indicating 'Queen Victoria's Journal').

10 June 1840 had been a mixture of statecraft and pleasure. The Prime Minister, Lord Melbourne (widower of Lady Caroline Lamb), was also the Queen's political mentor. He had called at Buckingham Palace just after lunch to discuss the Corn Laws debate. At tea-time, Victoria sang duets with her Consort, Prince Albert, whom she had

married exactly four months earlier and by whom she was already pregnant. After the tea and the duets, the couple set out by carriage to visit the Queen's mother.

> We had just left the Palace and about half way up the road, before Constitution Hill, I was deafened by the loud report of a pistol and crouched involuntarily ... Albert was sitting on my right. We looked round and saw a little man on the footpath with his arms folded over his breast, a pistol in each hand and before a minute had elapsed, I saw him aim at me with another pistol.
>
> I ducked my head and another shot, equally loud, instantly followed ... While he fired, dear Albert turned towards me, squeezing my hand, exclaiming 'My God! Don't be alarmed.' I assured him I was not the least frightened, which was the case ... We only stayed a short while with Mama and drove through Regent's Park and Hyde Park.
>
> On our way home, just at the Arches in Hyde Park, we found an immense concourse of people on horseback, on foot and in carriages who were most enthusiastic ... Followed us the whole way home like a triumphal procession, shouting and cheering – really most gratifying ...
>
> I gather the pistols were loaded so our escape is indeed providential ... We stayed up till 11. Oh! How thankful must I be, and am, to the Almighty who has so wonderfully spared me. How often has He not transported me through dangers and trials. (RA QVJ, 10 June 1840.)

The assailant, a young revolutionary named Edward Oxford, was seized by onlookers and arrested within seconds of the shooting. Surprisingly little was revealed about him, although he was initially charged with high treason. The charge was consistent with the view that the monarch is not only head of state (as is, say, a republican president) but the embodiment of the State itself. The British monarch is also head of the established church and – uniquely among the remaining European royals – is consecrated and anointed at the coronation ceremony and thus invested with a sacred as well as a political identity.

Oxford was acquitted of the charge – for which the punishment was death – because of insanity, although he took the surprisingly rational view when others followed his example that, if he had been hanged, 'these other attempts would not have taken place'. Oxford was released from Broadmoor Asylum twenty-seven years later, on condition that he emigrated to Australia and promised to stay there for good.

Two years after the first attack, the royal couple were riding along the Mall in the same vulnerable coach on a fine Sunday towards the end of May when Albert saw a man step from the crowd and point a pistol at them.

'I heard the trigger snap but it must have missed fire,' he wrote later. (See *Life of the Prince Consort* by Theodore Martin: letters from Prince Albert to his father.) 'I turned to Victoria who was seated on my right and asked, "Did you hear that?" She had been bowing to the people on the right and had observed nothing. I said, "I may be mistaken but I am sure I saw someone take aim at us."'

Back at the Palace, Albert asked the footmen who had been riding with them if they had spotted a man 'step forward and stretch his hand towards the carriage as if he wanted to throw a petition into it.' They had seen nothing, either. Albert alerted his military equerry, Colonel Arbuthnot, the Inspector of Police, and Sir Robert Peel. He then ran out to the balcony to see if the man had been seized. Apart from offering himself as a long-range target, he achieved nothing more than a sight of a quiet crowd dispersing.

By the following morning, the Prince Consort was beginning to doubt his own observation. But at 9 am a fourteen-year-old boy arrived at the Palace to describe how he had seen a man point a pistol at the royal coach. The man had departed, murmuring, 'Fool that I was, not to fire!' Patiently, the Scotland Yard protection officer followed the witness as he struggled through this alliterative sentence in spite of a painful stammer.

Victoria was 'very nervous and unwell' to learn that another assassin was waiting for her. Yet she was not willing to shut herself up like a prisoner, possibly for months. Both the Queen and Albert therefore decided to ride out as usual that afternoon. She confided to one adviser that for some time she had been expecting 'one of these mad attempts' and 'would much rather run the immediate risk at any time than have the presentiment of danger constantly hovering over her.' (Martin, *op. cit.*)

Many people seemed to want to walk in the royal parks that Monday afternoon. Most of them were thinly disguised police officers. But far from taking a protection officer with her in the coach, the Queen's precautions seem to have been limited to three simple expedients. She excluded her lady-in-waiting, Emma, Lady Portman. She instructed the coachman to drive faster than usual. And she invited two military equerries, Colonels Wylde and Arbuthnot, to act as outriders near the coach. Her response to the threat, as quoted by Elizabeth Longford (*op. cit.*), was that 'I must expose the lives of my gentlemen but not those of my ladies.'

Albert, the only person, aside from the stuttering boy, who could identify the assailant, later recalled (Martin, *op. cit.*):

> You may imagine that our minds were not very easy. We looked behind every tree and I cast my eyes round in search of the rascal's face. However, we got safely through the parks and drove towards Hampstead. The weather was superb and hosts of people on foot. On our way home, as we were approaching the Palace, between the Green Park and the Garden Wall, a shot was fired at us about five paces off. It was the fellow with the same pistol: a little, swarthy, ill-looking rascal.

The shot must have passed under the carriage for he lowered his hand. We felt as if a load had been taken off our hearts and we thanked the Almighty for having preserved us a second time from so great a danger.

The assailant on this occasion was a 22-year-old joiner named John Francis. A policeman 'immediately seized him but could not prevent the shot. It was at the same spot where Oxford had fired at us two years ago.'

The Queen was cheered by some original but sage advice bestowed by her German uncle, Count Mensdorf, an experienced old warrior, who was riding behind her. He asserted that 'one is sure not to have been hit when one hears the report, as one never hears it when one is hit.' (The advice still holds good. In January 1973, Lieutenant Henry Upton of the Queen's Lancashire Regiment was leading his platoon down Leeson Street in Republican West Belfast when he was ambushed by the IRA and shot through the neck by a high-velocity Armalite bullet. He did not hear the shot, though he had a sensation of somersaulting backwards before losing consciousness. With immediate medical treatment, he lived. Later he compared notes with other gunshot casualties who also noted they heard no shot. Possibly the victim is already in a state of shock from the bullet's impact by the time the sound wave, moving more slowly than the bullet, reaches him.)

In 1842, the Queen noted, 'I was really not at all frightened . . . Thank God my angel is also well but he says that had the man fired on Sunday, he must have been hit in the head. God is merciful. That indeed we must feel daily more and more.' (RA Y 90/49) Meanwhile this latest unsuccessful assassin, John Francis, gave 'coarse and witty' answers to his interrogators. Within two weeks he was on trial, accused of high treason and mocking his judges until they sentenced him to death, whereupon he fainted. The sentence was commuted to banishment to 'Van Diemen's Land' – Tasmania – for life.

The day after the death sentence on Francis was commuted, yet another assassination attempt was made upon the Queen as she drove across the park. By now, faith and fatalism were blended into a doctrine that remains the philosophy of the House of Windsor. Doubtless, practical security might be enhanced by a ruler's adoption of unspecified entrances and exits. True also, the assassin could be eluded if his VIP target vanished from public gaze down devious back-street routes. That is not the style of British royalty in such matters.

This third attempt was a farcical affair in which bystanders appear to have had more sympathy with the assailant than with two youngsters who made a citizens' arrest. The attacker was a seventeen-year-old hunchback named John Bean, a chemist's assistant. After a family quarrel a week before, when the newspapers were still full of John Francis's trial, Bean left home to brood. He also left a note to his father in which he threatened to do 'something which was not dishonest but desperate'. He begged to be remembered to his brothers, who had never treated him as a brother, and signed himself, 'Your Unhappy, but Disobedient Son'.

Bean purchased a cheap, powder-fired pistol without too much trouble and waited for the Queen to emerge from the Palace. At the critical moment, the pistol misfired. A youth of sixteen named Bassett seized Bean but, Prince Albert records, the bystanders laughed and shouted, 'Give him back his pistol. It's only a joke.'

The diminutive Bassett and his younger and even smaller brother clung to Bean until the police took notice. The police also thought the affair a bit of a joke and pushed the trio away. Surrounded by the crowd, Bassett now released the assailant and clawed his way through to the nearest officer, to show him the pistol he had taken from Bean. The officer promptly arrested the good citizen Bassett. Some hours later, the truth established, the police traced and arrested Bean.

Beyond the farce, a serious legal debate was developing. If the law provided only that a would-be assassin must be charged with nothing except high treason, and he was then shown to be mentally unbalanced, he would be acquitted and, in the fullness of time, set free to try again. So it was that when, later that day, the Queen learned of the latest incident, she observed that she expected similar attempts on her life so long as the law remained unaltered.

(The law was defined by the McNaughten case the following year, but not in the direction the Queen desired. McNaughten, a 27-year-old Irishman, shot Peel's private secretary, Edward Drummond, after mistaking Drummond for Peel, then Home Secretary. McNaughten was declared 'not guilty by reason of insanity'.)

In August 1842, Bean was convicted of 'shooting at Her Majesty' (a misdemeanour) and sentenced to eighteen months' hard labour. Although the sentence was comparatively light, it had the merit of distinguishing between an attempted *coup d'état* and a despairing gesture by a disturbed adolescent.

The new prescription was not needed again for seven years. This did not mean that there were no anxieties about the Queen's safety. In the spring of 1848, martial law was imposed on the realm by a government nervous of the working-class Chartist movement.

The British royal family, having just played host to an assorted collection of royal refugees from France (while observing the republican tidal wave running over most of Europe in 1848), retreated to their Isle of Wight home, Osborne House, two days before a workers' rally in South London. The Chartists, noting the efficacy of street politics in bringing down King Louis-Philippe in Paris in February of that year, were preparing to demonstrate for the right to vote. In the capital, fearing the worst, great families imported their gamekeepers and farm foremen, armed with shotguns to defend the town-houses from the rabble on the streets. In the event, the great rally was non-violent. But the Queen's prudence, a month before she gave birth to her sixth child, was not excessive.

Elements of the Chartist movement had enjoyed a reputation for mob violence at least since 1839, when forty London constables were bottled up by demonstrators in a Birmingham police yard for nearly two hours. The police finally fought their way out of the siege by using cutlasses. At other times in the 19th century, from the 1830 Reform Bill onwards, Downing Street was regularly under siege, and military guard.

A year after the Chartist scare, when Victoria's self-confidence was beginning to flow back, an Irish bricklayer named William Hamilton tried to kill her. Hamilton was not an immediate victim of the Irish famine of the hungry forties, but the bitterness of that country was spreading like a stain across the political landscape of England.

The Queen's Journal for 19 May 1849 noted that the weather was dull in the morning and became fine later. 'My birthday was kept officially today . . .' After the artillery's twenty-one-gun salute, the crack of a pistol was unmistakable, and much more threatening.

'As we were coming home and going down Constitution Hill we heard the report of a pistol quite close to us and on turning round, saw a man being seized wearing a coarse flannel jacket. No-one was hit, thank God . . . I was not frightened but it is painful that these sorts of things should begin again. These last two years and particularly this year, I was beginning to regain my confidence when driving out, though I always thought of the thing and looked at the people I passed.' (RA QVJ, 19 May 1849)

When she returned to the Palace there was such a fuss that 'I felt more agitated and nervous by all this than by the event itself.' (Ibid.)

Hamilton personified Irish despair. He told his police interrogators that he did not care whether he was hanged or drowned. There was also some doubt about whether the pistol was loaded. The report that the Queen had heard might have been nothing more than a percussion cap. Next day, Victoria noted this and observed:

'It was a wanton act to frighten me and everyone else, which is very wicked . . . It has been finally decided to try the man for misdemeanour, not for high treason, which is far better. Under Sir R. Peel's new Act a man will be sentenced either to seven years' transportation or imprisonment with flogging. We went out for a short while in the garden. No one extra for dinner.' (RA QVJ, 28 May 1849)

Less than a month after the attack, Hamilton was sentenced to seven years' transportation to an Australian penal colony. He had pleaded guilty. No one suggested that he was of unsound mind. His political significance for the future of royal security went unremarked. No one except the Queen herself seemed to observe that 'Hamilton lives with Irish people and associates with them.' It is a measure of her courage, if not her judgement, that within a few weeks, she became the first British sovereign since George IV to visit Ireland. The visit was a popular success.

The assault on the Queen which came most near to causing permanent injury was carried out not by an Irish rebel but by a former 10th Hussars lieutenant, aged 30 and the son of a former High Sheriff of Cambridge. His name was Robert Pate and he seems to have nursed some grievance involving the monarch personally rather than any political motive.

On 27 June 1850 the Queen, now a 31-year-old mother,

rode from Buckingham Palace with her two youngest sons to Cambridge House, Piccadilly, the home of her Uncle Adolphus, Duke of Cambridge, who was dying. Buckingham Palace had now taken to giving some advance warning, however brief, to the police about the Queen's movements around London. Before Victoria's reign ended there would be a police contingent based at the Palace itself, with standing orders to take any available transport so as to reach the royal venue ahead of her Majesty.

On this particular occasion the Queen noted:

A crowd had collected to see me go out again and as no one knew that I intended going to Cambridge House, no police were there. The gate is very narrow so that the Equerry could not keep close to the carriage and the crowd got close up to it, which always makes me think more than usually of the possibility of an attempt being made on me.

A little in front of the crowd stood a young gentleman whom I have often seen in the park – pale, fair, with a fair moustache and with a small stick in his hand.

Before I knew where I was or what had happened, he stepped forward and I felt myself violently thrown by a blow to the left of the carriage. My impulse had been to throw myself that way, not knowing what was coming next – till I was roused a moment afterwards by poor Fanny (Jocelyn, her lady-in-waiting) saying 'They have got the man.'

My bonnet was crushed and on putting my hand up to my forehead I felt an immense bruise on the right side, fortunately well above the temple and eye! The man was instantly caught by the collar and when I got up in the carriage, having quite recovered myself, telling the good people who anxiously surrounded me, 'I am not hurt,' I saw him being violently pulled about by the people. Poor Fanny was so overcome that she began to cry ...

I ordered the coachman to drive home and sent for Colonel Grey, who was greatly horrified, to find Albert, who was riding in the Park with the Prince of Prussia ... Upstairs to my room

to put arnica on my poor head, which was becoming very
painful ... (RA QVJ, 27 June 1850)

Astonishingly, the Queen's doctors – evidently unaware of
the insidious dangers of concussion – allowed her to go
that evening, as arranged, to the Royal Opera House,
Covent Garden.

'We saw the second act of the "Prophète", coming away
after the third. My beloved one so dear and kind. We both
felt so deeply how mercifully I had again been protected
and what an escape my poor eye had had! But it leaves a
very painful impression.' (Ibid.)

The Queen's courage was acknowledged by the opera's
Italian cast, which sang 'God Save The Queen'. Victoria,
as well as being gratified, applied her mind to the risk she
ran. Her journal offers no comment about Hamilton other
than that he was Irish. But of the ex-Hussar Pate she noted:

'Certainly it is very hard and very horrid that I a woman
– a defenceless young woman and surrounded by my children – should be exposed to insults of this kind and be
unable to go out quietly for a drive. This is by far the most
disgraceful and cowardly thing that has ever been done; for
a man to strike any woman is most brutal and I as well as
everyone else think this far worse than an attempt to shoot
which, wicked as it is, is at least more comprehensible and
more courageous.' (RA QVJ, 27 June 1850)

Implicit in this comment is a value structure which
suggests that dogs are whipped while horses and monarchs
die more gracefully and cleanly. It was also the case that
there were numerous assassinations during this time in
which the pistol was the instrument of destruction, and no
example of a head of state's being beaten to death with a
cane.

That aside, the Queen's evaluation of her own security
in earthly as well as celestial terms was improving: the

carriage, the narrow gate, the consequential absence of an outrider, the familiar face in the crowd and the hand holding the stick were all subtle early warning signals which, in some measure, she picked up. (In a later age an SAS veteran – himself the elusive target for an assassination plot – told the author, 'If you are even half intelligent, you can pick up the signals of an impending attack.') It is reasonable to assume that when the blow fell on Victoria, she was already moving away from it, saving herself from worse injury.

The following day the Queen repeated her journey to Cambridge House and stayed twenty minutes with her uncle. Pate followed his predecessors down the long road to the Tasmanian wilderness and seven years' transportation. Three years after his sentence, in December 1853, he petitioned the Crown for mercy and was refused.

It would be another twenty-two years and the onset of a decade of terrorism (the 1870s) before there was another breach of Victoria's personal security. But they were turbulent, dangerous years all the same, which saw the birth of assassination philosophies sired by revolutionaries such as the Russian anarchists Ishutin and Mikhail Bakunin, as well as the rise of Irish Fenian terror. Ishutin advocated a purifying course of isolation to be followed by the assassin in preparation of his deed: an assumed name, no family ties, no friends or marriage. In his book *Terrorism*, Professor Walter Laqueur notes: 'On the day appointed for the assassination, he was to disfigure his face with chemicals . . . In his pocket he would carry a manifesto explaining his motives and once he had carried out his attempt he was to poison himself.'

It was just the stuff to inspire the more gloomy Russian literature as well as the mad, the desperate and the regicides such as Ishutin's cousin, Karakozov. In 1866 Karakozov shot at (and missed) Tsar Alexander II, a man with whom

Victoria flirted and quarrelled during a forty-year acquaint-
anceship.

If they were years of growing danger for any sovereign,
they were also a time in which the English Queen's extravag-
antly extended mourning for her late Consort Albert, from
his death in 1861 until around 1872, probably enhanced
her personal security. Out of public life, she was not a
target. Yet the threat of an Irish assassination, represented
by the Fenian dynamite raids in England after 1867, generated rumours of plots against the Queen that were hard
to pin down.

The Queen discounted them, but one of her inner circle
– General Sir Charles Grey – took them seriously. As
recounted by Elizabeth Longford (*op. cit.*) Grey surrounded
Balmoral with soldiers in October 1867. A month later, as
the Queen moved to her Isle of Wight estate at Osborne, a
very colourful tale reached Grey's ears. This was that eighty
raiders were to stalk the Queen from the sea. They would
approach up the Solent, rowing with muffled oars, to land
stealthily on the Queen's private beach.

'Next morning, when she was driving in the woods, they
would snatch her out of the pony chaise from under John
Brown's nose . . . Grey besought her on his knees to leave
Osborne.' The Queen refused, but agreed to a series of
improved security measures including official passes for
visitors, police patrols, static sentries, and the presence of
substantial elements of the Brigade of Guards and the Royal
Navy. Later, she learned that the story of an abduction plot
was false. The invasion of her cherished privacy which it
provoked did not make her more ready next time to tolerate
expert opinion about her personal security. Indeed, her
relations with General Grey, once a favourite, never seem
to have been solidly re-established after this episode.

The Queen's scepticism was apparently undented by an
attempt to kill one of her own children – her second son,

Prince Alfred, Duke of Edinburgh – a few months later in the spring of 1868. As he opened a public event in Australia he was shot in the ribs. With good luck and careful nursing, he survived. The attack, by a Fenian gunman, was meant to revenge the hanging in Britain of three Irish terrorists six months earlier. (The Queen, endorsing those executions as a last but necessary resort, had also said prayers for the condemned men.)

Following the shooting of her son, Queen Victoria refused to accept the political message it was meant to convey. In her eyes, Alfred was entirely unconnected with the Irish or political life generally. He was an uninvolved, innocent bystander, and the only explanation for an attempt to kill him must be something close to original sin, or 'wickedness'.

As it happened, the international terrorism of the 1870s coincided with a decline in Queen Victoria's popularity. Her long retreat from public life, combined with colourful rumours about her relationship with her Scottish servant and companion John Brown, an unofficial but effective bodyguard, gave anti-monarchists an opening for savage public criticism. In 1871 an approach to Parliament for an annuity for the 21-year-old Prince Arthur, the Queen's seventh child, provoked a pamphlet critical of the £385,000 Civil List. Its title: 'What Does She Do With It?'

The Queen's refusal to open Parliament in 1870 had not dampened such criticism. But Edward, Prince of Wales, a cigar-smoking man's man, was popular and when he seemed likely to die, like his father, from typhoid, public sympathy for Victoria returned. All the more ironic, then, that when the Prince's unexpected recovery was celebrated with a thanksgiving service in St Paul's in February 1872, an assassin should be waiting for the Queen in the cathedral.

This time it was a 'slight, delicate' 17-year-old who would threaten royal security. The youth, Arthur O'Connor, was a descendant of an Irish Republican named Fergus O'Connor, who had died insane after attacking an MP in the Commons Lobby. Like Fergus, young Arthur was very mad indeed.

He was discovered in St Paul's at 2 am on the day of the thanksgiving, and released. Six hours later he returned but was unable to get near the building because of the crowds. As one biographer (Dorothy Marshal: *The Life and Times of Victoria*) describes the arrival of the Queen and her heir: 'They received a thunderous welcome as they entered the City at Temple Bar, that marked the reconciliation between a frustrated people and a secluded Queen.'

Two days later, O'Connor climbed the railings of Buckingham Palace armed with a pistol of sorts, and a petition. This the Queen was to sign, agreeing to the release of imprisoned Fenian terrorists, while O'Connor held the pistol to her head.

The Queen's carriage halted just inside the Palace Garden Entrance. The first to dismount was John Brown, the gillie and servant who was the latest in a series of surrogate father figures in Victoria's life. Brown's habit of addressing Victoria as 'Wumman' shocked protocol yet helped to reassure the Queen of Brown's total devotion to her. No orthodox close protection officer would come so close to the Queen. He was with her when she arrived unannounced and incognito at Highland inns. He was with her now as O'Connor prepared to kidnap her.

Brown let down the steps of the carriage. The Queen remained seated, waiting for the footman to remove the rug wrapped about her legs (a task sometimes consigned to the protection officer in the present reign). It was some seconds before Victoria comprehended that the man approaching her was no footman:

I perceived it was someone unknown peering above the carriage door with an uplifted hand and a strange voice . . . calling out and moving forward. Involuntarily, in a terrible fright, I threw myself over Jane C. [lady-in-waiting] calling out, 'Save me!' and heard a scuffle and voices.

I soon recovered myself sufficiently to stand up and turn round where I saw Brown holding a young man tightly, who was struggling . . . Brown kept hold of him till several of the police came in. All turned and asked if I was hurt. I said, 'Not at all.' Then Lord Charles, General Hardinge and Arthur [her son] came up saying they thought the man had dropped something . . . Cameron, the postilion, called out, 'There it is!' And looking down, I there did see, shining on the ground, a small pistol!!

This filled us with horror. All were as white as sheets. It is to the good Brown and his wonderful presence of mind that I greatly owe my safety for he alone saw the boy rush round and followed him! I remained a little while standing in the carriage whilst the grooms, two footmen and Flemming, the page, all rushed out amazed and horrified. General Hardinge came in bringing an extraordinary document which this boy had intended making me sign! It was in connection with the Fenian Prisoners! . . . Then the boy was taken away by police and made no attempt to escape. (RA QVJ, 29 February 1872)

O'Connor was charged with treason-felony and pleaded guilty, although his pistol was unusable. He was sentenced to a birching, which was not inflicted, at the personal request of the Queen, and twelve months' imprisonment followed by enforced emigration to Australia where he could live as a free man.

Evidence of his madness, given at his trial by eminent doctors, was crushed by the Attorney-General, Lord Coleridge, who also destroyed the credibility of the psychiatrists. It was a misguided effort to make even the mad responsible for their actions and thus to deter others but in this case the tactic backfired. As Dr Harrington Tuke, one of the expert witnesses, observed in a letter to *The Times* three years later, 'While in Australia . . . among other eccentricities, O'Connor wrote letters to Her Majesty, one of which suggested that he should be made Poet Laureate in succession to Tennyson.'

Whatever the lawyers might think about O'Connor's sanity, Scotland Yard believed, correctly, that he was still a danger to the Queen. In 1875 O'Connor left Australia and returned to London. He lived in poverty in the East End for some time, always under discreet surveillance and each day becoming evidently more disturbed.

On 5 May he made his way to Buckingham Palace and waited near the spot where he had made his first assault. He offered no resistance when two detectives, awaiting the Queen's return from a reception at St James's Palace, arrested him. His insanity was recognised officially at last and he was consigned to the Hanwell Asylum, Middlesex.

Ironically, the only fatal casualty of the O'Connor affair appears to have been one of the first of Victoria's close protection officers, Inspector Frederick Baker. Born at Melbourne, Cambridgeshire, Baker's period as the Queen's official protector covered nineteen years from 1853 to 1872. They were years in which his quiet surveillance coincided with a total absence of any public assault on the Queen, ending the run of five assaults in ten years which began with Oxford in 1840 and concluded with Pate in 1850.

Baker was responsible for a monarch who did not encourage her protection officer to come too close. The official bodyguard was then, as now, a member of the London police force and not one of the royal household, a permanent under-stairs visitor known to the others as 'the Policeman'.

The low profile, arm's length approach to personal security worked well for a Queen whose pursuit of privacy invariably overcame her fear of assassination. She seems to have reasoned that in the last analysis, if she kept her eyes open and shouted 'Save me!' when she saw the threat coming, then one of her chosen, inner circle would do just that.

The strategy actually worked, as in the case of O'Connor. But for the protection officer formally responsible for the Queen's safety, the stress was too much. On 2 May 1872, less than a month after O'Connor's trial, Sir Thomas Biddulph, one of the Queen's aides, sent for Inspector Baker at Windsor.

An official note observes that Baker, 'a quiet, zealous and efficient servant', came as usual and said nothing about himself. So Sir Thomas did not know that Baker had been unwell. The following morning the Inspector, aged fifty-six, was found dead in his bed at Windsor. The resident Medical Officer, Dr Fairbanks, 'did not appear to think a post-mortem examination necessary'. (RA Z195/8)

Baker, a bachelor, was buried at Tottenham, North London. Queen Victoria placed a monument over his grave on which was inscribed:

'Erected by Queen Victoria in memory of Frederick Baker . . . who for 19 years faithfully and zealously discharged his duties as Inspector of Police in the Royal Palaces . . . "Be thou faithful unto death and I will give thee a crown of life." (Reve. 2–10)' (RA PPVic. 11974 (1872)

Less formally, the Queen wrote to her eldest daughter Vicky, the Princess Royal, the day after Baker's demise: 'Another loss I have had which has pained me much and which you will regret, good Baker my trusty and faithful Police Inspector for eighteen or nineteen years – who was about with me everywhere – was found dead in his bed yesterday morning. A great loss.' (RA Add, U32 4 May 1872)

Another ten years passed before the seventh and final assassination attempt against the Queen. Although an Inspector Baldry had succeeded Baker, Victoria still depended for her close protection upon members of the royal household rather than professional bodyguards. In old age, her faith still lay in the power of the Almighty in heaven backed up by a legal framework of deterrence on earth. In the backwash of this last attack on her, it would be the state of the law and the attitude of the judges and the Liberal Party which were exposed to the formidable weight of her criticism.

At 4.30 in the afternoon of 2 March 1882, Her Majesty stepped out of a special train at Windsor railway station. She had come down from Paddington on her way home from Buckingham Palace to Windsor Castle. She was now keenly aware of the danger attending every public moment. Exactly a year earlier her friend and occasional rival Tsar Alexander II had been murdered, at the third attempt, by Russian revolutionaries. (Of the two men who hurled the bomb that did the trick, Karl Marx wrote – from a safe distance: 'Sterling, businesslike people . . .') As well as anarchists and nihilists, there were also the Fenians.

In the Windsor station yard, the boys of Eton College were prominent among a crowd of loyal spectators. So were several civilian-suited Metropolitan Police officers including Inspector Charles Fraser of 'A' Division, whose parish includes the capital's royal palaces. The men of this division, known as 'Royal A', still provide the family's personal bodyguard although they are not, by vocation or training, detectives nor – to begin with – firearms specialists. They are ordinary London bobbies who know their place. They have no pretensions about controlling their 'principal' as do some other close protection teams.

Queen Victoria's Journal records that she set off for the Castle, accompanied by her daughter Princess Beatrice.

'Just as we were driving off from the station the people, or rather the Eton boys, cheered and at the same time there was the sound of what I thought was an explosion from the engine. In another moment I saw people rushing about and a man being violently hustled and people rushing down the street. I then realised it was a shot which must have been meant for me though I was not sure.' (RA QVJ, 2 March 1882)

This time it was Beatrice who displayed a regal calm. 'Great excitement prevails. Nothing can exceed dearest Beatrice's courage and calmness, for she saw the whole thing: the man take aim and fire straight into the carriage, but she never said a word, observing that I was not frightened.' (Ibid.)

In the crowd, Inspector Fraser was close enough to pounce upon the gunman as soon as the first shot was fired. Fraser reported later: 'Roderick McLean, a clerk by occupation, age twenty-seven, born in Oxford Street, London and having been residing at No. 84 Queen Victoria Cottages, Windsor, attempted to shoot Her Majesty the Queen . . . Just as HM was leaving the station yard, a most unusual cheer was got up which caused me to look from whence it came and at the same moment I noticed something resembling smoke and instantly a report and in three seconds I should say, I had in custody with Superintendent Hayes, McLean who was held by the right collar by Supt Hayes while I seized him by the left.' (RA L14/102)

Another who intervened was an Eton College boy who, according to the courtier Lord Bridport, 'had rushed up and beaten him with an umbrella'. (RA QVJ, 2 March 1882)

McLean was armed with a new revolver loaded with two unfired rounds. Two cartridges had been discharged. The shot fired at the Queen had passed behind the royal carriage and was later recovered. On their way to the police station, Fraser wrote later, 'McLean said that he had done what he had done because he was starving. If he had money he would not have done such a thing.' (RA L14/102)

As a result of Beatrice's studied silence the Queen was still uncertain, when she reached the massive sanctuary of

Windsor Castle, whether she had been the target for another gunman.

'Brown, however, when he opened the carriage, said with a greatly perturbed face, though quite calm, "That man fired at Your Majesty's carriage." Sir J. McNeill jumped out of the second carriage in a great state, hoping we were not touched and saying that the man had been caught. When we got upstairs, Horatia S. rushed up to ask if we were not hurt. I pacified them and went to Arthur and Louischen and told them what had happened . . . Took tea with Beatrice and telegraphed to all my children and near relations. Brown came in to say that the revolver had been found loaded and all chambers discharged.' (RA QVJ, 2 March 1882)

Next day, the indefatigable Brown was back with the gun itself.

'Brown afterwards brought the revolver for me to see. It could be fired off in rapid succession with the greatest facility. Quite small, but with six chambers. I saw the bullets. Was much relieved to hear that the missing one was found for it proves that the object was not intimidation but far worse.' (RA QVJ, 3 March 1882)

Initially, the Queen denied that the attack had affected her. On the day of the attempt she wrote:

'Was really not shaken or frightened, so different to O'Connor's attempt, though was infinitely more dangerous. That time I was terribly alarmed.' (Ibid.)

But she offered her thanks to God in a particularly poignant style and wrote next day:

'God has indeed mercifully protected me. The loyalty manifested on all sides is indeed most touching and gratifying. Walked with Beatrice down to the mausoleum and here I knelt by my beloved one's tomb and offered up prayers of thanksgiving for my preservation to God our heavenly father.' (Ibid.)

The euphoria of the latest survival was given public expression by the cheers of the Eton College boys – through whose neighbourhood the royal carriage was carefully routed that first day after the shooting – as well as telegrams and letters from all over the world. ('I heard from all the sovereigns, from the President and people of the United States . . .') (Ibid.)

It was a month before the Queen's anger and fear were to manifest themselves. McLean was acquitted on grounds of insanity on the direction of the Lord Chief Justice, Lord Mansfield, who was obedient to the rules which had emerged from the McNaughten trial. Anyone who was incapable of perceiving the consequences of his act, or of perceiving that his actions were wrong as a result of his insanity, could not be culpable of the criminal act of murder. As in the case of O'Connor, the battleground was the grey area where the emergent science of criminal psychopathology collided with the conservative, institutionalised tradition of the law. (Similar considerations would apply a century later to the case of the man who shot, but did not kill, President Reagan.)

Queen Victoria had no doubt about what was to be done. Madness was no excuse for wickedness and public policy should acknowledge that truth. A note drafted (probably by her private secretary, General Sir Henry Ponsonby) on her behalf, dated 19 April 1882, said:

'The Queen must say she is much shocked as well as surprised at this verdict. She feels there is now no security for her! And depend upon it, the Queen will be exposed more than ever now! She really thought this time the people would feel for their poor Queen who never injured anyone and escaped narrowly . . . Till the Queen be wounded or killed, this will go on! . . . And this always happens when a Liberal government is in!' (RA L14/134)

Ponsonby took up her cause with Sir William Harcourt,

Home Secretary, who observed that, if McLean had been sentenced to death, 'he would probably have heard that sentence commuted to imprisonment and continued efforts made for a further commutation.' In other words, the outcome – incarceration for a long time, followed by ultimate release on licence – would be the same. McLean, after all, was to be detained in an asylum for an indefinite time.

This did not satisfy Her Majesty, who wanted criminal responsibility to be publicly identified as such. A note on her behalf to her Liberal Prime Minister, Gladstone, on 23 April observed:

'Punishment deters not only sane men but also eccentric men, whose supposed involuntary acts are really produced by a diseased brain capable of being acted upon by external influence. A knowledge that they would be protected by an acquittal on the grounds of insanity will encourage these men to commit desperate acts, while on the other hand a certainty that they will not escape punishment will terrify them into a peaceful attitude towards others.' (RA L14/141)

The notion that deterrence works even for the insane was not original. In this case, however, the potential victim was uniquely placed to make her opinions stick. And as it happened, the emergence of the Irish Republican Brotherhood made deterrent sentencing a particularly topical matter. The Queen got her way. On 4 May, Ponsonby reported to Victoria:

'The judges have admitted the force of Your Majesty's arguments and are ready to consider the best mode of altering the recent verdict.'

The result was the Control of Lunatics Bill, introduced into the House of Lords soon afterwards and read a third time in the Commons on a Saturday morning. The effect was that anyone found to be insane at the time of committing crime would not be acquitted on the ground of insanity, but would be convicted of committing the criminal act. Insanity as such now constituted a 'special finding' causing the accused person to be detained 'at Her Majesty's pleasure'. The formula is still in use.

CHAPTER 2

Playing it Cool with Umbrella – A Style is Born

After the carnage of the First World War a historical myth took root. This was that the turn of the century, La Belle Époque, had been a time of somnolent ease and careless laughter, a cultural Eden in which even the serpents were friendly.

In practice, the three or four decades before 1914 were a time of increasing terror for many people, particularly the ruling class. Though some were slow to wake up to the fact, they were becoming the quarry of a burgeoning terrorist culture which included resentful Armenians, Indians, Egyptians, Serbs, Irish, Russian, Spanish and even English female upper-class dissidents. Dynamite (a substance credited with near magical properties by such revolutionaries as the German-American publisher Johann Most) and the modern pistol were tipping the balance in favour of the assassin for the first time since the emergence of the nation state.

But there was more to this development than technology. As in the 1980s, regular warfare was remote from the comfortable societies of Europe and North America. British historians of the time, when they referred to 'The Great War', had in mind the rout of the French army by Bismarck in 1870–71. The Americans had not found an equal battlefield opponent since they fought their fellow Americans in the fratricidal struggle of 1860–64. (Wars against the Amerindians, the Spanish in Cuba and in the Philippines counted as little more than journalistic adventures.)

For some people, the substitute for the collective violence of general war is the individual violence of assassination.

Or, to put it another way, assassination, like suicide, is not usually a symptom of the indiscriminate slaughter which accompanies national armed conflict. It is the political intoxicant of a society not threatened by a larger struggle for survival.

Whatever the threats to other heads of state, the British remained outwardly complacent. After the last attempt on Queen Victoria in 1882 her Prime Minister, Gladstone, observed that foreign assassinations had a political motive but 'in England, they are all madmen'. Only the previous year America's President Garfield and Russia's Tsar Alexander II ('The Liberator') had fallen victim to the assassin's art.

Over the next twenty years or so both assassination and its antidote, Close Protection, were to become growth industries. The Garfield and Alexander murders were followed by those of President Carnot of France (knifed by a man who leapt into his carriage) in 1894; Prime Minister Antonio Canovas of Spain in 1897; Empress Elizabeth of Austria in 1898 (also knifed); King Umberto of Italy in 1900 (shot through his carriage window); US President McKinley in 1901; King Alexander and Queen Draga of Serbia, 1903; King Carlos and Crown Prince Louis-Philippe of Portugal, 1908; King George of Greece, 1913, and, most fatal for the rest of Europe, Archduke Ferdinand and the Duchess of Austria at Sarajevo in 1914, followed four sanguinary years later by the elimination of the entire Russian royal family in the massacre of 1918.

British royalty encountered some of these events close enough for it to hurt. In 1898, the future George V with his wife Princess Mary of Teck were with a party of European nobles aboard a lakeland steamer at Geneva as guests of Baron Adolf de Rothschild. As another guest, Empress Elizabeth ('Zita') of Austria, was about to step on board, an Italian anarchist named Luigi Lucheni obstructed her path and drove a stiletto into her heart with such silent precision that at first no one comprehended what had happened. The victim herself walked on, unaware at first that she had even been wounded. An eye-witness wrote later:

'She dropped quietly down on the Quai de Mont Blanc, so quietly that the people around her thought she had fainted. They carried her on board but when they bent over her they found that Elizabeth, the beautiful Empress of the House of Habsburg, was dead.'

(Later, King George – faithful to Belle Époque mythology – would assert that in a world of beautiful women, the world of his youth, 'the two most beautiful were the Empress Elizabeth and my own mother.')

At first it was unclear whether Elizabeth's assassin was an official guest. An attempt by 'one of the family' (as in Plantagenet England or contemporary Saudi Arabia) still provokes disquiet among close protection officers responsible for British VIPs, from whose church services and other quasi-public occasions the bodyguards are often excluded.

Gladstone had chosen his words carefully in declaring that *in England*, regicides were madmen. He did not exclude a political attack on a British monarch outside the realm. The experience of the 19th century seems to be that a sovereign was most at risk during the comparative freedom that went with being Prince of Wales, an uncrowned king at large in a wide world. So when the future Edward VII went to India in 1876 it was noted that he was under a surprising degree of surveillance. As Philip Magnus describes it in *King Edward VII*:

'Edward Bradford, "the head of the secret police in India", who never left the Prince's side, was made responsible for security. The suite had orders to surround the Prince at all times, and its members took turns in sitting up all night outside any room or tent in which he slept. Those precautions fidgeted the Prince much less than did the innumerable telegrams about his health which Queen Victoria despatched constantly, often *en clair*, and sometimes so worded as to provoke ridicule.'

Such security was not possible throughout an adventurous, zestful life. On 4 April 1900, Edward – now aged fifty-nine and still Prince of Wales – was on his way to Copenhagen. His train stopped at Brussels and he strolled round the railway station. His diary, in which he referred to himself in the third person, noted drily:

'Just as train is leaving, 5.30, a man fires a pistol at P. of W. through open window of carriage (no harm done).' (RA, Prince of Wales's diary, quoted in Magnus, op. cit.)

The shot was fired by a fifteen-year-old anarchist named Sipido, whose revolver still had five bullets left when the stationmaster pounced and wrestled the gun from him. The Prince's Special Branch bodyguard, John MacCarthy, seems to have played no part in an affair which, politically, was just beginning. At first, Edward – who had shot elephant, cheetah, black buck, numerous tigers, including an eight-foot pregnant tigress carrying three unborn cubs, bear, chamois, crocodile, deer, elk, wild boar, grouse, partridge and pheasant – made elaborate jokes about Sipido's poor marksmanship. He even suggested clemency for the youth but was furious when Sipido, placed under relaxed police supervision, fled to France and freedom.

When the Prince of Wales returned to London sixteen days after the shooting, cheering crowds greeted him at Charing Cross, their faith in the mystical capacity of their royal family to frustrate an adversary's knavish tricks entirely confirmed. Elsewhere, the parliaments of Greece and Portugal recorded congratulatory votes as their contribution to the applause.

The British Parliament (to Edward's annoyance) said

nothing, the Cabinet having taken the view that it was not known, on the proper day to discuss such matters at Westminster, whether Sipido's gun was actually loaded. Edward's response was to carry the bullet which had missed him as a souvenir for the rest of his life, a token, perhaps, of the frailty and uncertainty of a life spent in the public eye rather than a symbol of regal magic.

Even in the British Isles, behind the confident front presented by Gladstone and his successors, the British were responding to the growing threat to their sovereign. In the same year as McLean's attempt at Windsor, Irish republicans had murdered Lord Frederick Cavendish, Chief Secretary for Irish Affairs, and his Under-Secretary, Mr Burke, as they walked to Phoenix Park, Dublin.

A direct result of the Phoenix Park murders in 1882 as well as a Fenian bombing campaign in Westminster a year later was the formation of an élite team of underground detectives drawn from the Royal Irish Constabulary. This was the Special Irish Branch, later known as the Political Branch and finally renamed the Special Branch. One of its first special duties was to provide better close protection for the Queen. As a result, the most dedicated guardians of royalty and leading politicians alike were Irish police officers such as Sergeant Patrick Quinn from Mayo and Detective Sergeants John Sweeney, John MacCarthy, George Riley and Dan MacLaughlan.

Quinn would become the first police officer to be knighted as well as the second head of the Special Branch (from 1903 to 1918) while MacLaughlan was the first of this new generation of protection officers to die in action, alongside his charge, Lord Kitchener, in 1916 (see Part II). In 1909, when Queen Victoria's grandchild, the eighteen-year-old English Princess Ena Battenberg, married the Spanish King Alfonso in Madrid, Quinn as head of the Special Branch went to some trouble to ensure that her security was impenetrable. He failed, but it was not for want of effort.

The close protection team included John MacCarthy and a French detective named Xavier Paoli. Paoli was a favourite of the English King Edward VII because of his knowledge of the interesting low life of Paris. As a close protection officer the Frenchman was also one of the first to appreciate that good intelligence in advance of an assassination attempt was worth a brigade of men after the killing had happened.

It was symbolic of the international complexion of European royalty at that time that Paoli was attached to the Prince and Princess of Wales (George V and Queen Mary) for the procession from Los Geronimos church to the Royal Palace. MacCarthy, in the fourth carriage, followed the newly-wed monarch and his bride. For good measure, the bridal coach was surrounded by a team of officers from the British 16th Lancers as outriders and four Spanish cavalrymen.

According to Superintendent Edwin T. Woodhall (in *Guardians of the Great*) an explosion just in front of King Alfonso's coach provoked pandemonium.

'Screams, shrieks, yells, shouts and orders were heard on every side. Horses plunged and reared, shied, kicked and bolted in terrified alarm. Plunging through the maze of horses and horsemen, MacCarthy made straight for the door of the royal carriage . . . As he helped the Queen from the carriage he could not but help seeing that on the train of her bridal gown there were ominous splashes of the life blood of one of her unfortunate bodyguard who had been blown to pieces.'

The Prince of Wales heard the explosion and thought it was the first gun of a royal salute rather than a bomb that had just killed twenty people and wounded about sixty others. Ena and Alfonso brushed the glass away and were propelled by MacCarthy into another coach. Two streets away the public were ignorant of what had happened. The couple, MacCarthy said later, were 'simply marvellous'. He added:

'Up to the gates of the palace, the Queen kept her composure. Then, as soon as she was out of sight of the public, she fell into the arms of the King in a dead faint . . .'

The anarchist bomber had breached security by the simple expedient of hurling his dynamite from a roof overlooking the processional route. Some hours later, acting on information provided by the wily Frenchman, Paoli, Civil Guard officers cornered their man. He was shot dead from the saddle by a Spanish officer who had taken part in the wedding procession. This did not inhibit the future George V's criticism:

'Of course the bomb was thrown by an anarchist, supposed to be a Spaniard, and of course they let him escape. I believe the Spanish police and detectives are about the worst in the world. No precautions whatever had been taken . . . Naturally, on their return, both Alfonso and Ena broke down, no wonder after such an awful experience. Eventually we had lunch about 3. I proposed their healths, not easy after the emotions caused by this terrible affair.' (RA)

The threats were multiplying in England also. In part this was due to an increasing access to foreign travel throughout much of Europe without tight border controls, compounded by terrorist abuse of neutrality and the wilfulness of some VIPs reacting against the restrictions imposed by constant protection. Such problems would be the bread and butter of a later generation of protection officers.

In a shopping street in placid Southsea, Hampshire, one Edwardian summer afternoon, John Sweeney, now an inspector, was in charge of the heir to the Russian throne, the haemophiliac Tsarevitch Alexis. The protection officer was dressed in civilian clothes. Alexis wore a sailor suit. Sweeney observed that they were being followed by two men. Obeying the Irishman's whispered instruction, the child's tutor led Alexis into a nearby shop. Sweeney waited outside and watched the reflection of the two men in the front window, fingering the white silk handkerchief he was to wave as a signal to other officers shadowing him if he needed their help. Both men, armed with sheath knives, were then arrested and questioned. They were Nihilists from Odessa and Riga respectively and were promptly deported to Russia.

Other Russian exiles such as Lenin and Trotsky were kept under Special Branch observation while in England but so long as they merely preached revolution without actually trying to conduct it, they were free to enjoy the status of political refugee. Other governments were more nervous. The nervousness showed during the London funeral of Edward VII in 1910.

A total of forty-eight European royalty (including eight kings and an emperor) walked in the funeral procession. Immediate close protection was provided by four Branch officers led by Quinn and MacCarthy but Kaiser Wilhelm brought his own close protection team of a dozen armed men. It was not the first time foreign bodyguards would carry weapons in public in London and assuredly not the last: the practice continues. At the time it was the most heavy display of its kind, yet it did not assuage the Kaiser's unease while in England. Possibly this had something to do with the spy network he had just set up in Britain, a network promptly penetrated by his Branch bodyguard.

On his way home, as the German monarch left a train at Harwich railway station, a stranger leapt a barrier and ran towards him. According to Woodhall, the Kaiser grabbed his ivory stick and held it aloft.

'"God, I will smash you," was the look in his face. The

man was seized by the police and searched. He had no weapons. He was a German and wanted to pay his respects . . .'

It seemed that Wilhelm, like – in a later generation – King Hussein of Jordan, was a sovereign who was prepared to defend himself if the occasion arose.

With the conflagration of general war in Europe from 1914 to 1918, the fashion in assassination declined. There are several reasons, among them the popularity of the national leadership in time of grave crisis and the convention, in Europe anyway, that leaders regard their opposing peers as a protected species until the war is over. Hitler, it is true, was the target of a bomb plot when he had clearly lost the war, but the plotters were disowned by the Allies. The Kaiser, like his English relatives, died peacefully in bed after the war.

In spite of such considerations risks touching the British élite had to be considered. One of the most obvious was how to restrain the enthusiasm of Edward, Prince of Wales, son of George V and (later) the first English monarch for centuries to abdicate. This prince relished the role of star performer in the royal playpen. When he wanted to go up to the battle front to fight his German cousins during the first weeks of the war, he was told by General Kitchener: 'If I were sure you would be killed, I do not know if I should be right to restrain you. But I cannot take the chance, which always exists until we have a settled line, of the enemy taking you prisoner.'*

Yet the authorities could not resist the Prince's demands to visit the front, even if he were not to join it. He might visit the battleground so long as he got into no danger. The man charged with the impossible mission of assuring this was the Prince's close protection officer, Edwin Woodhall.

* Source: *A King's Story*, by HRH the Duke of Windsor.

A Branch officer before hostilities, Woodhall served with the Cameronians for the first few months of the war, then transferred to the Intelligence Police (Royal Military Police) in 1915 with the rank of sergeant. He would see more action through his attempts to keep the Prince out of trouble than had fallen to his lot in a front-line infantry unit.

He had already come in for criticism from the Assistant Provost Marshal, Major John Solano, for having permitted the Prince to get into danger. So when they next visited the front, Woodhall was ordered not to answer any questions the Prince might ask about the local situation. All went well until they reached reserve trenches occupied by Australian troops, whose cheers, it seemed, caused the Prince's horse to bolt.

Woodhall later recounted (ibid.):

'The Prince's horse galloped over shell holes, across wide gaps, over a broken fence in its frenzied fright. My animal was well trained but it jibbed three times at wide leaps and at a fence it caught its hoof in the wire and I was shot off 10 ft clear! I picked myself up, remounted and again took up the pursuit. Many of the Australians were now in full cry after the Prince . . . watching His Royal Highness subdue and control the fear-maddened animal . . . within the sound of the Ypres guns.'

The Prince was not always an unwilling participant in such adventures. Soon after the bolting horse episode, he borrowed a staff car and set off for the front again, leaving Woodhall to follow him on a borrowed motor cycle. Soon, like other members of the royal family, including Lord Mountbatten, he shook off his bodyguard. It was some time before Woodhall found the car, smouldering on one side of the road and wrecked by shellfire. As the protection officer braced himself to retrieve the Royal remains, a familiar voice chirruped from a nearby trench: 'Hello, Sergeant! They've done it this time, haven't they?'

It seemed that after the Prince of Wales had left the car to speak to a wounded man, the vehicle had become a target for the German gunners. Woodhall added: 'The Prince laughed . . . I was so shaken that it took me all my time on my way back to collect my nerves . . .' There was time enough for this process, for 'HRH went back to headquarters on my motor cycle.'

Woodhall was discovering an uncomfortable truth about the life of a close protection officer to a member of the British royal family. Royals are the stuff of popular legend and are under pressure to make the legend a reality, particularly in a danger zone. Protection officers are in the business of containing risk. The roles are intrinsically incompatible and regularly prove fatal to the health of the bodyguards.

As Cockney soldiers of the 56th Division, encountering the Prince of Wales in the trenches during the second week of the Somme battle (on 16 July 1916) put it: 'Blimey, if 'e gets killed 'e's all right. But what abaht us?' (ibid.)

Even George V himself was not immune from the risk of injury. In 1915, a horse provided by General Haig reared up and rolled on him when he was cheered by a group of Royal Flying Corps aviators. Doctors diagnosed as simple bruising what was, in fact, a fractured pelvis. Still conscious and in pain he was lifted into a service ambulance for a two-day journey to England. The ambulance was a flatbed with canvas flaps bearing the Red Cross and no special suspension, a type used to carry all wounded Tommies. For security reasons, it was said, no special escort was provided. The decision might also have had some link with Haig's failure to acknowledge for three days that the King had been hurt, and seriously so.

After the war, the Prince of Wales's close protection team remained doggedly with him through visits to the homes of unemployed miners in the grey days of the Depression. His police bodyguard at the time, Jim Robson, observed the

Prince's determination to sell his racehorses so as to contribute to the miners' distress fund. Leonard Burt (head of Special Branch from 1946 to 1958) was with him in a squalid Chilean village in 1925 when a man staggered out of a wine shop and collapsed in the road before them. The attacker withdrew into the wine shop as the Prince, impulsive as ever, rushed forward to examine the casualty.

'He's been stabbed!' said the Prince.

The royal party administered first-aid, but it was insufficient to save the victim's life.

Like his grandfather Edward VII, the future Edward VIII enjoyed a frisson of excitement from the exotic pleasures of France. The first of these monarchs had had the omniscient French detective Xavier Paoli to guide him. The younger Edward had Commissaire Charles Sisteron, whose philosophy in caring for visiting royalty was 'to satisfy desires while warding off the impecunious'.

Referring to himself in the third person, he would say:

'It is Sisteron's duty to see that their incognitos are strictly safeguarded . . . The habits and amusements of the visitor are ascertained from members of the entourage so that every desire may be met at once and even in advance.'

This was all very well for the French. According to British style, as Woodhall revealed, 'our detectives send a report to the superintendent of the Special Branch who in turn is directed to the Commissioner and through him to the Home Secretary.'

George V died in January 1936 and was succeeded by Edward, who abdicated to marry Mrs Simpson and become Duke of Windsor the same year. As Rupert Allason has observed in his history of the Special Branch, a close protection team stayed with him long afterward: 'Prior to the abdication, Superintendent Storrier of London's "A" Division had been allotted the task of guarding Edward VIII, but soon after that traumatic event the Prime Minister [Mr

Baldwin] requested the attendance of a Branch officer and Detective Sergeant Atfield was appointed. When the Duke was sent to Nassau as Governor in 1940 he was accompanied by a new Branch officer, Detective Inspector Harry Holder.'

It seems likely that such protection was withdrawn after 1945, when the Duke of Windsor retired to live in some degree of seclusion for the rest of his life. The progression is a model of how close protection is afforded members of the royal family. The officers of Royal 'A', such as Storrier, are occasionally despised by some members of the Special Branch, who describe them as 'uniformed officers in plain clothes'. The apparent paradox is reconciled by the absence from the Royal 'A' cadres of the detective training which all Branch officers undergo before they hang up their uniforms.

Although the close protection team guarding the royal family – drawn from 'A' Division – do not wear uniform, much attention is paid to dressing them correctly. They in turn will ask what is the peculiar potency or even relevance of detective training to close protection, and an honest Branch officer will admit that there is very little, except in so far as it enables the CID-trained bodyguard to talk to some local police chiefs on equal terms.

More to the point in this context, perhaps, the Branch is concerned with political subversion. That is its *raison d'être*. When Edward ceased to be king, he did not qualify for protection as a member of the royal family, since this is normally accorded only those who have some constitutional claim to succession to the throne.

Traditionally, the Branch has protected politicians who are not held to be at risk throughout their lives. Thus the decision to afford Branch protection to the ex-King Edward put him firmly in the category of political VIPs who qualify for protection for the time being. Further, Edward's links with the Nazi leadership before the war might have made it seem at least prudent to attach to his personal staff in the Bahamas during the war years, one man who could be relied upon to report back to his superiors in London.

In Britain during that war, the rest of the royal family were in the front line along with those of their subjects who had not fled to North America or South Africa. It was known as the 'Home Front' and during various Blitzkriegs it was where the main action was to be found. A Heinkel bomber contrived to hit Buckingham Palace itself in 1940, only to be stalked through appalling visibility by the son of a Yorkshire cattle dealer, the RAF fighter ace Sergeant Ginger Lacey. Lacey used peculiarly lethal tracer bullets at ultra close range to destroy the raider, only to be shot down himself in the encounter. He lived to fight and survive to the end of the war.

By sharing such dangers with their people, the Windsors earned their total loyalty. There was more. To George VI – the decent man who stumbled doggedly through each Christmas Day broadcast in spite of a frightful speech defect – the common man extended a peculiarly protective affection. He was a living example of sacrifice and a sense of duty, virtues much in demand and in fashion as Britain fought for survival without allies. So the paradox of war was fulfilled: whatever overt dangers existed, the threat of terrorism, including Irish terrorism, expired like a punctured balloon.

It is also worth noting that despite his natural modesty the King was not a believer in mere passive resistance. As the historian A. J. P. Taylor has noted, throughout the bleakest period of Britain's wartime isolation, 'The King practised revolver shooting in the grounds of Buckingham Palace and intended to die there fighting.'

By the end of the war, the Special Branch had come to dominate the close protection of every politician from

Churchill to such visiting Russians as Molotov. Their men were increasingly responsible for the royal family also. Leonard Burt, already head of the Branch, accompanied Princess Elizabeth to South Africa in 1947 on one of her first overseas tours.

The first terrorist threat to the Windsors was detected a year later. It came from an unexpected quarter. 1948 was the year in which, amid much bloodshed, Britain withdrew from Palestine and the Jewish state of Israel came into being. Just before the British Mandate ended in May, letter bombs were received by several people including a former military commander in the Holy Land, General Sir Evelyn Barker. The Barker letter bomb was dismantled and found to contain a French detonator. France was the next destination of Princess Elizabeth and the Duke of Edinburgh.

Superintendent George Wilkinson and his Branch colleague Tom Barratt arrived in the French capital shortly before the royal visitors and the Princess's protection officer, Inspector Aleck Usher. Astonishingly, the French government was able to reassure the British security men that it had reached an understanding with the Zionist terrorist movement, the Stern Gang, which guaranteed 'a temporary truce' for the visit.

Wilkinson recorded in his book, *Special Branch Officer*: 'On our journey from Paris, the Princess endeared herself to the French people . . . Although we were behind schedule, the royal cars slowed down for every group of children, no matter how small . . .'

Wilkinson, like his successors who found themselves holding posies of flowers handed out of the crowds to Elizabeth as Queen, was aware of the calculated risk involved in such a human gesture. He might also have reflected that, in this case, the threat reflected a curious turn of events. Had the British, including the royal family, not resisted in 1940, France might not have been liberated and many of the Zionists would assuredly have mouldered in the death camps.

But if the Branch was becoming concerned about a new breed of terrorist as a threat to members of the British royal family, the family itself was not convinced. Soon after the war it acquired from 'A' Division a protection officer universally known as 'Perkins'.

Perkins – Superintendent Albert Perkins – was an unlikely choice as a royal bodyguard, though he must have met criteria laid down by the Palace to have been promoted to the job by the top brass of Scotland Yard. He spoke in monosyllables, and as infrequently as courtesy allowed, in a flat, adenoidal voice. He was tall but somewhat stooped. He disdained firearms, reasoning that the use of such weapons was for lesser mortals than those charged with royal protection. Although the royal bodyguard was issued with such a weapon, Perkins discouraged its very presence unless it was tucked out of sight, and reach, in a briefcase.

'What do you want that thing for?' he would sneer when confronted by one of his juniors who believed – as they say in the trade – in 'carrying'. Perkins advised any CP officer escorting the Queen to carry an umbrella instead, since this monarch, like Victoria, tended to worry about weather. Also, the role of Umbrella Man helped the protection officer to stay close to Her Majesty, but unobtrusively so.

Such advice was delivered just once and then not always too clearly. In 1966 one newcomer to royal protection was told simply to be at the Chapel Royal, Windsor, for the Garter ceremony. The new recruit stood near Perkins throughout, awaiting some illumination. As the ceremony ended, the Queen's personal detective (an honorary title inscribed, nevertheless, above the door of his cabin aboard the Royal Yacht *Britannia*) murmured in his sepulchral tone, 'Follow me.'

The recruit did so. At an administrative wing of Windsor

Castle, the new man, a rising young inspector called Michael Trestrail, was told to wait while Perkins conferred with an Assistant Commissioner from Scotland Yard. Some time later Perkins re-emerged and told Trestrail to present himself at Buckingham Palace the next day.

Perkins was much criticised by his close protection rivals in the Branch. The scorn was mutual. The Branch officers, who invariably 'carried' in that intransitive sense, questioned the expertise of someone who seemed dedicated to tucking in the travel rug as the Queen settled back into her Rolls. Perkins's hostility towards Leonard Burt was particularly sharp. He especially resented the Branch chief's claim to carry out most risk-evaluation reconnaissance in advance of a royal trip overseas.

Perkins also had great strengths, however. He never allowed his attention to flicker from the job. He used the royal preference for flunkeys rather than an overt bodyguard to enhance the opportunity to stay close to the monarch on terms she would accept. And there was something of Victoria's gillie Brown in his flashes of paternal bullying: 'You're not going out without your raincoat in this weather, Ma'am?' Above all, he had a better chance than any more professional bodyguard of obtaining royal acquiescence in a crisis.

In postwar years, the royal protection team found itself increasingly enmeshed in a web of protocol. It was formally and actually responsible for guarding members of the royal family from assassins, kidnappers and terrorists. But it was also the screen between the family (particularly the sovereign) and the 'Thugs' (her word) representing other arms of VIP protection, led by the Branch. The royal protection officer was increasingly caught in the conflicting aims of royal security as perceived by the Metropolitan Police commissioner and others responsible for the monarchy as a state institution, and the Queen as a human being who – like most of the family – detests pomposity and empty ceremonial.

The task of liaison with other security authorities has been derided by its critics as that of 'protocol officer'. But in the circumstances which prevailed before the attempt to kidnap Princess Anne in 1974, it was the best that could be achieved.

Certainly Michael Trestrail, when he succeeded Perkins in 1973, maintained the status quo. He was known to Thames Valley Police, covering the Windsor area, as the man who urged less tight control of civilian traffic as the Queen drove out to the races. Prince Philip, according to Palace folklore, asked: 'Is it really necessary to stop the whole of the Thames Valley traffic because we are going to Ascot?' The local practice of closing a public road crossing the grounds of Windsor Castle well ahead of the royal limousine's appearance promptly ended.

The alternative to this consciously unpretentious style was to make virtual prisoners of the Queen and those who might be in line of succession. It was one which started to acquire an alarming reality in the 1980s and it is with that change that the following chapter is concerned, a change which arguably embodies the most profound revolution in the British royal lifestyle since an executioner's axe in Whitehall ended the concept of divine right.

CHAPTER 3

Search for Sanity,
with Horse and Sugar Lumps

The atmosphere in which Albert Perkins and his immediate successors in royal service functioned from the fifties to the late seventies was not so very different from that of the officers who had responsibility for Queen Victoria's security. As policemen, they have never been members of the Household, and the Household, for its part, does not hesitate to remind them of their status as outsiders if some small privilege (such as who sits next to whom at table under stairs at Balmoral Castle) seems in any way endangered. Nor are the protection officers courtiers, though they rub shoulders with the equerries and advisers.

Even as protection officers, they are not expected to claim the godlike power to take drastic initiatives permitted the US Secret Service, including the right to hurl the head of state to the floor and lie upon him if that is required to save his life. The British royal protection officer may only advise (perhaps urge vigorously) his charge to change course. The task requires tact, watchfulness and – above all – accurate advance warning so as to elude trouble before it happens. It is supremely a job of personal relations.

Commander Michael Trestrail was to prove good at this, but when he started as a newly-promoted inspector in 1966, the auguries were not good. Several members of the royal protection team had submitted a respectful memorandum to Scotland Yard in which they invited 'the system' to examine overwork and prolonged absence from home. Perkins had interpreted the request as a minor mutiny. Three officers were promptly transferred to other duties.

Trestrail has told intimates, with characteristic candour,

of his first days in the job. Perkins, it seems, told him, 'You're with Prince Philip. Take him down to Windsor. If he asks if you are the officer on duty, you address him as Your Royal Highness and you say, "Yes, Your Royal Highness, I am on duty." You don't volunteer anything else.'

After a week at the Palace, Trestrail did not know what type of vehicle would be used for this trip to Windsor. He was untrained in close protection techniques and the use of a firearm, though he had been issued with a Walther self-loading pistol. Prince Philip had an open-topped Alvis sports-tourer. Trestrail waited uneasily beside it. When the Duke's valet, Joe Pearce, emerged Trestrail asked him what the form was. Pearce, an ex-Royal Marine, grinned and said: 'I sit in the back. You sit in front, with the Prince.'

The Prince drove fast, expecting his protection officer to act as navigator on twisting back roads. Trestrail was to learn that the last thing Philip wanted was a bodyguard. The protection officer was known simply as 'The Copper' and was expected to make himself useful in other ways. One capable man did not last long because he could not break out of a near-silent, gloomy embarrassment at 'mucking in' with Philip during a bird-watching trip. The party lived in Scottish bothies and took turns with the cooking. Human warmth was as vital as other fuel.

So when, after driving for some time, Philip asked Trestrail during that first journey, 'Are you on duty this weekend?' and received a reply that sounded like a robot – 'Yes, Your Royal Highness, I am the protection officer on duty this weekend, Your Royal Highness' – the Prince looked at him somewhat searchingly. Subsequently the relationship improved, for Trestrail was a quick learner.

If at first sight this seemed to outsiders to be a less than perfect prescription, then British monarchs and their families have tended to answer, 'So be it.' Like Queen

Victoria when faced with the threat presented by John Francis, they have preferred to take their chance and live some of the time, at least, as normal, free people. This meant that they rather than their bodyguards were in charge of the minutiae of their lives, particularly on those days not devoted to affairs of state.

This left the protection officers with a dilemma. To be sure, they were responsible for guarding the royal family from assassins, kidnappers and terrorists. But they were also the screen between the family and other security agencies. Essentially this conflict of roles reflected the need to protect the monarch as a state institution (the responsibility of the Metropolitan Police Commissioner) and the desires of the Queen as a human being who detests undue fuss. (She once told an editor of the *News of the World*: 'Oh, what a pompous man you are!')

Rare public statements about their security by members of the royal family reflect the protection officer's problem. Shortly before his assassination by Irish terrorists in 1979, Lord Mountbatten shrugged off Special Branch pleas that he should go somewhere other than Ireland for boating holidays. In May 1986 during a television interview, Princess Anne observed: 'If someone decides it is worth his while either kidnapping or just killing you, I don't think there is anything constructive either we or anyone else can do about it.'

(By a sad irony her interviewer was Terry Waite, special envoy of the Archbishop of Canterbury, who was kidnapped in Beirut after discharging his British-trained Druze bodyguard.)

Almost a year after that interview, in an unattributable talk with Spanish journalists, Prince Charles declared that he was less likely to be a target of the Basque terrorist movement, ETA, than of the IRA or one of its offshoots. 'I'm not much of a target,' he declared. 'If it came it would be from the IRA. If your name is on the bullet, there is nothing you can do about it.'

Publication of those remarks with full attribution to source by journalists who betrayed the terms agreed for the interview provoked a diplomatic rumpus. Such royal fatalism, at a time when ETA gunmen were stalking the Spanish monarch, King Juan Carlos, Prince Charles's host, was not in itself surprising. Some observers detected a consistency in royal attitudes to personal safety that even touched the Queen's own driving habits when she was observed driving home from Sandringham church, a protection officer in the passenger seat alongside her ('on the box' in royal parlance), neither of them restrained by a seat belt.

The selection and training of royal protection officers, until around 1980, was artfully arranged so as to ensure that the right sort of personality was recruited. During Perkins' reign, freshly-promoted young inspectors with a sound background in the obedient rota of duties in the uniformed service, far removed from the cleverness of Special Branch, were most favoured. They had to be of good appearance and be able to merge into the scenery of royal public engagements with the elegance of canapés at a cocktail party.

Since they would rarely see their own homes, unmarried men had an advantage over their more domesticated colleagues. One of the team recently estimated that in an average year he would expect to be overseas 125 nights and another forty away from home within the UK. Unlike Special Branch men doing a similar job, members of the Royal and Diplomatic Protection Group were (and are) not paid overtime, though they do receive a modest allowance to compensate them for 'unsocial hours'.

For all those working close to the monarchy, the travel is formidable. Former press secretary Michael Shea accompanied the Queen to fifty-three countries. Trestrail's service took him to Argentina; Canada; Yugoslavia (three times); Hungary; West Germany repeatedly, for the royal family's blood relatives are still there; France; Norway; Sweden; Holland; Switzerland; Italy; Malta; Finland (twice); Tunisia; Algeria; Morocco; Tanzania; Malawi; Zambia; Botswana; Canada; the USA (twice); the Caribbean (several times); Japan; Hong Kong (twice); Australia and New Zealand (more than a dozen times); Tonga; Fiji; Papua-New Guinea; Christmas Island; Norfolk Island; Hawaii; Samoa; Mexico ... and so on, through sixteen years of royal protection, nine of them with the Queen, with whom he is still a favourite. In most cases, the protection officer had made a preliminary trip to the territory to be visited, to check the security arrangements in advance.

Once the visit was under way, the bodyguard's demeanour was vital. Trestrail, faithful to the Perkins code so long as it was practicable, would instruct newcomers to the team: 'It doesn't matter if there are thirty thousand Hottentots running towards you with blunderbusses: you will smile as if it is the greatest joke on earth. That is what They expect. The last thing They want from Their protection officer is a face that suggests the world is about to end.'

He was tested by his own counsel in Papua New Guinea. The Queen was receiving a traditional welcome from the island's primitive (and recently cannibalistic) 'mud men'. She stood at the rear of a Range-Rover, with Trestrail in the front of the vehicle. The ceremony included a series of war charges by the dancers. They were armed with spears which they thrust vigorously towards the Queen, swivelling the spear by its haft, in tribute to the monarch, at the last second. She accepted these and handed them to Trestrail, who tried not to appear anxious.

It is open to question whether such deliberate exposure to danger would now be permitted the Queen or her protection team. Times change. In the sixties and seventies, although the bodyguards' firearms training was minimal, much attention was dedicated to *dressing* the officers correctly. One man with experience of that time recalls his growing astonishment at the size of his wardrobe, for which he did not pay.

'On a particular day I was sent to a leading military tailor in London to be measured for formal dinner suits (full tails and white tie; morning dress and black tie); lounge suits; tropical wear; country and mountain gear suitable for the shoot . . . even a shooting seat/stick. The idea was to make me "part of the wallpaper".'

When the tailor archly enquired whether any special provision was to be made to accommodate Sir's firearm, the reply was, 'That's not your problem. You leave that to me.'

The same officer confesses that when he was issued with his first firearm, he was instructed to carry the pistol in one pocket and the bullets in another, to avoid accidents. Later he attended the basic Metropolitan Police firearms course, target shooting twenty-five yards from a stationary target while maintaining what cynics describe as the 'stand-and-deliver' posture. Derived from competition shooting, it required the bodyguard to assume a stance with one hand on his hip while the other held the gun single-handed and, it was hoped, decorously.

The reality, as Inspector Jim Beaton, George Cross, was to discover in the Mall one night in 1974, was anything but elegant. The postwar pioneers of close protection received no professional training other than basic pistol practice. The manifold protection skills of evasive driving, threat analysis, close escort, resuscitation and so on were learned, if they were learned at all, from more senior colleagues on the job.

Such colleagues, part of a very small team indeed, were

often grossly overworked and the example they set was occasionally bizarre. One veteran was famous for switching off the light in his hotel room with his pistol. He shot the bulb out. Even in the remoteness of northern India this aroused some comment. The Foreign Office duty 'dog' was up much of the night composing a diplomatic signal to London to explain the circumstances surrounding the incident.

Another protection officer, whose advances to a young woman attached to the staff of Gordonstoun School were rejected, threatened to do something rash with the weapon he carried. He was persuaded to change his mind and was posted elsewhere.

Yet others were not fit or young enough to cope with the prolonged stress and immense fatigue that went with days of endless vigilance. In 1975 a sergeant in his mid-thirties joined Princess Anne in some routine gardening on a fine August day. She then noticed that he had fallen victim to a seizure which might have been epilepsy. Certainly he was foaming at the mouth. She coolly administered first aid and, having somehow got him into her car, drove him to hospital.

Two protection officers have died prematurely during service at Balmoral: one (like Queen Victoria's Inspector Baker) in his sleep; the other – for many years the Queen Mother's bodyguard – died in the late 1970s while walking on the hills overlooking Balmoral. At least one royal chauffeur responsible for Prince Charles also suffered a heart attack, though not a fatal one. To the problems of physical health in royal service can be added those of low morale resulting from marital breakdown, a condition which itself is a cliché of the protection officer's lifestyle.

There is still no mandatory medical examination for members of the Royal Protection team other than the basic test which they pass on joining the police as raw recruits. And though the vocational training of bodyguards has improved, that of the key chauffeurs has not: efforts to encourage them to attend evasive driving courses at the Hendon police driving school made little headway. One veteran told the author, 'Only junior Royal Mews drivers could be spared, it seemed. The Queen's chauffeurs were always too busy.'

Such experience sharply contrasts with the belief of military protection officers who sometimes guard members of the royal family, that a bodyguard should be physically fit and strong enough to carry his charge to a place of safety. Nor do such incidents seem to have aroused any unease on the part of the Home Office, the Metropolitan Police, the Household or the royal family itself. Not even the explosion of violence in Northern Ireland in 1968–69 triggered off a response, although politicians such as the Home Secretary and Northern Ireland Secretary were deemed to be in need of armed guards and bullet-proof cars.

The official assessment of the Irish problem was that the IRA could not afford the loss of sympathy it would suffer among its North American supporters if it attacked a member of the popular British royal family. In the light of events in August 1969, when the Royal Ulster Constabulary found it necessary to take to the streets of Belfast with armoured cars, and to use .50 Browning machine guns at short range in the Lower Falls area, this was breathtakingly optimistic. The policy remained unchanged until the assassination of Lord Mountbatten, a distant cousin of the Queen and her husband's uncle, in 1979.

As it happened, 1968 was not only the year in which modern political terrorism first became manifest in Europe and – as it hit European interests through hijacking – in the Middle East as well. It was also the dawn of greater exposure of the royal family to public contact, and therefore risk, through the institution of the 'walkabout'.

A walkabout, in spite of its nuance of aboriginal solitude,

may be defined as a set-piece occasion in which the VIP –
if he is a politician – shakes hands and 'feels the flesh' or,
as the Queen has developed the art, accepts an amiable
closeness to people which gets no more visceral than the
acceptance of posies of flowers. The relevance of this ritual
to close protection is that it brings a large number of people,
not all of them security-screened, within the potential killing
zone of ten feet or so within which the assassin has a fair
chance of causing deadly harm with a pistol, hand grenade,
knife or – as in Pate's case – even a cane. When the close
protection officer is kept busy accepting the posies as well,
as sometimes happens, it reduces his chances of responding
instantly to an emergency. This is well known in bodyguard
training schools, which have photographs of some leader,
on a walkabout, surrounded by people whose hands are
stretched towards him. The professionals have a phrase to
describe the risk. It is, 'Watch the hands!'

If, in spite of being a receptacle for floral tributes, he does
respond to an apparent assault, the royal bodyguard's
efforts do not always win him applause. At Bristol University some years ago a man dressed in Puritan garb vaulted
a crowd barrier and moved towards the Queen. A Special
Branch officer attached to the local police brought the man
down with a Rugby tackle while another official gently
touched the Queen's shoulder to guide her away.

Flushed with anger, the Queen paused conspicuously to
talk with a pensioner in the crowd. By now, it was apparent
that the 'Puritan' was an American and a dedicated royalist
who wanted to pay homage in a manner which has been
out of style for the last century or so. On board the royal
yacht *Britannia* that evening the guests included the Chief
Constable of Avon and the official who had broken the
basic, if unwritten, rule that the Queen is not to be touched.
At first it seemed as if each of them might be on the receiving
end of a royal rebuke. But instead, the Chief Constable and

Trestrail, her personal detective, were able to discuss the incident as fellow professionals. The Queen was respectfully told that there would have been greater reason for criticism if the police had not intercepted the exuberant American. Historical overtones apart, there was no guarantee that this Puritan was not a regicide.

The Queen's visit to the Royal Tank Regiment's fiftieth anniversary parade at Reinsehlen, West Germany, on 14 July 1967 was an illustration of the new trend towards more exposure and less formality. An elaborate Anglo-German security plan included a ten-man Royal Military Police escort team on roads to and from the nearest airfield. The plan failed because of regal spontaneity and lack of horsepower. When the Queen stopped her car to receive yet more flowers, or slowed down the procession to acknowledge the crowd, the British escort lacked sufficient acceleration to catch up with the royal convoy as it sped away, comfortably accompanied by German police Mercedes limousines. By the time the party reached Wietzenbruch airfield for the flight back to Britain, the Military Police escort was a full twenty minutes behind. ('We were,' said one, 'just out of sight.')

In the fullness of time, the walkabout would become a formal part of the programme, using – if circumstances warranted it – a 'sanitised' crowd of people such as military families who would pose little or no risk. But the scale of most royal tours still renders it impossible to eliminate the risk completely. Since 1977 at least, those charged with royal protection have been engaged in a battle of wits with terrorists hoping to make political capital from a spectacular assassination.

The comparatively open lifestyle enjoyed by the Queen and her family received its first body-blow in 1974. Just as the Windsors had shared the risk of the 1940 blitz with their people, so events would now demonstrate that (like other Londoners) they could not count on safety a few yards from home in a country not formally at war.

Until the kidnap attempt on Princess Anne in March of that year, the Queen and others felt free to drive out of Buckingham Palace into London's traffic and down the familiar road to Windsor, unencumbered by radio contact with the police, and certainly unescorted by a back-up vehicle manned by additional bodyguards. One personal CP officer usually, though not invariably, went with him or her. Perkins had retired a year earlier in 1973 and had been succeeded by his deputy, Michael Trestrail, but the Perkins–Windsor style of security was still intact. (At that time, any efforts to change the system would have encountered vigorous resistance and would probably have led to the removal of the officer who tried.)

Princess Anne, for her part, was memorable as a sportswoman who presented special problems for her less fit bodyguards. She was the royal skier who borrowed a motorised skidoo during a trip to Austria, to the dismay of her military escort. They, on humble skis, could not stay with her. She solved the problem by towing them. The escorts' task of staying upright without losing weapons, while travelling at high speed in a blur of snow, was a unique experience.

In 1974, in keeping with the Perkins-Windsor style, it was left entirely to the discretion of the protection officer whether he carried a firearm. As it happened, the courageous man travelling with Princess Anne on the night of 20 March 1974 did have his gun with him. Unfortunately, it did not work.

Inspector Jim Beaton was a good example of the best that the Perkins–Trestrail system could recruit to Royal Protection. Smaller and more slightly built than most police officers, he is of dapper appearance and quick intelligence.

His soft Aberdonian accent renders him classless south of the border. He would pass for a Civil Service mandarin or – in a certain light – for the former Liberal leader, David Steel.

He had used a shotgun regularly before joining the police in 1962, at which point, as a young probationer, he was plunged into the bewildering dirt of London's King's Cross area. Out of curiosity and because he wanted a day away from the seedy routine of the capital's most unlovely red light area, he went for a basic police marksman's qualification, shooting the .38 Colt revolver one day a year.

The Royal Protection Group regularly runs short of suitable volunteers and 1973 was no exception. The established strength then was as follows: the Queen, one officer, known as the 'personal detective'; Prince Andrew, Prince Edward, the Queen Mother and Princess Margaret, one personal protection officer each. The Duke of Edinburgh, the Prince of Wales and Princess Anne were each allocated two officers. In practice, the thirteen full-time Royal Protection officers covered for one another, particularly at weekends. It was perhaps symbolic that the Queen's personal protection was minimal, just as her limousine was not armoured long after those of some of her ministers had been.

Inspector Beaton had joined the team as No. 11 in March 1973 after some training with a self-loading pistol (often inaccurately described as an 'automatic'), the 9 mm Walther PPK. This is a Franco-German weapon and a favourite of many plain-clothes security teams because of its comparatively slim profile. The more bulky revolver has to be carried on the belt, as some Special Branch men were to discover the hard way. But like all self-loaders, the Walther has a magazine spring which might malfunction unless the magazine is emptied frequently, relieving the continuous pressure of ammunition compressed on top of it. Some

Metropolitan Police firearms instructors found a more serious fault: hairline cracks in a number of their training weapons.

Having completed his introductory training with the weapon, Inspector Beaton did one or two sessions of refresher training, firing at a static target from a standing position. Malfunctions – known in the trade as 'stoppages' – were not covered in any detail. Once the refresher training with the Walther was completed, the weapon was loaded, holstered and carried with a full magazine.

This refresher training required expenditure of around fifty rounds in contrast with the 108 bullets expended on a four-day basic course introduced in 1967, long after Beaton had first qualified as a marksman, and dramatically fewer than the 1,700 rounds fired in basic training by Royal Military Police bodyguards who, as soldiers, are already familiar with small arms.

On the night of Wednesday, 20 March 1974, the Queen was visiting Indonesia with the faithful Michael Trestrail as her guardian. Princess Anne and her husband Captain Mark Phillips had attended a reception and film in the City to help a disabled riders' charity. Inspector Beaton had asked for a soft drink but none was available. His thirst was hardly quenched by the single glass of wine he permitted himself.

At 7.50 pm they were in the Mall in the antiquated but comfortable limousine used by the Princess and a few minutes away from Buckingham Palace when the driver stopped abruptly. Beaton observed that a car had stopped on their offside, barring their way. He concluded that this was a routine brush with another neurotically reactive London driver who felt slighted. The driver of the other car was out of his vehicle now and approaching them.

Beaton, leaving it to his own driver to exchange the usual insults, darted from his front passenger seat, round the rear of the royal vehicle, and positioned himself protectively outside the rear offside door. Behind that door sat Princess Anne, Captain Phillips and a lady-in-waiting, Miss Rowena Brassey, facing Captain Phillips. Beaton was responding to instinct rather than knowledge, for none of the royal limousines was fitted with a rear-view mirror for the protection officer. Also, he had no radio with which to summon assistance. Throughout the dramatic events which followed, his impression of the other driver – Ian Ball – was of 'a tall, thin shadow'.

The chauffeur, a fellow Scot, Alexander Callender, had a better chance to know what was happening, that Ball's white Ford Escort had deliberately cut across the front of the limousine, forcing it to stop, and that Ball himself, as he stepped out, was armed with a pistol. Had he had the benefit of modern training, Mr Callender might have tried to reverse the vehicle out of trouble but those familiar with that particular vehicle question whether the reverse gear was in sufficiently reliable working order to respond to an emergency manoeuvre.

As soon as Inspector Beaton rounded the offside corner of the Rolls and came into Ball's sight, the assailant's gun flashed. Beaton felt the thump of the bullet against his chest. He ducked back out of sight and drew his gun, his mind working in a slow, deliberate fashion. He told himself, 'Now you're being shot at. You could shoot back.'

Only when he was again exposed to Ball's fire did Beaton discover that his arm was so weak that he could not easily lift the Walther pistol with one hand. He tried, but the weapon went off before he could take aim. The Princess later told the author Nicholas Courtney:

'The policeman got off one shot which I am convinced came through the back window of the car as something hit me on the back of the head – so I thought that was a good start.'

It is a fair guess that Princess Anne was struck by a piece of debris, but was evidently unhurt.

Doggedly, Beaton tried again, lifting the pistol with both hands, pointing at his assailant with some care and pulling the trigger and . . . Click! Nothing happened. The round had come up from the magazine a fraction of a second too slowly and, instead of moving smoothly into the breech to be fired, was trapped like a crumpled cigarette between the head of the magazine and the slide mechanism above it.

A well-trained pistol handler would have snatched the slide with his left hand and worked it vigorously backward to clear the obstruction, but Inspector Beaton was already losing blood. He returned to the nearside of the car and did make some attempt to follow this drill.

From within the car, Princess Anne and Captain Phillips were holding the door closed as Ball tried to open it. This led to a tug-o'-war for possession of Princess Anne as Ball tried to haul the Princess from the car by one arm while her other was anchored by her husband. Throughout, Anne calmly repeated that she was not going with the man, as he was insisting. Then her blue velvet dress split at the shoulder and the sleeve came away. The Princess and her husband promptly slammed the door shut again.

Beaton, meanwhile, emerged from the nearside of the car to confront Ball, who snarled at him, 'Put your gun down or I'll shoot.' The protection officer did so, worrying – as he told a friend later – that 'someone would then kick my gun and it would start working, so I would never be able to prove that it had jammed.'

Unarmed and still bleeding from his chest wound, Beaton now clambered into the rear of the limousine to sit alongside Princess Anne, whose security he was still determined to defend. Rowena Brassey, the lady-in-waiting, was now outside the car and moving towards the discarded pistol herself (like, in an earlier age, Queen Victoria's amateur but loyal bodyguards) only to be told by a female spectator, 'Don't touch it!'

Not everyone chose to regard the incident as casual entertainment. A freelance journalist named John McConnell had heard the shots and ordered his cab to stop while he investigated the fuss. Ball's response was to produce a second firearm, a .22 revolver, with which he shot McConnell in the chest. As the journalist staggered away, Ball turned his attention back to the Princess. He shouted at Beaton to open the door and threatened to shoot again.

Beaton's instinctive reaction when he saw the muzzle at the window was to raise his hand, palm outstretched. In the same instant, Ball fired once more. The shot came through the window and tore into the inspector's right hand just below the thumb. Princess Anne had been in the line of fire. It seems certain that if Beaton did not save her life in that moment, he assuredly averted her grievous disfigurement.

Yet another would-be rescuer now arrived. A uniformed officer, PC Michael Hills (on duty at St James's Palace nearby) alerted neighbouring Cannon Row police station on his personal radio – the first time the incident was officially noted – and then, as he moved towards Ball, he too was shot in the stomach. Hills bravely tried to use Beaton's discarded Walther but he collapsed before he could touch the weapon. Since it was not working, this was just as well.

Increasingly desperate, Ball now shot the chauffeur Callender in the chest as Callender opened the car door. At the rear of the vehicle, in a confused mental state resulting from loss of blood and shock, Beaton convinced himself that there was a crowd outside which was likely to be friendly. Ball was now on the other side of the door and he was trying to open it.

Beaton told Captain Phillips to let go of the door handle, then opened the door himself and kicked out at the same time from a sitting position on the floor (which he shared with the two royal passengers). Ball's response was to shoot the inspector a third time. This bullet entered the officer's stomach causing a potentially lethal wound. Beaton slid out of the car and on to the pavement, all but unconscious.

Yet more people were now taking notice of the mêlée. A second driver, Glenmore Martin, a chauffeur, was the first person on the scene to use his vehicle as a weapon against the kidnapper. He blocked Ball's Ford with the Jaguar he was driving but then dismounted, to be threatened by Ball. As Martin retreated, Ball again tried to drag Princess Anne from her car. She told him, politely but obstinately, to go away.

Now Ronald Russell, also passing the scene in a taxi, intervened and punched Ball who fired a shot which missed and splintered the taxi's window. Russell was still struggling with Ball when police cars descended. Princess Anne, as quoted by Nicholas Courtney (ibid.), said that at this point she reached for the door handle behind her head.

'I opened the door and literally did a back somersault on to the road and then waited, because I thought that if I was out of the car he (Ball) might move and he did eventually, and went to the front of the car. I got back into the car and shut the door.'

Russell was still struggling with Ball when the first police car arrived. Ball broke free and ran towards St James's Park. The Princess emerged. 'Go on!' she shouted to the police. 'There's your chance!'

Seconds later, the fugitive was flattened in a flying tackle by a burly Detective Constable Peter Edwards.

In court subsequently, Ball entered pleas of guilty to two attempted murder charges and a series of other offences. He was ordered to be held for an indefinite period under the Mental Health Act, 1959. Yet there was much evidence that he was not acting on some insane impulse. Using an alias, he had rented a house in Fleet, Hampshire, and had made clear preparations to use it as a prison. Like Arthur O'Connor in 1872, he carried a note demanding a free pardon for the kidnap and other crimes, as well as a ransom demand for £3 million. Like Edward Oxford in 1840, he had come armed with two pistols. He was acting alone and yet was able to follow the Princess unobserved and come close to a successful kidnap.

The response of government was illuminating. It very properly recognised the courage of those who had intervened, notably Inspector Beaton, who was awarded the George Cross and appointed the Queen's protection officer in succession to Commander Trestrail in 1982. Other awards were made to Russell and Hills (George Medals) and to McConnell and Callender (Queen's Gallantry Medal). The authorities also scapegoated the Walther pistol carried by Beaton and other protection officers, including Special Branch officers guarding government ministers.

Gould and Waldren point out in *London's Armed Police*:

Within days, D11 staff [firearms specialists] had been ordered to implement a crash training programme to instruct protection officers on the Smith & Wesson .38 Special, Model 36 – a short-barrelled revolver. One of the problems associated with a self-loading pistol had always been the time required to clear a stoppage and fire another shot. If a round failed to fire in a revolver the firer merely squeezed the trigger again, which caused the cylinder to revolve and brought another round in line with the firing pin. By contrast, when a pistol malfunctioned it was necessary to pull back the slide to its fullest extent, which ejected the unfired round, and then release the slide . . . Failure to pull the slide fully back against the stop, either through stress, injury or maladroitness, resulted in the dud round's failing to be thrown clear through the ejection port.

In fact, another vital change was made even before the switch from the Walther self-loading pistol to the American Smith & Wesson revolver. Protection officers assisting the Metropolitan Police inquiry at the time noted that tests of ammunition imported for the Walther revealed a surprising number of duds.

'Until that night, the ammunition issued to protection officers was rubbish, but it was cheap rubbish,' one commented. 'It was rapidly withdrawn and replaced with much better, more expensive stuff even before the revolver replaced the Walther.'

Other security agencies, including SAS soldiers in the high risk business of undercover, plain-clothes surveillance in Northern Ireland, continued to rely upon a self-loading pistol, the Browning 9 mm (and still do). Such is their confidence in the fourteen rounds the weapon holds that each man might carry two Brownings during Q-car patrols round Belfast. And another government protection group is thought to be on the point of ordering a batch of new Walthers . . .

But the soldiers are aware of the limitations of a self-loader. When they regain the sanctuary of a safe base, the weapon is unholstered, the magazine extracted and the individual bullets expelled so as to remove dust and ease the magazine's spring. For a Royal Protection officer on call twenty-four hours a day, often performing duties which have nothing to do with security, this is not a practicable option. As a result the slim-line Walther, when it was carried at all before that night in the Mall, might remain for weeks undisturbed in its holster, the oiled mechanism collecting a harvest of pocket fluff. Nonetheless, the Walthers were withdrawn from police service . . . and issued to members of another high risk profession, the Northern Ireland Prison Service.

In the light of the Ball outrage, a Home Office study

produced other recommendations. For the first time, the Queen's vehicle was equipped with a police radio whose call-sign, 'Purple One', was tested by the Queen and her protection officer, Trestrail, from the Edgware Road, London. Trestrail later told a colleague that when the test succeeded, 'I knew how Marconi must have felt when his first signal got through.' For her part, the Queen wanted reassurance that she would not be pestered by radiotelephone calls as a result of this new security measure. For her, a car journey was one of the rare opportunities for respite from public attention.

As well as radios, royal limousines were also fitted with bullet-resistant glass and automatic locks on all doors. Even more important, Royal Protection officers were now given some formal training in bodyguard techniques for the first time. Early in 1975, Trestrail attended an SAS course in Herefordshire not as a student but as a 'VIP' whose protection from kidnap or assassination is the object of a three-day exercise. Live ammunition is used in the training and Trestrail had a unique exposure to the perception of his craft by the cleverest, most aggressive military minds.

It was not the first time that Metropolitan Police officers had trained with the SAS. Since 1970, police firearms instructors had been taught tricks of the trade on pistol courses run by the regiment. But across-the-board training in close protection encompasses more than weapon training. At Hereford it has even included the art of detecting poison in the principal's soup. One officer has been obliged to act as an operational taster when no chemical method of analysis was available to the people he was responsible for.

The bodyguard trainees who followed Trestrail to Hereford after 1975 were also given the chance to use a variety of exotic weapons held there, including machine-gun shotguns (a deadly close-quarter weapon, available for high-risk environments overseas) as well as Russian and Chinese automatic rifles. The reason for this was that in some Third World countries, heavy weaponry is politely deposited by the host government on the floor of the visitor's limousine, almost as discreetly as flowers at the bedside. One Royal Protection officer visiting Mexico had trouble persuading his hosts that he really did not wish to keep an automatic rifle as a permanent souvenir.

All this was light years from the low-profile approach favoured by the Palace. There, even a glimpse of visiting Special Branch officers dining below stairs without jackets, shoulder-holsters in view, was regarded with distaste. Pioneers such as Superintendent Brian Jeffery, then the Duke of Edinburgh's protection officer, returned from SAS training to a Palace regime still resistant to the Hereford style.

Equally significant was the Home Office's failure to amend its evaluation of the Irish threat to the royal family. The Whitehall line was unchanged. The practical response to Ball's assault was a narrow, minimal reaction to the menace posed by one determined, armed man acting alone, a man later deemed to be mentally unbalanced. The response, as it happened, preserved the public purse as well as the private preferences of the monarch and her nearest kin.

Yet if the domestic scenery around the royal family remained almost unchanged in so far as it was plausible, those conservative folk of the royal household had started to perceive security in a new light. For the first time for generations, as Beaton slowly recovered from his wounds, the Palace staff welcomed the protection officer not as 'The Policeman', or 'The Copper', an alien being, but as 'one of us'.

In 1977, celebrating twenty-five years as a monarch, the Queen undertook an elaborate programme of Silver Jubilee appearances. In Northern Ireland, at the height of the Protestant marching season, she opened the new University of Coleraine. The Army and the Royal Ulster Constabulary combined to provide an apparently impenetrable security screen, a task which the Queen's small personal protection team was happy to leave to those organisations.

The security reconnaissance, at which the Palace was represented, was memorable for a throwaway remark by an RUC threat evaluator.

'We expect no serious trouble,' he announced. 'Just, maybe, a wee demonstration somewhere.'

'What sort of "wee demonstration"?' Trestrail asked him.

'Well now, they might just blow up the oil refinery.'

Coleraine was far from the nearest refinery. Nevertheless, the precautions included a rehearsed evacuation by helicopter of a WRAC officer who acted as the Queen's stand-in. She later made some interesting observations about the ergonomic disadvantages of running in high heels and tight skirt to clamber into a machine whose rotor blades were already turning. What the men with stop watches made of it is not recorded.

For weeks before the visit, intelligence sources had concentrated upon the possibility of a bomb attack but there was no tip-off about this threat from any of the usual sources. Then on 29 July, almost two weeks before the Queen was expected, a routine search uncovered a bomb hidden in a lavatory on the campus. It was disarmed and then examined by a leading Army life-saver, the senior Ammunition Technical Officer for Northern Ireland, Lieutenant-Colonel Derrick Patrick OBE. Patrick, a dedicated pro who had grown up in London's dockland during the wartime blitz, noted that the bomb contained a new type of timer, first discovered in an Ulster arms dump nine months before. Patrick later wrote in his memoir, *Fetch*

Felix – The Fight Against the Ulster Bombers, 1976–77:
'This timer worked electrically instead of mechanically, and its main advantage to the terrorist was that it could be set to function a considerable period after the bomb had been hidden and with a fair degree of accuracy regarding time.'

Patrick named it the Sleeping Bomb. It had been first used shortly before, in Canada. In Europe, his warnings about it had not disturbed most security experts. This was surprising. To the back-street bomb-maker's art, such a device was arguably the greatest technical advance offered to terrorism since the invention of high explosive itself by Alfred Nobel in the nineteenth century. The full impact of the new weapon would not be felt until the Grand Hotel in Brighton erupted in 1984, almost obliterating an entire British government. It would be ten years before the prospect of a technical counter to the Sleeping Bomb started to come into use.

At Coleraine in 1977, saddled with a royal visit, the authorities began a careful search of the grounds on 4 August and the university buildings three days later. By now three additional bomb detection teams had been flown into the province. The royal visitors were to move by helicopter from that luxurious liferaft, the *Britannia*, itself moored beyond the range of mortar or land-based missiles, its specialised sonar identifying metal on the seabed nearby.

The vessel would accommodate numerous receptions during this risky visit but that in itself was not enough to guarantee the security of local VIPs embarking at Bangor and Portrush. Port facilities and the launches themselves were checked below the water line. To the normal difficulties of bomb hunting under water (for which Royal Naval clearance divers were flown in) was added the instruction that 'any devices found during the royal visit had to be cleared without alarming the royal party.'

Lieutenant-Colonel Patrick observed: 'The last requirement could be construed only as, "If you have to make a noise, make it quietly . . ."'

It was now 9 August, just forty-eight hours before the Queen was due to open the university. Patrick visited the scene to check again on the work of the team sweeping the place. All seemed normal. An hour after he left, a bomb exploded in the university grounds. The bomb was another sleeper.

Parallel with these events, in that cultural no man's land where the only independent source of debate available to the IRA leadership was a few half-trusted journalists, a Provisional chieftain was twitted by a liberal reporter who liked living dangerously. With twenty-four hours remaining before the Coleraine appearance, the reporter said something to the effect that the Provisional IRA seemed to be allowing the royal visit to pass off without so much as a puff of protest.

The IRA commander was unamused. Glancing at his watch he said, 'You'll be laughing the other sidea ya face this time tomorrow.' It was 10 am.

On the day of the royal visit, a formidable college of military talent assembled on the roof of the university alongside Lieutenant-Colonel Patrick. They included the GOC, Lieutenant-General Sir David House; the Commander, Land Forces, Major-General Dick Trant and the Chief Constable. On the floor immediately below prowled the Labour Secretary of State for Northern Ireland, Roy Mason, a pugnacious ex-miner who took a hard line with terrorism.

Patrick later described how the waters of the River Bann (a good fishing river, as Mason, an enthusiastic angler, noted) sparkled beyond the trees that morning. 'But someone reported that a bomb had been hidden somewhere . . .'

Mason, not the security experts, had to take the finely balanced decision to let the visit proceed. To cancel it at the last moment would be a propaganda coup for the IRA. To expose the monarch to death or mutilation would be an even greater disaster. Mason gambled on an unchanged programme. By 10 am, the affair would be in full swing . . .

Spectators admitted to the event, far from the treacherous streets of Belfast and Londonderry, were carefully vetted by security officers who passed them through a tight Coldstream Guards cordon. Once inside, their loyal applause was broadcast around the world's television networks, no less sincere for having been pasteurised. They, after all, were as much at risk as their royal visitors.

The moving finger reached 10 o'clock and the reporter telephoned the police information room in Belfast. No, nothing untoward was happening. No news was good news, was it not?

The royal party left amid the strained courtesy that passes for jocularity on such occasions, high heels crunching the gravel, protection officers looking nervously away from the VIP party as if searching the crowd for a friendly but elusive face. The Queen departed and the garden chairs were folded away.

That night, just before dusk, another bomb exploded in the shrubbery on waste ground near the university. It caused no damage and the RUC information department said dismissively that some rascal had hurled a device over a fence. The cognoscenti knew otherwise. Lieutenant-Colonel Patrick was in no doubt that this was the third, undetected sleeper. And the liberal reporter observed that the explosion had occurred at 10 o'clock, but at 10 pm and not, as intended, at 10 am.

'If the device had exploded at the correct time, it would have caused panic, but probably no casualties,' the reporter recalls. 'This was the political use of the new weapon, not a military operation. The authorities were right in thinking that at that time, the IRA could not risk a direct attack on a leading member of the royal family and certainly not one of the females.

'But the inhibition was not about the effect on American sentiment. What mattered far more to them – and what still counts – is the weight of opinion among the Catholic mums. Even in 1987 such newspapers as the *Irish News* [Ulster's leading republican newspaper] devote a lot of sympathetic coverage to the activities of Princess Diana and the Duchess of York. They do so because they know how popular the women in the royal family still are among the "republican" women of Belfast. It might not be good political logic, but that's how the sentiment is.'

But to any prudent risk analyst, the message was clear enough. In spite of the Catholic mums' vote, and in spite of Cousin Elmer in Boston, the IRA and its splinter groups were now beginning to regard the royal family as targets of some sort, even if – at first – the exercise took the form of impudent, republican playfulness.

There was also an element of military experiment at work. The third Coleraine bomb exploded twelve hours late but if it had been implanted several weeks before, this was not absolute technical failure. The teething troubles were still showing when the Brighton bomber, Patrick Magee, placed a sleeper in the Blackpool Imperial Hotel in 1983 at a time when the Conservative Party conference was taking place. That bomb failed to explode. It was 1984 before the sleeper's awesome potential was fulfilled at Brighton. By then, so much innocent blood had been shed in other ways that few people other than those who made or dismantled bombs, were concerned about the evolution of this weapon.

Later in that jubilee year the Queen visited the British Army of the Rhine at Sennelager and Paderborn in West Germany. For this event an entire para battalion – 2 Parachute Regiment in their blue lanyards – was required to man an outer cordon. Security *en route* for the British Queen and the German President was shared between German civil and British Royal Military Police, who were now increasingly taking over the direct role of military close protection from the SAS.

These men were implanted at every level of the ceremonial and its infrastructure. One armed sergeant major, disguised as a chef, was ordered to carve a salmon for the top table. When he admitted he knew nothing about cuisine, an irate Army chef roared, 'Then for goodness' sake get out of my way and make a cup of tea!' Another of the protection team stood behind the distinguished guests at the main banquet disguised as a flunkey.

After years of undercover work in Ireland the Army – and not just the SAS or Intelligence Corps – was familiar with clandestine activity. But there was still much to learn. The most hazardous issue on such a big occasion, involving so many armed spooks, was identification, or lack of it, among the people wearing civilian clothes. If someone produced a firearm from beneath his sports jacket, how could the security team be sure that this was an assassin rather than, say, a close protection officer belonging to another team, suddenly concerned about the condition of his pistol?

Distinctive lapel pins were issued but then it was discovered that German Boy Scouts were wearing the same identification. The solution chosen by Major Nicholas Crew RMP (now boss of the security firm Winguard International) was to mark the barrels of all bodyguard small arms with a luminous orange strip. In later years his successors adopted a counsel of perfection, insisting that every security agent should be able to recognise every other security agent, irrespective of service or nationality. For similar reasons the London police would insist that firearms were to be carried almost exclusively by uniformed officers.

In Germany in 1977, however, the hard fact was that on an occasion attended by 25,000 guests of whom 5,000 were German, it would be impossible to be absolutely certain. German police officers were instructed to carry a pamphlet entitled 'Special Investigations of Members of Baader-Meinhof Gang' as well as their firearms, but they were not expected to display the documents as a secret sign to their British colleagues.

Another problem for Crew was that the Queen's notorious (and rational) reluctance to travel by helicopter meant that, as usual, all her movement was by road, escorted by the faithful Michael Trestrail and an eminent Army doctor carrying resuscitation gear. To limit the risk further, members of the Army's Intelligence and Security Group kept 'selected houses close to the royal and presidential routes' under surveillance, while heavily armed close protection officers hovered over the royal route high enough to be unobtrusive but with a god-like perception of what was happening.

In the event, only one security scare occurred during that long and potentially dangerous day. At 1.45 pm, as the VIPs were assembling for lunch, a lance-corporal manning the police desk received a telephone call. The voice was male and the accent unmistakably Irish. It said:

'Hello. Listen carefully. There is a big bomb in the officers' mess.'

The corporal replied: 'Who is this calling?'

'The Provos,' said the voice.

Two messes which had been swept already as part of the general preparations were cleared and checked again within thirty minutes by a dog handler, sniffer dog and explosives expert. The call, from a public telephone in Germany, was a false alarm. But it should have been another warning to the Home Office threat evaluators, as well as the royal family itself, that they were being stalked by the IRA.

*

Shortly before he was blown up by Irish terrorists in 1979, Lord Mountbatten was a guest of the Scotland Yard Luncheon Club, an exclusive gathering limited to Metropolitan Police officers above the rank of inspector. By tradition, guests do not respond to their hosts' toasts by making speeches. Lord Mountbatten decided, nevertheless, to offer the assembly some reflections on close protection as he had known it.

As someone who was neither a prominent politician nor a member of the royal family who just might succeed to the throne (he was a grandson of Queen Victoria and the Duke of Edinburgh's uncle), he did not qualify for a police bodyguard in the United Kingdom. Ironically, it was when he visited the Irish Republic that the rules changed. His wife, who died in 1960, had inherited a Victorian mansion near the Atlantic coast in County Sligo, a home built originally for Lord Palmerston. In his years of widowerhood, Earl Mountbatten was still a regular visitor to his Irish estate. The Dublin Special Branch regarded him as a foreign dignitary who was at risk and – sometimes without saying so – discreetly attached a protective tail.

At the police Luncheon Club, Mountbatten boasted that he had soon rumbled what was going on and had decided to play games with his unrequested, unwanted escort. (Possibly, too, he had in mind the fate of the last British VIP to enjoy Garda protection, the British ambassador Christopher Ewart-Biggs who was assassinated while in their care in 1976.) Whatever the truth of that, Mountbatten drove fast and evasively across the wilds of the rural west, and the tail stayed with him, though only just. At last he halted on a deserted track under a bridge, as did the team detailed to follow him.

He now descended from the car and asked his pursuers what the hell they wanted, adding mischievously, 'You *are* journalists, I suppose?'

What they said in reply and what transpired as a result, history does not record. Soon afterwards, Mountbatten ignored suggestions by British Special Branch that it would be unwise to make his usual August pilgrimage, declaring, 'But they love me there!' When he arrived the Irish millionaire who rented the estate, Hugh Tunney, had also suggested that it was no longer safe, but this warning was also shrugged off.

In his biography *Mountbatten, Hero Of Our Time*, Richard Hough describes how the Earl acknowledged his escorts, Garda Kevin Henry and a fellow protection officer, at breakfast time on 27 August 1979. They were equipped with pistols, binoculars and a Ford Escort saloon car and they had been on duty since 6 am. Mountbatten bade them good morning and explained that he and his party were going out in his 29-foot motor cruiser, a converted fishing craft named *Shadow V*. The bodyguards would not be wanted on board. They would stay ashore in their Ford.

As Hough explains it: 'Until recently the boat had been guarded night and day and an officer had always gone out with Mountbatten. But he had asked for security to be relaxed – "Whoever would want to murder an old man like me?"

By now, the *Shadow V* had concealed beneath her decking a bomb which was detonated by a radio command triggered from a car ashore. The police escort, on the coastal road overlooking the scene (like the bombers, as it turned out), watched the catastrophe through binoculars but were unable to do anything about it. It was left to civilians in other boats nearby to retrieve the dead and the dying, including Mountbatten.

Mountbatten was a favourite uncle to the whole royal family and none of the Windsors was untouched by the shock of his loss, one made even sadder by the massacre, on the same day, of twenty Parachute Regiment soldiers at

Warrenpoint. The Duke of Edinburgh, who is normally less sensitive than a well-used bulldozer, was as wounded as the rest by his uncle's murder. The task of breaking the news to him, while he was on a private visit to friends in Normandy, fell to his personal protection officer, Superintendent Brian Jeffery, a veteran of twelve years' royal service.

When Jeffery gave his boss the message that he should telephone the British Ambassador in Paris, Philip said Jeffery should handle it. Politely but firmly Jeffery said, 'I think you should call him yourself, sir.'

The Duke raised his eyebrows, looked searchingly at his bodyguard and said, 'Why, exactly?'

The issue could not be ducked. Jeffery replied bleakly, 'I understand Lord Mountbatten is dead.'

As he learned the full horror of Mountbatten's murder, Philip was close to tears.

Jeffery observed later: 'The assassination of Lord Mountbatten changed our thinking about both our intelligence and theirs, and the degree to which the family were at risk.'

It did not help that the republican movement itself disclaimed 'credit' for the killing, blaming it on a breakaway faction which would be 'punished'.

Yet if the thinking about royal protection changed, not much else did. The Metropolitan Police Commissioner, Sir David McNee, set up a working party to scrutinise urgently the whole issue. The recommendations which resulted a few weeks later, in September 1979, proposed electronic defences at Buckingham Palace and elsewhere. However, as Gould and Waldren noted:

'Nearly three years later, despite efforts by Scotland Yard, officials of the Royal Household, the Home Office and the Department of the Environment were still juggling with the hot potato. None of the suggested security measures had been implemented by 6.40 am on Friday 9 July 1982 when Michael Fagan walked into the Queen's bedroom. Fagan was no stranger to Buckingham Palace, which he had entered a month previously. On that occasion, the court found him not guilty of the offence with which he was charged, but guilty of another matter unconnected with the Palace . . . He was committed to a mental hospital; it had obviously been a short stay.'

Some hours before, cloaked in darkness, Fagan had penetrated the place via a window near the Royal Gallery, housing the Queen's art collection. This had triggered off an electronic alarm. The uniformed police night watch looked around and discovered nothing amiss. This was no surprise. Fagan had already retreated again, closing the window as he left. The night watch concluded that the electronics had developed a fault.

Fagan then returned to try his luck a second time. He climbed railings near the front of the building and, from a concealed vantage point, he saw a car arrive. This brought one of the Royal Protection officers on his way to work. Fagan's luck held: he was not detected by an electronic beam which should have registered his presence.

The Queen was half awake and her bedroom was unguarded. At her suggestion, a uniformed constable formerly posted outside the royal bedchamber had just been replaced by a liveried footman. But at that hour, the footman was also absent, taking the royal corgis for their walk in the gardens.

Fagan now chose, apparently at random, a drainpipe, which he climbed to reach the second floor. The Royal Protection team had recommended the use of a special, slippery paint which would have rendered the pipe unclimbable but this initiative was quashed by Environment Department bureaucrats.

The window Fagan chose to enter the Palace main building was a few yards from the royal bedchamber. In the corridor on his way there, the intruder passed two cleaning women. In spite of his unkempt appearance — he was an obvious tramp — they made no comment and did not report on what they had seen.

It is anyone's guess how Fagan came to choose the door to the Queen's bedroom. The Queen was expecting the chambermaid, who would normally draw back the main curtains, silently deposit a cup of tea by the bedside and withdraw. When Her Majesty sensed that a stranger was in the room, which was almost immediately, she softly pressed a button to summon the footman. He, of course, was absent.

Next, the Queen kept Fagan in conversation about trifles, particularly his need of cigarettes. He, sitting at the end of the bed, blood dripping from a cut wrist, said he could certainly use a smoke. As if ordering a packet for him, the Queen lifted up her bedside telephone and told the switchboard, 'Send a policeman up here immediately.' The switchboard relayed the message to the police post in the Palace, but because such a request was alien to the usual practice of preserving a decent distance between the sovereign in her bedchamber and the police, no one responded until a new duty shift came on duty a full half hour later. The response of the incoming officer, studying the jottings of the night's official log and, finally discovering a note of the call with a blank still under the box marked 'Action Taken', may be imagined. Things now moved fast and Fagan was taken into custody.

In the clamour which followed, another report was drawn up, this time by an Assistant Commissioner. It was circulated to the royal family but not to their individual protection officers. Individual reactions varied. The Duke of Edinburgh wanted to hand the entire protection operation over to the Army but that overstretched service, with commitments in Ireland, Germany, Belize, the Falkland Islands, South Georgia, Hong Kong and elsewhere, was not anxious to take on this additional chore. Only minor changes resulted, including the more frequent movement of uniformed police officers from Palace duties to general work elsewhere. Until then, some Palace protection work had been becoming a sinecure.

'The old, grey veterans were able to mark time at the Palace to the end of their careers,' one senior bodyguard commented. 'It was a much-needed change.'

If an unemployed tramp destroyed one royal taboo (that the law did not permit trespass into the Queen's bedroom) it was a squeaky-clean ex-Army cadet who had damaged another facet of the legend a year earlier. In June 1981 the Queen was riding on horseback in the Mall, on her way to review the Colour as every sovereign has done since 1743. On this occasion, six shots exploded near her. The cartridges were blanks fired from a starting pistol, but horses are not entirely predictable beasts.

The youth responsible, Marcus Sarjeant, was pounced on by soldiers and one close protection officer planted in the crowd by Michael Trestrail. Sarjeant, like Arthur O'Connor a century earlier, was imprisoned under the Treason Act (for five years) but later, as his mental condition deteriorated, he was locked up in a secure hospital from which, shortly before the 1986 Trooping, he briefly absconded.

In spite of the atmosphere of danger evoked by the shots, the Queen, with characteristic courage, ignored advice to make the one-mile journey back to the sanctuary of the Palace in a closed coach or a limousine. Her back straight, chin up and riding side saddle, she guided her dignified old horse Burmese at a pace which seemed to some of her security advisers to be too measured. The Queen would give up riding Burmese publicly a year or so later for reasons which had nothing to do with security. But in 1981 the crowd, and millions of television viewers, adored this fastidious display of regal sang-froid. More sober minds perceived that the conflict between royal risk and royal exposure was becoming acute.

In October 1981, the Queen visited Dunedin on New Zealand's South Island. Three schoolboys took a .22 rifle to the Octagon area of the city where the Queen staged her first local walkabout. The leader of the three, an inventive seventeen-year-old named Christopher Lewis, had tried to stab his stepfather two years earlier. He was now a fascist who was about to launch his own terrorist movement. His first victim would be the Queen.

The adolescent hit team's first choice as firing point was so perfect that it was soon visited by two policemen looking for a good vantage point from which to enjoy the spectacle. The boys left quietly, taking the weapon with them. Next, young Lewis went to an office rented by a friend's father near the local university, where the Queen again went on a walkabout. This time, he levelled the weapon on a carefully chosen trajectory down to the open space the Queen would cross.

As she moved into the target area, his finger closed gently round the trigger but at a range of 600 yards, the low calibre bullet fell short. Police, including the local commissioner walking immediately behind the Queen, heard the shot and dismissed it as a backfiring car. Lewis concealed his rifle and fled.

Several weeks later Lewis, who was readily identified by his red hair, was arrested with his two followers after carrying out an armed raid on a post office during a school break. The theft of £8,000 was serious enough, or so the police thought. They found his assertion that he had also tried to assassinate the head of the Commonwealth scarcely credible. The full truth of the affair was hushed up until Lewis escaped from a secure psychiatric hospital six years later in 1987.

As a result of the hunt to recapture him, a former detective sergeant named, coincidentally, Tom Lewis, announced that every detail of the assassination story had been confirmed. Christopher Lewis had raided a gun shop near the Queen's route in another town to steal the weapon. This was recovered from the hide where he had planted it. The ex-detective added:

'Christopher Lewis had worked out the firing angles and there is no doubt that at his first attempt, he would have got her. The shooting was played right down because it was political. We wanted to throw the book at him. This was a case of treason and it is the only offence carrying the death penalty in New Zealand. But there were messages from Wellington. The police were told they couldn't charge him with that.

'We were told not to mention anything to anybody about it. Our security had been found wanting. There was a possibility there would never be another royal tour without changes to our security system.'

Lewis was tried in December of that year for unlawfully and dangerously discharging a weapon and received a remarkably lenient three-year sentence. Only then was anything said to the royal security team in London about the affair. The team had learned, by now, the dangers of being less than earnest about such problems in New Zealand. On an earlier visit, fireworks had been hurled at the Queen and Prince Philip at Waitangi, scene of the first treaty between Victoria's representative and the Maoris. During the same tour a chain was raised as a barrier in an effort to halt the royal car. But when Albert Perkins expressed concern to his charges about such lapses of security, he was advised to preserve his sense of humour.

In 1983, during a visit by the Prince of Wales to New Zealand, Christopher Lewis tried to escape from a secure psychiatric ward to which he had been transferred from prison. His namesake, the former detective Tom Lewis, commented, 'Drawings and notes in his hospital cell showed how he intended to kill Prince Charles ... The guy is absolutely nuts.' Nevertheless, Christopher Lewis was released from hospital in 1986. He promptly resumed his career of armed robbery (and also became an exponent of an oriental martial art named 'Ninja'). During the hunt which followed his latest crimes he rammed a road block with a stolen car and escaped on foot into dense rain forest. Eleven days later, he was arrested when he tried to buy a second-hand car.

The threats to royalty represented by Lewis, Sarjeant, Fagan and the killers of Lord Mountbatten could not be assessed in isolation from what was happening elsewhere at the same time, any more than the attacks on Queen Victoria could be distanced (as Gladstone sought to do) from the political assassinations of the nineteenth century. In 1976, Ewart-Biggs was killed by a car bomb. In 1979, Airey Neave was similarly murdered. The Egyptian President Anwar Sadat was assassinated by troops on parade before him in 1981. In October 1984 the Indian Prime Minister, Indira Gandhi, was gunned down by her own Sikh bodyguard. She was a graduate of Mrs Thatcher's Oxford college, Somerville, and the death was felt severely by her British counterpart. Within weeks, the bomb at the Grand Hotel, Brighton, came close to wiping out most of the British government including Mrs Thatcher. President Reagan (March 1981) and Pope John Paul II (May 1981) miraculously survived assassins' bullets which struck their targets.

By an interesting irony, the Palace acquired as its new Press Secretary in 1978 Michael Shea. When Mr Shea left the job in 1987, the *Observer* editor, Donald Trelford, noted:

> Fifty years after the Abdication crisis, republicanism has died as an issue in British politics. Even the radical *New Statesman* had to admit that it put on sales when it pictured Princess Diana on the cover. Twenty years after the decolonisation of the Commonwealth, the Queen is still head of state in eighteen countries.
>
> Satellite television has turned the British royals into global media megastars. The Queen's visit to the United States attracted four times as many pressmen as any other head of state in the world, and twice as many as the Pope. The first of Shea's royal tours attracted only half-a-dozen pressmen; for the US and China there were over 3,000. He has accompanied the Queen to 53 countries. Shea professionalised media access and facilities for trips like these, opening doors and drawing back curtains as far as he possibly could ... The Queen cannot effectively rule without the media – they control her access to the people and condition public attitudes towards her.

The delicate task of megastar management fell upon the protection officers. It was an unwritten but clear condition of their employment that they should be non-threatening, unremarkable figures who would not be caught out by media cameras while carrying firearms, police radios or other gadgets of the trade. In the matter of public image making, aesthetics mattered more than security at the very time when the risk was growing faster than for a hundred years.

Trestrail, an intelligent and sensitive man who won the grudging respect of his Special Branch rivals, followed the advice of his tutor Perkins and carried that peculiarly English symbol of authority, the umbrella. He even sometimes opened it over the Queen when no rain was falling.

Like his porterage of the Queen's bottle of Malvern Water ('Call me Aquarius!' he joked) and the careful arrangement of Her Majesty's car rug, the umbrella was a means of staying close to his principal. He once stopped some flying eggs as a result. It might equally have been a fragmentation grenade. As he put it in a talk to the Branch, 'Close protection is ultimately about being in the right place at the right time.'

A sharp-eyed journalist in Japan identified the brolly, with its discreet gold band marked 'E II R', as the latest short range 'umbrella-rifle'. That the British monarch preferred to be unencumbered by security was simply not credible to the Japanese, or to others. During the Queen's visit to the US in 1976, to celebrate the American Revolution against an earlier British sovereign, she was on a balcony in Philadelphia. In the far distance was a forest. An American security officer quietly lamented that he did not have enough men to 'fill the wood' while a second suggested using napalm to clear it if necessary. It is thought that this was a joke.

On the same trip, the royal motorcade moved through Manhattan. The Queen and Prince Philip were in an open-topped limousine, moving at walking pace, flanked by Secret Service agents on foot. At the Prince's suggestion, the procession moved faster, the agents first running and then scrambling into vehicles in an effort to stay with the party.

Each time the Queen rose to acknowledge the cheers of New York an American bodyguard made his presence felt. 'She's up!' he intoned into a microphone. As she resumed her seat, he announced, 'She's down!' They were approaching Harlem now and the locals were demonstrating on behalf of black power.

An increasingly nervous Secret Service chief, believing that Buckingham Palace and the White House shared a common culture, asked Trestrail, 'Mike, will you tell them to sit down? There's a political demonstration up ahead.'

The Queen rose and waved. 'Is that a demonstration?' she inquired innocently. The demonstrators waved back. The Secret Service, still haunted by Dallas, shook its head. Possibly it did not appreciate that while an American president might tolerate the straitjacket (and bullet-proof waistcoat) that accompany his maximum eight years in office, a British monarch is a full-time professional for life. It means that a British queen acquires more experience and a greater sense of occasion – the dangerous as well as the secure – than a temporary head of state can hope to absorb before he takes the presidential oath.

The significance of Queen Victoria's testimony is that there is such a learning curve. Yet the Thatcher years of government have seen the greatest revolution of all in the royal lifestyle in bringing about a movement away from the tradition of a sacrificial, risk-taking monarchy towards one which is increasingly hedged about with armed protection. In part this represents a genuine growth in the threat, a threat undiminished by Britain's part in the US bombing raid on President Gaddafi's home while Washington was selling arms, secretly, to Iran.

But there was a more general problem, not much touched on in public. In 1987, even the editor of *Burke's Peerage*, Harold Brookes-Baker, expressed dismay at the comparatively poor security around some royal houses, adding opaquely, 'The royal family have been the subject of more kidnap attempts than any of us could ever imagine.'

The changes which occurred during Mrs Thatcher's second term of office were also a measure of how the government's *perception* of the threat was changing. So it was that in 1986, the Cabinet was able to announce the Palace's acceptance of the proposals provoked by the

Mountbatten murder in 1979 and Fagan's intrusion in 1982. An additional £1 million was to be spent within twelve months to provide electronic surveillance around the homes of the royal family. A similar amount was voted by Parliament to protect its own Palace of Westminster.

One of the first fruits of the new policy, in July 1986, was an attempt by Chief Superintendent Alfred Longhurst to lure more men into royal service. Off-duty attractions, he promised, included fishing, golf and hillwalking in Scotland and elsewhere. This brochure did not convince everyone. Ten months later, under the headline, 'Queen's Cops Queue to Quit', the *People* newspaper asserted that twenty protection officers now wanted other work. The report added:

'The bobbies claim morale is at an all-time low because they are desperately short-staffed, have had overtime slashed and are worried about the Queen's security ... One disgruntled officer said, "We are twenty-three men short and that creates enormous pressure when you are the first line of defence guarding the Queen. On my watch, five lads have asked for transfers and we have four watches in all. Overtime cuts have cost some lads up to £70 a week."

'Another officer added: "After Michael Fagan broke into the Palace, security was stepped up. No expense was spared. Now they've whittled things down again. Anyone determined enough would get past the bobbies on the perimeter because there aren't enough of us."'

The weight of evidence elsewhere, however, suggested the opposite. The change of perception about royal security since the late 1970s – when a Special Branch officer was warned not to disturb the peace of Balmoral by walking on the gravel or switching on his personal radio – could not have been sharper. A century of sang-froid had been traded in for less aristocratic, somewhat blunter instruments of defence. Here were a few signs of the changing royal lifestyle:

●During the wedding procession of Prince Andrew and Sarah Ferguson in London in July 1986, a flunky whose eyes moved as nervously as those of a croupier in a dubious casino was identified as one of three armed Special Branch men close to the couple as they were married;

●After the wedding, Deputy Assistant Commissioner Brian Worth of Scotland Yard confirmed that the IRA had planned to blow up Westminster Abbey during the service, a potential outrage one degree worse than the Madrid wedding attack by anarchists on Princess Ena in 1909;

●In 1987 the first female protection officer was appointed to the team in spite of the Queen's known distaste for armed women in her entourage. (In this both sovereign and police were overruled by the Equal Rights Commission.) The new-comer's task was protecting Prince William, aged four and second in line to the throne;

●Men already on the team were now trained with German Heckler and Koch carbines, firing single rounds, as well as the American Smith & Wesson revolver;

●Strongpoints appeared at the gates of Buckingham Palace and were identified by the press as high technology machine gun posts to halt a Beirut-style assault on the Palace by lorry bomb and kamikaze driver;

●In London, Princess Diana – driving without the presence of her close protection officer, Inspector Alan Peters – had to accelerate her Ford Escort to high speed to elude Arab pests pursuing her in a white VW.

Soon, however, it was clear that the royal family, led by the Queen, had again set firm limits on the intrusion of the new security regime. A proposal to place barriers all round the Buckingham Palace area, including the gardens and the Queen Victoria Memorial in front of the Palace ('a potential sniper position', said the security wizards), was vetoed by Her Majesty. While threat evaluators studied worst-case scenarios and lines of fire, the Queen was more concerned about the damage that might be done to the concept of accessible monarchy by hiding behind a stockade. The Queen would tolerate the proposed *cordon sanitaire*, her staff revealed, 'under no circumstances'. 'We don't want to be hidden from the public,' she added. 'They must be able to see us.'

Meanwhile Princess Diana, the Princess of Wales, launched her own, highly effective counter-attack on the subject of security. She observed that the elderly support cars carrying back-up teams of armed bodyguards to escort royal limousines to public engagements broke down regularly. As a result she and the Prince of Wales as well as their sons Prince William and Prince Harry were sometimes protected by a single, personal bodyguard who travelled 'on the box' in their own car. His one gun (witness the events in the Mall in March 1974) might not be sufficient, particularly if they came under attack from several well trained terrorists.

In July 1987, during an official visit to Brixton police station, South London, the Princess surged through the protocol to express her concern to London's police commissioner, Sir Kenneth Newman, who was about to retire. She was most anxious, she said, for the safety of the children. Couldn't something be done? Something was. A shiny fleet of new Rover Vitesse cars was conjured out of Scotland Yard's budget.

Of all the events within the realms of public knowledge which might explain the Windsors' qualified acceptance, however reluctant, of orthodox but 'unfriendly' close protection, none registers more vividly than the IRA plot to murder the Queen Mother. Evidence given at the trial of the Brighton bomber Patrick Magee and his accomplices revealed that Peter Sherry, a Republican assassin known as the 'Armalite Kid' had planned to stalk the dowager Queen among the broad, peaceful and publicly accessible acres of Balmoral during the family's annual visit there.

Such a threat might have come from a film script. But in a world where violent fiction and reality were increasingly blurred, it was as frighteningly credible as Mountbatten's murder. Soon after the plot became known, the Queen Mother attended a Royal Command performance. Backstage, she met the script-writer Johnny Speight, whose bigoted but loyal character 'Alf Garnett' was the conduit for some outrageously racist insults. Not surprisingly, Speight had received threats from minorities who did not appreciate his irony. The threats made him wince somewhat until he encountered the Queen Mother.

'She told me she herself had been told that her life was in danger if she attended the theatre that night,' he said later. 'She said she always ignored threats and just carried on with her life. After that, they never bothered me.'

In June 1986, riding Burmese at her final review of the Colour Trooping from horseback, the Queen might have reflected that at her first such ceremony in 1952 a single personal security officer had sufficed. In 1986 some 3,500 police were on duty. Many were armed detectives mingling with the crowd. The number of the royal family inner circle requiring protection had grown to about twenty. Their security demanded the services of up to sixty full-time police bodyguards. As one commentator remarked: 'What a price to pay for the kind of world we have become.'

Politicians, including high profile home secretaries and prime ministers, do not have to sustain such pressures all their lives. Even in office they can adopt the style of Mrs Thatcher in the 1987 general election and arrive at a public occasion without advance notice.

This the Queen could not do without becoming a cypher. Her engagements, as well as those of other members of the royal family, are published in the Court Circular weeks before. Combined with the potential of the sleeper bomb, this ritual is the greatest single cause for concern among the Queen's guardians, but it is also a symbol of the public affection and public access that is at the heart of constitutional monarchy.

Royal security now has to reconcile that paradox with political persuasion to play it safe. The signs are that under pressure from Downing Street and Fleet Street, emerging security solutions are making unique inroads into the freedom of the monarch and the 'megastars' who will succeed her. Some of those changes manifest themselves in quirky fashion. It has been customary for several years for members of the family visiting Northern Ireland to do so without advance public notice. While they are in the Province, security precautions now extend even to the lunch menu. Soon after the Enniskillen cenotaph massacre in 1987, for example, the Princess Royal, Princess Anne, visited a training centre for delinquent youngsters including youths convicted of terrorism. Her lunch was prepared by four young women who were not offenders but trainee caterers from Antrim on a government youth training programme. Nevertheless, they were not told they were preparing lunch for a princess 'for security reasons'.

As the security tightens, it should not be surprising if some of those imprisoned by it seek asylum in either fatalistic acceptance of risk or temporary respite, somewhere where they may enjoy without restriction the humdrum small change of daily living which others take for granted. What is cruel as well as surprising is that certain newspapers should lampoon the heir to the throne for his entirely sane efforts to taste the freedom of a Scottish croft or the Kalahari bush. Such an activity, even taken in the company of a protection officer, might not make sense to Lunchtime O'Booze and his fellow headline writers of the night subbing shift. For Prince Charles it is the logical response to the threat to life generated by the terrorist and the threat to freedom posed by the government's quest for failsafe security.

Perhaps it is as well that Charles preserves a better sense of proportion than some of his critics. Riding with the Beaufort Hunt on a nineteen-year-old horse named Mexico, His Royal Highness was heard to summon his protection officer for an urgent mission. Clearly, the situation was critical and the detective did not hesitate. With the polish that comes only from years of quick-draw practice, the officer produced the sugar lumps needed to keep Mexico awake.

PART II
Politicians

CHAPTER 4

Suffragettes, Dog-whips and Bloodless Coups

If monarchs repose their chances of survival in the laps of fate or the Almighty, politicians tend to rely upon body-guards. Possibly this is because sovereigns have their role thrust upon them from birth and usually learn to accept it even when the role leads predictably to a bloody and premature end.

Politicians, by contrast, have not become potential targets of an assassin entirely by happenstance. They have learned to influence the course of events. They are actors, not audience, and they usually take some positive action to ensure their security. As a rule of thumb, the more devious and unpopular the politician, the more bodyguards he will tend to have about him. Julius Caesar had 2,000 and was assassinated. Huey Long – the man who made graft a respected art form of American politics – had about twenty-five, some of whom probably participated in his gory death. Sir Winston Churchill depended upon one good man and both of them died quietly in bed, at home.

In 1830, a year after the foundation of the Metropolitan Police, the Duke of Wellington – now a defeated prime minister rather than a victorious general – was obliged to convert his Hyde Park home, Apsley House, into a fortress and to arm his servants. A year later, stones crashed through his windows for an hour before help arrived. In 1832, the Duke was almost lynched in Central London, but was saved by an *ad hoc* bodyguard of Chelsea Pensioners, a magistrate, and his own sang-froid.

Slightly more professional security was provided by the militia so that when Reform Bill demonstrators surged into

Downing Street that year to bawl 'Liberty or death!' they encountered a row of muskets and an evil old veteran of the Napoleonic campaigns. 'Liberty I don't know much about,' he growled, 'but if you come any further I will show you death!'

It was as part of the slow process of civilising British politics that the first modern police force, the London Metropolitan, was created. Sir Robert Peel, the Home Secretary, explained to the Commons that the presence of an effective civilian force would mean that the Army was no longer required to keep 'the tranquillity of the Metropolis'.

This would go some way towards stilling an English hostility to a professional, standing army (and by extension, all things military) since the days of Cromwell. But personal protection remained the prerogative of the powerful for some decades after the creation of the Met., in a city where one in ten of the population – 115,000 people – depended upon crime for their daily bread, a city faithfully described by John Gay's *The Beggar's Opera.* In keeping with the spirit of the age, and less than a month before he sanctioned Peel's Police Bill, Wellington (as Prime Minister) was engaged in a duel in Battersea with his critic Lord Winchilsea. (Both men's shots missed, probably by design.)

The risks to health of politics as a career were already well known. In the late 18th century, Lord North as Prime Minister was attacked by an angry crowd of supporters of John Wilkes, the libertine prophet of press freedom. North's carriage was broken to pieces around him in a London street and he was repeatedly struck with truncheons taken from the Westminster constables who intervened. ('Wilkes, you will die of the pox or upon the gallows!' North had told his enemy, who responded, 'That, my lord, depends upon whether I embrace your mistress or your principles!')

Prime Minister Pitt was besieged in Downing Street by a

crowd demanding the end of the French war. In May 1812, Pitt's successor Spencer Perceval was shot dead in the Commons lobby by a Liverpool merchant, John Bellingham. Bellingham had a grudge about five years he had spent in prison in Archangel for debt, and for which he irrationally blamed the London government. After he had murdered Perceval at point blank range with a single shot he was immediately seized and brought before the Commons. He was tried and hanged within a week.

It was not until 1883 that a special team of professional close protection officers emerged to become a permanent and distinctive feature of British political life. Like so many aspects of political violence, this sprang from the dialogue between most of the British and some of the Irish.

The Liberal Prime Minister of the day, William Ewart Gladstone, was credited with a famous aphorism that 'Every time the English find an answer to the Irish Question, the Irish change the question.' In the 1880s the Irish were seeking various answers. One British response was intended to reduce the hardship suffered by Irish tenant farmers evicted by English landlords. This was the Land Bill. However, it all ended in tears and the arrest of Charles Stewart Parnell, the colourful leader of the Irish Party in the Commons.

Gladstone arranged for Parnell to be released on 6 May 1882, hoping that the gesture would reduce Irish tempers. But the British had underestimated Celtic zeal for lacing their politics with blood. Four days after Parnell's release a young, newly-arrived Irish Secretary of State named Lord Frederick Cavendish strolled towards Dublin's vast Phoenix Park with the Permanent Under-Secretary to Dublin, Thomas Burke, but without an armed bodyguard. This was unwise.

Within sight of the Secretarial Residence, both men were hacked to pieces by a gang armed with knives. Passers-by dismissed it at the time as just another drunken Dublin brawl. The gang was led by a 20-year-old builder named James Carey. In due time, Carey would turn Queen's Evidence and go free while his accomplices hanged, only to die mysteriously himself soon afterwards aboard a ship off the Cape of Good Hope.

Gladstone had regarded Cavendish as a son rather than the nephew he actually was. When the Prime Minister and his wife learned of the murders on their return to Downing Street from an Austrian Embassy reception, they sank to their knees in the entrance hall of Number Ten to pray. But Gladstone, a less than passive politician, did not leave vengeance entirely to the Lord. He offered a huge public reward of £10,000 for the identification of the killers who had struck under the *nom de guerre* 'The Invincibles'.

He also appointed a former military attaché in Paris, Colonel Henry Brackenbury, to be Under-Secretary for Police in Dublin to improve security there. Brackenbury reported that orthodox police methods were not an effective antidote to secret societies. A separate, special organisation was required to infiltrate the terrorists and 'break their nerve'. Brackenbury got his organisation, in which were to be found the seeds of the Special Branch, and his start-up budget of £20,000.

Any distaste the British public might have had about an alien 'secret police' was allayed a year later when one bomb exploded near Whitehall and another was defused outside the offices of *The Times*. During the following two years, Fenian bombs exploded in London on average once a month in a campaign more sustained than anything matched by later generations of republicans. Targets ranged from the Commons crypt to Nelson's Column, by way of Scotland Yard itself.

Almost 1,000 Metropolitan Police constables were hastily equipped with firearms and sent to guard key points such as the Palace of Westminster, the Thames bridges and even the Royal Gunpowder Factory at Waltham Abbey. Meanwhile ninety-three of the more senior men, including sergeants, were appointed as close protection officers for the duration of the emergency.

Of these, fourteen were allocated to the Home Secretary. Even this number would provide continual cover of less than four officers for an eight-hour shift. The German Ambassador was also on what the Ministry of Defence would now categorise as the 'A' list of VIPs, but that envoy enjoyed only a low priority, qualifying for the services of a single bodyguard.

These efforts were insufficient to contain the burgeoning crisis that preceded the failure of Gladstone's Irish Home Rule Bill to pass through Parliament in 1886. So the Home Secretary, Sir Matthew White Ridley, authorised a unique request from the capital of the empire. London sought the help of the Royal Irish Constabulary, thirteen of whose best detectives were sent on loan to stiffen the newly established Irish Special Branch. They included a dedicated sergeant from the wilderness of Mayo, Patrick Quinn, who would act on state occasions as Queen Victoria's bodyguard, and become the first police officer to receive a knighthood.

Additional RIC teams were set up in provincial British cities, such as Liverpool, with large Irish communities. In a parallel operation, RIC sharpshooters in their green uniforms helped to guard the capital's key points.

The new undercover team, meanwhile, adopted Brackenbury's methods of penetrating terrorist groups in order to keep them under observation for weeks before arresting anyone. After operating for twelve months as the Irish Special Branch under the leadership of a Scot, Chief Inspector John Littlechild, the new organisation was renamed the Special Branch. But it was some months before the public learned from *The Times* that 'the authorities have . . .

summoned to London a large number of detectives from the South of Ireland for the purpose of assisting in watching and detecting the supposed dynamite conspirators.'

The bombing campaign ended abruptly in January 1885. By then two bombers were dead as a result of an 'own goal' explosion and four were serving long prison sentences. Two of the prisoners were Irish Americans. The uniformed RIC teams returned home but by now the Branch was emerging in the public mind as an English answer to the Irish question, even if the answer was to use more Irishmen.

An important part of this response was close protection of the people who mattered. Quinn and his fellow countryman John Sweeney joined the team of experts brought in to guard the Queen on special, high-profile occasions, although the day-to-day management of royal security remained in the hands of Inspector Baker's long-suffering successors.

As it happened, there were no confirmed attempts upon the Queen after 1882. But Quinn and Sweeney, together with James McBrien, George Riley and John MacCarthy, were the cement which held together not only the security of Queen Victoria but also that of her successor Edward VII, particularly on his trips abroad. Sweeney and Riley were with Edward aboard a train in Belgium in 1909 when a Belgian anarchist named Sipido fired at him. (Edward retained the bullet as a souvenir.) Quinn and MacCarthy were also prominent in the escort at the late King Edward's funeral the following year, which was attended by forty-eight European royalty including Edward's nephew, Kaiser Wilhelm.

Perhaps it was a coincidence that politicians, having first introduced the Irish connection into British close protection, chose to dilute the Gaelic contingent for their own security; men with non-Irish Branch bodyguards bearing such names as Woodhall, Andrews, Nalty, Randall, Sandercock, Brust, Thompson, Lobb and Wilkinson. But this was no guarantee of purity, for the latest threat bore names such as Pankhurst, Lady Constance Lytton and Emily Wilding Davison.

The paradox of the Suffragette protest was that it was led by a middle-class élite which, in other circumstances, would be the essence of respectable, law-abiding, police-supporting society. At no time was the paradox more neatly illustrated than when a Special Branch cordon around Buckingham Palace in the early summer of 1911 was effortlessly penetrated by a debutante who was admitted to the royal presence by invitation. As Edwin T. Woodhall recounts in his memoir *Guardians Of The Great*: 'Just after her presentation [to George V and Queen Mary] she was heard to utter quite clearly the clarion call of the movement, "Your Majesty, when are you going to give women the vote?"' She was removed in dead silence and escorted off the premises. 'No other action was taken,' Woodhall reports, 'at the express wish of Their Majesties.'

Four years later Lady Blomfield's daughter, Mary, interrupted her presentation at Court more dramatically. She dropped to her knees in front of the King, saying, 'For God's sake, Your Majesty, put a stop to forcible feeding!'

Although the Suffragettes assassinated no one – the only public mortal injury was inflicted by Emily Davison upon herself, beneath the hooves of a royal racehorse at the 1913 Derby – it was the women's ability to get near to political figures, in spite of much close protection, that made them dangerous in the eyes of the bodyguards. As potential assassins using their wits to score bloodless coups against security specialists, they have no equal in history (unless it is among the lesbian alpinists who abseiled into the Lords Chamber in 1988).

The women's threat of close-quarter violence was backed up by real destruction of property which, in an epoch whose apparent stability and public order was threatened first by

Chartism, then by Anarchism and finally by Irish Republicanism, is hard to underestimate. Woodhall spoke for all his Branch colleagues when he wrote, one world war later:

> The women's suffrage movement when it was at its height was the sharpest thorn the Special Branch ever had in its side ... Suffragettes were more troublesome than all the other problems put together. It was so difficult to know who was or who was not in the movement ... Titles conveyed nothing at all ... They steered clear of assassination but they burned down public buildings and churches, waylaid Royalty and Cabinet ministers, blew up the Coronation Chair in Westminster Abbey; damaged priceless national treasures and pictures; set valuable property on fire; shouted down judges and magistrates; fought and assaulted the police on many occasions; smashed half the plate glass windows along Piccadilly, Regent Street and Bond Street and finally made an attempt to throw the King's horse at the Derby, where ... Emily Davidson [sic] was killed.

The active, violent phase of the campaign began outside the London home of the Liberal Home Secretary, Herbert Asquith, on 21 June 1906, when Theresa Billington, a Manchester school teacher, slapped a policeman's face. It reached its peak between 1912, when Cabinet ministers sought Branch protection, and the beginning of the First World War. By 1918 when women had shown their attachment to traditional values by supporting the war, most of them over the age of thirty were enfranchised.

The women were uniquely dangerous because of their intelligence and courage and because they followed no predetermined rules of engagement. They would attempt assaults against public figures which more experienced practitioners of violence might discard at the planning stage as too complicated, or too optimistic, or both. Once they had penetrated the security screen they would use psychological terrorism as well as physical violence. Not surprisingly, the bodyguards opposing them were sometimes brutal also, and being male, expressed masculine brutality. What began as a political argument often became a war of the sexes.

In 1910, after a limited suffrage bill was abandoned, leading to violent scenes on the day that became known to both sides as 'Black Friday', Harold Brust of Special Branch was keeping watch on the Commons terrace, beside the Thames. In his book, *In Plain Clothes*, Brust recalled:

'One night . . . I observed a boat of the fast motor-launch type stealing along from under the shadows of Westminster Bridge . . . When it came sidling in towards the terrace wall I motioned to my colleague, the late Inspector Riley . . . "Bob down. Out of sight," muttered Inspector Riley. "I don't like the look of this." . . . Suddenly came a dull bumping noise and the sharp tinkle of metal impacting on stone, repeated several times. "Grappling hook!" muttered Riley. "Funny business!"

'Again and again the grappling hook, attached to a length of rope, was tossed up . . . At last it hooked . . . and up a stout rope-ladder came climbing two strapping young ladies – right into our arms! I shudder to think of the havoc these two Amazons could have caused had they gained entrance to the Members' dining room.'

As one of the movement's pioneers, Mrs Emmeline Pethick-Lawrence, had said at the beginning: 'We look to none but ourselves. We appeal to none but women to rise up and fight by our side . . . The harder the fight the better. What we are going to get is a great revolt of the women against their subjection of body and mind to men.' (Quoted in Roger Fulford's *Votes for Women*.)

During the twelve-year agitation which followed, three politicians were singled out for violent attention. These were Herbert Asquith, Liberal Prime Minister from 1908 to 1916, his successor David Lloyd George and Asquith's

Home Secretary, Winston Churchill. During the two turbulent general elections of 1910 (campaigns which were matched for their security-consciousness only by that of 1987) the enemy arrived disguised as anything from telegraph boy to match-seller. She hid in the organ at the Albert Hall during political rallies and hurled slates through the roof of Bingley Hall in Birmingham.

Brust was at Number Ten to intercept a 'strangely excitable sort of nun' who had called to see Mrs Asquith. He summoned a police matron from Cannon Row. The matron 'found a prominent suffragette and a dog-whip concealed under the nun's robe'. For some who yearned to penetrate the armour of government, the whip became an almost routine method of making a political point. Churchill was nearly scourged in a railway carriage until Detective Sergeant Tom Nalty, his Branch bodyguard, intervened. The protection was insufficient at Bristol station in December 1909, when Miss Theresa Garnett slashed at the Home Secretary with the words, 'Take that in the name of the insulted women of England!'

Fulford observes that Churchill pocketed the whip but 'he might have been a little more flustered if he had known that his assailant had lately been charged with biting a wardress.' (She was acquitted.)

Asquith, in spite of having been pursued by angry women on the golf course as he partnered Herbert Gladstone, was one of those VIPs who liked to 'do a runner' to evade his bodyguard. As Brust (ibid.) recalls: 'Premier Asquith was very partial to a little game of "hide and seek" . . . He would slip out behind the Speaker's chair and hurry forth by a back way, emerging from the Victoria Tower . . . and I would sprint across Palace Yard and catch up with the Minister at the gate, to his great surprise.

'"Sorry," he would say with his affable smile. "I ought to have let you know I was leaving." And off we would go ... I had a reputation to maintain and a job to lose ...'

On Black Friday in 1910, when 300 women demonstrated at Westminster, 1,500 policemen were concealed in the crevices of Parliament. But away from Westminster's saturation security, the women continued to make fools of the protection teams. One of them followed Lloyd George out of an election rally and into his limousine, locking the door behind her as she did so. A protection officer's nightmare ensued.

'She gave him a severe lecture,' Fulford recounts, 'followed by a good shaking, while the chauffeur struggled to undo the car door. As she stepped triumphantly out, she narrowly escaped some mischief from the crowd ...'

Not all the assailants were women. Andrews and Woodhall, then Branch sergeants guarding Churchill, intervened to stop a male sympathiser of the campaign from whipping Lloyd George at Gatti's Restaurant in the Strand. But it was the women who came in for the roughest handling by the protection squad. The government's bodyguards, debagged if not emasculated as professional guardians, met psychological assault with sexual warfare. Quinn, normally the most courteous of men in his dealings with the opposite sex, but now facing a suffragette who screamed, 'Keep your hands off me!' murmured, catlike, 'Tut tut! I would never see a *lady* handled,' then, turning to his junior, 'Do your duty.'

Fulford describes Black Friday from the demonstrators' viewpoint:

'The wife of a Dublin professor had a punch on the nose and was hurled by a constable in front of a mounted policeman, with the encouraging order, "Ride over her." The gallant Mrs Leigh, ever at the heart of trouble, was knocked flat in the road by an inspector who said to a constable, "Take the cow away." A lady, unmarried and

verging on middle age, was grasped with firm affection by
a young policeman ... She screamed, "Unhand it, sir,"
only to be told, "My old dear, I can grip you where I like
today."'

As the campaign progressed, militant extremists of the
Women's Social and Political Union turned (like the *pétro-
leuses* of the 1871 Paris Commune) to arson and (like the
IRA) to high explosive as a medium of protest. The targets
were still inanimate if valuable items of property, but the
destruction was on such a scale as to become a form of
terrorism. Had not the First World War intervened, it was
only a matter of time before life as well as property were
destroyed. According to Sylvia Pankhurst, a total of 141
acts of suffragette destruction were logged during the first
seven months of 1914. She wrote later, in *The Suffragette
Movement*:

Three Scotch [sic] castles were destroyed by fire on a single
night. The Carnegie Library in Birmingham was burnt. The
Rokeby Venus, falsely, as I consider, attributed to Velasquez,
and purchased for the National Gallery at a cost of £45,000 was
mutilated by Mary Richardson. Romney's 'Master Thornhill' in
the Birmingham Art Gallery was slashed by Bertha Ryland ...
Many large empty houses in all parts of the country were set
on fire including Redlynch House, Somerset, where the damage
was estimated at £40,000.

Railway stations, piers, sports pavilions, haystacks were set
on fire. Attempts were made to blow up reservoirs. A bomb
exploded in Westminster Abbey and in the fashionable church
of St George's, Hanover Square, where a famous stained-glass
window was damaged. There were two explosions in St John's,
Westminster and one in St Martin's in the Fields and in Spur-
geon's Tabernacle. The ancient Breadsall Church near Derby
was destroyed and the ancient Wargrave Church. The organ
was flooded at the Albert Hall, damage amounting to £2,000.
The bombs and other material used were of a much more

professional and formidable character than those of the early period of secret militancy.

Hospitals as well as churches were burned down at this time by middle-class women, while doctors' wives were setting fire to private houses including a bungalow belonging to Sir William Lever (later Lord Leverhulme). But direct violence against individuals was still tuned to provoke embarrassment rather than casualties, in spite of the brutality expressed towards Suffragette prisoners by their gaolers and, through self-inflicted injuries, by the women themselves.

'Old ladies applied for gun licences, to terrify the authorities,' Sylvia Pankhurst records. '... A large envelope containing red pepper and snuff was sent to every Cabinet Minister; the Press reported that they all fell victims to the ruse ... Lloyd George's new house in process of erection ... was injured beyond repair by a bomb explosion.' And so on.

The authorities tried to take the leaders out of circulation by short-term imprisonment, sufficient to disrupt the campaign but not long enough to enable the women to die on hunger strike in captivity. The Suffragette response was to create their own bodyguard. This was sometimes one hard man such as the East End prizefighter 'Kosher' Hunt (whose arrest required the services of ten police officers), but later a Praetorian team of female bodyguards emerged, armed with Indian clubs. These women fought police trying to arrest Emmeline Pankhurst in Campden Hill Square, London, in February 1914. In Glasgow soon afterwards, one of them fired blank rounds from a revolver, from behind a platform draped with barbed wire.

When the war with Germany began, the extremists of the WSPU were the most ferocious in their support of blood-letting. In August 1914 Suffragette prisoners were released under an unconditional amnesty. Less than a month later, their demand for the vote shelved, Emmeline Pankhurst's militants, in Sylvia's words, 'handed the white feather' – symbol of cowardice – 'to every young man they encountered wearing civilian dress, and bobbed up at Hyde Park meetings with placards, "Intern Them All".' It was a vivid, if sad example of the fascination exerted by a general war over the extremist who resorts to terrorism at home in the absence of such a conflict.

As the tension generated by both Irish republicanism and the suffrage movement diminished, an overstretched Special Branch, countering the German espionage effort in Britain, was also obliged to provide four officers – Detective Sergeants Andrews, Nalty, Randall and Sandercock – to protect the Prime Minister, Lloyd George. In spite of the WSPU's change of direction, a residual threat remained from a small minority of Suffragettes who had made common cause with conscientious objectors to the war, men who were now on the run. This alliance generated the only case in which – if the prosecution was telling the truth – one of the women was prepared at last to become a political assassin. The intended victim, it was alleged, was Lloyd George and it was one of the most ambiguous episodes in the history of the Suffragette movement.

Towards the end of 1916, when the carnage at the Somme was beginning to make some impact on public support for the war, Mrs Wheeldon, a politically active Derby woman, and her two adult daughters, Harriet and Winnie, were militant suffragettes. Winnie's husband, George Mason, was a chemist based in Southampton. In December, Mrs Wheeldon received through the post from her son-in-law four phials of the lethal poison, curare. These she handed to 'Comrade Bert', a man who had befriended her and who was, in fact, a Special Branch agent named Herbert Booth.

According to the prosecution at Mrs Wheeldon's subsequent trial, Mrs Wheeldon intended the curare to be used to assassinate Lloyd George as he played golf at Walton Heath. It was to be applied by a dart fired from a blowpipe, attached to nails driven into the soles of his shoes or used to impregnate pins hidden in his hat. The exoticism of the scheme was in keeping with some of the militants' wilder schemes elsewhere and therefore not implausible. (Another suffragette, Catherine Griffiths, was jailed in 1912 for trying to put nails into Lloyd George's Commons seat, though without the garnish of curare. In 1988, now aged 102, she returned to Westminster to commemorate the suffrage campaign.)

Mrs Wheeldon was less fortunate. She claimed that Booth and others who induced her to obtain the curare for them were *agents provocateurs*. She had been misled into believing that the poison would kill prison guard dogs at a 'concentration camp' housing conscientious objectors, enabling the inmates to escape. Since her only son was a conscientious objector already on the run, the cause was one with which she sympathised. She was convicted of conspiracy to murder Lloyd George (and a Labour MP, Arthur Henderson, who had joined the War Cabinet) and sentenced to ten years' penal servitude. George Mason was sentenced to seven years' and Winnie to five years' imprisonment. Harriet, though charged, was acquitted. Mrs Wheeldon died soon after her release, prematurely, from prison.

The outbreak of the First World War generated a considerable spy fever throughout Britain. On the first day of the conflict, Brust arrived at Branch headquarters to find 'spy scares flooding in by thousands. Every few minutes, huge sacks of mail arrived.' The strength of the Branch was increased to 114. Soon MI5 would be created as a parallel organisation employing, by the end of the war, 800 people including some of the Branch's best talent.

With 45,000 aliens on a list of suspects compiled even before the war started, there was much to do. Mail intercepts and patient, old-fashioned policemanship uncovered a number of real enemy agents but it required the fortuitous capture of documents on the Western Front in August 1915 to neutralise a grandiose German assassination plot.

The scheme is of interest now as one of the first cases of state-sponsored assassination of a type familiar in the 1980s to be employed as one weapon in a more general conflict.

The German intelligence service conceived a grand design to assassinate, simultaneously, the soldier and War Minister Lord Kitchener, the diplomatist and Foreign Secretary Lord Grey, the French President Poincaré and the King of Italy. But if they were to acknowledge the unwritten convention that warring European leaders did not engage in anything so vulgar as personalised murder plots, the Germans needed a surrogate assassin. They found it in the Indian resistance movement which was second only in its anti-British sentiment to that of Irish nationalism.

The Indian extremists were fundamentalist Hindus who invoked the death cult of the goddess Kali for whom the murder of a foreigner was *jagna*, a ritual sacrifice. Their victims ranged from Sir William Curzon Wylie in London in 1909 (in mistake for Lord Curzon) to Mahatma Gandhi in New Delhi in 1948.

Germany set up an 'Indian Committee' charged with fomenting a revolution on the sub-continent, while Indians in Britain, Harold Brust observed, were to be supplied with bombs. Those under suspicion were watched and, when sufficient evidence had been obtained, arrested and interned.

The plot against Kitchener and others fell apart. Gandhi

denounced it in a Calcutta speech to students in which he described assassination as 'a western institution'.

Nevertheless, those on the German-Indian death list remained under close protection. Detective Sergeant Dan Maclaughlan was attached to Lord Kitchener. Less than a year later, he joined Kitchener's doomed expedition to Russia. The party started its journey from the British Expeditionary Force HQ at St Omer in northern France. Ex-Detective Superintendent Edwin Woodhall has described in his memoir how he parted from Maclaughlan. They stood chatting on the St Omer railway platform near Kitchener's compartment while waiting for the train to leave.

'"I have a sort of fancy that this Russian trip is going to be bad," the normally jovial Maclaughlan murmured. "I have a premonition we won't meet again, Ted."'

Woodhall dismissed the comment as nonsense, clapped him on the shoulder and went his way. Less than a month later, Maclaughlan was lost at sea along with his boss and many others from the cruiser HMS *Hampshire*. Amid mountainous seas, which had forced her destroyer escorts to turn back, *Hampshire* struck one of twenty-two mines laid by U-boat 75 shortly beforehand. The cruiser sank shortly before dusk within sight of the Orkney beach facing Marwick Head.

The cruiser's lifeboats could not be launched because of the storm. In *Kitchener, Architect of Victory*, George H. Cassar writes: 'Kitchener was last seen standing on the starboard side of the quarterdeck, phlegmatic, riding the doomed cruiser down. Fifteen minutes after the explosion, the *Hampshire* executed a forward somersault and plunged to the bottom of the sea.'

Alongside him stood Maclaughlan. Unusually for a body-guard who knows his time has come, he had an opportunity to reflect upon his fate, one which reflected the passive courage of thousands of men in the trenches who also had no choice but to bite on the bullet.

The loss of the ship, with the most popular of British generals on board, provoked at least as much noise and speculation as the destruction of the Argentine cruiser *Belgrano* almost seventy years later. Kitchener had fixed himself in folk myth as a survivor. His moustache and finger pointed at potential volunteers from a million posters, proclaiming, 'Your Country Needs You!' For someone so durable to die, some special dirty tricks department must be at work. The Goddess Kali again? The Bolsheviks? One of Kitchener's numerous political rivals at home? The conspiracy theories flourished for years. The absence of his body, when others were washed ashore, generated a belief that he was alive and a prisoner somewhere. With him went his man Maclaughlan, the first protection officer to die in action since the Branch was formed thirty-three years before, and one burdened with a premonition of doom.

A loss of a less permanent kind was that of Mr Lloyd George, successively Chancellor, Minister of Munitions and Prime Minister. He was still at risk from a minority of Suffragettes, as we have seen. He also had a voracious heterosexual appetite which seems to have been satisfied, most of the time, by numerous affairs. These most assuredly did not require the assistance of Special Branch bodyguards in spite of the fact that four were assigned to him.

So it was that he was without a protection officer, as usual, when being driven home to Walton Heath late one night in 1914 from a function in the City of London. The car broke down in an isolated spot. Uninhibited by the fact that he was dressed as a Privy Councillor (knee breeches, stockings and silver-buckled shoes) he descended from the vehicle to stretch his legs, or answer a call of nature.

He strayed too far, and the chauffeur, having restarted the engine, drove off into the night, alone. It was some time before the mistake was discovered and the chauffeur returned to discover a dogged figure, walking homeward. Lloyd George was an enthusiastic hillwalker, unlike most of his police bodyguards, who preferred to be with the less athletic Churchill.

The breakdown incident became one of Lloyd George's favourite stories. In its final version he used to add that he eventually came to the doors of a lunatic asylum and in desperation rang the bell:

'"I'm the Chancellor of the Exchequer," he announced as the warden answered the door. "Come in," invited the warden calmly. "The rest of the Cabinet is expecting you."'*

The Great War started with a double assassination at Sarajevo, manipulated by a bodyguard – the victims' security chief, Dragutin Dimitrijevic (Colonel Apis) – who betrayed his trust. It ended, in Britain at least, with a strike by police officers including Special Branch protection officers. The Branch had had a good war. It had detected and trapped Sir Roger Casement as he endeavoured to bring arms ashore in Ireland. It had caught many real German agents. It had picked up and released a fantasist in Mata Hari.

Pay and conditions were, however, woefully out of date for the responsibilities now borne by the best police officers. In 1918 their union spokesman, a calm, fatherly police constable, was dismissed for participating in an illegal organisation. The officers waited five months before reacting to official snubs. At the end of August, when the Commissioner went on leave to Ireland, their patience snapped.

Because of the overthrow of the Tsarist regime in a revolution involving Bolsheviks in the previous year, governments throughout Western Europe were phobic

* From *The Prime Ministers*, edited by William Douglas-Home.

about any manifestation of militancy among public servants, particularly those in uniform, and most particularly when the uniform was plain clothes. In France, army mutinies (partly inspired by Russia's withdrawal from the war and the anti-Tsarist revolution) generated a grievous series of summary courts martial and firing squads. In London Lloyd George apparently panicked. He called out the special constabulary and summoned armed troops to guard government buildings. This action served only to aggravate the small-scale strike action at the Branch and the Yard, so that by the next day almost all the uniformed constables in the Metropolitan and City forces had come out.

Downing Street alone required around 500 soldiers — hidden in the neighbouring Foreign Office quadrangle – for its protection from the faceless anarchy of an unpoliced city. After three days, the strikers' demands were met almost without reservation. But for long afterwards, Lloyd George appears to have been haunted by that fear for his personal security that is characteristic of the loneliness of the long distance statesman. This nervousness was to have unexpected effects upon his Special Branch guardians.

An epidemic of strikes and continued fears of Bolshevik revolution immediately after the war had resulted in a new independence for the Branch as the nation's first line of defence against 'Red machinations'. For almost three years from May 1919 the Branch was an autonomous organisation commanded by Assistant Commissioner Basil Thomson who was answerable direct to the Home Office. Thomson, son of the Archbishop of York, former Colonial civil servant and ex-governor of Dartmoor Prison, was uniquely placed to influence Lloyd George. Ever since the politician had been Minister of Munitions in 1915, Thomson's reports on industrial subversion, real and imagined, were the government's only inside – and uncheckable – source of information. Furthermore, it was Thomson's team which had uncovered the 1916–17 plot to assassinate the Prime Minister.

By the time Thomson led the Branch out of Scotland Yard in 1919, emphasising his political independence of the 'Met', he had made some powerful enemies. These included his rival spy-catcher, Sir Vernon Kell, a soldier who rose from the rank of captain to that of major-general as the first chief of MI5, and General Sir William Horwood, the Metropolitan Commissioner.

CHAPTER 5

Have Gun, Will Govern –
Lloyd George to Churchill

It was a challenge to the credibility of Lloyd George's personal security in 1921 which started Thomson's downfall. The affair is a notable example of how a leader's close protection can become a political issue in its own right. As described by the radical journalist Tony Bunyan, in his book *The Political Police in Britain*, 'four young Irishmen got into the grounds of Chequers [the Prime Minister's official out-of-town residence] and painted "Up the Sinn Fein" on the summerhouse . . . Thomson . . . satisfied himself that it was only a prank and with a warning let them go.'

However, Lloyd George, who had not been at Chequers at the time, was very shaken that such a thing could happen. Supported by General Horwood, Mr Shortt, the Home Secretary, told Thomson he was to retire immediately at the age of sixty. He was offered a generous pension provided he left without a fuss.

The feud between Horwood and Thomson did not end there. In December 1925, Sir Basil Thomson was arrested while sharing a bench in Hyde Park with a prostitute named Thelma de Lava. The charge was one of offending public decency. Thomson denied it but was convicted and fined £5. 'Afterwards,' suggests Rupert Allason (ibid.), Thomson 'was to claim that he had been framed by General Horwood . . . and the police establishment whom he had criticised on numerous occasions'. Horwood, meanwhile, was the victim of an attempted assassination by poisoned chocolates, an event touched upon with excessive delicacy in his memoirs by ex-Inspector Brust.

The Branch's brief period of independence ended with

Thomson's *faux pas* over this simple matter of graffiti at Chequers. Yet Thomson's accuser Horwood, and Thomson's successor as Assistant Commissioner in overall charge of the Branch, Sir Wyndham Childs, were able to keep their jobs and pensions intact in spite of a spectacular political assassination near Scotland Yard less than a year after Thomson was sacked.

The victim was a distinguished soldier, Sir Henry Wilson. He died in the full dress uniform of a field marshal, sword in hand, on a pavement in Belgravia on the afternoon of 22 June 1922, having been shot down by two IRA volunteers who were also ex-servicemen.

Wilson was in uniform because he had just unveiled a plaque at Liverpool Street railway station in remembrance of the railway's war dead. He was ex-Chief of the General Staff, and an Ulster MP with homes in Ireland and Eaton Place. He was also an unofficial military adviser to the newly-independent province of Ulster in a freshly partitioned Ireland. By any standards, he was a prime target. But he had no bodyguard. That cover had been withdrawn when he retired from active military service, and at the very time he was more than ever at risk for sound, if brutal, political reasons.

An Anglo-Irish Agreement of 4 January 1922 had created the Irish Free State with its own parliament in Dublin, yet tied to Britain (like such dominions as Canada) with a Governor-General and oath of loyalty to the Crown. This was not to the liking of a nationalist faction fiercely dedicated not only to independence but to an independent republic. For a time this profound split in the IRA was papered over, but Wilson's murder was to be the catalyst which provoked civil war between the two factions, as well as causing Lloyd George's downfall and the re-emergence of the Conservative Party as a separate, governing entity in British politics.

Wilson's assassination was an operatic affair. He was hit by nine bullets as he stepped out of his taxi. The driver then fled in one direction as his two assassins, one of whom had a wooden leg, took off in another. A hue-and-cry pursuit ensued, passing the local police station and on around the elegant avenues of Belgravia during which a brougham was seized at gunpoint and abandoned, and three police officers shot. The assassins, Reginald Dunn and Joseph O'Sullivan, were hanged at Wandsworth on 10 August, as a crowd of sympathisers stood outside singing 'Wrap The Green Flag Round Me, Boys'. (The killers were reinterred in Dublin, attended by an IRA guard of honour, in 1967.)

Neither Dunn nor O'Sullivan ever revealed who had ordered Wilson's assassination. The truth became a historical time bomb since the man responsible was Michael Collins, the dark Hamlet of the IRA and, at the time of Wilson's murder, leader of the pro-treaty party in the Dublin parliament. As the historian A. J. P. Taylor reminds us in his *English History 1914–1945*, the Conservatives were furious and put so much pressure on Prime Minister Lloyd George that 'the British government were driven to threaten that their troops would be used in Dublin against the republicans unless the Free State acted. The Irish civil war was thus begun on British orders. All Irishmen resented this, even when they were fighting against each other.'

The British did not stop at threats. They provided artillery for use against a republican position in Dublin's main court building six days after Wilson's murder. Yet it is still a matter of speculation why Collins ordered the assassination. Collins was a former post office clerk who had fought in the 1916 Easter uprising. He was also a genius of irregular warfare who recognised that whoever mastered the intelligence network would win the match. He so mesmerised official security agencies in Dublin that at least one British staff officer was feeding him with classified information.

Collins would have known of Wilson's role in advising the Loyalist government based at Stormont. 'Perhaps,' speculates Taylor, 'the order [to kill Wilson] was given before the treaty and Collins had forgotten to countermand it; perhaps it was given in the belief that Wilson was organising Unionist forces in Ulster to resist Sinn Fein.' The second hypothesis is endorsed by the best-informed historian of the IRA, Tim Pat Coogan, who adds that certainly 'the indignation [in Britain] would have been greater still if it had been known that the assassination was ordered by Michael Collins . . .'

Collins's plot backfired for he, too, was killed in an ambush in Ireland at about the same time as Dunn and O'Sullivan were executed in London. The Lloyd George coalition fell apart in October 1922 and a general election a month later returned the Conservatives led by the dying Bonar Law. The only people unaffected by Wilson's death – which had brought down an administration on each side of the Irish Sea while detonating a civil war on one side of it – were the Metropolitan Police Commissioner, Horwood, and the man responsible for the Special Branch, Childs. Rupert Allason explains how this came about. His history of the Branch suggests that the detective formerly guarding Wilson had been transferred to the new Chief of the General Staff.

'It had apparently been the responsibility of the Irish Office to request another bodyguard. They had never done so, and the Home Office had never added his name to their list of prominent figures requiring Branch protection. Horwood and Childs insisted the fault lay with the Irish Office and both men escaped with their jobs.'

It is plausible that all security agencies concerned might have concluded that Wilson had made his own arrangements for staying alive, arrangements more effective than a cocked hat and a dress sword. He, after all, was the military expert who had advised the British government on its Western Front strategy and the man who had told Lloyd George that Ireland could be reconquered only by an army of 100,000 men after the limited independence of 1922.

The error would not be repeated by another controversial figure, Winston Churchill. In future years he would sometimes carry his own firearm or arm a private bodyguard when the threat to him was glaringly obvious. In 1922, however, he was Colonial Secretary when Ireland was still an emerging ex-colony. Not surprisingly, he was accorded an additional armed guardian just one week after Wilson was murdered. Gould and Waldren describe how Churchill was allocated a team from 'A' Division of the Met., the same 'Royal A' which provided day-to-day cover for the royal family, in addition to his existing Special Branch cover.

PC Smith, an authorised shot, provided the team's transport. This was his own motor-cycle combination. He drove the machine while PC Brook, 'an expert rifle shot', rode in the sidecar. The men wore civilian clothes and were armed with .32 pistols. An armoured Rolls-Royce mysteriously appeared and, equally enigmatically, was withdrawn.

'On 22 July at 11.10 am on the London road between Guildford and Ripley, Mr Churchill's driver overtook a heavy lorry, but as Smith attempted to follow the official car he collided with a vehicle coming in the opposite direction. Both the motor-cycle and sidecar were badly damaged and the unfortunate PC Brook sustained compound fractures to both legs and his left arm. The bodyguard later reported that when he noticed the escorts' absence it was assumed that they had either missed the way or sustained a punctured tyre.'

A year later, out of office and standing as an independent in a by-election, Churchill was still enjoying the protection of two Scotland Yard bodyguards. They were needed. In one ugly confrontation, Churchill's companion, Brendan Bracken, was stabbed in the thigh.

The Wilson assassination had one final and unexpectedly beneficent side-effect. It removed the pressure of Irish terrorism from British politics for the next seventeen years, until the IRA bombing campaign of 1939. During those years the Irish – republicans, fascist blueshirts, anarchists, social democrats and the Simply Muddled – were preoccupied in murdering one another as a result of the Civil War and its lingering cup of bitterness.

Kevin O'Higgins, one of the most promising young Irish politicians of his day, was murdered by the IRA (in an 'unauthorised' operation) near Dublin, amid much publicity, in 1927. As Minister of Justice, he was unwise to walk alone, unguarded and unarmed to Mass at Blackrock. He was hit by a total of seven bullets fired at point-blank range by three gunmen pretending to be Irish patriots. At the other end of the war, a minor IRA figure suspected of being an informer was followed to New York, spotted at the St Patrick's Day parade there, traced to his home with the help of a New York policeman and murdered with a police revolver. The case hardly rated a paragraph.

When British targets in Ireland came under attack they were soft ones, necessarily so since the last British soldiers had left the Free State in December 1922. Henry Sommerville, a mellowing old British vice-admiral living in unarmed retirement in County Cork, was gunned down on his doorstep in 1936 for the 'crime' of providing references for young Irishmen wishing to escape to the comparative freedom of service in the Royal Navy. (Like that other British sailor, Mountbatten, he thought he could trust his neighbours.)

More ludicrous was the threat pointed not at any

individual Britisher but at a British beer. De Valera, Dublin's Prime Minister, dismantled the legal trappings of the Free State to make Ireland (other than Ulster) an independent republic in all but name in 1932. A trade war with England followed in which the British imposed a twenty per cent tariff on Irish imports. Matters were made worse when an executive of the English brewing firm of Bass made disparaging remarks about the Emerald Isle. In retaliation, as Tim Pat Coogan recalls in his book *The IRA*, a lorryload of Bass beer was destroyed in Dublin on 14 December 1932.

As a result, future shipments of the beer were accorded an Irish bodyguard manned by the Army Comrades' Association, men who had fought against republicans and for the Free State during the civil war. History does not record whether the bodyguard were also teetotal members of the Pioneers movement.

The action was elsewhere, although the IRA had not forgotten Britain and wistfully constructed schemes ranging from a machine-gun attack on the Commons chamber from the visitors' gallery, to an aerial bombing mission using an aircraft flown direct to Westminster from the United States. But in the world of reality the war in Spain from 1936 to 1939 followed by the war between Russia and Finland and the Second World War all had the effect of conducting macho lightning which in other circumstances might have struck in the form of urban terrorism elsewhere.

In London, the quiet situation was symbolised by the discovery in 1939 of an 'A' Division constable in an obscure part of the Home Office. The constable was making tea. Inquiries revealed that he had been posted to the department on temporary close protection duties in 1921. As Gould and Waldren (ibid.) observe: 'For the past eighteen years the forgotten man had quietly drawn his pay every Wednesday and returned to his cubby-hole.'

This comparative calm had been unruffled by the General

Strike of 1926 (when Churchill, as A. J. P. Taylor puts it, 'tried to provoke conflict by parading armoured cars through the streets') and the rise of British Fascism from 1932 onwards. True, in the private sector, bookmakers at Doncaster racecourse and elsewhere required trained boxers and streetfighters to protect them from razor wielding gangsters, but the underworld always had such problems. And private bodyguards, unlike their government counterparts, could not legally carry firearms.

British protection officers could do no more than take note of the turbulence elsewhere, and sharpen up their responses when their principals went abroad. The overseas action was colourful and bloody: Sir Lee Stack, Britain's governor-general in the Sudan, murdered by an Egyptian nationalist in 1924; the Mexican guerrilla leader Emiliano Zapata, murdered by a guard of honour in 1919; French President Paul Doumer, unguarded when shot dead at a Paris book fair in 1932; the King of Afghanistan, assassinated in 1933 followed a year later by the Austrian Chancellor Engelbert Dollfuss (a victim of Nazi terrorism) and King Alexander I of Yugoslavia, shot by a Croat extremist as he drove in a state limousine through Marseilles.

In the United States, easy gun laws combined with an Irish tendency to lace politics with bloodshed meant that even the leading exponents of violence such as Al Capone needed armed protection.

The political victims included President Franklin Roosevelt, saved from an assassin's bullet as he stepped ashore in the Bahamas in 1933 from Viscount Astor's yacht. He survived because a spectator, a local doctor's wife, pushed the gunman's arm at the critical moment. Anton Cermak, Mayor of Chicago, was an alternative target and he died in Roosevelt's arms. Two years later, Senator Huey Long was also murdered by gunmen in his own office in Louisiana.

British Special Branch bodyguards picked up their education by proxy during visits to such Fascist dictators as Benito Mussolini. The Italian ruler was a formidable exponent of his own close protection. He needed to be: six attempts on his life had employed bombs, bullets, knives and poison. When Brust travelled to Rome as bodyguard to the Foreign Secretary, Sir Austen Chamberlain, forty Italian detectives were assigned to their hotel suite and arrested an Egyptian student armed with a revolver.

The Foreign Secretary was on sufficiently close terms with Mussolini in the 1930s to share family holidays with him. Thus, Chamberlain's bodyguard was afforded a unique insight into the arrangements Il Duce made for staying alive. He required a team of three hundred specialists and even this was not always sufficient.

As Brust notes: 'It did not surprise me, moving in Italian police circles, to hear talk of cohorts of the "Ovra" (Political Police) on guard about his person by day and night, to hear mention of food-tasters, of bullet-proof vests, of such precautions at times of public appearance as inspection by police of all lamp-posts on the line of route, of a law which insists that all householders shall bar access to their house roofs, and of frequent roof tours by police posses. Along the kerbs, drain-slits are fitted with close-meshed gratings to prevent the placing of concealed bombs.'

Mussolini was lucky, most of the time. A shot missed him, but killed his chauffeur . . . A Bologna boy fired upon him and the boy was lynched . . . A shot was fired at his car but it was his secretary who travelled inside and was wounded . . . A bomb hurled at his car in 1926 wounded eight people but left Mussolini unscathed. The same year, an Englishwoman tried her luck. Her bullet chipped a piece out of his nose. He went ahead with a visit to a battlecruiser, wearing sticking plaster over the wound. He disembarked at Tripoli and rode a horse through a cheering crowd, still wearing his plaster.

It was clear that Mussolini did not trust his own body-guard. Brust observed: 'The frequent last-minute changes of plan, of route, of departure time, is a source of worry to his guardians. Here again the protective methods are cautious, and routes are changed, mode of transport is altered ... Usually several [official] cars travel in close succession. It would be difficult for a would-be assassin to determine in which vehicle was the man he was after. Sometimes Mussolini bestrides his own motor-cycle, be-goggled and crash-helmeted; few would be able to recognise him in the garb, and he always drives furiously, notching the machine up to sixty miles per hour ... He feels safest in his own airplanes, with his own trusted pilot at the controls ... "I speak as a man who knows what protective surveillance means," he said with a smile, "but one must not complain. It is necessary, I suppose."'

Winston Churchill also anticipated trouble. In August 1939, a full month before hostilities began, he summoned his former Special Branch bodyguard, ex-Detective Inspector W. H. Thompson. In his book *The Gathering Storm*, Churchill says that there were 20,000 'organised German Nazis' in England just before the war began, ready to commit sabotage and murder.

'I had at that time no official protection and I did not wish to ask for any; but I thought myself sufficiently prominent to take precautions. I had enough information to convince me that Hitler recognised me as his foe. My former Scotland Yard detective, Inspector Thompson, was in retirement. I told him to come along and bring his pistol with him. I got out my own weapons, which were good. While one slept, the other watched. Thus nobody [intent on assassination] would have had a walk-over ...'

Thompson tells the story somewhat differently. That Thompson was now an ex-police officer into his fourth year as a greengrocer made no difference to the warlike preparations of Mr Churchill, then a back-bench MP. Churchill had already inspected France's inadequate defence against German invasion and told Thompson, 'The Germans believe I am one of their most formidable enemies. They will not stop short of assassination.'

During his trip to France, he told Thompson, a senior French politician had assured Churchill that his life was in danger. Churchill instantly cancelled a trip to see the Duke of Windsor, then living on the Côte d'Azur, and flew home. In his memoir *I Was Churchill's Shadow*, Thompson recalls a conversation with the great man soon afterwards:

'"I can look after myself in the daytime," he said, setting his jaw in characteristic Churchillian fashion. "Will you protect me at night?"'

For his services as a private bodyguard, Thompson was paid £5 a week and given a .45 Colt self-loading pistol drawn from Churchill's personal armoury. This also included a Mannlicher rifle and a .38 Webley revolver. For a time Thompson was running his shop by day and haunting Chartwell, Churchill's country home, at night. He describes living a 'strange role of an armed, *unofficial* bodyguard patrolling round the quiet of the Kentish countryside in peacetime, ready to pounce upon a would-be Nazi murderer'.

With the declaration of emergency on 26 August, Thompson was drafted back to police service. Churchill had a word with the Commissioner and the bodyguard's position was regularised. Thompson returned the big Colt and drew an official Webley .32 self-loading pistol worn in a patent chamois leather 'contraption' inside his jacket. It made for a faster draw, which was not invariably healthy: 'Once I found it too fast when, in a sudden movement, the gun slipped from its moorings and shot me in both legs.' In his overcoat pocket, while accompanying Churchill on foot at public ceremonies, the bodyguard also carried a revolver.

When Churchill became Prime Minister in 1940, a back-up police car was provided. Thompson, having ensured his own mirror was fitted above the front passenger seat, was able to use it to pass coded signals to this additional escort. But Churchill was invariably prepared to defend himself by the most extreme methods. At Chequers, he had a range constructed. 'He was most deadly with the Colt,' Thompson noted.

As the Battle of France raged in mid-June the Prime Minister prepared to fly for last-minute consultations with a French government already on the point of capitulation. At the last moment he told Thompson to collect his Colt. Churchill pocketed the weapon for what would prove to be a hazardous mission with the comment, 'One never knows. I do not intend to be taken alive.'

This made him a difficult case for any protection officer. During the London blitz, as an anti-aircraft shell exploded near Downing Street, sending lethal fragments of shrapnel in every direction, Thompson pulled the Prime Minister forcefully back into Number Ten. 'He was horrified. "Don't do that," he roared at me.'

Churchill became a spectator of the biggest air raids, which were attracting crowds of sightseers from safer parts of the country. Thus Thompson records:

His worse habit, from my point of view as his bodyguard, was of going on to the roof of the Downing Street Annexe to watch the raids. The harder the Germans hit, the more often he would go up there and nothing would dissuade him. He would stand on the roof in his thick siren suit, an RAF greatcoat and steel helmet, smoking a cigar and watching intently as explosions and fires lit up the battered sky.

On these occasions I used to take him to the top floor in the lift. Then with much exertion he would climb the winding staircase to the roof.

One night, after the bombs had come particularly close, he said, 'I am sorry to take you into danger, Thompson. I would not do it, only I know how much you like it.'

'I am not at all sure about that, sir,' I answered. 'But what I am concerned about is your safety. I do think that you should stop going on the roof and risking your life unnecessarily.'

Firmly and sincerely came the reply that overruled all my protests: 'When my time is due it will come.'

In December 1941, days after the Japanese attack at Pearl Harbor had brought the United States into the war, Churchill went to Washington. Thompson was stunned by the elaborate protection around President Roosevelt. While the Prime Minister could travel freely anywhere in England with two men from Scotland Yard, the President had an armoured car and between twelve and eighteen men 'constantly in attendance and armed to the teeth'.

For a Christmas Day church service, 'two long lines of uniformed police on motor cycles with armed men in the sidecars headed the procession. Immediately behind the President's car were two huge cars filled with Secret Service men. All traffic was stopped. All approaches to the church were under guard. Occupants of houses overlooking the church had been ordered to draw their blinds and keep away from the windows. Secret Service men stood in a semi-circle watching the windows.' Even in church the pews near the President and Prime Minister were filled with Secret Service men. 'As he got out of the car, Mr Churchill gave me a quizzical look which plainly told me his opinion of the turnout.'

America was a newcomer to this war and had a president who had already survived, but narrowly, one assassination attempt. It is possible that the Secret Service were at least as fearful for Churchill's safety, from sympathisers in America of Nazi Germany and Irish republicanism. Subsequently, as the Americans endeavoured to cloak Churchill's presence at Palm Beach with a veil of disinformation (the press were led to believe he had left for Europe) the Prime Minister cast all caution aside and dived naked into the sea. His bodyguard was waiting on the beach, holding the towel. It was one of the many idiosyncratic tasks that went with the close protection of a highly idiosyncratic personality.

In Moscow a few months later, Thompson learned that Soviet security could be even tighter than that around Roosevelt. Armed sentries were everywhere and when Thompson walked round the garden on a tour of inspection (his duty as Churchill's bodyguard) he was dogged by secret policemen in plain clothes. He was soon at odds with his hosts, who – having separated him from his boss during a visit to the Kremlin – suggested that he should return to the villa without Churchill. He did so only when the Russians confirmed that Churchill and Stalin were dining together in private. The style had not changed when, more than twenty years later, another British prime minister, Harold Wilson, made nineteen journeys to Moscow.

The pervasive risk of assassination was again brought home to Churchill and Roosevelt in January 1943 when they met at Casablanca. Two months earlier, an Anglo-American force had invaded French North Africa. To reduce French resistance and Allied casualties, both Churchill and Eisenhower, commanding the task force, were prepared to do a deal with Admiral Darlan, an enthusiastic Nazi collaborator. After French opposition to the invasion had evaporated, but before the dirt could stick to the Allies, Darlan was conveniently murdered by a French loyalist on Christmas Eve. Meanwhile, on the Allied side, the victorious Eighth Army commander General Montgomery would soon be so much at risk that a Pay Corps officer, a

Montgomery 'lookalike', would be the star performer in an intelligence bluff directed by MI5.

For the Casablanca conference, therefore, the security experts sanitised a campus area, put barbed wire round it and told everyone to stay inside. Churchill went for a swim and then led his team back over the wire. They were spotted by some sentries armed with tommy-guns and admitted, with some loss of dignity, by a young officer who drily explained that his men had been ordered to shoot on sight anyone trying to penetrate the area.

About a month later the Germans, who took their killing more seriously, shot down a transport aircraft (VIP flight 777) out of Maison Blanche airfield, Tunisia, in the belief that Churchill was a passenger. In fact the aircraft carried a well-known actor, Leslie Howard, who had been entertaining the troops.

It was at about the same time, as Paul Johnson has noted in *A History Of The Modern World*, that the Americans determined to kill Admiral Yamamoto, the inspiration behind the Japanese navy. The Americans, like Yamamoto, believed that God was on their side in the conflict. Johnson writes: 'But all war-leaders had become assassination targets. That was why Hitler and Stalin never left their working headquarters. Churchill took the most risks. After the Washington Arcadia Conference in December 1941 he returned by an unescorted Boeing flying-boat, which was nearly shot down, first by the German defences in Brest, then by intercepting British Hurricanes. "I had done a rash thing," he admitted.' (His bodyguard, Thompson, who was left behind on that occasion, protested that the transatlantic flight was too dangerous, but he was overruled.)

In the same month that the Americans were plotting to murder Yamamoto, Johnson continues, 'the Germans destroyed a British flight believing Churchill was aboard: in fact they killed the film-actor Leslie Howard. The difference was that, on the Allied side, morality was reinforced by technical superiority. The Germans did not know of Churchill's flights, whereas Yamamoto's movements were studied in advance by America's code-breakers.'

Yamamoto's aircraft was shot down on 13 April 1943, on Roosevelt's personal order. Success was signalled to Washington in a coded message that said 'Pop goes the weasel.'

It was in Tunis towards the end of that year that Churchill appeared to be about to die of pneumonia rather than enemy action. Thompson and another Special Branch man, Sergeant Cyril Davies, stayed at his bedside through the long nights of this crisis, reasoning that he would not be disturbed by their presence. At the darkest moment of this crisis, Churchill's massive self-confidence faltered.

'In what better place could I die than here, in the ruins of Carthage,' he told his bodyguard.

'Don't say that, sir,' Thompson replied. 'The world needs you.'

Churchill was in no greater obvious peril after that until he visited Greece as that country reeled into civil war after the German withdrawal. In an effort to end the fighting and forestall a Communist takeover, Churchill flew to Greece on Christmas Eve 1944 for a conference of the rival factions.

In Athens snipers tried to shoot him and the other British delegates and on the night after the conference 'three-quarters of a ton of German dynamite was discovered in a sewer' not far from the hotel where the Greek moderate George Papandreou and the British party were believed to be staying. Churchill, however, slept on board HMS *Ajax*, which was moored offshore.

In victory, Churchill was still a protection officer's lost cause. Surrounded by a noisy multitude in London after the defeat of Hitler in May 1945, the Prime Minister climbed on all fours along the roof of his chauffeur-driven car, then sat with his legs dangling over the windscreen, waving like a football hero.

Thompson and his successor, Detective Sergeant Edmund Murray, enjoyed a relationship of domestic intimacy, if not cosiness, with Churchill. Murray's account of his life with Churchill from 1950 until 1965 is replete with stories of errant false teeth and spectacles as the old lion drifted into his dotage and required a bodyguard as nurse/valet rather than bullet-catcher. By contrast, the task of their Special Branch colleague Superintendent George Wilkinson was dour indeed. Between 1942 and 1948 he became a specialist in looking after distinguished Soviet visitors to Britain, starting during the Second World War with Foreign Minister Molotov. Wilkinson's own memoir records a professional feud of epic proportions between the Branch and Molotov's protection team in London in 1946.

The Soviet bodyguards were led by Major General Shadrin, a man built 'like a traditional Russian bear', weighing around sixteen stones and imbued with a massive, imperturbable indifference to any plans Scotland Yard might wish to make. Shadrin believed he was in charge of security and that the Metropolitan Police would choreograph London's traffic, including traffic lights and police escort, accordingly. Wilkinson asserted that on British soil, he was in charge. His escort car would not precede Molotov, as Shadrin decreed, but would follow immediately behind. Liaison deteriorated so badly that Wilkinson and his men were obliged to sit in their vehicle, lurking near the Soviet embassy in Kensington, in an effort to guess what Molotov would do next.

'We sat in the car for hours at night when we could have gone off duty had we known Mr Molotov was not to leave the Embassy again . . . We missed meals and generally were disorganised, frustrated and annoyed . . . We felt on the verge of doing something desperate. All the necessary ingredients had been mixed up for us that day to have justified our throwing a brick through the Embassy window before going home and waiting for the sack.'

At 9.30 the next morning, Molotov was due for a bilateral meeting with French Foreign Minister Georges Bidault at Claridges, a rendezvous which was not part of the official international conference programme at Lancaster House. That did not start until 11 am. So – in the absence of any consultation – Wilkinson arrived at the Embassy at 9 am and kept out of sight. The Russian cars left at 9.15.

'They went towards Bayswater Road, which was a mistake, for a stretch of it was under repair, necessitating single lane traffic and inevitable delay . . . At 09.30 we pulled up into our usual place within sight of the Embassy and waited. Fifteen minutes later a figure came running out.'

It was the Ambassador in person, to ask the Branch team to pick up Molotov at Claridges. By the time Wilkinson got there, a row had developed about the stationary Soviet convoy in front of the hotel. Among the queue of vehicles which spread out into the Strand was one containing Lord Montgomery. A chorus of motor horns added to the confusion. Order was restored with the assistance of a uniformed constable.

There were similar rows at the Savoy before relations started to improve. When they did, it was in a burst of cordiality as sudden as snow melting in a Moscow spring. Wilkinson, awash with vodka, was helped home by his driver, Sergeant Lobb, a non-drinker.

CHAPTER 6

The Postwar War –
The Class of '68

In the reconstruction years following the Second World War, most Europeans had had enough of violence, although Communist agents selectively used the tool of assassination to topple democratic regimes in such countries as Czecho-slovakia, where a nationalist leader, Jan Masaryk, was defenestrated.

In general, however, irregular warfare of that sort, with its concomitant need of bodyguards, was reserved for Third World countries which now wished to be ex-colonies, or which had just achieved that status. (A typical case was President Bongo of Gabon, who surrounded himself with big German veterans of the French Foreign Legion. They were sometimes heard in chorus in the main hotel singing the 'Horst Wessel' song, a Nazi favourite.)

In some turbulent areas such as Malaya the guerrillas who turned their guns on the old regime in postwar years had been trained and armed by the original colonial power to fight an underground war against the invading Japanese. In others such as Indo-China (now Vietnam) the arms and training were supplied during Japanese occupation by the United States. Throughout much of Occupied Europe, the Middle East and the Balkans, assassins who had been trained by British agents of Special Operations Executive (who in turn had received elaborate tuition in techniques of murder) soon recognised the power of such knowledge and declined to forget what they knew after 1945. It is not every day that one has a chance to learn the tricks of the assassins' trade – how to open a door stealthily with the right hand and to start shooting with the left because that is the most efficient way to despatch those inside, all courtesy of SOE and the Office of Strategic Studies.

A third group of revolutionaries – black Africans and Algerians among them – learned the art of modern regular warfare as soldiers with the Allied armies. It was this training, experience and armament which would rebound on the West, fanned by Communist doctrines of national 'liberation', more than a decade after the Second World War had ended. (Huge quantities of ordnance left by the British in Libya and Egypt in 1945, for example, were later used against a new generation of British and French soldiers in North Africa.)

The political irony of the new, changed world was personified by the award of an OBE to the Communist guerrilla Chin Peng before he appeared in the London victory parade and returned home to Malaya to make war on the British. (The fighting Poles, suspecting that their leader Sikorsky had been assassinated by Britain in 1943, as a favour to Stalin, did not march through London in 1945.)

To begin with, threats from erstwhile allies seemed remote to British politicians and those charged with their security. The IRA had had a bad war. The top German agent delivered by parachute to open up a third front at Britain's back door in 1940 – the doomed Captain Herman Goertz – committed suicide in despair, still in Ireland, two years after the war ended. A sporadic series of republican armoury raids in Britain and attacks on barracks in Ulster during the fifties fizzled out and left the leaders in Wakefield Prison, where they established cosy links with Greek Cypriots of the EOKA terrorist movement. Neither group seems to have considered assassination in Britain to be either desirable or necessary.

It was the new, assertive influence of the sixties which saw the first signs that the chickens of irregular warfare might come home to roost. In 1968, established governments in Germany, France, Britain, Northern Ireland and the United States were attacked by a virus of urban terrorism which, over the next twenty years, would emerge as a form of armed conflict routinely promoted by criminal cultures disguised as governments in the Middle East and elsewhere.

In a campaign which bore a striking resemblance to Suffragette violence, attacks were made on the homes of public figures including Sir John Waldron, Metropolitan Police Commissioner; Sir Peter Rawlinson, Attorney General; Mr Robert Carr, Home Secretary; Mr William Batty, Ford's Managing Director, and the Trade and Industry Minister, Mr John Davies. Other targets were a BBC mobile unit covering a Miss World contest and the Scotland Yard Bomb Squad headquarters (emulating an assault by 19th-century Fenians). Thus arrived the chic revolutionary – young, with no experience of general warfare – in London two years after the Paris Sorbonne was occupied by a mob singing the 'Internationale'. That event, in 1968, had coincided with the first tide of terrorist air piracy by Palestinians.

Bodyguards were back in fashion. The strength of the Special Branch increased from 300 in 1968 to 550 in 1975 but even that growth concealed a fourfold increase in the number of protection officers. Foreign ambassadors were protected by armed police of the Special Patrol Group. In February 1973 the group shot dead two Pakistanis armed with replica pistols at the Indian High Commission in London.

The SPG handed over embassy protection in November 1974 to a newly-created Diplomatic Protection Group. This team, operating in uniform and linked administratively to the Royal Protection squad, carries firearms and keeps private residences as well as public embassies under surveillance. It came into being soon after a sharp rise in the number of Western diplomats kidnapped in South America and elsewhere (see Part III) and is manned by decent, average policemen such as Police Constable Trevor Lock, the hostage and father figure of the Iranian Embassy siege in London in 1980.

High-risk foreign diplomats in Britain continued to enjoy armed Special Branch protection. In June 1982, a Jordanian assassin shot the Israeli Ambassador, causing him irreversible brain damage. From the scene of the attack (the steps of the Dorchester Hotel in Park Lane) Detective Constable Simpson chased the gunman to South Street, calling on him to stop. As the gunman turned to shoot at him, Simpson opened fire, wounding the Jordanian in the neck before arresting him.

The alliance between the new, chic revolutionary and the old nationalist gunman in his trenchcoat was consummated – where else? – in Ireland between 1968 and 1970. In 1968 an Ulster civil rights group, which enjoyed much goodwill from journalists, emulated French and German revolutionaries in politicising such issues as discrimination in jobs and housing. Behind the scenes, providing the 'marshals' for street protest marches, was the new, politically-oriented IRA shaped by a sophisticated leadership typified by Roy Johnston, a Marxist computer scientist. In 1969 the civil rights radicals, some of them student leaders such as Bernadette Devlin, confronted the Royal Ulster Constabulary with rocks (the wilder spirits preferred petrol bombs) just like the Sorbonne students opposing CRS riot police in Paris a year earlier.

The old guard of the 'Provisional' IRA – in fact, a deeply traditional, nationalist and reactionary faction of republicanism – soon followed through the student confrontation with bullets and nail bombs. This was inevitable. The Old Guard had to maintain credibility when the graffiti of Catholic ghettos read 'IRA = I Ran Away'. And anyway, even among the student revolutionaries, what one later described as 'the nationalist thing' was, she admitted, 'always there'. It was the same old cause disguised as a campaign for 'one man, one job' and 'one family, one house'; that is, equality within the United Kingdom.

If the British were slow to respond to this new Irish threat it was partly because the precise threat was hard to identify. Political agitation on the street – agitprop – had not been a manifestation of terrorism hitherto. On the contrary, in the British tradition, street violence below a certain level had been a constitutional (if informal) alternative to armed revolution, even a safety valve, at least since the Chartist demonstrations of 1848. Communist states – witness Budapest 1956 and Prague 1968 – took a different view. It is within this overall political context that the lack of a coherent response to the threat of individuals and the need for close protection of VIPs, British and Irish, should be examined.

Among the first to come under pressure in 1969 were moderate Unionist MPs, including a respected barrister, Richard Ferguson, from Loyalist extremists angry about concessions to Catholics. Some of the moderates left politics as a result. Next, there began an ugly campaign of sectarian assassination. Shortly before midnight on 23 December 1970 a Protestant company director, Andrew Jardin, was shot dead by masked gunmen who crept into his luxury home in a Belfast suburb. The police rushed out a statement in an effort to distance the killing from the Troubles. Most evidence suggested otherwise.

A few weeks later, in February 1971, British soldiers who had been hailed by the Catholics of the North as saviours less than eighteen months earlier, came under IRA fire. Gunner Robert Curtis, aged twenty, was the first of hundreds of victims of the new terror campaign. The Royal Military Police promptly resumed its wartime role of providing bodyguards for senior Army commanders and their VIP visitors.

In 1970, the Prime Minister, Home Secretary and Foreign Secretary had an automatic right to the protection of a basic two- or three-man team but not, surprisingly, the Secretary of State for Northern Ireland. The Home Secretary had a police car and a police-employed civilian driver with no knowledge of either mobile security techniques or firearms. Other senior ministers were driven by Government Car Service chauffeurs who tended to be elderly, dignified men (like their Royal Mews counterparts) with no security training and not much inclination to use their treasured limousines as weapons of war. (The GCS women drivers were nicknamed, on account of their uniforms and touch-me-not approach to everything, the 'Green Goddesses' of security by irreverent Branch bodyguards.)

One senior ministerial chauffeur had survived his first heart attack and was prone to paralysing pains in his right foot. A veteran of the police escort service told the author: 'In order to keep himself awake, this chauffeur kept accelerating and decelerating between sixty and ninety mph, leaving the escort cars backing and filling like a concertina. The close protection officers who were obliged to travel in that vehicle developed a drill to deal with the chauffeur's next heart attack, just in case it happened while he was at the wheel.

The Branch officer would practise the following manoeuvres:
1. Lean to the right while keeping eyes on the road ahead;
2. Left hand on wheel to steer;
3. If driver's foot still on throttle, lift with right hand and permit deceleration;
4. Turn off ignition *without* engaging steering lock;
5. Apply hand brake;
6. Pray! . . .

There were no special cars or briefings to avoid obvious pitfalls such as the same, familiar route to work. The vehicles were frequently parked at the chauffeurs' homes. As a gesture to security, after 1970 the cars were fitted with special locks and their garages protected with security devices.

The absence of mobile security for some ministers was still provoking anxiety as recently as 1984. After the Secretary of State for the Environment, Mr Patrick Jenkin, was left shocked, dazed and suffering from a fractured wrist caused by a collision between his chauffeur-driven Rover and another vehicle in Wapping, he was without a bodyguard and a potential 'pushover for abduction', as some back-bench MPs pointed out.

In the mid-seventies, the meagre coverage of earlier years was reluctantly extended to ministers connected with Northern Ireland and (after the Angry Brigade attack on his home) to John Davies also. In the aftermath of the Angry Brigade trials in 1972, a Metropolitan Police advisory team was created to give guidance to vulnerable ministers and other VIPs at risk who did not qualify for bodyguards. They were told to 'dial 999' in an emergency and to conduct their lives 'more securely'.

In some cases electronic security devices were fitted at the ministers' homes by the private security organisation Group 4. But anyone who wanted a firearms licence was told to go to his local police station, where he discovered that the unwritten policy in London was not to permit British politicians to arm themselves, however much they were at risk. Few, if any, followed Winston Churchill's example of discreetly acquiring armed bodyguards anyway.

The relaxed – some might characterise it as 'dilettante' – approach to the business manifested itself in various ways. The Metropolitan Police instruction book, a tome two inches thick, devoted just half a page to close protection.

The Princess Anne kidnap attempt came and went in March 1974 (see Part I) causing hardly a ripple on the surface of political protection a few hundred yards away at Westminster. Lack of firearms and firearms training was compounded by a virtual absence of dedicated radios, police drivers and, sometimes, intelligence. As one of the team veterans put it:

'We had two potential enemies: the assassin in front and the senior officer or bureaucrat behind who refused to allow change, but who would make us scapegoats if some tragedy occurred.'

Where there were reforms, the results were occasionally bizarre. After the attempt to kidnap Princess Anne, the Metropolitan Police issued the .38 Special Smith & Wesson revolver to most close protection officers in place of the slim-line self-loading Walther. The more bulky revolver could not be worn easily like its predecessor, in a shoulder holster. As a result many officers including members of the Branch carried the gun in a holster on the waist belt instead.

This was satisfactory until the officer was obliged to empty his bowels. Such were the ergonomic difficulties involved that if he was to avoid some accidental injury to himself, his revolver, or both, it was prudent to take the gun out of the holster and place it on the cubicle floor. Many actually tucked the weapon out of sight behind the pedestal. Not everyone remembered to retrieve his gun afterwards, for bodyguards, particularly political bodyguards, were invariably in a hurry.

During the following winter and spring two attempts were made to blow up former Prime Minister Edward Heath. On 22 December 1974 a bomb was thrown at the balcony of his house in Wilton Street, London, and exploded, seriously damaging the house. Soon afterwards a sleeper bomb was hung beneath his official Rover, parked unguarded outside his house. It fell off but did not explode as the vehicle was driven away and lay in its container, a duffle bag, until someone else drove another car into the same parking space. It was then discovered and made safe.

Heath lost a general election in March 1974. During the months that followed, an IRA onslaught on central London caused many deaths. The victims ranged from Professor Gordon Hamilton-Fairley, a cancer specialist who was taking his dog for a walk, to a civilian Bomb Squad specialist, Roger Goad, killed while defusing a device in Kensington Church Street.

The publisher Ross McWhirter was the victim of a carefully arranged assassination because he took his own counter-terrorist initiative. He offered public rewards for information which would identify IRA assassins and was promptly shot at his own doorway. After eight murders including the McWhirter killing, one of the IRA teams responsible for the latest campaign was besieged in Balcombe Street, Mayfair, for five days before surrendering to armed police specialists, including snipers of the London police D11 team.

That did not help the bodyguards, whose pre-emptive task was to intervene before the end-game of Balcombe Street or its equivalent was reached. But if by now the 'firemen' of D11 were well organised and beneficently budgeted, the protection teams were not. Even the newly elected Prime Minister Harold Wilson and his Home Secretary, Merlyn Rees, enjoyed only minimal cover except when an increased threat to them was clearly identified. Then a temporary, 'band aid' solution was sought. Wilson's Press Secretary at the time was Joe Haines, who wrote in the *Daily Mirror* in June 1987:

In 1975 Wilson and Rees were believed to be in grave danger of an IRA attack. The Special Branch guard upon them was doubled and wherever they went they were closely followed by security men in bullet-proof cars. Nothing, of course, was said about it but the *Daily Mail* printed the story when it spotted the cars. Immediately, TV cameras and press photographers descended upon Downing Street to picture the cars and the Special Branch. That could have been a disaster. If an IRA attack were to have been made, the guards would have been the first target, not the Prime Minister. He would be next. As Press Secretary, I phoned the editors of ITN, the *Evening Standard* and the *Evening News* and asked them not to use the pictures. They agreed.

The image of convoys of bullet-proof cars in Downing Street did not impress professionals in close protection, some of whom would vividly recall the ham-fisted efforts of Metropolitan Police technicians to armour just two VIP limousines for political use at about that time. Bullet-resistant windows attached to a Rover were so heavy that the doors sagged on their hinges and could not be closed. The same vehicle had a sun roof which had to be kept open much of the time as the only means of demisting the windscreen.

The other armoured vehicle, a Daimler, acquired the unexpected modification of doors which could not be opened from within. Once inside, the distinguished passenger was a prisoner.

When President Carter visited Britain in 1975 and went to Washington, County Durham, his Secret Service officers wanted to exercise their customary control over such key arrangements as who would drive the presidential limousine. Government Car Service chauffeurs strenuously resented this and seemed, for the first time in their history, prepared to go on strike over the issue. They were persuaded only at the eleventh hour to withdraw the 'Green Goddess' who had been nominated in exchange for a local police officer who was graded a 'first-class driver'. This substitute chauffeur handled the armoured Daimler with difficulty, driving a limousine for the first time and surrounded by a phalanx of armed Secret Service bodyguards on foot as Carter's motorcade moved through the homely streets of the little Durham town.

Meanwhile, in spite of the Irish tragedy, performed live daily before television cameras only ninety minutes' flying time from London, the division between military and police close protection remained all but absolute. The practical effect was that military guardians, such as the SAS Regiment or Royal Military Police teams, were trained to carry true automatic weapons such as the Heckler & Koch sub-machine gun. The civil police – in spite of the odds moving against them – were not permitted access to such military firepower.

In fairness, it should be noted that most British police officers are still dismayed by the un-British notion of carrying any firearm. Many still take the view that it is 'not law enforcement' and 'not what we joined the force for'. So until 1986, even the protection officers depended upon single shot weapons such as the revolver or self-loading pistol.

The Branch had a few good cards in its hand. One was that it was the collator of police intelligence on political matters. It could – and did – send a senior officer to have a discreet word with sources of trouble before a controversial foreign leader arrived. The emissary's message to Russian-Jewish emigrés and anti-apartheid groups alike was that legitimate demonstration was acceptable; the use of force was not. The activists were told to police their own hotheads at such times and they usually did so. It was sound, pre-emptive close protection.

This did not do much for exposed British politicians seeking police bodyguards, who in London depended upon the Metropolitan Police (and ultimately the Home Secretary). High-profile public appearances outside the capital were a different matter. Thus someone as contentious as Enoch Powell might qualify for temporary bodyguards while addressing a meeting north of Watford (and almost certainly in Bradford) but not in London. The situation was full of anomalies. Visiting 'friendly' foreign protection officers were and still are issued with temporary firearms certificates or carry unlicensed weapons to which the British police turn a blind eye.

By contrast with English practice, Northern Irish politicians such as Austin Currie, Paddy Devlin and Gerry Fitt of the SDLP and the Unionist John Taylor (almost all of them survivors of assassination attempts) were *advised* by the police to acquire firearms and were granted certificates to do so by the Royal Ulster Constabulary. Although they could legally carry their guns into Britain, most seem to have followed Fitt's self-imposed restraint in (usually) leaving the weapon with the police at Aldergrove airport before flying to London. Occasionally the restraint crumbled. As Fitt told the writer Richard West in 1981:

'Did I tell you about the time there were six of us at the airport – going through the metal detector – four politicians and two security men? Each of us had a gun but none of them showed up on the screen. But there was Cardinal Conway coming behind us. He showed up as covered with metal . . . All those religious medallions!'

During the years between 1972 and 1977, the Branch protection squad observed a series of spectacular assassinations and attempted assassinations around a shrinking world with increasing concern. The bodyguards knew that they were inadequately trained and equipped to match the sophistication of modern international terrorism; insufficiently informed to know from which direction the attack might come. In Madrid in 1973, the cycle began with a bomb placed by university-trained mining engineers in a specially dug tunnel which blew up Spain's Prime Minister, Carrero Blanco.

In 1975, an attempt by one of Charles Manson's tribe to shoot US President Ford at close quarters failed because of luck and incompetence by the trigger woman, 'Squeaky' Fromme. She was too weak to draw back the slide on her self-loading pistol to cock the firing mechanism. But the event signalled more than inadequate weapons handling. It was the use of a human zombie, conditioned to perform someone else's crime, that represented a peculiarly chilling threat as old as the Persian Assassins of antiquity, and (like them) representing a human being degraded by drugs to the status of a machine.

The attack on Ford was only one of thirty noteworthy assassination attempts, carefully logged by the CIA that year, ten of which were carried out on territory not controlled by the victim or the assailant. The reason was politically simple. The Third World was now settling its internal feuds on neutral ground where less oppressive security favoured such attacks. A year later, the worldwide total of such assaults increased to forty-four and another head of state, Argentina's President Jorge Videla, had a narrow escape when a bomb packed into metal tubing supporting a reviewing stand exploded moments after he had left.

The last straw for some senior bodyguards was the cold proficiency of the German Baader-Meinhof terrorists in kidnapping the industrial chieftain, Hans-Martin Schleyer, having first turned all their firepower upon Schleyer's four police guardians. Schleyer was in their care on 5 September 1977 because he was known to be at the top of the terrorist kidnap list. At least six terrorists took part in the attack, firing seventy rounds of mixed fire (HK .223, Polish M63 machine pistol, armour-penetrating solid shot and Colt .45) into the escort vehicle and only six at Schleyer's car, all aimed at the driver. Schleyer was murdered forty-three days later, but his bodyguard was the primary target.

A year later, a similar operation by the Italian Red Brigades using around forty-two terrorists (as compared with seven in the Schleyer case) kidnapped former Prime Minister Aldo Moro. The five-man escort had no chance and the body of Moro himself bore eleven wounds when it was found, fifty-five days later, in a car boot in Rome.

In the gloomy Palace of Westminster, a police officer responsible for the protection of Prime Minister Callaghan showed a colleague the London evening newspaper report of the Moro kidnapping with the grim comment, 'That could have been us and at the moment, there isn't much we could do about it.' At a time when politics was becoming a worldwide blood sport with no close season Special Branch protection officers did not even carry the personal radios issued to their more junior colleagues on the beat in uniform. Even the Soviet press had condemned the Moro kidnappers as 'pseudo-revolutionaries'.

The Prime Minister's Parliamentary Private Secretary, Mr Roger Stott CBE MP, took an interest in the problem because, as he told the author, 'I was the one who would normally sit behind the protection officer when we were travelling in the Prime Minister's car. Along with the driver and the protection officer, I would be the first to get it.

'I had been trying to persuade the "Old Man" to get a new official car but he was worried about the cost – exceeding £100,000 – required to get it properly protected. The fear was that the *Daily Mail* would immediately run stories about "extravagance". My response to that was that if the British Prime Minister were knocked off one day, the damage to sterling across the exchanges and consequent cost to the nation would be rather greater than the cost of a new armoured limousine. Mrs Thatcher's first move after her election was to get a couple of new armoured Daimlers and good luck to her.'

(Callaghan's instinct about Fleet Street was not so far off the mark. In February 1988, the *Daily Express* reported: 'The increasing cost of providing police protection for Mrs Thatcher is provoking a serious backstage financial row . . .')

From Callaghan's protection team, Stott learned that six years earlier, Mrs Imelda Marcos, wife of the Philippines president, had been attacked by a man with a knife in the presence of her bodyguard. It was the eighth such attempt on the Marcoses in two years. In spite of that, Mrs Marcos would not allow her bodyguard to be near enough to intervene in a close-quarter attack. The assailant, Carlito Dimailig, inflicted wounds on her arms and hands which required seventy-five stitches before Protective Force personnel brought him down. The most disturbing fact was that he had been shot five times by protection officers but their 9 mm pistols did not have sufficient stopping power to halt the attacker in his tracks. Some Branch officers, who preferred a self-loading pistol to the Smith & Wesson revolver, were still carrying the same weapon that had not deterred Dimailig.

Stott referred the matter to the Home Secretary, Merlyn Rees, without great expectation of change. He was not disappointed, for Callaghan's attitude to security appeared to be that he wanted as little of it as possible. This is a view which the former Prime Minister, now a peer, would contest years later. When the author raised the issue with him, Lord Callaghan replied: 'I am certainly not aware that I resisted any proposals that were put to me to improve my security, although it is of course true that until the Brighton bombing everyone's security was more relaxed than it has been since.'

Lord Callaghan does not contest another of Stott's recollections, an event in January 1979 during the Western summit at Guadeloupe attended by US President Carter, French President Giscard d'Estaing and Chancellor Helmut Schmidt of West Germany. The conference was staged behind a tight French security cordon around a vacation spot from which legitimate holidaymakers were excluded. When the statesmen took an afternoon off, most of their wives played Scrabble. Prime Minister Callaghan put to sea in a sailing dinghy, alone. His PPS and duty protection officer watched, dismayed, from the end of a jetty while their Prime Minister sailed away unguarded towards the horizon. The anxious pair of spectators even considered whether to commandeer a pedalo so as to shadow their charge.

Then President Carter emerged. He had chosen to go scuba-diving. He strode towards the sea wearing all that was necessary and carrying a maritime spear. He was also surrounded by a shoal of Secret Service escorts, also in diving gear, all armed with what appeared to be exotic underwater weapons and wearing waterproof radios which they were already testing: 'This is Red Baron One to Red Baron Four. Can you copy?' – 'Yeh, Red Baron One, we copy.'

(Deprived holidaymakers were not impressed. Fernand Estenne, a Belgian company executive who was peremptorily shunted out of his £100-a-day chalet, praised the British security team for their courtesy but said of the other protection officers, 'They were unspeakable.')

For a time, however, it was not apparent that Stott's initiative had fallen upon entirely barren ground. A high-level inquiry into prime ministerial security was conducted over a period of a year but – like the results of the inquiry into royal security following the attempt to kidnap Princess Anne – it appears to have remained an exercise conducted on paper with little practical effect. Protection officers who had received only one day's personal combat training in years of service were still left to 'pick things up as we went along'.

There was no intensive firearms training of the sort provided by SAS courses for Royal Protection officers: just the routine one-day refresher training on the range with a Smith & Wesson revolver, firing at a stationary target. Some of the most critical shortcomings were covered following a directive from the Cabinet Office. The Security Services and the Foreign and Commonwealth Office were able to provide a number of useful items including personal alarms and radio communication facilities. (Callaghan's predecessor as Prime Minister, Harold Wilson, carried one of these gadgets on his summer vacations to the Scilly Isles. He used it to let his bodyguard know that he was on his way to the Co-op store or the beach.)

After the security inquiry and the Security Services' renewed interest in Cabinet protection, the number and types of radio to be carried by the Branch bodyguards proliferated. One veteran of that period recalls:

'Our limousine resembled a technical workshop. We carried a big radio capable of linking to any police network in the country, but this was too heavy to be back-packed. In "A" Division, around Westminster, each man now also carried a portable radio linked with the police in the division when the protection officer stepped out of the car. Another type of personal radio was supplied for VIP walkabouts, able to communicate with sets of that kind, but no other. We had to be masters of radio communication, constantly switching from one set to another, hopping in and out of the vehicle to use a radio capable of linking with the local police.

'And, of course, we also carried personal "bleepers" (pagers) as well as radios. We were like electronic Christmas trees and yet we still did not have a set linked to an internationally safe network.'

In other respects, clear gaps remained. Some members of the team had suffered at least one heart attack and another, more than one. In spite of that, every time an Arab head of state known as 'the Emir' visited London, he demanded that this same officer should guard him. Such sang-froid depressingly replicated the approach adopted for royal protection and was in sharp contrast with the dynamic transformation taking place among parallel services in France, Germany (where Helmut Schmidt's personal detail totalled sixty men) and Italy.

Some British veterans wondered whether the problem stemmed from the fact that they were under the control of the Yard's Administrative branch (just like, in the Defence Ministry, their Royal Military Police colleagues) rather than Operations. One victim of this form of control describes it as 'a disaster'. At a rare meeting with their top brass, eight senior Branch bodyguards repeatedly proposed reforms. They suggested that no active protection officer should be older than forty; that all bodyguards should be obliged to take physical exercise and vocational drills at least once a week; that the team should control its own, dedicated drivers who were to learn mobile security techniques; and that firearms policy should be reviewed to make them better armed and more expert. These suggestions, like the earlier proposals which flowed from the Stott initiative, were stone-walled.

Some officers, observing a repetitive history, gloomily concluded that cost must be the underlying reason for the Yard's reluctance to take personal protection seriously enough. To run a three-man team (the minimum) required around £75,000. The royal family's rejection of tighter security — for other reasons — gave the Yard's budget controllers a respectability on this issue that they would not have enjoyed otherwise.

There was another, less rational obstruction to reform.

This was the phobia expressed by middle-ranking Special Branch administrators about the 'James Bond phenomenon'. The administrators – failing to comprehend the changes taking place around them – concluded that police officers in plain clothes who said they wanted more firepower must be brought back to the 'real' world.

For the protection officer, however, the 'real' world was the abattoir created by the IRA, Red Army Faction, the Red Brigades and the graveyard fraternities of the Middle East. Potentially, every public occasion, and many less public ones involving a politician under their care, could become personal tragedy and political disaster. To be prepared, they had to make certain working assumptions about their own safety. Unhappily, those assumptions were not shared – or even perceived – by their administrative masters whose signatures were required to authorise improvements.

British insularity was symbolised by a senior Scotland Yard officer who travelled to the United States and watched a Secret Service bodyguard training course. On his return to Britain, he reported in his debrief: 'We have nothing to learn from the Americans.'

Meanwhile, as the men in the front line of protection reminded one another, they would take the blame if – or, rather, when – an attempt was made to assassinate or kidnap a senior British politician.

Quite why the most senior politician of the period – Prime Minister Callaghan – should have resisted proposals to improve his security and that of other ministers remains a matter of surmise. Possibly he accepted assurances proffered from other security sources that all was for the best in the best of all possible worlds. Perhaps – aware as he was, by then, of the allegations by the MI5 renegade, Peter Wright, of a plot to destabilise the Wilson government – he had decided that *any* enhanced security was a potential threat. If so, he was confusing the politically loyal Special Branch protection team with the maverick spirits of military counter-espionage.

Paradoxically, it was often easier to control security around British politicians when they went abroad, or when they were entertaining foreign visitors to Britain since the cost did not fall upon the limited funds available to the Branch. At the 1979 Lusaka Commonwealth meeting, which preceded the independence of Zimbabwe, additional protection was provided by the regular SAS and by SAS veterans working for the private security company KMS.

An exception to the rule that it might be safer to be a statesman abroad was an economic summit in Japan attended by the Big Four Western leaders (Carter, Callaghan, Giscard and Schmidt) in 1979. Visiting protection teams, including the British, had to learn from local press reports that a bomb had been discovered in the delegates' hotel.

But misunderstandings in international customs cheerfully flow both ways in the security world. Statesmen visiting Britain brought (and still bring) guardians with them who are well armed and not always familiar with the British distaste for weaponry. One African president checked into the St Ermin's Hotel in Westminster with an entourage whose two armed guards visited a neighbouring store to purchase new suits. The sales staff, dismayed that the men were wearing shoulder holsters as well as tribal scars, summoned the local police who took the visitors into custody.

They were released after high-level diplomacy and the disingenuous suggestion that they were covered by immunity. Entirely unembarrassed, one of them told a British protection officer: 'Ho-ho! I should realise the staff in this store was alert people, because of the name, which is "Army & Navy Store".'

There was also embarrassment, normally concealed, about infelicities in relations between different British security agencies charged with close protection. When Callaghan visited his own constituency in Cardiff on one occasion, the local police back-up escort cars got ahead of the Prime Minister and his Branch bodyguard in circumstances of ludicrous confusion. The recollection of one participant is that the back-up cars, moving at speed, were then admitted to a local factory (where Callaghan was to be the visiting celebrity) while Callaghan and his party were refused entry by a uniformed police officer on the grounds that they were already inside.

The event is not one which Callaghan himself can now recall. But he observes: 'This sounds a very unlikely story because I was probably known as well as anyone else in Cardiff to everyone in the local factory and certainly to the local police.'

The event which started the change in perceptions of British politicians about their special freedom from the gun and the bomb, was the killing of Airey Neave MP. The bomb attached magnetically to his car by the Irish National Liberation Army (INLA) was a complex device, depending upon an electronic timer as well as a liquid tilt mechanism which shifted as he drove up the ramp from the Commons car park.

Neave was an authentic war hero, a Colditz escaper who had run the underground escape organisation MI9 in Occupied Europe. In March 1979, two months before the general election called by Prime Minister James Callaghan, Neave was the trusted guide who ran Mrs Thatcher's private office. His was the public, flamboyant killing which the Branch protection officers had expected and feared.

'It was on our own political doorstep and things had to change after that,' said one practitioner. In practice, the most necessary changes were not made until after the Brighton bomb attack on the British Cabinet in 1984. Yet in due course Neave's death would be seen to stand out as a

murder which would have as much impact on political
affairs as had the killing of Sir Henry Wilson in 1922, or
the Fenian bomb of 1884 which closed the Commons
Lobby to casual visitors.

CHAPTER 7

Land Where No One Is Safe – Ireland, 1968–88

Political assassination in Northern Ireland does not mean quite what it means elsewhere. Usually, the phrase describes the murder for political reasons of a political spokesman. In Ulster, by contrast, it might equally signify the random slaughter of a man or woman who happens to be a Roman Catholic or Protestant ... but an *unlucky* Roman Catholic or Protestant.

During the first four years of the recent Troubles – from 1969 to 1973 – there were at least 198 such victims, all civilians, most of them without any link to the paramilitaries. Only one of the dead, an elderly Unionist Senator at the Stormont parliament named John Barnhill, was a serious public figure. He was murdered by the IRA near the border with the Republic in 1971. The following year, in February 1972, Northern Ireland's acting Home Affairs Minister at Stormont, Mr John Taylor, was machine-gunned at close quarters while being pursued along a motorway in the province. He survived a classic mobile ambush in spite of having been hit by about six bullets.

Only later did selective assassination become the prime weapon of terrorism in Northern Ireland, creating a threat which belies the brave mask of normality adopted by Ulster's establishment. The toll of murdered VIPs now includes three judges, two stipendiary magistrates and six prominent politicians. Three other members of the judiciary have been injured in attacks and others have had narrow escapes. At least seven senior politicians have been wounded, while many more have been shot at or have experienced attacks on their homes. Anyone, of whatever religion or political party, who participates in public life in Northern Ireland, needs courage. The irrepressible Gerry Fitt MP (later Lord Fitt) sharpened a stock response for the dark, hate-filled but anonymous voices on his telephone:

'Fitt, you bastard, we're coming to get you!'

'Well then, you'd better join the queue,' Fitt would reply.

Because of the threats and the plain impossibility of guarding the multitude of potential victims, the RUC encouraged MPs and others at risk to acquire their own firearms, and provided some basic training in weapon handling. One of the few who declined the offer was Paddy Wilson, aged thirty-nine, a former Stormont Senator and Fitt's election agent in Catholic West Belfast. Wilson explained:

'I couldn't shoot anybody. How could you live with a thing like that afterwards? I couldn't sleep at night knowing I'd shot somebody's son, husband or father.'

At 11.30 on the night of 26 June 1973, Wilson left a Belfast bar which was also a popular political rendezvous with Miss Irene Andrews, a 29-year-old Protestant who worked for a local newspaper by day and gave most of her spare time to ballroom dancing. Two hours later, the Belfast *Newsletter* received a telephone message from the ubiquitous 'Captain Black' of the Ulster Freedom Fighters, a Protestant terrorist group.

'We've just killed Senator Paddy Wilson and a lady friend,' the voice said. 'The bodies are at Hightown Road. After the IRA have murdered a retarded boy we are not going to stand by for what those animals have done to us in the past four years. There will be more deaths in reprisal.'

According to one detailed study (*Political Murder in Northern Ireland* by Martin Dillon and Denis Lehane), an Army search team discovered the couple in a deserted quarry.

'Wilson's car was parked facing the road. Both doors were open and a few feet from the passenger door

Andrews's body lay. She had been stabbed twenty times in the head and chest. Fifteen yards from the driver's door was Wilson's body. He had been stabbed thirty times in the head and chest, and his throat had been cut from ear to ear. Wilson had apparently put up a struggle with his killers. His body showed the marks of a fierce struggle.'

Only twenty-four hours before, Fitt's daughter Joan had discussed with Wilson the threats against all of them. She had asked him if he was afraid of dying. His fatalistic reply – 'If you've got to go, you've got to go' – was evidently insufficient. During a gory departure from this life he had been all but decapitated.

The manner of the murder shocked Fitt into accepting the need to arm himself. As he told the author, to carry his own weapon would not necessarily avert assassination. But it would reduce the risk of being kidnapped and tortured to death like Wilson, as well as giving him a chance to take the assassin with him. So for the next ten eventful years, until he settled permanently in London in 1983, he routinely carried a 9 mm self-loading Browning pistol while he was in Ireland. In those years he was to become the most threatened politician in Europe, reviled alike by the IRA as well as by 'Loyalist' terrorism.

It was no coincidence that Wilson and Fitt were at the top of everyone's hate-list. Both were avidly anti-sectarian, prepared to criticise equally the extremists of both sides. Fitt's refusal to swallow every word of IRA propaganda generated an attack on his Belfast home by a mob on 9 August 1972, the first anniversary of internment.

The windows were smashed. The police warned him that, next time, petrol bombs might be used. There was a next time, and another after that. New glass panes – brick-proof, bullet-proof and resistant to petrol bombs – were installed while the rear of the building was protected by wire netting and a screen to direct any flow of burning petrol harmlessly into the street. (This is not as easy as it might appear at first. The Irish blend a common household substance with their petrol to ensure that, like napalm, it sticks to its — sometimes living — target.)

The environment was not the kindest. 'We lived like that from 1972 to 1983,' Fitt told the author in 1986. 'We had a hell of a time.'

Fitt was a threat to the IRA because of his excellent track record during the civil rights campaign of 1968–69. The leader of one of the first non-violent protest marches, he was bludgeoned by the truncheons of the regular Royal Ulster Constabulary in October 1968. He still had enough credibility to make him dangerous. His repudiation of violence made him even more so in the perception of men who lived by the gun. As he once put it, 'When you have walked behind as many coffins as I have you realise the futility of violence.'

In 1976 on the fifth anniversary of internment, the mob arrived, banging dustbin lids, screaming obscenities and kicking his front door. Repeated telephone calls to the police and security authorities produced no response. As the door collapsed, Fitt heard one of his daughters scream, 'Don't kill my daddy!' Dressed in his underclothes, he took up the pistol, went on to the landing at the top of the stairs. Later he said:

'I stopped the ringleader at the top of the stairs. There were about forty others behind him, some of them women. In that fleeting second three thoughts shot through my mind: First, "This is the way you die." Second, "My God, they will kill my wife and daughter." Third, "Gerry, don't pull the trigger. You'll have it on your conscience for the rest of your life."'

In the event, he roared at the leader, 'Get back or you're a dead man!'

The mob retreated, yelping, 'We'll come back!'

Fitt observed to a reporter next day, 'If I hadn't had a

gun they would have kicked me to death ... As it was, I was the fastest gun in a vest!'

The mob did return after Fitt made a speech on 10 November 1980 in which he said that the IRA hunger strike was wrong. He told the author:

'The republicans used to send big crowds around the house to stand there silently with flaming torches. My wife telephoned me from Belfast. At that time, I was the MP at Westminster for West Belfast. She said,

'"Gerry, for the first time, I am afraid. There is no one else in the house. I am looking out of the window. There are about a thousand of them out there. They have got flaming torches like the Ku-Klux-Klan. One of them hits a drum every five seconds. No one is shouting. They could take this place apart brick by brick."

'I flew home immediately.'

In 1983, the mob broke into the family house while it was unattended and started four fires. Fitt described the scene as follows:

'The furniture had been taken out of the house and systematically burned. There were holes in the walls. The banisters which my wife had polished every morning were all broken. The house was wrecked. After the television cameras went away I closed the door and tramped around among the ruins. I went into Geraldine's room ... I was a bit emotional and thinking, "This is what you get after all these years in politics."

'Then I looked down and saw some paper fragments. I picked these up and found it was the remains of my wedding album photographs. I was seething then. I decided to show them I was not finished.'

He had now been rejected by an increasingly nervous Social Democratic and Labour Party, of which he was the leader, and had lost his parliamentary seat to Provisional Sinn Fein.

'Hints had been dropped before the election by both leading parties at Westminster that I could be offered a peerage. I'd been less than interested until now. But faced with the wreckage of what had been my home I was determined not to be silenced. I said, "Right, I'll take my seat in the Lords."'

He became one of an increasing band of politicians on the British mainland who are so much at risk that they are deemed to require the unremitting protection of armed bodyguards. The change was more pronounced after the election of the first Thatcher administration in 1979, but the trend towards the Irish and American style of armed politics was first acknowledged after the killing of Airey Neave.

Fitt, with customary adaptability, started a new life in London with the constant attendance of two or three guardians. He observed that Provisional Sinn Fein had now codified its policy of 'Armalite and Ballot Box' into a unique fusion of the instruments of coercion and democracy symbolic of people who sought political power through a gun barrel. It was deeply ingrained in the Irish. At some SDLP caucus meetings, one of Fitt's colleagues had made his 'points of order' by producing his legally owned Browning and sliding a loaded magazine into the butt. Another demonstrated his marksmanship to a friend by shooting at a Dublin traffic signal. He scored a dead centre, first time. The friend fled.

The growth of the gun as a political instrument on both sides of the Irish Sea and the resulting importance of expert protection was marked by the change in terrorist tactics away from riots towards assassination. In Ireland the SAS was discreetly called upon to provide temporary protection for such unlikely figures as Bernadette McAliskey (née Devlin), briefly a Westminster MP, and Mrs Maire Drumm, who would regard any offer of police protection as a macabre joke. The first of these two was a Socialist republican; the second, an old-fashioned nationalist who believed that the English were born less intelligent than the Irish, as she once assured the author.

Soon after Mrs Drumm went into Belfast's Catholic Mater Hospital in October 1976 for routine treatment the bodyguard – more a security screen round the hospital, whose nurses detested the security forces, than a true close protection team – was withdrawn though on whose orders is not clear. Since the officer in charge of the team later died in Oman, it is unlikely that we shall ever know.

A day or so after the security around Mrs Drumm was reduced a Loyalist assassination squad arrived at the hospital dressed in doctors' white coats. Mrs Drumm, one of the most charismatic as well as personally generous republicans of her generation, saw the killers coming. She was hiding beneath her hospital bed when the fatal bullet struck her.

A protective screen placed at a distance around Mrs McAliskey's country home, probably without her knowledge, did not succeed in intercepting the assassins who came gunning for her in January 1981, but expert resuscitation by SAS soldiers on her and her husband as they were lifted by helicopter to hospital saved them. As they heard the shots, the soldiers sprinted 200 yards to the rescue after a night lying in the open in sub-zero temperatures. Mrs McAliskey was bleeding from eight bullet wounds. The gunmen were immediately arrested. Their judge said that first-aid had averted a murder trial.

Five days after the attack on Mrs McAliskey, it was the turn of Sir Norman Strong, Speaker of the already-defunct regional parliament at Stormont. He and his son James were together in the library of their home, Tynan Abbey, near Armagh, when a lone assassin broke in and murdered them. Later that year another mainstream politician, the Reverend Robert Bradford, Westminster MP for South Belfast, was shot dead as he arrived at his advice centre at Finaghy. An RUC police bodyguard with him was wounded. The RUC claims that he is the only politician it has lost while in its care.

The following year, 1982, witnessed another spate of killings, but this time, five out of six victims were acknowledged members of the IRA or INLA. They were unarmed when pursued and shot by members of a new counter-terrorist team (Headquarters Mobile Support Unit) run by the local Special Branch. On 11 November IRA volunteers Eugene Toman, Sean Burns and Gervaise McKerr were in a car which was hit by 109 bullets. Three RUC officers were tried and acquitted of their murders. The trial judge, Lord Justice Sir Maurice Gibson, commended the officers for bringing the three IRA men 'to justice . . . the final court of justice'. As a process of deterrence, it was not an effective operation. Gibson himself now became a top priority IRA target, stalked by terrorists for the next four years.

Two weeks after the first interception, a youth named Michael Tighe, aged seventeen with no terrorist connections, was shot dead in a hay shed. Another man with him survived. These shootings, also by an HQMSU team and apparently monitored by the Security Services, were to have remarkable political repercussions more than five years later.

In the last of this series of killings, INLA members Seamus Grew and Roddy Carroll were shot as they were on their way home. A police officer tried for their murders was acquitted. The trial judge, Justice McDermott, observed: 'While policemen are required to act within the law, they are not required to be supermen.'

These operations revived earlier allegations that the security forces were running their own form of dissuasion, a 'shoot-to-kill' policy of counter-assassination, instead of operating within the law. In 1978, for example, two SAS soldiers had staked out a cemetery and shot a youth who drew a weapon concealed beneath a tombstone. They also were tried for murder and acquitted . . . but were told by their trial judge, Lord Chief Justice Sir Robert Lowry, that the Army was 'not above the general law in the use of weapons'. Such sentiments were contradicted by political rhetoric from Westminster and Downing Street concerning a 'war' against terrorism. In the SAS trial, prosecuting counsel had denied the soldiers the legal immunity of the battlefield but as time passed and the judges themselves came under particular attack, the courts also appeared to be less confident than Lowry about a soldier's, or policeman's, duty to observe the law in all its fine particulars.

For politicians trapped by their own typecasting on the slippery slope of Irish history, the presence or otherwise of varying degrees of official muscle as protection was a focus for the stress under which they were now living. After a Democratic Unionist MP, Peter Robinson, had appeared to face public order charges in the Republic in 1986 he noisily denounced the withdrawal of his RUC security screen and alleged that the British government had hired an assassin to dispose of him. Almost two years later, without naming any names in public, the RUC let it be known that 'a loyalist politician was refused protection when he wanted to be driven to a rally which police held to be in breach of the law. Instead, he had to organise his own transport.'

Others were even worse off. In January 1987 Robinson's colleague David Calvert (a humble councillor) was shot in the head and stomach as he walked to his car in County Armagh. He survived. The terrorist group responsible, the Irish National 'Liberation' Army (no agent of Whitehall), said it had shot Calvert because of his 'outspoken and bigoted utterances'. The veteran correspondent David McKitterick concluded that the shooting was designed to goad loyalist extremists into a violent reaction. As Senator Wilson's murder had demonstrated, this was not unduly difficult. But the attack did signal a growing reliance upon political assassination in the Province. An official review of close protection was set in train and challenged spectacularly by the IRA.

By now the RUC's protection detail was trying to cover hundreds of potential victims. It was an operation which required more than a thousand officers, specially trained in close protection and directed by an Assistant Chief Constable. They provided a graduated scale of security, reflecting the current threat and the importance of the potential target. Such VIPs as government ministers and high court judges received total cover, twenty-four hours a day, while lesser fry had to be content with an occasional visit by a police patrol as it slowed down outside the front door.

Just three months after Calvert was wounded the IRA used a new plastic explosive called Semtex to murder Northern Ireland's Chief Justice, Sir Maurice Gibson, and his wife Lady Cecily in the no man's land between the two Irelands, near Killeen. A few hours earlier the Gibsons had driven ashore at Dublin, taking a circuitous route home from holiday in a borrowed Ford Escort as part of a security plan suggested by the RUC Special Branch.

About a mile to the north a bodyguard from the RUC's VIP Escort Branch was sent to meet the couple. One senior officer told journalists: 'We don't normally drive right up to the border to meet VIPs. We ceased this practice when three of our officers were killed in a 1,000-pound landmine blast some time ago. In a situation like this we are in constant close radio and telephone contact with the police in the Republic. We would know exactly when the judge and his wife were due to cross the border.'

On this occasion, the communication somehow overlooked the presence of a stolen car inserted between the two security forces and parked in dead ground, out of sight of an Army checkpoint half a mile away. As the Gibsons drove north, celebrating a safe homecoming, the bomb hidden in the parked vehicle exploded with terrible precision at the second they passed it, enveloping them in blast and fireball.

The bomber is thought to have been Brendan Burns, aged thirty-three when he accidentally blew himself to pieces with one of his own weapons at Crossmaglen, Armagh, in March 1988. Burns was also held responsible by security forces for killing eighteen Parachute Regiment soldiers at Warrenpoint in August 1979 (on the same day that Lord Mountbatten was murdered in Sligo Bay) and for another five soldiers blown up at Camlough, County Armagh, in 1981.

The weapon which killed the Gibsons employed a modern explosive almost certainly manufactured in Eastern Europe and supplied to the IRA by Libya in revenge for the American bombing of Tripoli from British bases. The tactic of planting a bomb between two linked but separate security forces was more venerable. In the early 1950s, as part of a Muslim Fundamentalist campaign against British troops in Egypt, a barrow loaded with explosives lightly garnished with fresh fruit was left for more than an hour on a bridge over the Sweet Water Canal while two British teams guarded each end of the bridge. The effect was similar to the Gibson bomb.

In the Gibson assassination it is not known who supplied another commodity, almost as deadly as the explosive itself. This was hard, timely and accurate intelligence about the victims' movements. Sir Maurice himself had booked tickets in his own name and title and that information was stored on the ferry company's computer on both sides of the Irish Sea. It was not the soundest security arrangement.

In the wake of this murder, police escort officers in plain

clothes took the daring step of travelling with their charges across the border to the nearest town. The IRA response and part of its war of nerves against selected individuals was to reveal that it had obtained advance knowledge (confirmed by an official police request for additional man-power) of a vacation in County Kerry by the British Ambassador to Dublin, Mr Nicholas Fenn. In a cool, damage-limitation interview Fenn played down the signifi-cance of a leak which might have cost him his life.

But it was clear that the terrorists were now sniffing the air for some other means of exploiting the recriminations which would result from the Gibson affair. In this area of psychological warfare – the propaganda follow-through – the IRA is often the master, but this time an unexpected gift descended from the opposing camp. It became known that Gibson's RUC protection officer, detailed to take on the job at the last moment, was being disciplined because he had arrived late at the agreed rendezvous. Punctuality would not have changed anything and the fact that the bodyguard appeared to be set up as a scapegoat did not make his police colleagues any more chipper about bullet-catching as a way of life, or death.

In December 1987, five days before the inquest into the Gibson assassination, the IRA breached security around the South Belfast home of a Crown court judge, Donald Mur-ray, and exploded a bomb near his front door. Murray moved home. His example was followed within a matter of weeks by two other judges, one of whom decided he would enhance his security by living in Scotland. Another Ulster lawyer who was intimidated into the 'comparatively safe anonymity of the English bar' by IRA death threats, told *Guardian* writer Gareth Parry:

'It becomes a living nightmare, looking around your shoulder each moment, considering: "Should I do this? Go there? Are the wife and children safe to take that picnic on the beach this afternoon?" You get tense, knowing the moment you relax and don't take simple precautions, like looking underneath your car before getting into it, could be fatal. In the end some, like myself, say life's just not worth living like that.'

The Gibsons were not just symbolic victims. In January 1973 Judge William Doyle had been gunned down on the sabbath, on his way to Mass, his police guard dismissed for the day. A few days later a Belfast magistrate, William Staunton, was shot through the head as he collected his young daughter from St Dominic's College in the Catholic and Republican Falls Road area. A year later another magistrate, Martin McBirney, was shot and killed in his East Belfast home and Judge Rory Conahan was also murdered at home. The next judicial victims were William Travers, a magistrate, and his young daughter, shot down as they walked away from the Catholic Mass on a Sunday morning. Mr Travers survived. His daughter did not.

By the time the Gibsons were murdered in 1987, several judges were carrying their own, licensed firearms. One of them, Ambrose McGonigal, was thought by some of his colleagues to conceal a tiny Derringer pistol in the capacious sleeve of his judicial robes in court and a heavier-calibre weapon beneath the raincoat usually slung over his arm in the street. The custom generated an unusual legal joke: 'If His Honour felt that counsel had really made a muck of presenting a case, he had an instant, final solution to hand. He could start shooting . . . again.' Except in the Wild West, such anecdotes would be related within a framework of invisible quotation marks, as apocryphal, might-be-true stories. But Northern Ireland is no ordinary place and McGonigal was no ordinary judge.

As Captain McGonigal, he had been an experienced guerrilla himself during 1944 and 1945. He was a member of the Special Boat Squadron when it was part of the original SAS and created havoc in Occupied Yugoslavia, blowing up railway tunnels and ambushing the German patrols sent to find him. In attacks on fortified houses he had led from the front with pistol and hand grenade to fight a determined enemy from room to room. In Ulster forty years on, judges and prosecuting counsel were preparing their own fortifications. Some deemed it prudent to build an additional small room at home: a 'keep' to which they could retire when under attack, like air-raid victims of the 1940 blitz or white farmers in the last days of Rhodesia. Such a shelter had walls reinforced internally to resist blast; an armour-plated door; food and water for a siege; cellular telephone for communication; and remote, closed-circuit television and video for observation.

How to live with such security was a matter of temperament. Some, like McGonigal, appeared to relish the challenge until they died peaceful, natural deaths in bed (in McGonigal's case, while pretending to be elsewhere). Others found such a style of life and death as unacceptable as the wallpaper overlooking Oscar Wilde's deathbed, provoking his last, sad joke: 'One of us will have to go.'

The quarrel between judges and bodyguards focused ostensibly upon the absence of sufficient protection rather than the smothering effect of having too much of it. After the attack on Judge Murray's home, Andrew Donaldson QC (once upon a time, the youngest sergeant in the RUC) resigned to resume his practice as counsel after five years as a County court judge. Donaldson blamed 'persistent inadequacies' in his protection for a decision which cost him a substantial pension. The RUC asserted that what really troubled him was that his security was 'too rigid'. Donaldson dismissed this, and other RUC claims, as 'evasive and deceitful'.

The catalyst for the last quarrel was a university evening class in maritime navigation at the University of Ulster which the judge wished to attend for purposes of recreation. For the first three classes, he was accompanied by an armed police bodyguard. But according to one version, 'as he was preparing to leave his house for his fourth class, an RUC officer came to the door and told him he could not go.'

Certainly the bodyguard was withdrawn after the judge's third lesson, when the risk of this innocuous outing had been evaluated anew. The university is sited at a place called Jordanstown. It has had a deadly reputation since three police officers were murdered there in two booby-trap explosions one of which injured a former Lord Chief Justice. The evaluators concluded that to deliver a judge and his bodyguard to this same place at the same time every week was to invite more trouble than the risk merited. Donaldson, for whom this was evidently an issue affecting the quality of life (and, arguably, some small part of his identity), disagreed and an unseemly public wrangle ensued. The *Observer* newspaper joined in to claim that six members of the Ulster judiciary had said that they had never been offered a guard on their homes, a story flatly denied by the police. The newspaper quoted a judge's wife: 'We feel isolated here, as though London doesn't care. They regard us as Paddies and we can take care of ourselves.'

In January 1988, while the quarrel was still smouldering, an RUC spokesman spelled out the implications of any security system which would be effective for the VIP without putting bodyguards' lives frivolously in jeopardy. He told the *Belfast Telegraph*'s Barry White that 'as soon as anyone agrees to be appointed to the Bench, he will be visited by the security branch for consultations on his personal safety. Fences and TV cameras will be installed and the social habits of a lifetime changed.

'Most people have a good idea of what is involved, and are prepared to accept the restrictions on their freedom, but it is only when they have direct experience of round-the-clock surveillance that they know how they react. Some find it too oppressive and may reject our advice. We will try to dissuade them, but we cannot force anyone against his will.'

The police, he emphasised, had to assess a risk which varied from day to day. The threat evaluator bore in mind the life of the VIP and his family 'and secondly, the lives of RUC personnel. If someone wants to play golf on a Sunday, we have to know where he is going. He may want to play at Course A, but because of its situation, we may advise Course B. Nearly always we reach an agreement. Very seldom is there a showdown. But since we are responsible for the individual's safety – and that of our own officers – our decision must be final. If the Man still insists on going his own way, he must do it without us . . .

'Our problem is that the public only hear about our failures. They know nothing – and in many cases neither do we – about the hundreds of lives that must have been saved, over the years, by our personal security cover.'

All this fuss was good news for the IRA, which, in a psychological stroke calculated to enrage enemies and encourage its few friends, proffered its own form of 'protection' to the judges. It offered an 'amnesty' to Judge Donaldson, provided (as well as resigning from the Bench) in his profession as an advocate, he refrained from acting on behalf of the Director of Public Prosecutions. It was another painful example of the growing significance of close protection as an instrument of political stability within the UK. If judges were no longer safe, who was? For some observers of the bodyguard business, this situation was reminiscent of the last days of British rule in what was once called Aden, when even newspaper correspondents were obliged to keep a revolver on the bar alongside their beer at their favourite watering hole.

The linkage between gun and ballot box was affecting a growing number of society's leaders and their families, in mainland Britain as well as Ireland, as the first decade of the renewed Irish 'Troubles' ended. An illuminating, symbolically important case was that of Roy Mason, who was still routinely accompanied by two armed men years after he completed thirty months' eventful service as Labour's Northern Ireland Secretary.

Five months after he left office as a consequence of the May 1979 election, he revealed that there was an assassination competition between the IRA and its rival republican terrorist group, the Irish National Liberation Army. It seemed that Mason was one of the prizes. The INLA had murdered Airey Neave in March of that year. Mason's murder was to be the IRA 'answer' to the Neave assassination, though in the event, Mountbatten was the next prominent victim.

The implications of this macabre game, not lost on the security services, included a challenge to the right to live of any politician who disagreed with terrorism. The knee-capping fascism of the 'no-go' areas was about to be imposed on Westminster. The threat was one which warranted the attention not only of Special Branch but of its big political brother, C Branch of MI5, responsible for protective security. The security services' answer to the Irish movement towards anarchy was revealed by Mason as one of its main beneficiaries. He had, he said, 'diced with death' for two weeks during the general election campaign of 1979 while an IRA hit squad staked out his Barnsley constituency.

Speaking to members of the Newspaper Society at a luncheon in his constituency, he described in some detail the way he now lived:

'Home, if that is what you can call it, has become a mini-fortress. The gardens are patrolled, floodlights are on all night, security men live in a hut outside the door, checking all visitors, even the postman and milkman, in a

24-hour vigil. The house is under total surveillance and my protection team never leave me alone. My wife walking the dog or shopping is protected all the time and within the house we have a multiplicity of devices which help assure our safety.

'I cannot live freely in London. Nobody will have me. The Government has provided out-of-the-way accommodation and I have to live like a recluse. Foreign holidays are impossible because a "hit team" might follow me. All this for doing my job. What a life and what a legacy.

'Hit squads came to Barnsley but my protection was so tight they were deterred and returned to Ireland. I shall be forever grateful to the police for their major exercise on my behalf, commandeering flats and rooms for surveillance, the use of bullet-proof cars and bullet-proof vests.'

For his wife, Marjorie, normal life was also hard to sustain. One newspaper reported:

'Every Wednesday Mrs Mason gets into a bomb-proof limousine and is driven off by three Special Branch detectives. "I can't think of anything that could stop me going to my Brownie night every week," she said, and tried to behave as if nothing special were happening around her. "I try to go everywhere I want to go, including doing the shopping and taking our dog for a walk. But, naturally, I'm always conscious of the bodyguards around me all the time. I couldn't cope with it if I was the hysterical type. But like most women, I have made my mind up that my family life must go on, no matter what . . . I do look forward to a time when we can get away from it all, but who can tell when that day will come. Until then, it is something I know I must put up with."'

Several years on, the presence of bodyguards around the Mason menage was given formal recognition of a specially British kind: Mr Mason issued a commemorative necktie to the fifty Branch officers who had taken care of him. It incorporated a Westminster portcullis and a Yorkshire rose. As he adjusted to his new title of Baron Mason in 1987, he started work to redesign the tie to incorporate a coronet.

In what Lord Fitt describes as the IRA's 'murderology', Mason's case is by no means exceptional. Those involved in the decision by Mrs Thatcher's first administration not to be blackmailed by the IRA prison hunger strike – Humphrey Atkins, Ulster Secretary at the time, the Home Secretary, William Whitelaw, and even certain junior ministers as well as the Prime Minister herself – are 'people who let the hunger strikers die and they deserve to be murdered themselves'.

Individual response to such personal malevolence varies and, as Mason's case demonstrates, is not invariably doomladen. Attorney-General Michael Havers (later Lord Havers) observed philosophically when he retired in November 1987: 'You know, in 1981 it was only a fluke that I wasn't killed when the IRA bombed my home in Wimbledon. I think that made me aware of what the priorities really are.'

Another target was Don Concannon, Minister of State at the Northern Ireland Office from 1976 to 1979. His wife, Iris, insisted on dispensing with bodyguards when she went shopping. 'I didn't want to be like my husband, who could not even go to the toilet without a detective following him,' she told a newspaper. In an interview with *Today*, she continued:

'I got used to having two policemen at the back and two policemen at the front of the house, night and day, but I always had the feeling we were being watched. One night I woke to the sound of policemen banging on the door. One of our children had left a window open. The police were worried that someone had crawled into the house.

'The next minute our home was taken over by sniffer dogs. They went into every room, including the bedrooms, but the children slept through it all.'

Others who have resisted Irish terrorism and are still at risk, still guarded, include the former Prime Minister Edward Heath. Like Mr Mason, Heath was obliged to add an additional structure in his garden. This was a sort of sentry-box colloquially known as a 'Wendy House' to accommodate the duty protection officers. In Heath's case it provoked grumbles from neighbouring aesthetes who felt that the structure was out of keeping with the style of a Queen Anne house in Salisbury. (The same folk, doubtless, had accepted the whiskery presence of sandbags around some cherished buildings when the war was public, official and patriotic.)

In this changed political landscape the new, pervasive presence of state bodyguards caught even the professionals of the secret world by surprise, none more so than Britain's most eminent spymaster, Sir Maurice Oldfield. From 1973 to 1978, Oldfield was chief of Britain's espionage service, MI6, after a lifetime devoted with bachelor zeal to the intelligence world. Soon after the general election of 1979, Mrs Thatcher visited Northern Ireland and was shocked by conflicting intelligence assessments she received from the Army and the RUC. Her response was to summon Oldfield from retirement to co-ordinate security policy. As the province's intelligence supremo, he would be a prime terrorist target, identified publicly for the first time as such and therefore needing a heavy blanket of protection.

Oldfield's various flats around Westminster had been used for a variety of purposes, official and domestic, over the years. Notable visitors had included the Soviet spy, Sir Anthony Blunt, and the spycatcher, Mr Peter Wright of MI5. No one noticed anything odd about Oldfield's lifestyle, however, until he was equipped with his Special Branch bodyguard, one of whom noted that Oldfield's library contained a quantity of books and magazines devoted to homosexuality.

As part of the protection, Oldfield's home was kept under constant surveillance and a steady flow of unofficial visitors was observed. They were young, mostly hard-up, and male. Some were questioned by the Branch and admitted they were homosexual prostitutes. In the scale of official indiscretion, such rough trade would be regarded as the most dangerous of all because of its potential for blackmail.

Oldfield's status as a person who could be trusted with official secrets was removed and he resigned within months, in June 1980. Less than a year later, in March 1981, he died.

The case was a cruel reminder of the implications of close personal security and the power the bodyguard might acquire over the principal he is protecting. It is sometimes a finely-balanced, politically-flavoured relationship and one which an increasing number of public figures have had to come to terms with in Britain during the Thatcher years.

The price of democratic government can be measured in other, more prosaic ways. At a cost of approximately £50,000 a year, including technical support, for each protection officer, the budgetary requirement for former ministers and other political figures such as Fitt now runs to several millions of pounds per year. Such expenditure does not run on unchecked, however, and those cases where the withdrawal of a bodyguard is attributed to political causes are more likely to originate in someone's effort to reduce the growing financial burden of protection.

In mainland Britain, a panel of Home Office experts regularly reviews the threat posed to individual VIPs and, where appropriate, recommends that protection be scaled down or removed. The final decision is left to the Metropolitan Police Commissioner as the man ultimately responsible for the Special Branch. Some statesmen have been known to argue forcefully and successfully that their bodyguards should be restored. Others defer to expert opinion.

The effect is that some former ministers 'wait at the bus stop like anyone else' (as a former home secretary put it) while others continue to command the official car and its two-man team, sometimes described by cynical colleagues as 'the chauffeur and the valet'. A minority of VIPs enjoy the best of both worlds, accepting the protection but not everything it implies, occasionally eluding the bodyguard in a deliberate search for privacy. Lord Fitt describes the custom as 'doing a runner'.

Not all politicians regret parting from their official guardians. Dr David Owen, Foreign Secretary in the last Labour government, relinquished his protection with some style. 'By the morning of the 1979 election I knew Labour had lost,' he told one interviewer. 'I said to my detectives, "Why don't you go back to London? You'll be needed there by my successor." And I climbed into my car by myself for the first time in two-and-a-half years and I remember singing at the top of my voice as I drove round Plymouth. There was an extraordinary sense of freedom. The sadness didn't hit home until later.'

In a subsequent discussion with the author, Dr Owen questioned the value of bodyguards in a democratic society. 'When I was Foreign Secretary, I spoke at the Cambridge Union. My protection officer was in the front row. A guy came in through the back door and hit me with a flour bomb. There is probably a case for guarding a prime minister or an ex-prime minister, if only to avoid ugly incidents on the street. But the point about democracy is that it is an open system.'

CHAPTER 8

Mrs T's Quest for Perfect Security

The Thatcher years have witnessed an extraordinary growth in governmental reliance upon close protection. For her own protection, as John Stott MP noted, the Prime Minister's first move after her initial election in 1979 was to get a couple of new armoured Daimlers, overriding her predecessor's misgivings about the cost and the way such cost might be exploited by Fleet Street. By 1984, the dozen Branch bodyguards dedicated to protecting top politicians during the Wilson era, ten years earlier, had increased to around a hundred. By 1987, a visiting statesman such as Mikhail Gorbachev was received behind a ring of steel at RAF Brize Norton in a meeting reminiscent of the Second World War, while journalists admitted (after stringent vetting) to Mrs Thatcher's press conference were searched as cautiously as if they were terrorists. Even the fact of the press conference itself was kept secret until the last moment, although it was taking place in a military zone amid people sanitised by X-ray and other forms of technology. In 1988, a metal detector was fitted to the door of 10 Downing Street.

Milestones on the road to this new model democracy are numerous. Not all of them followed that pivotal month of October 1984, when the IRA came close to wiping out most of the British Cabinet with a single bomb in a Brighton hotel, and when Mrs Indira Gandhi was slaughtered by her personal bodyguard in spite of warnings that she was living dangerously in allowing herself to be surrounded by potentially dissident Sikhs. The changes, some made before October 1984 and many afterwards, have included the following:

- Protection of British diplomats in high-risk areas overseas removed from the civilian firm KMS and taken over by the Royal Military Police;
- Continued SAS training – matching that of the RMP's own bodyguard school – of police officers guarding the royal family;
- Direct SAS protection, when needed, of a minority of high-risk/high-value targets in the UK, including Soviet defectors, senior Defence Ministry personnel on the 'A' List (but almost certainly not the Prime Minister herself during the 1987 election campaign);
- Arming of an inner elite of Special Branch bodyguards with twelve fully-automatic 9 mm HK MP5 (K) sub-machine guns as used by the SAS, GSG–9 and other special forces, to protect political VIPs;
- Increasing co-ordination of intelligence gathered by threat evaluators of MI5's C Department with that of other agencies dedicated to close protection (in effect, a marriage of several intelligence agencies);
- Opening of the first Metropolitan Police bodyguard training school, employing specialists from the Branch and D11's firearms teams as instructors;
- Recruitment of armed policewomen as bodyguards for the Queen and the Prime Minister;
- Allocation of £1 million of public funds to improve security at all four political conferences in 1986 with similar sums earmarked for the security of royal palaces and Parliament itself.

Before the Brighton bomb attack, some effort was made to keep such changes out of public view. For example, during the celebrations of the Prince of Wales's wedding in 1981, D11's police marksmen received with incredulity an order concerning weapon handling. As the people charged with the delicate task of picking off snipers who might try to emulate Lee Harvey Oswald's assassination of President Kennedy, they had a sufficiently difficult task in keeping potential killing zones under an unblinking scrutiny. The order which angered some of them dictated that, for fear they might be photographed by journalists, they could not remove their rifles from containers until the royal procession had entered the sector they were covering, as if this were some ceremonial drill rather than counter-terrorism. As Gould and Waldren (op. cit.) comment: 'Many of the riflemen felt that politics had unwisely taken precedence over protection.'

There was reluctance to bow to the change being wrought in the British approach to public order even after the Orwellian year of 1984. Following the Brighton outrage, one Conservative conference organiser declared: 'We must not be bombed into having no party conference or a different party conference which would be a sham.' The Home Secretary himself, Leon Brittan, observed in Parliament immediately after the Brighton attack that total security was impossible in a free, democratic society. He went on:

'Political and other leaders are vulnerable because they must be accessible. Everything which can be done will be done to prevent such outrages and to protect their targets. But we will not be bombed into bolt-holes by terrorists. Those who believe that terror can prevail against democracy understand neither the members of this House nor the British people.'

These were brave words, but the impact of the events at Brighton was to induce a new, defensive style into British politics at the ensuing Conservative conferences and the 1987 general election.

The bomb that was placed in room 629 three weeks before the Prime Minister was due to stay in the building for the annual Conservative Party conference was a fine-tuned 'sleeper' of the type first observed by Colonel Patrick in Coleraine seven years before. According to one informed estimate, it was set to detonate just 24 days 6 hours and 36 minutes after being activated, so as to explode at 2.45 am on the last night of the conference. When it tore the building apart, police lookouts were on the roof, studying an empty promenade through night-vision binoculars.

Such timing, in reasonably expert hands, was no longer a technical feat. The space-age chronometer built into, say, a video recorder could trigger an explosion as accurately as it could intercept the 'Muppet Show' or 'Spitting Image' – that is, with a margin of error to be measured in minutes rather than hours – over a twenty-eight-day period. A linked array of such machines would multiply the bomb's gestation to more than a year with only slight degradation of accuracy. At Brighton the 35-year-old former Norwich altar boy turned bomber, Patrick Magee, who was later convicted of the attack, kept it comparatively simple.

But if modern timers might now defeat contemporary security methods then the high explosive – in this case around 30 pounds of Frangex, made in the Irish Republic – should not have done. Even behind the plastic panelling of a bathroom, most modern HE will release a pungent odour resembling that of marzipan, an odour readily identified by a trained dog or even a good human nose. Anticipating this, the bomber insulated his HE with cling film.

The *Guardian*'s reporter Gareth Parry confirmed that the hotel was searched by police dogs before the conference, but 'no other bomb detection methods were used by the Brighton police . . . The sixth floor, where the bomb was planted, received scant attention . . . The police were in some difficulty over the conflicting demands of security and the Conservative insistence on an "open" conference, with the image at least of business as usual . . .

'But perhaps it is still odd that the pre-conference security checks did not take advantage of the enormous array of sophisticated bomb-detecting apparatus available from the

Metropolitan Police. This included equipment for making radio sweeps of rooms and highly sensitive chemical test machines which can "smell" any alien chemical. The police also consequently failed to use a battery pulse detector unit which might have picked up the low-level emissions from the long-delay battery which powered the IRA bomb hidden behind the bathroom walls.'

The precision of the Brighton bomb, four floors above Mrs Thatcher as she worked and her Cabinet as it slept, emphasised the growingly discreet character of a weapon of assassination which was able to kill long after the assassin had fled. It was technically appropriate, therefore, that the same terrorist team came to Britain equipped with an Armalite rifle intended to murder – among others – the Queen Mother in the grounds of Balmoral.

The Brighton bomb, when it exploded, blew out the front of the hotel and spread it across the corniche like a disembowelled body, but its moral and political effects were to create a conference 'spectacular' for the Prime Minister, an event whose potential public relations value was on a Churchillian scale. Mrs Thatcher naturally attracted all the sympathy going. The terrorists knew almost immediately that the operation was yet another 'own goal'. One of them was later to be discovered on the neutral territory of France, muttering to anyone who would listen, 'Don't worry, we'll get her next time ... We only have to get lucky once.'

For the incidental victims, including the four dead, the casualty rate was one hundred per eent. The fatalities included Sir Anthony Berry, the third Westminster MP to be assassinated in five years. The non-fatal casualties included the bonny, vigorous wife of the Conservative Party chairman, Mrs Margaret Tebbit. Until the blast crippled her, she had been an enthusiastic hill walker. Norman Tebbit, in spite of his own injuries, supported her and his Branch bodyguard supported him through the hard times that followed. Three years after the explosion he revealed:

'I don't think I am supposed to say how many bodyguards I have, but there is a team and I have got to know them very well over the years. They are all marvellous characters and there is a fund of family jokes that includes them. I have just lost the chap who was with me at the time of the Brighton bombing. I value them all tremendously and not just for the security.

'When Margaret was in hospital I was living a rather lonely life and at times a not very easy life. I was often very glad of their friendship and company as well as the security.'

He recalled an incident which occurred while he and Mrs Tebbit were undergoing some inevitably hard treatment by physiotherapists at Stoke Mandeville hospital. A protection officer, in a parody of his own profession, put his head round the door as the Tebbits were being pummelled and stretched and said in an intimidating police voice: 'If you sign the confession we'll call them off.'

The assassination of Mrs Thatcher and her Cabinet at Brighton in October 1984 was to have been only the first stage in the IRA's selective elimination of its most dangerous opponents. Eight months after that attempt failed, a police raid on a brownstone tenement building in the suburbs three miles south of central Glasgow – 236 Langside Road – put Magee into handcuffs along with three accomplices, one of whom carried a Browning pistol in his belt. There was also a 'bomb calendar' revealing a scheme to blitz a dozen British seaside resorts as well as a London hotel.

A week later another police team kicked down the cellar door of a basement in nearby James Gray Street. There they found 139 pounds of high explosive and other bomb-making equipment . . . and a page torn from the *Sunday Times* magazine for 24 March 1985. This was devoted to a day in the life of the Falklands military governor, Major-General (later Lieutenant-General) Sir Peter De La Billiere, an SAS veteran.

Gareth Parry suggested that the evidence pointed to a seaside bombing campaign as a diversion from the real target: the assassination of De La Billiere and others. The diversion would draw in one police force after another 'while the IRA moved against people they considered to be more sensitive targets . . .' Had such a campaign taken off, the threat to British society would have been as pervasive as some military thinkers now expect from Warsaw Pact commandos as the prelude to general war.

It is certainly true that early in 1985 a conference of terrorists representing most West European countries proclaimed political murder to be one of its tactics in 'a guerrilla war in Western Europe'. The French General René Audran, gunned down a few yards from his home in France, was one of the first victims. President Mitterrand's efforts to keep trouble at bay by granting amnesty to terrorist leaders clearly did not yield the desired result. Mrs Thatcher, by contrast, went on to the attack to hit those who supported terrorism, notably the Libyans, whose 'diplomats' had murdered Woman Police Constable Yvonne Fletcher with a burst of automatic fire from their London embassy on 17 April 1984.

Less flamboyant, but no less important, was Leon Brittan's initiative in setting up a Home Office committee chaired by a deputy permanent secretary to sharpen up co-ordination of counter-terrorism among agencies including MI5, the Army and the Royal Ulster Constabulary. In January 1985, in a linked operation to make political conferences safer, the Chief Inspector of Constabulary, Sir Lawrence Byford, led discussions among British police chiefs on lessons learned by the Army in Northern Ireland. The problem facing British threat evaluators was multiplying in direct ratio to the number and combination of Britain's enemies around the world. The Prime Minister's image had been burnished by the Falklands War in her response to Argentine aggression in 1981 and by the bomb that did not kill her at Brighton in 1984. The bomb that did not kill Libya's leader, President Gaddafi, was flown from Upper Heyford, Oxfordshire, courtesy of Mrs Thatcher, by the US Air Force in April 1986. It did cause the death of his adopted daughter, Hanna, aged sixteen months, and gravely injured his sons Saef al-Arab, aged three, and Khamees, aged four.

This was of less obvious benefit when the world learned that while bombing Libya the United States was secretly supplying weapons to another terrorist control centre, Iran; and later still, that a female *German* terrorist had been accused of the 1986 bomb attack on American soldiers in Berlin that had provoked Washington's reprisal. Evidence *for* Libyan involvement depended on radio intercepts.

The anticipation of threats – real, simulated and imagined – became a political factor in its own right, guaranteed a headline a day, which touched every aspect of democratic activity from that of the Palace of Westminster (where a passing pleasure craft triggered off an alert when it tickled an underwater security sensor) to the conduct of the 1987 general election. For years later, Gaddafi was ready to confirm in public that he was supplying the IRA with advanced weapons.

One of the most piquant pointers to the increased importance of the bodyguard in British politics concerned the security of a young car salesman in Texas. Until the USAF raid against Libya, the British Prime Minister's son Mark lived in a luxury apartment block in the élite Turtle Creek district of Dallas. His security was in the hands of the Secret Service, paid for by the US taxpayer.

In April 1986 the owners of the building insisted that he

should leave because – as they euphemistically put it – they could not guarantee his safety. The British consul in Texas, David Hollamby, promptly offered to pay for enhanced security including closed circuit television linked to the apartment, but to no avail. Mark now became, according to one correspondent, 'something of a recluse' and – still accompanied by bodyguards – organised his wedding the following year in the tiny Savoy Chapel, London, rather than in the bride's home town, with one eye to security.

On the face of it, such behaviour might have seemed excessively cautious. Mark, after all, was clearly not a political figure in his own right and Dallas was a long way from London or Libya. Nor was it immediately obvious why the protection accorded him was more noteworthy than that which enfolded his twin sister, Carol, a journalist.

Such security would make sense, however, if Mark Thatcher's disappearance or kidnap were to make the British Prime Minister uniquely vulnerable to blackmail. It is conceivable therefore that the threat evaluators in London, seeking chinks in the Iron Lady's armour, could find only one and that was not a fear for her own safety. Only two other prime ministers – Wellington during his duelling days and Churchill when he was prepared to turn his gun upon himself in France in 1940 – have equalled Mrs Thatcher's zest for combat. The only sign of melting iron occurred in public not after the attempt to assassinate her at the Grand Hotel but somewhat earlier, when Mark appeared to be lost while taking part in a motor race across the Sahara Desert in 1982. His mother wept.

Mrs Thatcher's approach to her own security was to embrace enthusiastically any proposal advanced by the growing number of specialists around her, while declaring publicly that she really did not much care about all the fuss. During the Commonwealth conference at Vancouver in 1987, for example, she chatted to her hairdresser, Derek

Lawrence. He in turn faithfully relayed the message: 'She talked and relaxed. She told me she was locked into air-conditioned cars and rooms all week during the beautiful weather and every time she tried to open a window a Mountie would rush up and make her close it.'

The reality of life back in Britain, both during the run-up to the general election and at the subsequent Conservative Party conference, was somewhat different. During the campaign the Prime Minister made public appearances without advance notice and was shadowed constantly by a variety of security agencies amid speculation about assassins from Libya, Ireland and Iran. Mrs Thatcher was even elusive when visiting her own constituency in North London. The *Observer*'s Simon Hoggart reported:

'Members of the audience whispered that they had been told not to breathe a word to anyone about the meeting. "A tragedy, really," said one. "She explained to us that she really wants to meet the people. She said she can do it in Moscow, but not in Finchley." As an avoid-the-people technique, the secret meeting is rivalled only by the mini-rally, which takes place in someone's sitting room in front of an audience of a dozen or so . . .'

No contemporary politician, however well entrenched, can dispense with journalists, and security arrangements were tailored to accommodate that fact. There was also the continuing embarrassment that, in a democracy, a general election is a very public occasion. So a special request went from Downing Street to the BBC that no forward details of the Prime Minister's programme should be included in election details held on the BBC News Room computer. The reason was to restrict such details to a handful of trusted political insiders and make it inaccessible to their less august colleagues.

An even greater novelty was that for the first time in Britain the gun was now an essential tool of the hustings.

At Chequers, where the Prime Minister played host to French Premier Jacques Chirac, passes were scrutinised by British bobbies wearing bullet-proof vests and armed with pump-action shotguns of a type soon to be prohibited to civilians. Even the Prime Minister's mobile campaign headquarters was armoured. For once, the cliché 'battle bus' was apt.

The Prime Minister's security was further hardened by the presence of London's first armed woman protection officer, a six-footer named 'Rosemary'. This Special Branch bodyguard was promptly photographed and identified by the London *Evening Standard*, which had not yet learned from the Martin Schleyer kidnap that the bodyguard is the first target. A photograph of the victim is always helpful to an assassin and 'Rosemary' could be readily identified six months later, hovering over Mrs Raisa Gorbachev when the Soviet first lady visited an Oxfordshire primary school.

The new high-risk/high-security style, superficially so like the thicket of muscle around Madonna and other pop stars, was a socially infectious influence for a time as a younger generation of high flyers, most of them from north of the Thames, concluded that they had to be under threat to enjoy any sort of significance. Many of these 'Yuppies' (or, in their own phrase, 'Young Masters') now clamoured for property in combative Lambeth precisely because, as they admitted to puzzled but delighted estate agents, it *was* a dangerous area. A sort of mid-Atlantic, high-adrenalin chic had replaced traditional English sang-froid in one of many changes to the British lifestyle wrought by Thatcherism. It provided a target for the fast-growing anarchist movement comprising angry young men of the same generation.

During the summer and autumn of 1987, the momentum of psychological warfare between assassins and guardians accelerated in the run-up to the Conservative Party conference at Blackpool. There were many reports, selectively leaked, about SAS bodyguards, some of which surprised the SAS itself. Others identified by name an IRA assassin who had once served in Britain's élite Royal Marine Commando, and who, it was said, was now gunning for the Prime Minister.

Mrs Thatcher herself, flatly rejecting the cool, royal approach to personal security, adopted a theatrical style when – as the *Daily Mail* crime writer Peter Burden noted – she 'switched cars taking her to Crathie Church' during her annual stay with the Queen at Balmoral. She ended the journey 'travelling in a green Range-Rover instead of the grey Ford Granada she normally uses'. Veterans of the close protection world observed that she had not yet adopted Mussolini's trick of riding in her own motor-cycle escort, but nevertheless, this oriental touch of evasive government, more in keeping with Morocco than the Highlands, is believed to have surprised her hosts. There was, it is true, reason for the tension: three people accused of a plot to assassinate the Northern Ireland Secretary, Tom King, had just been taken into custody.

There was also, at last, good news: a sign that the technological edge enjoyed by the terrorists since the innovation of the sleeper bomb in 1977 was at last about to be blunted. A Defence Ministry invention, the Hydrogenous Explosives Detector, was coming into use to pick up the presence of high explosive even when it was hidden beneath layers of masonry. According to the veteran defence writer Ellis Plaice, 'it fires a low-level radioactive beam which can detect bombs in buildings . . . It can be fired through walls and floors and is "tuned" to spot the atomic particles present in explosives.'

The device had been used operationally some months previously, during a high-profile visit by the Queen to Berlin. For that occasion, British protection officers had adopted some imaginative if unorthodox methods of disguising their presence. Many were dressed in German uniforms.

The 1987 Blackpool Conservative Conference itself consummated a marriage of several styles of political security. It required, in addition to the usual assemblage of men and women with guns under their civilian clothes, the presence of a Royal Navy minesweeper, the *Cuxton*, bristling with anti-aircraft missiles, standing a few hundred yards offshore. Between the *Cuxton* and the beach, two Royal Marine Commando inflatables bounced from one wave crest to another, to the delight of television crews. A Defence Ministry spokesman issued the deadpan statement:

'We have been requested by the Lancashire Constabulary to provide HMS *Cuxton*, together with a Royal Marine contingent with two inflatable boats. They are to provide assistance to the police during the Conservative Party conference in Blackpool. We can give no further details.'

The Prime Minister's other defences included hidden television monitors and video recorders and around three hundred uniformed police officers including snipers armed with rifles. There was even a public telephone 'hot line' to receive calls from members of the public who thought they saw a terrorist. (The line was disconnected after the conference.) The total cost, around £1 million, was one for local ratepayers, a situation which moved the Police Superintendents' Association at its more modestly guarded conference at Torquay to consider a permanent cadre of specialist teams, centrally financed, to take over the job of protecting such events.

Certainly the Conservative Party conference in October and the meeting at RAF Brize Norton between the Prime Minister and Mr Gorbachev two months later, were both endowed with a gladiatorial style of security far beyond the means of the average town council, and far beyond the limited security envisaged by Leon Brittan in October 1984.

For the Gorbachev visit, two venues made identical preparations, including, according to one report, a 'twin' to
present a bouquet to the Soviet leader's wife. Some miles
away from the first choice, RAF Brize Norton, at RAF
Lyneham in Wiltshire, 'Nicola-Jane Batchelor, aged six,
was ready on the tarmac with a posy of flowers, but no
VIPs dropped in.'

Paradoxically, Gorbachev needed only four personal
bodyguards (his permanent inner circle) when he touched
down in Oxfordshire and a modest enough team of 135
KGB security men including 'sweepers' when he travelled
on to the US to sign the INF treaty. There, to the surprise
of some, he went on a public walkabout around central
Washington. The irrepressible Simon Hoggart, writing in
the *Observer*, explained: 'In Russia, the head of government sometimes finds it necessary to have people shot.
Here it's the other way around, which is why presidents,
unlike Communist Party bosses, no longer meet the
people.'

By the time Gorbachev arrived, at least three innovations
could be identified in the security surrounding Mrs
Thatcher. First, there was intensive screening of journalists
and others admitted to the sanitised zone through X-rays
and metal detectors, a process familiar to many hacks since
body searches were instituted in Belfast from around 1970.
This, plausibly, was the result of the study which, as we
have seen, Sir Lawrence Byford conducted from January
1985.

Second, there was the 'double venue' bluff favoured by
such elusive targets as King Hassan of Morocco and King
Hussein of Jordan, possibly recommended by MI6 or the
SAS international protection specialists.

Third was the total military envelope, including air cover,
divers and maritime patrol, provided for the Blackpool
conference. The author of this might conceivably have been

the Prime Minister herself, for she had been the centre of a dazzling security display provided for her by the combined intelligence services of Israel, the United States and Britain only eighteen months earlier in May 1986. In that month she flew by RAF VC10 on an official visit to embattled Tel Aviv, a few weeks after the USAF raid on Tripoli.

Trusted correspondents were briefed to the effect that spy satellites were eavesdropping on telephone and radio calls in the area; CIA station chiefs in Lebanon, Israel, Syria, Jordan and Cyprus and US Navy electronic surveillance ships in the Mediterranean had all been ordered to log suspect messages and report them to a secret intelligence 'clearing house'. There, desk analysts worked to relate such messages to the movements of known terrorists.

The *Sunday Express*'s man, Michael Toner, wrote: 'With Arab factions forever disintegrating and re-forming, their own signals – often passed by hand-held radios – might supply the only advance warning of a murder bid. Then intelligence analysts based at the GCHQ out-station in Cyprus would have only minutes to alert the Prime Minister's guards on the spot.

'A chilling illustration of how great the risks are considered was the specially equipped ambulance awaiting Mrs Thatcher's arrival in Israel. That ambulance, carrying supplies of her blood group, will shadow her wherever she goes.'

Clearly not even the Lancashire Constabulary could match such an effort. Nor would anything so vulgar as a public ambulance be placed prominently outside the conference hall. A Special Branch medical team using an armoured Daimler limousine would be more in keeping with the Downing Street style, together with a strong, six-foot woman able to carry the Prime Minister to a place of safety if need be, plus, say, a flight of helicopters for swift evacuation. Electronic surveillance including signals interception and direction finding are skills to be found in the armed services, MI5 and GCHQ rather than a county constabulary.

The security machine surrounding the Prime Minister which has started (one can argue justifiably started) to emerge since 1984 is almost certainly more refined than even the Police Superintendents' Association knows and certainly far removed from Mrs Thatcher's eyelash-fluttering comment to her Vancouver hairdresser about the Mounties who make her close windows on a fine day. A few weeks after the successful Brize Norton operation an airport-style 'walk-through' metal detector was installed behind the front door at 10 Downing Street. A spokesman explained that this was to counter the fear that 'a terrorist posing as an aide to foreign dignitaries could smuggle a gun inside'.

(Another, more enigmatic change at Downing Street was the disappearance of Wilberforce, a thuggish black and white cat which once harassed Esther Rantzen. Wilberforce, it was said, had not been banished along with other veterans of government, but retired. He died soon afterwards.)

A further glimpse into the reality of protecting political power in Britain was afforded by R. M. Whalley of the Home Office emergency planning division, who informed local authority officers about a series of eight exercises planned to run in various parts of Britain, under various code names, during the autumn of 1988. At a time when relations between Soviet Russia and Britain appeared to be more cordial than at any time since 1945, Mr Whalley suggested that 'Soviet Special Purpose forces might be infil-trated during a period of tension to engage in sabotage against targets of military significance.'

Initially, the police would bear the brunt of such attacks but 'it is thought likely that a stage could be reached when the police considered that they did not have the capability to deal with the threat to life and property posed by Soviet

Special Forces. The police might then have to ask the Army for help.'

A network of police forces and local authorities in Britain trained to repel Soviet saboteurs and assassins would clearly be an appropriate mechanism to deal with other threats from the enemy within. Such a marriage of security, long resisted by both civil police and military authorities, would go some way towards converting the whole country (save for those remote patches of mountain and inner city jungle not regularly patrolled by the forces of law and order) into a sanitised security zone. The only recent models have come from strategic clearance and resettlement programmes derived from wars in Algeria and Vietnam. An effort to create a British model might be less evidently brutal in its effects but, equally, it would mean that terrorism had won some sort of victory in Britain after all.

PART III
Diplomats

CHAPTER 9

Sweet Reason v. Smoking Gun

Diplomacy was always a dangerous occupation but during the past twenty years it has become a front line profession more exposed to violence than the exercise of monarchy, politics, the stage or Mafia administration. For anyone with ambitions to join his country's foreign service, the profession's mortality and kidnap statistics should offset even the enticements of a state honour and an index-linked pension.

Between 1968 and 1987 approximately 500 diplomats were killed and 1,500 wounded in terrorist incidents throughout the world. Almost 170 of these were victims of assassination and twenty-three were ambassadors. Many others have been kidnapped and illegally imprisoned for months on end. In a single guerrilla operation in 1980 – a raid on a reception taking place at the Dominican Embassy in Bogotá, Colombia – eight ambassadors and four lesser mortals were seized as hostages and released, at a price, in Cuba, two months later.

Although the diplomatic species is not so much at risk that it is likely to become entirely extinct, it surely needs protection. Recognition of that fact by the British and some other Western governments has been a slow process, painful for the front-line victims of the changing times.

For three centuries, until the end of the Second World War, diplomats were protected by international agreements whose cornerstone was the Treaty of Westphalia at the end of the Thirty Years' War in 1648. But the self-imposed constraints the game required were essentially European in character and gentlemanly in orientation.

After 1945, with the end of imperialism, the number of states more than trebled. Most of these new nations came out of post-colonial Africa (fifty new governments) and Asia (more than forty). In a changed international community, international manners also changed. In the 1950s, when Fidel Castro was still a rebel guerrilla leader in Cuba, his people kidnapped at least forty-seven US citizens, creating a fashion which others still follow. By the 1980s the diplomats were stalking one another in a macabre parody of Buñuel's film *The Discreet Charm of the Bourgeoisie*: Robert Lamp, chief of the US State Department Bureau of Diplomatic Security, was heard to observe angrily in 1987 that Iranian agents including accredited diplomats had been 'casing' American embassies in search of soft spots, vulnerable to attack.

With the post-colonial conflict came also international terrorism for which the symbolic value of the ambassador, as representative of a system, was an irresistible target. One of the first was Charles Elbrick, US Ambassador to Brazil, seized in Rio on 4 September 1969 and held prisoner until fifteen political prisoners were released. This capitulation generated a market in tethered diplomats which grew faster than Kentucky Fried Chicken outlets in Latin America. In *Terrorism and the Liberal State* Paul Wilkinson estimates that seventeen out of twenty-one diplomatic kidnaps during the years 1968–71 occurred in that region. He also observes that 'for the release of Ehrenfried von Holleben, the German Ambassador to Brazil, the ransom price climbed to forty prisoners. And when the Swiss Ambassador, Giovanni Bucher, was kidnapped on 7 December the same year, the price paid for his release had escalated dramatically to seventy prisoners.'

Not all the victims survived. Early in 1970 the German Ambassador to Guatemala, Count von Spreti, was abducted and murdered. On 31 July a terrorist commando in Uruguay tried and failed to kidnap both the US second secretary and the cultural attaché in Montevideo.

Another target, Dan Mitrione, was an American security expert who performed a Houdini-like escape from the flat, open-topped truck in which he was being carted away. In spite of being bound hand and foot, he contrived a back-flip and side roll from the moving vehicle. This incensed the terrorists, who were made to look foolish, and Mitrione (the father of newly-born twins) was promptly assassinated.

The most celebrated victims of this new form of terrorist blackmail, however, were British. In Quebec in October 1970, James (Jasper) Cross, British Trade Commissioner, was held prisoner by French Canadian separatists for more than sixty days in Montreal. The operation was a failure since the Wilson administration, like all British governments, would not trade diplomats for concessions to another country's terrorists. Cross himself resisted all pressures. His captors merely obtained safe conduct to Cuba rather than the $500,000 they demanded, together with more political objectives.

Back in Uruguay, the British Ambassador, Geoffrey Jackson, wrote to Cross soon after the latter was released, 'to welcome him to the world of the living'. Soon it would be Jackson's turn to be entombed in the small, dark hole of a 'People's Prison' beneath the floor of a factory lavatory whose sewage occasionally leaked upon him. Jackson's eight-month passive resistance – a Jesuitical blend of humour, Catholicism and psychology which virtually hypnotised his youthful captors – has become part of the folklore of diplomacy and textbook material for the directing staff who run courses in close protection.

The Ambassador, subsequently knighted, speaks eloquently for himself about his captivity in his book *People's Prison*. What is relevant to this study is the period before he was seized, for it, too, is a model of a sort.

For months before his vehicle was ambushed in the crowded streets of Montevideo, Jackson knew that he was a target. An essential part of any course in mobile security – the art of not being kidnapped while on the road – is counter-surveillance. It is now as basic to a high-grade, professional chauffeur as an ability to find reverse gear. While the threat to all foreign VIPs built up during that tense summer and autumn of 1970, the intelligent diplomat applied his mind to the task of observing the little people around him, to spot the face that recurred. Queen Victoria had acquired the same skill as a result of the hard lesson of being a target for assassination. Jackson was a candidate for clandestine imprisonment. He noted:

'It was quite early in 1970 when I began to sense that accumulation of recurrently anomalous situations which the late Ian Fleming defined so neatly. His James Bond says somewhere that "Once is happenstance, twice is coincidence and three times is enemy action." When, after a relatively quiet life, nocturnal telephone calls begin to proliferate; when one's hitherto pleasantly solitary walks along beaches and sand-dunes and in pine-forests begin to bristle with horizon-marching silhouettes and sudden encounters with the courting young in unlikely trio formation; when one's golf-game – and not only one's own – begins regularly to be intercepted by casual youthful spectators on remote fairways; when for the third time one's path is crossed by professional violence literally on one's own doorstep – by this time the least perceptive of mortals begins to grasp that, however much the world around him may be changing, his own private world is changing still more.'

The experience of being buzzed by the same vehicles, observed by the same faces in different places and times, to test his reactions and those of his driver and bodyguard, the Ambassador likened to 'the presence of mice, or rats, behind the woodwork, that certainty of an intelligence and strength always invisible, but always there, present, vigilant, somehow malignant'.

He contrived a plausible reason to fly back to London so as to report personally to the Foreign Office. The Department was sympathetic ... and laconic. The Department hoped that 'things were not too unbearable'.

Jackson returned to his post. The mice continued to nibble and the squeaking grew louder. The Ambassador observed that 'if this was normality, it was normality of a totally new dimension.' As some Special Branch teams were discovering back home, people's perception of risk was not uniform. Jackson expressed the problem with customary precision: 'In fairness to myself, when one visitor begged me not to see a Tupamaro (terrorist) behind every tree, it was barely a day or so later that they emerged in force to wrench me away from my accustomed reality.'

Anticipating the calvary of Terry Waite some seventeen years later, Jackson specified that there would be no deals for his freedom (though an escape by a hundred terrorists from Montevideo prison, coinciding with his release, was widely seen as evidence of a secret exchange deal). Jackson also took a crucial decision about his own security which a professional bodyguard would assuredly contest. He forbade any of his three guardians (one who travelled with him, another pair in a back-up car) to carry firearms.

The day came when the Ambassador called goodbye to his wife and was driven into a shoal of traffic filtering through the back streets of central Montevideo. Between two lines of parked vehicles, there was only one constricted artery where any movement was possible. With great deliberation one of the parked vehicles, a red van on the limousine's near side, moved out and blocked the way, crushing the car's wing. As the chauffeur got out, so a team of young men appeared from nowhere, firing automatic weapons one of which had been camouflaged, until now, by a basket of fruit.

No one interfered as Jackson's chauffeur was beaten up. The four young terrorists now swarmed into the limousine. One fired two shots as he did so. Jackson, fastidious throughout, resented the unnecessary damage they caused to the vehicle and even to their own hopes of taking him unscathed. The unarmed bodyguards, clambering out of their back-up car, could only watch helplessly as their boss was clubbed with a pistol. The limousine drove away, unpursued, in the wake of the terrorists' van. Montevideo had few police reserves available for a chase. The President was out of town and, sagely, had taken with him a substantial part of the local constabulary.

As abductions go, this one had everything going for it. But specialists in the protection field thought it bizarre that only the side panels of the limousine were armoured, with the result that shots fired through vulnerable parts of the car would ricochet from one panel to another *inside the vehicle*.

In the circumstances, the Ambassador's decision to go unarmed and virtually unescorted still looks like an unsound choice, yet it was vindicated by events. Jackson ultimately relied upon the weapon he knew best, which was the diplomatic art of influencing other people even when they did not realise that he was doing it. Regrettably, his non-violent option required eight months to be effective and imposed a stress upon Jackson which even he could not assess. It required his unique strength and cunning (though it is to be hoped that Waite will follow the same successful road) to make it work. It did not scatter the corpses of bodyguards in a futile but under-gunned operation of the kind that accompanied the abductions of Hans-Martin Schleyer and Aldo Moro in Europe.

'The kidnapping of diplomats,' observed an Australian

specialist in diplomatic protection, '. . . represents a flat rejection of the diplomatic option of peaceful negotiations and mutually satisfactory compromises . . .' Jackson, sharing that view, insisted while in captivity upon retaining the status and protocol due to Her Majesty's representative in Uruguay, in conversations with his captors and others. But the gesture of disarming the bodyguard was not universally understood.

One of His Excellency's most galling experiences during his confinement must have been the attention of a visiting journalist, trusted by his self-appointed gaolers, who asked him:

'Ambassador . . . It's been said you didn't take any precautions. Deep down, did you want to be kidnapped?'

Possibly she had heard a British criticism that this was the world's first 'psychosomatic' – i.e. self-induced – kidnap.

Jackson replied that this was crazy. He took 'reasonable precautions' but did not go around 'as if I were in a state of war'.

The next question was even more wide of the mark.

'Let's suppose that you are one of the top British secret agents and that you managed to get yourself kidnapped to learn from the inside the mentality of this unknown people, their methods and some way to uncover them. Is it another crazy idea?'

Jackson replied: 'James Bond has been so successful that people are likely to believe anything . . . No, I am strictly an English diplomat.'

The notion that the political prisoner has engineered his own loss of freedom for some ulterior motive is not unusual. The author, held without charge for a time by the Lagos regime during the Nigerian civil war, was later alleged by that regime to have been engaged in some journalistic manoeuvre in getting himself locked up. For some people, the plain truth is too simple. In fact, the cool and phlegmatic approach adopted by Jackson before and after his abduction was in keeping with a patrician style that was as well tested as His Excellency's Daimler and probably even more out of date.

Just seven years before Jackson's abduction, the style was vividly demonstrated in the Indonesian capital, Jakarta. A mob intending to burn down the British Embassy was opposed by just one SAS major – a Scot named Roderick ('Rory') Walker – who marched up and down in front of the building as if this were Inverness Castle, firing warning bursts of bagpipe music into the air. This gesture secured the building for about twenty-four hours, or long enough for the most sensitive papers to be destroyed or evacuated. Then the mob did finally break down the gate and the place was gutted.

It happened that in 1972 the Parliamentary Under-Secretary in the Foreign and Commonwealth Office was Sir Anthony Royle (later Baron Fanshawe of Richmond) whose own military service had included four years (from 1948 to 1951) with 21 SAS Regiment (Territorial Army). As Royle prepared to make a ministerial tour of South America, when memories of Jackson's ordeal were still fresh, he was offered a Special Branch protection team.

The Branch, as we have seen elsewhere in this history, was not the most efficient protection agency at that time. Royle insisted that if he were to have a bodyguard it must be an SAS officer. The regiment nominated Andrew Nightingale, a young major whose good looks added zest to any diplomatic gathering. He was not one of his generation (such as the late Simon Garthwaite) who preferred to wear boots without socks while immersing themselves in the flea-bitten politics of the Omani mountains. Through Royle and Nightingale the SAS found a foothold as the protection agency for the upper echelons of the Foreign Office.

As it happened, a few months earlier, in January 1972,

the regiment had already started to survey areas where British envoys were most exposed. This move was a response not only to the Jackson kidnap, but also to threats against Sir David Hunt in Rio later the same year. The task was not to provide direct protection but to identify and evaluate the threat for others to counter.

The surveys were undertaken by Captain – later Major – David Walker, a friend of Nightingale, who turned his ingenious sapper's mind to the embassy security problems in Uruguay, Argentina, Brazil and Bolivia. He still recounts with relish the experience which put the 'superman' image into a decent, jokey perspective. Arriving at La Paz to ease the anxieties then being exercised by the British Ambassador, Walker discovered a cocktail reception in full swing. La Paz, like many South American cities, is at an altitude (around 13,000 feet) which makes it less than comfortable for the unacclimatised and unwary, particularly those who bounce with fitness at sea level. In the worthy cause of promoting His Excellency's confidence in his adviser, Walker attacked the stairs two at a time all the way up to his room . . . and then collapsed, breathless, on his bed for a considerable time.

Other memorable points on Walker's itinerary were Turkey and Iran, where he advised the Shah about his personal security. But it was in Buenos Aires that he discovered a new career in a profession which did not yet properly exist: that of kidnap negotiator. After advising the British Ambassador, Sir Michael Haddow, he participated in a security seminar in the Argentine capital for the leaders of expatriate British industrial and commercial life. Argentina was already plagued by kidnaps that were the work of left-wing guerrillas, including the ERP (Ejercito Revolucionario del Pueblo), a group which, in 1974, would pick up a ransom of $14 million in exchange for an oil baron. In due course, the country would suffer even more from right-wing death squads, whose activities would create a new, sinister noun: 'The Disappeared'.

Walker's lecture drew a capacity audience, one which included representatives of isolated teams working across the border in Uruguay as well as in some of the more lonely crevices of Argentina where some of the neighbours spoke English with German accents, though settled in South America since 1945. As Walker later told a friend:

'People wanted advice about every aspect of security. They wanted me to visit their factories. I was convinced that there was a real need for this sort of help.'

The result was Walker's resignation from the Army in October 1974 and the foundation of a colourful and successful company named Control Risks, discussed in Part IV.

At the time of the Royle/SAS initiative, the regiment had been in the bodyguard business since 1966, but apart from the Jakarta adventure, had not yet spent much time on the diplomatic circuit. The year 1966 was one in which – exceptionally – there was no local war in which Britain's interests demanded an SAS presence. In its search for a new role, the regiment observed that its founding father, David Stirling – no longer a regular soldier – was running a security company called 'Watchguard'. Alert to a growing trend among newly independent but still nervous governments, Watchguard was preparing to train bodyguards in some of these countries, sometimes to protect an emerging prime minister from the excessive loyalty of his new subjects.

Democratic Kenya was the first to accept such a contract. The Foreign Office perceived it as a harmless export of British expertise which had some political potential. Before Watchguard could actually put its men on the ground, however, the Regulars of 22 SAS Regiment moved in and took over this pioneering training programme. To ensure that none of the trainee bodyguards got it wrong, each novice was obliged initially to wear a numbered vest and to retain the same, pre-scripted role in subsequent escort exercises.

A Close Protection Cell was created within the regiment's Counter Revolutionary Warfare Wing at Hereford and the programme took off. Its purpose was to protect friendly foreign heads of state whose goodwill Britain needed, rather than her own diplomats. Some of the first rulers to enjoy SAS protection were in the Far East. In the UK, hyper-sensitive targets such as Warsaw Pact defectors were also guarded by the SAS.

Not everyone cared for this role. One Director of SAS later described it as 'a boring, policeman's job' and – in a classic phrase – 'not an SAS task'. Those who know the regiment understand the distaste. The bottom line of a bodyguard's job is his willingness to stand in front of a bullet meant to kill someone else. The unofficial motto of the SAS, by contrast, is along the lines of 'I will die for my country if absolutely necessary, but I prefer to help my enemy to die for his, instead.' SAS soldiers are not natural sacrificial victims.

A minority of SAS men, including some of the original training cell, took a different view of the bodyguard's role. They discovered a magic in the apparent boredom which had to do with evaluating the threat correctly and dealing with it before the shooting started. One of these pioneers told the author, 'The job is as boring as you choose to make it, as I still tell my pupils.'

The comparative tranquillity ('boredom' in SAS-speak) of training bodyguards was disturbed in 1970 by an interesting and bloodless coup. In Oman, the medieval despotism of Sultan bin Taimur was brought to a sudden end by his Sandhurst-trained son, the present ruler, Qabus, with the complicity of British intelligence. Even before the coup had happened, an SAS bodyguard was on its way to ensure the security of the young Sultan. As he conducted his first public audiences – receiving personal petitions in the manner of a Plantagenet monarch – the bodyguard stood behind him, concealed by a two-way mirror. The safety catches came off whenever a petitioner made a gesture that was too emphatic, or ambiguous. Possibly the team had been briefed about an attempt to kill the 'Old' Sultan, bin Taimur, in 1967. On that occasion, it was the ruler's own Omani bodyguard which turned its guns on its master at a range of a few feet . . . and missed.

One lesson of the Omani coup of 1970 was that close protection was now an international diplomatic card of some importance. It was ironic that the British government could recognise this in Oman while shrugging off the risks facing Geoffrey Jackson in Uruguay in the same year.

The coup averted – though only just – outright victory by Communist rebels who were aided by the government of South Yemen (formerly the British Protectorate of Aden). After the SAS bodyguard came the regiment's training teams, and then the involvement of a squadron or more to fight a full-scale, modern war for the next six years. The professional vacuum which had been filled by bodyguard-training programmes was over. The SAS, having started to train Royal Military Police soldiers in the art of close protection (for work in Northern Ireland) as well as royal bodyguards from the Metropolitan Police, could no longer meet the growing demand in this area. Yet in an increasingly turbulent world, more and more diplomats and their families were at risk.

For some time, the question of diplomatic protection was allowed to drift on a gentle tide of *laissez-faire* although terrorist attacks on embassies raged on. In late 1974, for instance, the Japanese Red Army seized the French Embassy at the Hague, while the terrorist 'Holger Meins Kommando' took over the West German Embassy in Stockholm in April 1975. There was no reason to believe that British diplomats would be immune to the virus.

At the request of the Foreign and Commonwealth Office, a joint conference took place between FCO security advisers (largely former Special Branch officers) and a team from 22 SAS. The diplomats took the view that the task of the armed forces was the defence of the realm and that they were part of the realm to be defended, even if they did happen, somewhat inconveniently, to be in Ulan Bator, Uttar Pradesh or Ouagadougou.

The SAS response was to propose a sort of 'Centurions' Guard', employing retired warrant officers and senior NCOs drawn from all Britain's special forces. This idea foundered because of the need to provide such men with regular salaries and allowances as full-time members of the FCO staff. What was needed, in a fast-moving area of surrogate warfare, was an irregular force able to work on an in-and-out basis, without dependants, at short notice. The force also had to cost as little as possible.

Besides, the FCO already had its quota of retired sergeant-majors working as doorkeepers for its Security Officer branch.

Faced with this impasse, the Foreign Office mandarins decided to deal with the irregular warfare being waged against them through the novel means of hiring trusted private security specialists. They took advice from the security service MI5 and, in 1975, contacted a private company known by the cryptic initials 'KMS'. This had once been an informal codeword among SAS veterans for 'Kini Mini Services' or deniable operations. ('Kini Mini' was a Swahili phrase describing the silent, sinuous approach of a snake through the long grass.)

The legal formalities to incorporate KMS were still

incomplete when the Foreign Office made its move. The new firm was run by a remarkable trio: a swashbuckling royalist veteran of the Yemen civil war of the 1960s and former Lloyd's broker, Colonel Jim Johnson; an SAS name from the Radfan (Aden) campaign, Brigadier Mike Wingate-Grey; and the up-and-coming David Walker, now a major. Subsequently, Wingate-Grey retired and Andrew Nightingale joined the firm two years later.

One person alone seems to have had reservations about using KMS, the Foreign Secretary, Dr David Owen. Nevertheless, KMS got the contract to protect the most vulnerable diplomats. The only possible alternative – Control Risks – was preoccupied with the delicate work of charming wealthy kidnap victims out of captivity. KMS was the sole qualified horse in the race. The firm immediately despatched its first protection team to the Argentine capital of Buenos Aires.

During the next three years KMS worked with quiet efficiency at British embassies all over the world, including Argentina, El Salvador, Uganda, Holland and Thailand. Not all the threats were politically inspired. In Bangkok, the Thai capital, threats to the British Embassy resulted from a criminal prosecution against the local Chinese tong, a Mafia-like secret society. The case had its origins in British-controlled Hong Kong. The threat of retribution was intense but short-lived and would not have justified the heavy administration of a permanent cadre of people on the government payroll.

Only one high-risk zone was a no-go area for the ex-SAS men. This was Dublin. The firm was told that if it operated in the Irish Republic, even within the British Embassy, offence might be caused to the Republic's own police force, the Garda. Added emphasis was given to this message when it became apparent that the messenger was a representative of MI5. This evaluation of risk *v.* political advantage would become a life-or-death gamble for Britain's newly appointed ambassador to the Irish capital, a gamble he was to lose.

In 1976, about a year after the link was forged between the FCO and KMS with the express purpose of keeping British diplomats alive, London's man in Dublin, Christopher Ewart-Biggs, was murdered by an IRA culvert bomb placed under the road leading to the British residence. He had been in the post for just sixteen days. Ewart-Biggs's widow, later created a baroness, noted in her memoir, *Pay, Pack and Follow*:

> The security arrangements . . . were oppressive. Garda officers roamed the garden night and day, the entire house was brightly illuminated during the darkness hours and Christopher shadowed by security guards wherever he went on foot or by car . . . On 12 July he described [in his own diary] a meeting with members of the Garda immediately concerned with his security at [the residence] Glencairn:
> 'See two officers of the Garda, to try to learn something of the rationale behind the measures taken to protect me and what should be done in emergency, about which there seemed to be no instructions. They are not very reassuring. They assess that I, but not Jane and the children, am distinctly at risk from the Pira [Provisional IRA]. They don't seem to have given much thought to the scenario of attack. They thought for some reason that an attack on the car was unlikely. ("It hasn't happened yet.") I asked them to keep us informed about any changes in their assessment of the risk.'

When his wife asked him whether it would not be wiser to reduce road travel by moving to a residence closer to the embassy, he replied: 'They [the Garda] say that as this house is particularly well placed and designed with a view to protecting us, we should stay here.'

Only two routes led from Glencairn to the Dublin road, one of which passed over the culvert containing the bomb.

Remarkably, it was not spotted by the Garda in spite of the presence of a police escort car behind the Ambassador's distinctive blue Jaguar. Shortly before, a military security expert brought from London had advised the embassy to find some alternative route. Since there was no suitable alternative at ground level, he suggested lifting the Ambassador out by helicopter. It is not clear what became of that proposal, which is not discussed in her book by Baroness Ewart-Biggs.

There were special reasons for treating Anglo-Irish relations with kid gloves rather than knuckledusters at that time. Shortly before Ewart-Biggs's arrival, Prime Minister Harold Wilson had publicly committed the SAS to battle against the IRA in Northern Ireland. Many Republicans, paranoid about the activities of other British undercover groups operating in Ulster, responded: 'The SAS is here already.' Diplomatic bodyguards who had just left the regiment to join KMS would have been objects of more than passing interest — and targets in their own right — in Dublin at that time.

Elsewhere, however, KMS was extending its cover of British envoys to include roving ambassadors who might stray into tricky situations, as well as those who were more static targets. In 1977, when Field Marshal Lord Carver was about to visit Rhodesia in the twilight period before it became Zimbabwe — as part of a tour of Black Africa — the Foreign Office shopped around for a reliable, personable bodyguard to go with him.

Someone recollected the Royle mission to Latin America five years earlier and suggested 'that chap Nightingale'. Nightingale had decided to follow Walker's example and leave the Army, but the formalities were not yet complete. As a regular officer, working on a KMS contract placed him in a somewhat irregular situation. He gave the issue serious consideration (all of two minutes) and accepted.

In a gossipy world, word of his decision reached Westminster and parliamentary questions were drafted. But gossip flows both ways and Nightingale became aware of this looming embarrassment before he flew to Rhodesia. As one of his friends put it, 'When he took off he was still Major Andrew Nightingale. By the time the aircraft had reached its cruising altitude of about 39,000 feet, he had been discharged . . .'

The parliamentary questions and answers went ahead all the same, though somewhat later than expected, in July and August 1978. On the face of it, they seemed unremarkable. On behalf of the Foreign Office, Mr John Tomlinson replied: 'Abroad, guards have been obtained through one private firm – KMS Ltd – to protect ambassadors at a very few particularly exposed posts . . . The department looks for reputable firms able to provide a good and consistent standard of service.'

Next, Defence Secretary Fred Mulley was asked specifically about the Carver mission. Did the Minister have a policy about 'serving officers acting for hire through private companies?' Mulley replied: 'There are no regulations to prevent people in this category from taking up civilian employment in advance of their release dates.'

Implicit in these questions and answers was the deadly flaw of legal status. What would have been the position of an armed bodyguard who might be obliged to open fire on alien soil? Would he enjoy full diplomatic immunity? Such appointments, Mr Tomlinson promised, were 'with the agreement of the governments concerned'. But once the parliamentary whistle was blown in 1978 it became notionally possible that the diplomatic bodyguard might become a diplomatic embarrassment.

Money was also a consideration, in spite of the cost-effectiveness of the private sector. Each KMS bodyguard cost the taxpayer £20,000 a year, paid offshore. But the cost in blood of not having expert protection also rose in 1979 with the murder of Sir Richard Sykes, Britain's Ambassador to Holland, eight days before Airey Neave's murder at Westminster. He was assassinated 'on behalf of the IRA' by Dutch members of the Red Brigades in a chilling example of the Terrorist International's murder exchange. According to the French counter-terrorist specialist Captain Paul Barril, the murders of Sykes and Neave were the work of the Irish splinter group, the INLA.

Whatever the truth of that, after Sykes's killing the Foreign Office promptly sought the advice of KMS and others. One expert forcefully recommended the provision of an armoured Rolls-Royce costing around £100,000. There were some in the department who suggested a penny-saving compromise. Would it not be appropriate, they suggested, to follow the precedent set by the existing Daimler fleet, with armour only on the doors of the new limousine? In theory the occupant would survive a burst of gunfire perfectly well, so long as he ducked in time. This was the theory which gave rise to the bodyguards' description of Foreign Office close protection policy: 'Duck – and write a memo.'

Of the twenty-five or so Rolls-Royces still in British diplomatic service abroad, only a handful have been ar-moured, and those in the areas of highest risk. But as a Foreign Office spokesman admits, 'The killing of Sykes did concentrate minds. What had been only a threat until then, became reality. The trouble with armour-plating is cost: it's all a question of cash.'

There was one other secret foray into the complex world of international protection made by the SAS during the 1970s. This was its campaign to defeat hijackers. Air piracy is almost as venerable as powered flight: the first political hijack occurred in Peru in the 1930s. But until the late 1960s it was not a weapon of international diplomatic potential. The innovation of worldwide, live television news by satellite changed all that.

In September 1970, a Palestinian woman named Leila Khaled and a South American named Patrick Arguello attempted to seize an El Al airliner which they had boarded at Amsterdam. They were members of a Marxist splinter group of Yasser Arafat's Al Fatah movement, named the Popular Front for the Liberation of Palestine. They encountered a professional Israeli sky-marshal who shot Arguello dead and disarmed Khaled before she could detonate a hand grenade.

Khaled was detained at Ealing police station after the aircraft landed at London Heathrow but was set free after a British VC10 flying to Bahrain was hijacked by other PFLP members. The British hostages were eventually freed, but the destruction of the aircraft, along with a TWA Boeing and a Swissair DC8 on the friendly soil of Jordan, led to the short war between King Hussein's largely Bedouin army and the swaggering, armed mass of Palestinians who believed they had taken over Jordan permanently. The Palestinians lost that war and have known the event as Black September ever since.

Behind the scenes, as the stakes rose in this deadly international game of beggar-my-neighbour, a grim and angry British government set about repairing the damage done to its credibility by the propaganda-by-deed of the alluring Miss Khaled and her comrades. During the struggle for Jordan, for example, it became known that King Hussein had by his side a British military adviser. That was only the beginning of Britain's response.

Foreign Office ministers concluded that the hijack instrument would now prove irresistible to terrorists of all kinds in future since it provided a portable propaganda platform from which to command a worldwide audience. The formation of a specialist hijack-busting team was a necessary counter to this, and the unit most suited to do it was the Special Air Service Regiment based at Hereford.

The unit took three years – from 1970 to 1973 – to establish itself, under the overall command of Brigadier Simpson. In 1972–3, when Britain joined the European Economic Community, the SAS supplied training teams to assist other European nations in setting up their own anti-terrorist units, and by the mid-1970s the training programmes were a going concern.

The first and most vivid fruit of this initiative was the storming of a Lufthansa Boeing airliner hijacked to Mogadishu, Somalia, in October 1977. The assault was led by two SAS soldiers, Major Alastair Morrison and Sergeant Barry Davies, and followed through by a German counterterrorist team, GSG-9, commanded by Ulrich Wegner. Three terrorists were killed and a fourth, a woman, was wounded. The operation was a body blow not only to the Palestinians (whose hijack leader had assassinated three people in London shortly before) but also to three West German terrorists who hoped to blackmail their way out of Stammheim prison as a part of the hijack strategy. The three – Andreas Baader, Gudrun Ensslin and Jan-Carl Raspe – were found dead in their cells soon afterwards.

This was the beginning of the end for such spectaculars. The series had started in the darkness of early morning at the Munich Olympics in 1972. Terrorist leaders gradually abandoned hijacking until conditions (among them, the design of larger passenger jets) changed in their favour again. The change occurred only after a revolution in Iran and the dismemberment of Lebanon provided logistics, bases and bolt-holes. By 1988, in entirely different conditions, the quick solutions available to end this form of terrorism seemed suddenly less clear. But then, in the 1970s, the war without frontiers was only in its infancy.

CHAPTER 10

Redcaps Shoot Back

A change of direction away from privatisation in Foreign Office protection began with the election of Mrs Thatcher's first administration in 1979. As we have seen, only a month before that election, Mrs Thatcher's aide, Airey Neave MP – a former escape expert in charge of MI9 – had been murdered by a tilt-bomb attached magnetically to his car by Irish terrorists. The Neave assassination was the first of several which would make the war against terrorism a highly personalised combat between terrorists and Prime Minister. In those circumstances it was no longer credible that Britain's diplomats should depend upon a team of irregulars, however experienced, for their security.

In 1979–80, in the absence of other takers, the only agency with the experience, manpower and credibility to tackle this new political minefield was the Royal Military Police. Aficionados of irregular conflict savoured the fact that, in spite of its distinguished and often sanguinary history, the 'Bloody Provost' was not formally a combat unit. It was, and is, part of an empire ruled by the Defence Ministry's Adjutant-General and therefore a microchip within a machine controlling everything from pay and allowances to the prosecution of homosexuality in the armed forces. That, at least, is the theory.

In practice, the greatest single percentage of RMP man (and woman) power has been engaged in front-line counter-terrorism for many years. It has a record of clandestine operations in this field which reflects its investigative skill as well as its military role. Having been trained as bodyguards by 22 SAS (in a course which included a class in detecting poisons), by the mid-seventies the Redcaps had more close protection teams trained than were required in Northern Ireland. The move to diplomatic protection made economic sense.

The transition period in which KMS gradually gave way to RMP bodyguards continued until 1982. The warriors of the private sector then said a stylish farewell to the Foreign Office. In the spring of 1982 the Falklands crisis exploded, surprising the British government but not the country's journalists, some of whom had travelled specially from Britain to photograph the Argentine invasion. One ingredient of official dismay which followed was the slow-dawning realisation that certain British embassies in South America – particularly in Argentina's neighbour, Uruguay – would be at risk.

The Foreign Office appealed to the Royal Military Police for a team to fly immediately to protect our men in Montevideo. But this was the time of the biggest military operation since Suez (1956) and the RMP could not oblige. KMS, unhampered by the needs of longstanding training and leave commitments, was able to muster experienced bodyguards within hours. At Heathrow Airport, they checked through the firearms supplied by the FCO's own armoury and, within a few days of the original signal, were in position in Uruguay.

In spite of such enthusiasm (of which critics of KMS are usually unaware) assessments of the firm's performance vary considerably even among military men. According to one seasoned military correspondent, Christopher Dobson, writing in *You* (the magazine of the *Mail on Sunday* newspaper):

They were the very antithesis of the thuggish, overweight bodyguards employed to look after pop stars. Quiet, mature men, at home in a dinner jacket and on the diplomatic cocktail circuit where they were able to chat in more than one language, they made sure that their pistol holsters did not spoil the line of their well-cut suits. Their presence was usually sufficient to ensure the safety of their clients.

Word of their prowess flew round the Lebanon when a group of Arab notables called on Sir David Roberts, then ambassador, at his villa outside Beirut. The sheiks brought their own body-guards, armed with silver-plated Kalashnikovs, who tried to demonstrate their expertise by blasting away whole magazines at tin cans. Their shooting was abysmal.

Sir David then asked his 'gunslingers' if they would like a little target practice. Rather reluctantly, they drew their Browning pistols and neatly drilled each can. One shot, one can.

The contrasting experience of someone who followed them into Beirut was conveyed by the following anony-mous anecdote:

David Roberts wanted to do some Christmas shopping at Beirut's famous Hamra centre, where there was some nice, turquoise jewellery. The shop was entered by four heavies carrying automatic weapons who ushered the customers out. Then three more people entered, as bodyguard to a shorter man. The shopkeeper was somewhat amazed when it was explained to him that this was basically a normal shopping expedition by a customer who wanted to pay for the goods he was taking. That was the KMS way of doing things.

In parallel, the RMP was also growing steadily into its new role as the leading military exponent of close protec-tion. Since 1970 the Corps had been in the front line of counter-terrorism in Northern Ireland as the guardians of senior officers. This in turn had led to the foundation of the Corps' first training course in the subject at Werl in West Germany, conducted by men who had received SAS training at Hereford. In 1977, these pioneers proved capable, during the Queen's Jubilee visit to the British Army of the Rhine, of a big, set-piece bodyguarding operation to the satisfaction of everyone except Prince Philip, who fussed over two minutes lost in convoy on German roads, under German escort.

It was the appointment of RMP volunteers to take over the task of guarding diplomats in certain high-risk areas of the world which brought it out of the purely military sphere into the risky, ambiguous milieu of political warfare. As some soldiers in Northern Ireland were also discovering, they could be penalised for shooting at the wrong time as well as for not opening fire when required.

From 1980, when the RMP formally became the operational leader in military close protection, the Corps evolved a programme on two parallel but sharply different tracks. It guarded, as before, military commanders at risk and VIPs temporarily in military care. It now also ran teams on six-month Foreign and Commonwealth Office tours of duty without wives and often with little chance to relax. In the words of one distinguished Provost Marshal (or Military Police chief), a Brigadier, 'The lads had to become social chameleons.'

A team guarding the General Officer Commanding Northern Ireland usually wore uniform and carried weapons as publicly as those wielded by the group which enfolded Montgomery in his desert days. By contrast, the men serving on FCO tours wore civilian safari suits and shoulder holsters and learned a complex body language of weapon display in Beirut which sometimes fell short, just, of opening fire. (When these 'games' began, the RMP crew made sure that potential opponents knew that their weapons were loaded with live rounds.)

In Germany, by contrast, the protection teams had to operate in a mist of Anglo-German legalities which meant that success depended almost totally upon identifying a threat even before the potential victim set foot on German soil. Contrary to the Beirut style, weapons such as the HK 53 tend to be concealed rather than brandished during operations in public places.

The men tended to be popular with their principals, the people whom they guarded. When the late Sir Timothy Creasey left the British Army to command that of the Sultan of Oman, he formally requested that his RMP bodyguard should go with him. The protection officer was a diminutive figure who had been in the General's looming shadow throughout a hard Ulster tour. The request was refused.

Initially, there was less comprehension of close protection among 'the helmets', those parts of the Corps not involved in this arcane trade. Captain R. J. Evans, writing in the RMP *Journal* in 1982, quoted some of the epithets. The more polite ones were 'Hit Man for Mothercare' and 'Plastic SAS'.

The more exposed the clients, the less persuasion they required of the bodyguards' utility. When King Hussein visited an air show at a military base near Middle Wallop in 1980, a Territorial Army battalion provided a cordon three miles from the event; a 120-strong company, also composed of reservists, one mile away; and the Redcaps, in various forms of dress, the close protection. To avoid accidents, the King had also brought his own bodyguard of twenty armed men.

Elsewhere, in a series of sensitive and dangerous operations, RMP bodyguards came under fire in San Salvador, Beirut and parts of Africa. When they returned fire it was with a carefully disciplined minimum force which the irregulars ranged against them would find impossible to match.

At first there were doubts about whether men who were policemen by training and inclination – and therefore more than usually conscious of legal inhibitions on the use of force – would shoot to kill without hesitation. One young veteran, who did so when the time came and won a gallantry medal, told the author: 'During my close protection training course in 1985, I was asked during an interview known as "the Stress Interview", "Can you kill someone?" The honest answer was, "I don't know."'

Hard, public proof of the teams' ability to make a snap decision to open fire when necessary came dramatically one day in September 1984 on a dusty street in Beirut. The British Ambassador, Mr (later Sir) David Miers, was paying a courtesy call on his opposite number from the United States, the Honourable Reginald Bartholomew. He had arrived accompanied by a team of five RMP bodyguards, all corporals. The usual team leader, a staff sergeant, was on temporary duty in Britain.

That day one NCO stayed at Sir David's side as he travelled by lift to the fourth floor of what had been an apartment building in non-Islamic East Beirut. The other three corporals remained near the Ambassador's armoured Ford, in the car park.

Corporal R was the first one to observe that something was wrong. Probably this was because he was standing on a bank at the edge of the car park. This vantage point, eight feet above road level, gave him a bird's eye view of events. He noticed some sort of commotion at the embassy entrance check point just over 100 yards away to his right. A Chevrolet van moved through the check point and halted at a barbed-wire chicane. Then there was a shot and the van accelerated towards him.

The corporal instinctively moved the lever of his HK-53 to 'automatic'. He knew what had to be done. As the vehicle drew level he fired a burst of five rounds into the left hand door of the vehicle, the driver's door. The driver slumped forwards and sideways and the van careered to the right, out of control. It bounced against another parked vehicle and travelled perhaps ten yards more before exploding.

Mobile bombs of this type, delivered by kamikaze drivers persuaded, drugged or blackmailed into believing that this was a short cut to paradise, had already inflicted grievous damage on the Americans in Beirut. On 18 April 1983 a similar bomber had killed sixty-one people at the embassy including Charles Ames, the CIA station chief, and nine of his agents. At a stroke, much US intelligence about Lebanon was paralysed.

The latest bomb was more ambitious. It was calculated to carry not less than 2,000 pounds of high explosive. Probably it was destined for the embassy's underground car park. Detonated there, it could have brought down the entire building, causing hundreds of deaths. That it did not was due to the intervention of the British corporal.

An expert assessment after the event was that the bomb was triggered by a 'dead man's hand' device which, once released, caused detonation. As it was, nine people were killed in an awesome blast which blew Corporal R more than ten yards across the car park and left him with permanently impaired hearing. The corporal had no recollection of being knocked unconscious. He saw one of his colleagues lying on the ground, flattened by the explosion but apparently uninjured, and shouted, 'Get the Ambassador!'

While two of the British team made their way towards the building through a dust cloud, Corporal R pressed the call button on his radio, praying that it would still function. He spoke tersely to the British Embassy, requesting emergency services, and then followed his companions towards the shattered American headquarters. On the way he counted three bodies. There were also a lot of people running in various directions, screaming.

R's police training took over. He directed people away from the building and waited for things to calm down a little. Then, finding a young woman lying badly injured and unattended, he picked her up and carried her a short distance to a sandwich bar which was now being converted into a casualty station.

Soon, he hoped, he would see the rest of the team emerging with the British envoy. They would need instant transport. He hailed a vehicle and – with the aid of his weapon – made it clear that he was taking it over for the time being. The driver shrugged acceptance. By now Phalangist Militia – non-Muslim irregulars controlling the area – had started to appear on the scene and a semblance of order was emerging. But inside the embassy the British team had come face to face with one of the classic problems discussed during their bodyguard training: the obligation to rescue a VIP in dangerous circumstances, only to discover that he would not go willingly.

Sir David was unwilling to be evacuated immediately – and for good reason. His fellow diplomatist, the American Reginald Bartholomew, was lying on the floor of what had been his office, his legs trapped beneath the weight of a steel girder which had been brought down by the blast, along with one complete wall. The British envoy said regretfully that no one was going to leave until they had extracted Mr Bartholomew.

Of the four who now set to work to clear the rubble one man, Corporal B, had been in the car park when the bomb exploded, hurling him over the British Ambassador's vehicle. He was coming to the conclusion that this was going to be one of those days. One of his comrades, Corporal I, was already at work putting a tourniquet on the arm of a wounded American bodyguard. That job done, the British NCO said quietly, 'Get out of here and into a hospital, my friend. And do it *now*.'

After some time and the expenditure of much sweat, if few words, they contrived to prise Mr Bartholomew free. He was incapable of walking unaided. The biggest and strongest man on the British team, Corporal McB, handed his HK MP-5 sub-machine gun to a colleague and, with the help of the others, lifted the burly American on to his back. Then, as Corporal B led the way to clear survivors, bodies and rubble from the path, they walked gingerly down the stairs.

At ground floor level they gathered round Bartholomew and chaired him in a cat's cradle of arms to the car which Corporal R had already seized for use as an ambulance. The area was still crowded with the shocked, the curious and the morbid. Somehow, a way had to be cleared and fast. It was the Phalange Militia who provided it: a running escort of militiamen firing weapons into the air accompanied the vehicle much of the way to hospital.

Meanwhile, one of the British team remained at the scene, treating the most seriously injured people he could find, injecting morphine when necessary. He was still assisting the casualties some time later, when one of the British Embassy staff arrived to collect him.

At the headquarters of the French contingent of the International Peacekeeping Force in Lebanon, efforts were now made to determine whether that establishment would also come under attack, and if so, how. Experience had shown that in their search for the element of surprise, terrorists adapted their tactics as one method lost its bite. What, wondered the French, would be an alternative to a car or lorry bomb?

'We concluded,' a highly placed French military source told the author, 'that the risk now was from a light aircraft loaded with high explosive which might be crashed on our building. We placed a machine gun on the roof and this was manned night and day.'

With that rationality with which non-Frenchmen credit the French, some of the mission objected that the terrorists would not employ an aircraft bomb since 'flying an aeroplane is a technical matter, requiring rational modes of thought, which would make it unlikely that a pilot would be willing to destroy himself.' Either they had not heard of Japan's wartime kamikaze pilots or chose to reject this evidence. It seemed that the sceptics on the team were vindicated one moonless night, soon after the gun was mounted, when an unlit light passenger plane flew straight at the headquarters at low altitude. The gunner fired a long burst and winged the aircraft, which then landed at Beirut international airport. It turned out to be a party of journalists, endeavouring to make a discreet and trouble free journey back to Lebanon. As journalists sometimes do in such situations, they had pooled their expenses and clubbed together to charter the machine. They showed no lights because of the fear of terrorists.

In 1986, a young RMP corporal who had been a Sheffield police constable until four years before found himself in a nightmarish situation. With the clients in his care – six British diplomats including two women, plus a woman secretary – he had just watched five rebel African troops murder the people who lived next door to the British residence in a normally quiet road on the fringes of the city. The neighbours were local people, an African executive with the country's electricity board, and his wife.

While the British watched through the curtains of their villa the victims were marched on to the front lawn, forced to kneel down and shot in the back with Kalashnikov assault rifles. In a country then in a state of anarchy, there was no police force to defend them. Potentially this was a replay of the ghastly first days of post-independence Zaire, with its regression to ritual blood sacrifice. The corporal, some years younger than his charges, had never been under fire. He'd had no service in Northern Ireland or the Falklands. Nevertheless, he told them, 'I think everyone should go upstairs.' He meant everyone except himself.

The upper part of the building was a collective strong room, the stairs to which were protected by a massive, barred gate. The young bodyguard ushered his civilians to sanctuary behind it, locked the gate from outside and then tossed the key through the bars, up the stairs. He was now like Horatius on the Tiber bridge, but without Spurius Lartius or Herminius to share the impending combat. He had one advantage over the Romans, however. He was armed with a Heckler & Koch 53, a weapon of formidable firepower if there is enough ammunition to hand to match its phenomenal rate of fire. On this occasion, the corporal had four magazines, about 100 rounds of 5.56 mm. When that was gone he had a Browning pistol with three magazines – thirty-six bullets in all – of 9 mm. The high velocity 5.56 mm could kill at any range up to 400 metres. The 9 mm was recommended for its stopping power at shorter distances. He hoped he would not need to test it.

He now chose his firing point: a small window above a hand-wash basin in the main ground floor loo. He had arrived at the residence only the day before, but there had been time, just, to check potential fields of fire. He knew that when he smashed the window of the loo with the butt of the HK he would overlook the main gate. He smashed the window.

A muddled battle had been going on around the house all morning and mortar fire was passing over it from time to time. But when the local rebels opened fire and high velocity rifle shots whistled into the residence walls, there was no doubt that it was the British diplomats who were now the target. The corporal sighted his gun on the gate. He did not have to wait long. A brown hand, then a muscular forearm in drab olive-green combat gear appeared over the top of the gate, followed by a shoulder and a head. The intruder was a big man, his face glistening with the effort of hoisting himself up. He now sat astride the gate, an arm outstretched to receive the Kalashnikov rifle being passed up to him by his accomplices.

'That's when I opened fire,' said the corporal. 'I aimed for the chest, squeezed the trigger and fired a long automatic burst, a complete magazine. He wasn't hurled backwards. The bullets just passed straight through him. He just released his hold and toppled slowly backwards.'

The remaining attackers withdrew back across the road fronting the house, into the rain ditch and the trees behind it. Then they opened fire with Russian-made anti-tank RPG-7 missiles. At short range the raiders missed the house and, instead, demolished a tree. The corporal had a personal radio, carefully netted into that of other members of the close protection team who were in charge of another British establishment a mile or so away. His message was crisp.

'We are under fire at the house from an unknown number of enemy troops. We shall have to evacuate the diplomats. Over . . .'

By now, the corporal estimated, there were perhaps four rebel soldiers close to the house among the trees and two or three more, armed with RPG rockets, somewhere on the hill behind the first group. But on the summit, perhaps a mile away, an army barracks was full of rebels.

He was still giving answering fire to the wild shooting from the first group. If a massacre of diplomats was to be averted, they would have to move quickly. At the second British location, the rest of the protection team bundled into two armoured Range-Rovers with a variety of weapons and swept down the road. The team comprised a staff sergeant and three corporals. As they turned into the drive of the beleaguered house, another RPG was fired at the building.

The newcomers returned fire and for some minutes a venomous little battle was fought across the narrow road fronting the villa. Two of the corporals held their ground on the road as a sacrificial perimeter guard while the staff sergeant, as team leader, and one other NCO entered the residence garden to aid the evacuation. As they did so, two long bursts of fire from the roadside defenders caught the RPG team.

The diplomats were now summoned from their strongroom sanctuary on the upper floor. They had not forgotten to bring the key. Their guardian was waiting as they emerged. Then he opened the front door for them. It was a simple enough gesture, but symbolically important while shooting continued. If 'their' corporal was signalling that they were about to survive this nightmare, they knew they would do so.

Seconds later they were aboard one of the Range-Rovers as it accelerated out of the drive under covering fire from the bodyguards, one of the women wincing at the sound of the guns. That vehicle was followed closely by the second, the team scrambling aboard and still firing to discourage thoughts of pursuit as it rolled forward. This time no one shot back at them.

Later, the British team would learn that four rebel bodies had been recovered from the scene. But for now it was sufficient to follow the drill. The envoys were taken to a secret location, an RMP safe house specifically prepared for this 'doomsday' contingency. The punishing training sessions in an English country house, including retrieval and evacuation of a VIP party, were paying off.

Many months later the corporal's courage and his staff sergeant's leadership were officially, if somewhat discreetly, acknowledged. The corporal received a Queen's Commendation for Brave Conduct, accompanied by a citation which spoke of his 'unhesitating courage, devotion to duty and military skills in responding to a serious threat to the lives of civilians . . .' The staff sergeant was awarded a Queen's

Gallantry Medal for 'outstanding leadership, personal example, technical skill and calm direction of the RMP close protection team' engaged in the same operation.

In a parallel operation in the Ugandan capital, Kampala, KMS bodyguards protecting an EEC economic aid team repelled an attack on the Eurocrats' residence by rebel soldiers armed with Kalashnikov assault rifles. It was one of several gun battles which prompted the EEC team as well as the British High Commissioner, Sir David Roberts, to propose an OBE for gallantry for Norman Duggan, leader of their British bodyguard. The Whitehall government did not respond to this novel suggestion. Had it succeeded, this would have been only the second time that a British mercenary soldier had received official recognition from his own government for an act of gallantry on foreign soil. (The first case was that of John Ford Elkington, a Foreign Legion soldier who was also a cashiered British lieutenant-colonel, in 1915. The British restored Elkington's name and added a DSO to Légionnaire Elkington's Croix de Guerre.)

During the civil war which led to the takeover of Uganda by President Yoweri Museveni, a British security team came under fire while trying to rescue its charges, shot back and killed two rebel soldiers. Concerned for the niceties of law and order, the British team leader delivered one of the corpses to the local police station for identification. The police response was dismissive: 'Put that thing back in the gutter where you found it.'

The therapy of action is not given to many bodyguards. The psychological effect of the job upon most of them is somewhat like that imposed upon a fireman or police officer called out to a particularly macabre event, such as a suicide on an underground railway, only to discover that the original summons was a false alarm. Almost by definition the military bodyguard – armed and hyped up for action – is a victim of a series of controlled, preplanned false alarms. Nowhere are the constraints on reaction more apparent than in West Germany.

The average non-German soldier in the Federal Republic, of whatever nationality, tends to remain behind his own cultural stockade. Entire non-German communities with schools, churches, tennis clubs and knitting circles cluster around some military nucleus. There are, for example, US air bases at Ramstein and Bitburg which from within are indistinguishable from Tinker, Oklahoma. But VIPs visiting Germany as icons of Western solidarity cannot remain behind the stockade, feeding dimes into vending machines. They must go out and about to participate in public life as much as they do back home in the US or UK.

Where'er they walk, exposed to the joint scrutiny of the IRA and the descendants of Baader-Meinhof, so their protective shadows go also. The British are a very special case, since the royal family maintains close links with its many blood relatives of the House of Coburg in Germany, links expressed in regular private as well as public visits. The RMP role in that country has been described by one of its practitioners as follows:

'We are a private Praetorian Guard, not on hire but on loan. People come into our area and we are loaned to them as their Praetorian Guard. We have no element of surprise. The press are briefed months in advance of a VIP visit. (That is partly the point!) Even before the visit begins, a Security Advance Party (SAP) will carry out a careful search.'

The close protection group will be augmented for this sanitising task by an Engineer Search Team and a pair of Army Explosives Search dogs. The safe area then has to be kept that way until the visit is over.

'The job is 95 per cent boredom but everyone finishes it

"knackered". It is not like Beirut, where you get cumulative fatigue building up over a six-month period. In one recent visit to Germany, the Prince of Wales went to twenty-six places in five different major locations.

'This meant twenty-six different operational moves. We did not have twenty-six SAP teams. We had two teams which operated in turn and where necessary as either SAP clearance squads or Personal Escort Security [PES] groups. They moved at high speed around a large area of West Germany, leapfrogging one another in order to provide the cover that was needed.'

As well as the British military escort on such occasions there are various local security authorities, including the Kriminalpolizei (abbreviated nickname, 'Krepo') and criminal intelligence, or SEK (for Sondern Einsatze Kommando).

After a month's preparation for a routine royal visit, the tension is valuable human fuel to overcome the desire for rest in the vital forty-eight hours or so of the official programme. In Germany, unlike Beirut, it is not a good idea to carry weapons too demonstratively, particularly if you are a foreigner in civilian clothes. But the weapons have to be carried, all the same.

Equally important is the ritual of relaxation after the operation, to siphon off the adrenalin. (After all, everyone was wound up and ready to shoot, but that proved unnecessary.) The relaxation drill is done in stages. First comes the official debrief, followed by the informal drinks party in the NCOs' club. The Prince's personal police bodyguard's insistence on following his master in a second tank, deep inside a secure military zone, does not come in for comment here even if it later makes modest headlines in London. But as the RMP team complete the task of disarming themselves, formally inspecting one another's weapons to ensure that no live round is left in any of the guns waiting to kill the unwary, there are things they want to get off their chests.

'That dog was knackered after the first day.' – 'He's getting too old for it, like you!'

'"Krepo's" too "heavy".' – 'Their country, cock, not ours.'

'That civvy with the video camera was asking for trouble, leaning out of that window.'

The stress of military close protection, like its civilian counterpart, can be destructive. In 1986 a 31-year-old 'former bodyguard to a high-ranking British Nato officer' appeared in court in London to admit handling stolen goods. He had quit the Army in 1983 after nine years as a military policeman in West Germany and was now 'very much at a loss, living in squats, unemployed and depressed'. He had become a civilian, said his counsel, because of 'an incident' when the man discovered that his second wife was having an affair with a bodyguard to a high-ranking American officer. It was, Judge Christopher Compston agreed, a genuinely sad story. The man was conditionally discharged.

At the RMP's close protection training wing in Britain, stress is a constant factor during a selection period of three weeks followed – for those who pass the complex psychological screening as well as physical aptitude tests – by a further five weeks of basic training. Weapons instruction is intense. Using the 9 mm Browning self loading pistol and the superfast HK 53 sub-machine-gun, the student has to average a 75 per cent hit rate. Trainees shoot to 'kill' at cut-out targets. The HK's 5.56 mm round is lethal at 400 metres but on this course it is sufficient to do it effectively at close quarters. Each student will fire a total of 1,700 bullets, some of them in terrifyingly close proximity to other students and instructors.

Faced with a close-in assassin (which most are) the trainee

uses a composite martial art technique known as Kempo Katzu Mo to punch or kick his opponent while thrusting his principal (the person he is protecting) out of the firing line. Then he draws and starts shooting, aiming off just a foot or so. The live bullets are actually fired into a target resembling the assassin.

No surprise that there is no ready forgiveness on this course for the careless handling of a firearm. Until recently a single, accidentally discharged bullet led to instant dismissal. The guilty man (or woman) had a maximum of two hours to get packed and on the road back to his unit of origin. If that unit happened to be part of a friendly but foreign army, the embarrassment was considerable.

Automobile escape techniques using bootlegger handbrake turns and fast, reverse flick turns are on the curriculum not only for potential bodyguards but also for those taking the two-week Royal Corps of Transport evasive driving course or a similar, shorter training offered to people, usually foreigners, working as British embassy drivers abroad.

An RMP tutor told the author, 'We have trained soldiers from a lot of countries. British students range from corporals to majors. We train Royal Air Force, Royal Marines and even the Royal Navy.'

From the first day the soldiers have to learn to suppress a basic law of the profession of arms, which is to take cover when under fire *before* shooting back. The military bodyguard, in the last analysis, is a 'bullet-catcher', an alternative target to the VIP whose life he has chosen to protect as a more valuable one. The psychological profile required to meet this saintly doctrine ('Greater love hath no man . . .') together with many other strains of the job, is not easy to fill, particularly in someone still in his twenties. The least desirable personality is a ramboesque character secretly inhabiting a death-wish fantasy world.

The bodyguard, when he goes to work in earnest, will carry high-powered weapons in a crowded civilian environment. That requires control and mature judgement, the exact opposite of the personality usually prepared to stand in someone else's killing zone. Significantly, the more experienced the bodyguard, the greater his impatience with a VIP who says, 'I don't mind dying; there is nothing I can do about it anyway.'

Not surprisingly, the RMP has discovered that there is a shortage of the right timber. Simultaneously there has been a sharp growth in demand for trained men as terrorists have increasingly turned to assassination as a propaganda weapon as well as a fulcrum to destabilise the state. 'Controlled aggression is what is needed from our people,' said one expert. 'The police psychology is ideal for the job.'

But so is the military response, which does not come naturally to a civil policeman. 'Terrorists,' commented one RMP weapons training expert, 'do not expect the intended victim to adopt military tactics in shooting back accurately, aiming to kill. This is not in the terrorist's rule book. He regards it as rather unfair and packs up and goes home.' The instructor concerned spoke from experience, having been shot in the neck during a tussle in Africa.

The training concludes with an exercise lasting up to six days in which a four-man protection team plus team leader will 'cover' a real general, or civilian equivalent, as he goes about his normal routine at work and at home. The delicate problems such intimacy can create for both parties might become apparent only much later, in a posting far from the expertise of the training school. One practitioner explained:

> The close protection officer might be responsible for someone who does not want protection. The wife doesn't want the team around. They are a drag on her rations. They interfere with her smooth-run household. She is advised to acquire, say, net

curtains to reduce the danger of flying glass if there is a bomb attack because you cannot have the main curtains drawn all through the day (and that, maybe, is not aesthetically pleasing). Yet you have to reduce the chances of the house being observed or, worse, being made a target.

The house is checked, swept for security and then maintained that way so that each time the housewife visits, let us say, the attic to collect something there is a protection officer following her to make sure that the place has been left properly secure. He also pokes into places the householder doesn't necessarily want people to see. And not everyone wants his cellar occupied by a couple of people he would initially regard as 'hoods'.

Back at the training school, the end-game is played out in a solid Victorian country house standing in its own grounds. The bookshelves carry works ranging from studies in divinity to *The Thorn Birds*. Less evident are the microphones and video cameras to record every wince, every nervous updraught in the bodyguard's voice as he moves about the house waiting for the attack which is coming. Up to the moment of the assault, he has to remember his 'house training'.

'During the protocol lecture,' one veteran explains, 'we teach them about living with VIPs. A young corporal who has never even seen a general learns to stop picking his nose. He needs to learn dress sense. We have to mature a man ten years in eight weeks and "grow him up". We do not want him standing outside his principal's bedroom at 3 am, farting.'

That part of the job becomes easier as the average educational level of trainee bodyguards increases. Some of the corporals these days are university material. One is certainly a graduate. Others probably have had police experience in civil life, and a spell of legal studies behind them.

Stress is another matter. The VIP might be the target of an expert kidnap or assassination attempt at any time.

When it happens, special forces personnel often play the role of the enemy and all hell breaks loose. Concealed chemical dispensers fill the country house with smoke; the disorienting, pulsing whirr of high-powered burglar alarms and the crack of gunfire (usually blanks) are the cover under which the general is being abducted. The trainee bodyguards have a choice: to remove the Man under guard to a safer environment, leaving a sacrificial rearguard to cover the withdrawal, or to fight to sustain the status quo while hoping for reinforcement.

The 'enemy' do not play fair. They have been known to use CS riot gas from a concealed eyrie in the roof space. At least one VIP needed first aid for a nasty gash on the forehead inflicted as he was hauled into a getaway car. It could be worse. One of the lessons of Beirut is that medical training has become an essential element for any bodyguard team in such an environment. Casualty-management of a seriously wounded man or woman might have to be sustained for thirty-six hours or more as a larger battle rages round the VIP and his team. Most of that time they might have to remain at floor level, moving about on all fours. During one civil war action in the Lebanon, seven RPG rockets slammed into the British Embassy.

An RMP failure rate of forty per cent of its trainee bodyguards is not surprising if the object of the training is to produce a 'Rolls-Royce' class of protection, capable of guarding ageing monarchs as well as adventurous lieutenant-colonels who wish to lead from the front. But as this book seeks to explain, the essence of close protection is that it reflects, ultimately, the lifestyle and personality of the person being protected. This requires a specialisation on the part of the bodyguard within the overall task of protection which is almost biological in its intensity.

The forty per cent failure rate has concentrated minds upon what, within budgetary constraints, official bodyguard priorities should be. The shortfall is compounded by a wastage of men for the best of reasons. The most able recruits are now selected for protection work as a matter of policy. It follows that they will also be those most likely to win promotion to higher things, out of the close protection manpower pool. It is a paradox of the trade that the high-risk job of bullet-catching carries the lowly rank of corporal.

The ultimate issue raised by the spectre of insufficient RMP bodyguards is one of supreme importance. During the grey, 'no-peace, no-war' period known to professional soldiers as Transition to War in Europe, terrorism would shade over into urban guerrilla warfare in a way which would put even more people at risk from selective assassination. One RMP expert estimates that 'our system of society and government is essentially directed by about 1,500 top, key people. The elimination of those would in itself create havoc.'

In an effort to increase the number of military bodyguards available to the British government, there is talk of a two-tier system in which a less elaborate training would suffice for the straight military bodyguard, while the existing training course, with some further refinements, might be necessary for the cream of each generation dedicated to Foreign Office protection or some similar, specialised purpose.

What is clear is that the Royal Military Police, having been appointed the leading British agency in the apparently boring business of bodyguarding, has struck political gold. Since the election of Mrs Thatcher's first administration the strategic importance of the lean, hard young man armed with pump action shotgun, or the dapper figure with its Heckler & Koch thinly camouflaged in its sports bag, if camouflaged at all, has grown dramatically. Because of the way the world is changing, the political leader's bodyguard is becoming a person of political importance in his own

Above: In 1850, as Queen Victoria emerged from Cambridge House, London, in an unguarded, open coach, 'a young gentleman' whom she had often seen in the park rushed forward and crashed his stick on to the Queen's skull, knocking her unconscious. The man, ex-Hussar Lieutenant Robert Pate, was sent to Tasmania. The Queen, having treated 'my poor head' with arnica (a herbal remedy), went to the Royal Opera House, Covent Garden, as planned. *(Mary Evans Picture Library)*

Below: In March 1882, as Queen Victoria left Windsor railway station for the Castle, the cheers of Eton schoolboys were pierced by gunshots which the Queen thought was 'an explosion from the engine' of the locomotive. Roderick McLean, a clerk, fired two revolver shots before plain-clothes police bodyguards, aided by the schoolboys, seized him. McLean was judged insane and acquitted. It was the seventh and last attempt to kill the Queen and led to changes in the laws governing the criminally insane. *(Mary Evans Picture Library)*

Left: The only known occasion when the popular sporting Prince of Wales (later Edward VII) was the target of an assassination attempt was at Brussels on 4 April 1900 when a 15-year-old Belgian anarchist named Sipido fired a shot through the open window of Edward's carriage. Edward was accompanied by two Irish veterans of the Special Branch, John Sweeney and George Riley, but Sipido was disarmed by the local stationmaster. Edward kept the bullet as a souvenir and joked about Sipido's poor marksmanship. *(Mary Evans Picture Library)*

Above: Abraham Lincoln, the President who dismissed a White House guard because it made him feel 'like an emperor', was unarmed and unguarded the night he was shot (Good Friday, 1864) in Ford's Theatre, Washington, by John Wilkes Booth, an actor. With the President were his wife and an unarmed ADC, Major Rathbone, plus Rathbone's companion Miss Harris. One result of the killing was the creation of the Secret Service to safeguard future presidents whether they wanted protection or not. *(Mary Evans Picture Library)*

Above: The scene (reconstructed as photo-montage) outside the home at Eaton Place, London, of Field-Marshal Sir Henry Wilson after Wilson was assassinated by two IRA men in 1922. Wilson's bodyguard was withdrawn when he left the regular army, although he was still clearly at risk. The killing triggered off a civil war in Ireland. *(Popperfoto)*

Below: Winston Churchill testing the Sten sub-machine-gun, his bodyguard Detective Inspector Thompson beside him (in pinstripe suit). This wartime picture was probably taken during preparations for the D-Day landings in occupied Europe in June 1944. Churchill had his own armoury (like the King) and was respected as a marksman by Thompson.

Foot: Winston Churchill – taking chances ducked by other Allied war leaders including Josef Stalin – visited the Soviet sector of Berlin just after the war ended in 1945. Behind him in the vehicle sat Foreign Secretary Anthony Eden and an escort including (in trilby hat) Churchill's devoted bodyguard, Detective Inspector W. H. Thompson. The party's jeep was driven by a Royal Military Police NCO. *(Topham Picture Library)*

Left: St Peter's Square, Rome, 1981, and Pope John Paul II has responded to warnings of a plot to assassinate him by telling his Swiss Guard: 'Let us pray that the Lord will keep violence . . . far from the Vatican's walls.' Outside the walls a hand reached from the crowd, but not in greeting. Mehmet Ali Agca (hand ringed), a Turkish Moslem, was pointing a Browning pistol at the Pontiff. The Pope, though wounded by 9mm shots from close range, survived. Mehmet went to prison. His fellow plotters did not. *(Camera Press)*

Left: In the first tragic seconds after the slaughter of President John F. Kennedy at Dallas in 1963, a Secret Service bodyguard – Jacqueline Kennedy's protector, Agent Clinton J. Hill – leapt aboard the presidential limousine as it accelerated away from the killing zone. His objective was to put himself in front of any other guns brought to bear on the party. Exactly how many assassins there were that day is still a matter of conjecture. Certainly there were insufficient bodyguards, and those who were present were not close enough to 'the Man'.
(Topham Picture Library)

Below centre: Gerry (later Lord) Fitt relives a political nightmare: the night in 1976 when, as a local MP, he stood alone against a republican lynch-mob as it swarmed up the staircase of his Belfast home. Twelve years later, living in England, he was still protected by armed guards. *(© Daily Express)*

Below: Big Ben, symbol of democracy, looms above the scene of a momentous political assassination. Airey Neave MP – a personal friend and close ally of Mrs Thatcher in opposition – was murdered by a tilt bomb attached magnetically to his car by Irish republicans while it was parked beneath the Palace of Westminster just before Mrs Thatcher's first election victory of 1979. For her it was the first practical lesson in the link between politics and terrorism. *(Popperfoto)*

Above: The Grand Hotel, Brighton, October 1984: the bomb laid by IRA terrorist Patrick Magee (a former altar boy from Norwich, England) almost succeeded in killing most of the Thatcher administration. A sophisticated timing device enabled Magee to walk away from it twenty-five days before the explosion and still to strike without warning, under cover of darkness.
(Frank Spooner Pictures)

Left: 'I am not supposed to say how many bodyguards I have,' said Norman Tebbit, Conservative Party chairman in 1987. 'But there is a team and I have got to know them very well over the years. They are all marvellous characters.' Before 1984, a British politician surrounded by protection would have been regarded with curiosity by journalists and voters. But not any longer. *(Rex Features)*

Above right: February 1988: Mrs Thatcher with her personal team of Special Branch bodyguards at Salford University during a vociferous student protest in which eggs flew. She is among the democratic world's most intensively targeted leaders (for assault and protection) but the cost of her protection is beginning to provoke critical comment even in right-wing newspapers. *(Press Association)*

Right: 'Rosemary', a recruit to the inner circle of Special Branch protection officers in 1987, was publicly identified as a bodyguard by a newspaper as soon as she joined the team. Six months later she loomed over the First Lady of the Soviet Union Mrs Raisa Gorbachev, during the Gorbachevs' flying visit to Britain.

(© Mail Newspapers plc)

Above: President Gaddafi of Libya is guarded at a reception by one of his daughters of the revolution. Like another (now retired) head of state, Idi Amin of Uganda, Colonel Gaddafi places much faith in women as bodyguards. It is, in part, a political gesture to assist control of his country internally. The other Mediterranean power which enthusiastically arms its women is Israel. Australia and the UK also have a few females in close protection, in Britain's case because both head of state and head of government are female. Some British professionals question whether a woman would have the upper body strength needed to carry a wounded principal to a place of safety in an emergency.
(John Hillelson)

Above: The moment of death for President Anwar Sadat of Egypt in 1981. The soldiers who assassinated him were converts to Islamic fundamentalism; he had made peace with Israel. The assassins' fanaticism was concealed until the last, fatal moment. Some close protection experts believe that Sadat did not trust his personal bodyguard, and the reason they did not open fire to defend him was because their weapons were loaded with blank cartridges. *(John Hillelson)*

Left: India's Prime Minister, Mrs Indira Gandhi, photographed in 1980 with the Sikh bodyguard Beant Singh, whom she trusted implicitly but who became her assassin in 1984 under pressure of Sikh demands for an independent state. *(Frank Spooner Pictures)*

Top: General Frederick Kroesen, commanding the US Army in Europe, had known for weeks that he was being shadowed by German terrorists. Yet his German police driver, specially allocated to him for the danger period, was unprepared when an RPG-7 anti-tank missile hit his armoured Mercedes near Heidelberg. The first missile exploded through the boot and exited just above the wheel arch on the other side of the car. The General's driver then switched off the ignition and remained a static target until Kroesen, deafened by the blast, ordered him to drive away. *(Popperfoto)*

Centre: Italy's former Prime Minister, Aldo Moro, with Oresto Leonardi (holding umbrella), the senior bodyguard who was as close to him as a son. On 16 March 1978, Leonardi was one of five bodyguards slaughtered in Rome as a preliminary to Moro's kidnap. *(Camera Press)*

Foot: In March 1981 John Hinkley shot at President Reagan as the President walked out of the Washington Hilton. In the chaos that followed, Jerry Parr, special agent in charge, noted blood on Reagan's mouth and identified probable lung damage. He pushed Reagan into his limousine and rushed him to hospital, probably saving his life. Meanwhile other members of the team floored Hinkley but kept their cool. *(Camera Press)*

Top: In March 1974, Ian Ball tried single-handed to kidnap Princess Anne. She was half a mile from Buckingham Palace, a passenger in a venerable Austin Princess limousine and accompanied by an armed bodyguard, her husband Captain Mark Phillips, a chauffeur and a lady-in-waiting. Ball, armed with two firearms, wounded the bodyguard, Inspector Jim Beaton, the chauffeur, another policeman and a passing author who 'had a go'. At no point was the limousine used (as it might have been by the chauffeur) as a battering ram out of the situation or as a weapon to run over Ball. The vehicle (above, after the incident) was extensively damaged by the bullets in spite of its passive role. Ball was arrested after a prolonged struggle and detained for an indefinite time under mental health regulations. *(Camera Press)*

Centre: October 1977: from the gloom of illegal captivity, the West German industrial leader Hans Martin Schleyer stares out of his propaganda photograph at a world he will never see again. His four-man police bodyguard has been murdered with military efficiency. The bourgeois terrorists holding him have just linked his kidnap to a Lufthansa hijack going on in the Middle East (shortly to be ended at Mogadishu). Soon Schleyer's utility as a pawn will be at an end and he, too, will be murdered. His killers are still at large. *(Popperfoto)*

Foot: Terry Waite with Druze bodyguard in Beirut in January 1987, just before his 'calculated walk in a minefield'. British representatives advised him that he was pushing his luck. Waite, who felt himself compromised by the Irangate scandal, was determined to re-establish trust with his contacts so as to negotiate the release of other hostages, including the British journalist John McCarthy. Waite was persuaded to leave his bodyguards behind when he went to his contacts' rendezvous and was promptly betrayed. More than a year later his fate was unknown. *(Associated Press)*

The Queen, with escort 'on the box' (in the front passenger seat) beside her, drives out to a polo meeting – without safety belt. Similar photographs taken on her Sandringham estate also show the monarch and her police bodyguard travelling in this way. This practice is, perhaps, symbolic of the Queen's dislike of 'fuss', particularly about her personal security. *(Rex Features)*

The Queen with her subjects, as she likes it: a single protection officer to whom she can hand the flowers, and a contact with the crowd which falls just short of intimacy. The gap preserves royal mystique and is carefully judged, but it leaves the sovereign well inside a potential killing zone. For the bodyguard, the motto is now, more than ever before, 'Watch the hands!' *(Camera Press)*

Right: A personality abroad, with escort, on the dangerous streets of London, March 1987: Boy George (the name on his chest means that no one can fail to identify him) goes shopping around unsalubrious Camden accompanied, so the photographer believed, by 'his personal bodyguards' *(Frank Spooner Pictures)*

Below: The protection around the stars attending Bob Geldof's English wedding in 1986, provided by forty bodyguards, was so heavy as to divert everyone's attention from the main event and towards the security arrangements. The *Daily Mirror* cartoonist, Griffin, commemorated a public relations disaster in his own way. *(© Daily Mirror)*

"Still no sign of the bride yet, Sir Bob. Only some weird looking blonde in a red dress – we slung her out."

Top: One popular performer (known simply as 'Prince') follows the logic of bodyguard-as-accessory to its logical conclusion and has his protection team in the wings and even on stage while he performs. But then everyone expects a prince to have a bodyguard. *(Rex Features)*

Below left: Singer Michael Jackson, waiting for baggage at Tokyo Airport in 1987 with (as one reporter noted) 'just one black bodyguard, seven feet tall and wearing a top hat'. The bodyguard, in spite of showbiz razzmatazz, shapes up like a professional on a high-profile assignment: his principal may sit but he does not; the eyes are alert; he is not overweight. His hands are near enough the belt to draw a weapon (though we do not know if he carried one) in a variant of what some professionals describe as 'the bodyguard stance'. *(© Mail Newspapers plc)*

Below: Leslie Grantham, the colourful personality known to addicts of the EastEnders soap opera as 'Dirty Den', is escorted to the opening of a shopping precinct. His bodyguards, in a land which does not permit them to carry firearms, have dedicated themselves to building up nature's body-armour instead. But they also seem to know their escort drill: one walks each side of 'the Man', and a third is at his back, hands out of pockets. In an emergency one of the three could ward off trouble, moving in front of Grantham, while the others would carry him to safety. *(Rex Features)*

Right: Most religious leaders have disciples, but Bhagwan Shree Rajneesh, guru of enlightenment-through-promiscuity, also had unofficial armed bodyguards. When these proved insufficient to keep trouble at bay he attempted to fly out of the US without pausing to complete emigration formalities and claiming his life was under threat. This might explain why, after his arrest at Charlotte, North Carolina, in October 1985, the US Marshals' Service accorded him an official bodyguard armed with automatic rifles. Bhagwan was convicted of arranging sham marriages and deported. *(Topham Picture Library)*

Below: Sylvester Stallone, as tough-guy guerrilla on location in Israel for Rambo III, with bodyguards. The London showbiz writer Victor Davis noted: 'Sly Stallone moves in a miasma of fear and paranoia. Eight bodyguards, at least one packing a pistol, are always at hand. Their behaviour is appalling.' *(© Mail Newspapers plc)*

Above: On state occasions, government bodyguards are camouflaged to blend into the background, whether at the banqueting table or in the guise of a liveried footman riding on a horse-drawn carriage. This armed officer, a Special Branch sergeant, was planted in the team accompanying Prince Andrew and Miss Sarah Ferguson at their London wedding in 1986. Behind the bodyguard's watchful, ever-moving eyes is a memory that has just recorded the faces of perhaps a dozen potential assassins. If nothing happens, that is fine; but for the bodyguard the stress is just as great.
(Syndication International)

Below: Prince William discovers snow, February 1986. The prince is shadowed by a large, usually amiable man who is not quite one of the family. Barring accidents, that man, or his clone, will be present throughout the Prince's lifetime and at his graveside. For both parties the relationship is special, and difficult.
(Frank Spooner Pictures)

right as guarantor of the most basic integrity of government, keeping the government itself alive. The men doing the job see their role in slightly less messianic terms.

'You cannot win in close protection,' one veteran told the author. 'You "lose your name" if you lose the principal, the Man. If you make a mistake by opening fire at the wrong moment, you create a scandal and you also lose your name. If necessary, we will step in front of a bullet. So why do normally sane, above-average-intelligent guys volunteer for a no-hope game like this?

'It has to be said that it has become a respectable career option. There is some glamour. The decisions you make – whether to shoot someone or not – are big, life-or-death decisions. It is potentially extremely exciting. The fact that the action hardly ever happens is neither here nor there.

'You get to deal with people you would never meet otherwise. A colonel will take the advice of a corporal in this game. In Beirut a British staff sergeant, in civilian clothes, virtually took over the deployment of an American Marine battalion sent to guard the British Embassy perimeter. He gave some crisp, expert instructions about where this and that observation post should be placed. The American colonel was happy to relay these orders with a "Yes-sir!"

'It beats ordinary soldiering, or police routine. But it isn't a job for idiots, or for the nervous.'

The protection of British diplomats is not exclusively, or even primarily, the responsibility of the RMP, who are currently serving the Foreign Office in Kampala, Khartoum, Nicosia and Beirut. The department's own tiny team of security consultants – most of them ex-Special Branch officers invested with the Civil Service rank of Senior Executive Officer – is engaged in an operation analogous to repairing the Forth Bridge. Its members move endlessly round the globe from one UK embassy to another, looking for gaps in security and suggesting improvements.

Their knowledge has to include means of detecting hostile electronic surveillance such as telephone bugs as well as personal security. The search for the totally secure embassy has created a new style of architecture and a drastically changed lifestyle among British diplomats. In such high-risk cities as Bonn (dangerous in spite of its statue of Beethoven and its village atmosphere) and Amman, the British envoy works within the hi-tech equivalent of a medieval castle, with an electronically-sensitive outer fence, electronically controlled ramps at the entrance and the equivalent of a portcullis beyond that. Communication with the reception desk inside the foyer is via a voice amplifier, through bullet-proof plastic or glass. ('So very different,' mourns one of the old school, 'from the handsome glass and concrete designs of Basil Spence.')

Such protection cannot be afforded the Queen's Messengers during their long, solitary journeys around the world, carrying diplomatic mail so sensitive that it cannot be entrusted to coded radio signals. The QM is a retired military officer whose bladder is still in sufficiently good shape to make it necessary for him to visit the loo (a vulnerable, unsupervised area) only in moderation. An unarmed embassy escort meets him at the airport of the country to which he is delivering his documents so as to release him for a loo stop 'in the event that he has a "gippy" tummy'.

Neither the security consultants (whose knowledge of embassy security should make them prime targets for kidnap) nor the QMs (whose documents are exquisitely sensitive) nor the ex-NCOs of the Security Officer Branch, on the front door, rates a bodyguard. Nor are these targets themselves permitted to carry firearms, in spite of their years of experience in handling personal weapons. As one insider explained to the author, 'The FCO takes the view that anyone over the age of forty is incapable of using a firearm properly. After all, the Metropolitan Police won't issue firearms to anyone over forty. We think they are more of a nuisance with a gun, after a certain age, than without it. They are not in the fisticuff business.'

CHAPTER 11
The Enemy of My Friend . . .

At the other end of the process, up in the thin political air of geopolitics, the linkage between British and American foreign policy has become ever more intimate during the Thatcher–Reagan years, apparently untouched by either the US invasion of part of the Commonwealth (Grenada) or the Falklands War and Britain's first armed conflict in South America (apart from the River Plate battle) since 1776. Therefore it should not be surprising that a British enterprise emerged as the protector of some key US embassies.

The company concerned is Defense Systems Ltd, founded in 1982 by an amiable, restless and workaholic Scot named Alastair Morrison. Morrison became famous on a dark night in Mogadishu in 1977 as the SAS major whose boot crashed through the door of a hijacked Lufthansa Boeing jet. The boot was swiftly followed by a stun grenade, to signal the start of a close-quarter firefight which rescued more than a hundred innocent people from terrorists who had murdered the aircraft's skipper.

After becoming second-in-command of 22 SAS Regiment at Hereford, Morrison left the Army, worked for a time as a representative of the German gunmaker, Heckler & Koch, and then started his own protection company. A few years later, he was reputed to be a millionaire. His spectacular success was due not only to an exhausting life of endless jet-setting round the world, but also reflected the increasing need, internationally, for reliable security against blackmail and intimidation as well as kidnap and assassination.

Much of Morrison's work is for commercial companies, many of them multinational. The diplomatic contracts are in high-risk areas of the Middle East. In Amman, for example, in conjunction with the Jordanians, Morrison's company runs guard teams recruited from Jordan's special forces (many of whom were trained by the SAS in the first place) and from King Hussein's Royal Guard (ethnic Bedouin and Circassians, unsympathetic to the Palestinians or born-again fundamentalists).

Morrison told the author: 'The guards wear our uniform with the badge of rank they had in the Army.'

DSL also protects a US embassy in the Gulf. 'We provide ex-British-Army Gurkhas in an Arab country to protect a US embassy. British officers in Nepal recruit for us. When they retire from the Army, they are delighted to work on these things. They are earning good money. The job is very popular and they are damned good at it.

'The US foreign service is not as reluctant as Britain to use commercial organisations for security. US missions overseas include 141 embassies; 11 missions (US–Nato, US–Unesco, etc.), 75 consulates-general, 34 consulates and one or two other interest sections. Out of those, 130 employ a local guard overseas.

'The reason is that they decided that the Marine Corps security guards should not in future face angry mobs as in Teheran, or terrorist outrages. They are inside the building sitting on the real secrets. Responsibility for the outer perimeter lies with the host government. The building itself is under the control of the Marines. But there is a potential gap between the two lines of defence and that is where they employ their local guards.

'The State Department is now trying to standardise the ground rules for all US embassies. Companies like ours are informed where there is a particular problem. We offer advice.

'We did this in the Gulf, where we had good relations already with the public security authorities. We were able to say to the Minister of the Interior, "The Americans have a problem. We don't think it is a good idea to employ local people. Whom can we employ?"

'It was a choice between Baluchis or Gurkhas. They said, "We give you the authority to bring in third country nationals." The Americans cannot do this sort of thing because they would be exposed to political pressure. We are employed on the same basis as, say, a cleaning company. We do not have access to high-risk areas such as the Registry . . . We set up a suitable local company and we say to local sources, "Combine with us and we think you will have a chance of a contact with the US Embassy." We offer our management skills and we set the thing up.

'One of the major training skills we offer is personal protection of VIPs. We run courses lasting six weeks or three months, normally in the host country. We have trained the bodyguard for high-risk Middle East leaders as well as other teams in the States and in Jordan. We have run one course in Britain. You are restricted in the training you can do here because of firearms control.

'Nor do we like training out-of-country because the students are in a different environment. It is better to do it in the country concerned because of the general work environment, etc. Our two experts are Dave Abbot, ex-SAS and formerly chief instructor with the Nato Long Range Patrol School; and Tony Labus, a former major in the RMP, in charge of the close protection school. They train people who have gone out to protect ambassadors.

'We also advise government security services, particularly in the Middle East, about protecting official buildings, personal response to threats, etc. Labus runs all of that.'

Not all freelance security officers hired in the host country – and in 1985 there were more than 10,437 of them serving US missions around the world – are as efficient as the DSL team. An American public watchdog, the General

Accounting Office, notes that at one post a guard assigned to a US embassy school left his gun in the washroom, where a child found it. 'At another,' the GAO continued, 'the ambassador required the guards to walk his poodle.'

Hiring local protection is merely one item among many on a $4.4 billion shopping list of items intended to enhance diplomatic security in the wake of the Beirut bomb attacks of 1983 and 1984. (It is not just in the Middle East that the risk is high. In Lisbon, two mortar attacks were launched on the US Embassy in 1984, and in 1986, a car bomb was exploded just outside it.) Personal security guards apart, the other items include façades set up at least 100 feet from public areas; outside walls reinforced to resist high-explosive blast and secure zones where visitors' vehicles can be searched.

Senate critics argue that the cost – around $275,000 for each State Department employee outside the US – is disproportionate, while *Newsweek* journalists ask what is the point of such expenditure when 'for $1,000 anyone can legally purchase detailed architectural blueprints for any overseas mission to be built, giving potential foes a guided path for infiltration and attack . . . Over the next five years [ending in 1991], the US intends to erect 79 new missions, beef up 175 existing facilities and launch programmes ranging from buying fleets of armoured vehicles to hiring thousands of local guards.' Even friendly congressmen cannot quite understand why the new embassy at Muscat, Oman, will require 'granite floors 40 mm thick . . . when a normal 12 mm thickness would cut costs by 80 per cent'.

The answer, possibly, is that the American 'can do' philosophy reaches first for a hardware solution to a threat, rather than careful selection and training of the right people in the European tradition.

The inner circle of US embassy security (though not the last line of defence) – the US Marine Corps – enjoyed an invincible reputation for remaining immune to all outside influences (including, sometimes, the Congress itself) until 1 April 1987, when it became known that the entire twenty-eight-man contingent guarding the Moscow Embassy had been recalled for interrogation. The allegations ranged from espionage in collusion with a voluptuous KGB officer, Violetta Seina, to black-market currency deals. One well-briefed correspondent reported that the resultant Soviet bugging operation had shut down the CIA's electronic communications. Secretaries had been banned from using electric typewriters and all sensitive material was being transported by hand on flights to Frankfurt. 'It is astonishing that one woman could have done so much damage,' said a Pentagon chief. 'We have to assume that every means of communication has been compromised.'

In the event, only one Marine guard – Sergeant Clayton Lonetree, an American Indian – was court-martialled for spying. His lawyer claimed that Lonetree was being made a scapegoat because of his race since 'all he ever handed over were unclassified documents, junk like public telephone books'. The court martial did not agree and sent Lonetree to prison for thirty years.

The checks and balances of the American system ensure that (as in Caesar's Rome) the ultimately sensitive business of close protection is shared among many agencies. Threat evaluation is one of the growth areas. Since the bombing of Tripoli no prominent American travelling abroad would consider the trip before he (or, preferably, his security adviser) had made a reconnaissance and touched base with the FBI representative in the country to be visited. The purpose of this would be to collect from the FBI (often disguised as the Legal Attaché's Office) or the State Department's Regional Security Officer (RSO) the latest risk assessment report. Even evangelical church organisations such as the Mormons find it necessary to observe this non-religious ritual as a necessary prescription for not prematurely departing this life.

But the evaluation is only as good as the data base from which it is extracted and that, in turn, depends upon the people collecting the information. Here the US suffers from a self-imposed handicap. This is an Executive Order signed in 1975 by President Ford, after an exhaustive congressional inquiry into CIA dirty tricks, banning the agency from involvement in assassination. In an interview with the Washington-based British writer Peter Pringle, a senior White House adviser on terrorism, Michael Ledeen, explained the implications of the order for US security.

'Mr Ledeen said the order meant you could not infiltrate terrorist groups to recruit agents because terrorists were regarded as assassins and, as a result, US intelligence on terrorism was mediocre.'

During 1986–7, events in the Middle East forced an even closer marriage between the counter-terrorist forces of the US and Britain. Ever since the political potential of diplomatic hostage-taking on a grand scale had been demonstrated by the seizure of the entire US Embassy in Teheran, close protection of Americans overseas had become a major preoccupation of US domestic as well as foreign policy. The Americans had no more relished the image of their Marine Corps guards being overpowered by a hundred or so scruffy students in Teheran on 4 November 1979 than did the British the photographs of Royal Marines lying prostrate under Argentine guns in the Falklands three years later. For President Carter the outcome of his response (at Desert One) was disastrous; for Mrs Thatcher (through Operation Corporate in the South Atlantic) triumphant.

Another potent if subjective element in the changes now affecting government attitudes to personal security was that in President Reagan and Mrs Thatcher, each country had a leader with recent experience of surviving, though only just, an assassination attempt. One of the central themes of this book is that the bodyguard can only function as efficiently as the person being guarded will permit. With these two Western leaders, the special relationship between them and between some of their armed guardians, beyond the immediate circle of close protection officers, was very special indeed.

On the British side, administrative reforms aimed at creating a more catholic special forces team for use outside the Nato area to rescue Western hostages. As part of that programme the Royal Marine Special Boat Squadron was brought under the operational control of SAS Group headquarters in London in a new 'Directorate of Special Forces'. The new strike-and-rescue concept seems to have been exercised, under the eyes of Soviet observers, for the first time in UK waters in November 1987. Liaison between the SAS and its American cousin, Delta Force – loosened somewhat after the Desert One débâcle – was also improved.

Such links were part of a more general, strategic response to the geopolitical problem of how to stem the aggressive tide of Islamic fundamentalism, a threat more immediately destabilising than Communism. With the kidnap of US and other Western hostages by the pro-Iranian Hizbollah movement in Beirut, the Anglo-American linkage increased at other, less official levels. Evidence to Congress about the 'arms-for-hostages' deal spearheaded by Colonel Oliver North linked revenue derived from arms sales to Teheran with a slush fund set up by the Contra guerrilla and terrorist force in its war against the Communist (but properly constituted) government of Nicaragua. According to North, some of the resultant military action in Nicaragua – attacks on military aircraft – were farmed out to David Walker of KMS. If true, it was an interesting example of the 'seamless robe' of Anglo-American policy outside the Nato area.

As the Beirut hostages crisis deepened in the summer of 1987, it became clear that while Hizbollah was an agency practising kidnap for political ransom in the Middle East, it was also the weapon of assassination which was now turned like a smoking gun towards London. An Iranian exile and leading opponent of the Ayatollah living in the British capital, Amir Parvis, was blown up by a bomb hidden in his car. At the age of sixty-three he survived in spite of suffering grievous injuries.

Soon afterwards a detailed review of the risks to the West resulting from the Iranian crisis took place at Downing Street in private talks between Mrs Thatcher and Mr Frank Carlucci, chief of the US National Security Council. The meeting occurred under the shadow of the latest Iranian threat. Because 275 Iranians had been slaughtered in an obscure but bloody affair during the annual pilgrimage to Mecca, Teheran leapt to the conclusion that the deaths resulted from a US plot.

The Downing Street media machine discreetly briefed trusted journalists to the effect that 'there is special concern in Whitehall that prominent figures such as Mr Charles Price, the US Ambassador to Britain, should have heavy protection whenever he is outside the embassy in Grosvenor Square.'

The agencies responsible for such protection, outside the embassy, would be the Special Branch and uniformed bodyguards of the Diplomatic Protection Group. But in the climate which now existed it would be surprising if well armed American Secret Service or State Department protection officers were not also licensed to take whatever steps might be necessary to keep their man alive. Libya, as well as Iran, had scores to settle with the American 'Satan' wherever it had the chance.

Such fanaticism, as well as the unique political significance back in Washington of the security of its public representatives around the world, meant that the stakes were very high indeed; so high as to transcend the individual target's choice about his own security. Gone were the days when Geoffrey Jackson (or his US counterpart) could order his bodyguard not to carry a firearm. In London, where some streets display only Arabic and other non-European newspapers and where the Palestine Liberation Organisation was able to buy a five-storey office block (at Clareville Grove, South Kensington), the risk of a politically disastrous assassination was vividly obvious.

There was no obvious resentment about the new security measures although protests about armed American bodyguards in London would hardly be novel. In June 1984, Mr Gerald Kaufman, the Labour 'shadow' Home Secretary, had accused the government of insulting the Metropolitan Police by allowing two of President Reagan's bodyguards to carry firearms during a brief presidential visit to an economic summit at Lancaster House.

Initially, it had seemed that this would not be the case. Mr Robert Innes, deputy assistant commissioner at Scotland Yard who was in charge of security for the conference, had stated that visiting security officers would not carry guns and that no exception would be made in the case of the US. Soon afterward, Scotland Yard released a terse statement saying that a few days after Mr Innes had spoken, the British and US governments had reached an agreement under which 'just two of President Reagan's bodyguards will be carrying handguns. Nobody from any other country will be armed.'

The *Guardian* subsequently reported:

'When the President left the ambassador's residence yesterday to go to Buckingham Palace, he was accompanied by eight motorcycle outriders, two marked police cars, an open-top limousine thought to be carrying security personnel, a police Range-Rover, five assorted cars, a press bus and a police van bringing up the rear. His route to the palace was made known only to a few key police officers minutes before his departure. Police marksmen watched from the roof as he left to begin the journey along roads on which, reportedly, sewers had been checked and lamp-post inspection panels sealed with metal strips.'

In Parliament later, Mrs Thatcher denied that any precedent had been broken by the presence of armed American bodyguards on London streets. She said:

'The Government is, of course, ultimately responsible for the security of visiting statesmen in London. Decisions on arming bodyguards are taken after full consultation and in the light of all the circumstances. I am advised that in this case, no precedent was broken.'

After the USAF raid on Tripoli in April 1986, American diplomats worldwide required the protection of firearms controlled by American bodyguards. In June of that year, America's Ambassador to Sweden, Gregory Newell, was one of the guests at a dinner party given at the luxury lakeside home of the shipping magnate Bo Alexsson Johnson, a member of Lloyd's. Newell's bodyguard spotted two men crouching in shrubbery near the dining room. One of the men had an assault rifle, the other a shotgun. The bodyguard came out shooting and the mystery men lighted off through the forest. As the bodyguard closed the gap, the intruders uncovered a high-powered motor cycle and roared away. A huge police search began but in spite of enjoying almost twenty-four hours of daylight at that time of year, the Swedes were no more successful in this endeavour than in finding the assassin of their own Prime Minister, Olof Palme, a few months later.

Sweden might seem to be an eccentric place for anyone to try to kill an American diplomat, but in fact, it is the home these days of many people of Middle Eastern origin. Four months after the attempt to stalk Ambassador Newell,

six members of the Abu Nidal terrorist group were intercepted in Britain and deported. One of these was flown to
Stockholm. He was an Arab 'refugee' who was granted first
political asylum, then full Swedish citizenship. ·

If visiting American diplomats sometimes suspect that their
personal security in Europe lacks fragrance, they might do
worse than consider the plight of their senior soldiers, who
spend somewhat longer in the region and are regarded, by
reason of their profession, as fair game by every revolutionary undergraduate on the block. It was General Alexander
Haig who, having just survived the blast of a culvert bomb
detonated under his back-up escort car in Belgium on 25
June 1979, made a joke in the deadpan tradition of Bob
Hope: 'I guess if you can get through Monday you're gonna
survive the rest of the week.' The joke was apposite. Haig
was to retire from his post of Supreme Allied Commander,
Europe, and from the profession of arms at the end of that
week.

But on the Monday, he horrified professionals in the
deadly new world of surrogate warfare by halting his unscathed car after the explosion, dismounting and returning
to the scene in order to express concern for his US-Belgian
police escort. Generals, since they are soldiers, are supposed
to know how to defend themselves and to take appropriate
steps to do that. To some terrorists they represent a special
challenge, as General Frederick Kroesen, Commander-in-
Chief of the US Army in Europe, discovered in West
Germany on 15 September 1981.

There was, it is true, a threat assessment which said: 'A
terrorist attack, preparations for which have already taken
concrete form, is planned against one of several high rank-
ing officers of the HQ of USAREUR in Heidelberg. According to reliable information, a US officer is to be attacked
somewhere between his home and his office. Indications

are that the attack will take place before he starts work.'

Any doubts about the seriousness of the threat, by the Red Army Faction, were dispelled on 31 August when a car bomb exploded inside a high-security area at the US Air Force base at Ramstein, wounding twenty people. Kroesen reported early in September that he was under surveillance. He accepted the offer of an armoured Mercedes with a German police driver. Other measures included a German civil police 'sweep' car and an unmarked US Military Police car with a two-man crew.

Like many other kidnap and assassination targets, Kroesen was most vulnerable on his way to work. Short of air lift, he could not vary the route from his residence along the B37 into Heidelberg. Near the ancient city, the River Neckar enters the town at Karlstor, where there is a Y junction controlled by traffic lights. Beside the lights is a building from which the river lock gates are controlled.

At the end of the second week in September, four terrorists, one of them female, arrived in the area and pitched an igloo tent on the steep hillside about 180 yards from the lock control building. The campsite was in a densely wooded area about fifty yards below a student centre and some 250 feet above road level. The hit team attached a rope to a railing round the student centre car park to provide an escape route. Next they set up a firing point about ten yards below the camp site, clearing foliage to provide a good field of fire on to the road below. They then settled down to wait for several days, listening to the static on their radio link with a look-out post further up the B37.

On 15 September, as the General's car halted at the traffic light, the terrorists opened fire with two rounds of RPG-7 anti-tank grenade and a long burst from a high-powered HK 53 sub-machine gun. An official report concluded:

The first grenade struck the top of the vehicle's boot, passed through the boot and exited through the right rear quarter panel just above the wheel. The grenade shattered the rear window causing the General and Mrs Kroesen to suffer minor cuts from flying glass. Both suffered temporary hearing loss. The driver and the General's aide were both entirely unhurt.

The second grenade overshot the car and exploded on the road near the lock control building. From the burst of automatic fire, four rounds hit the Mercedes but were unable to penetrate the armour, and four hit the USMP car, damaging the front end but causing no injuries to the crew.

When the first grenade struck the General's car, the two-man crew dismounted from the back-up car, coming under fire as they did so. They did not return fire but in any case the terrorists began to bug out after firing the second grenade.

For reasons which have never been explained, General Kroesen's driver switched off the ignition as soon as the car was hit. It was the General who recovered his presence of mind and ordered him to restart the car. The driver then took General and Mrs Kroesen to the US military hospital in Heidelberg.

The terrorists escaped. Forensic evidence left behind indicated that the sub-machine gun had been used in the 1977 kidnap and murder of Hans-Martin Schleyer. Fingerprints on the radio and a getaway car belonged to two women terrorists of the Red Army Faction.

The official analysis of the attack noted that the German civil police sweep car had gone over the route fifteen minutes before the General. 'It saw nothing suspicious. Even if the ambush had been at street level and at close range, the chances are that the crew of the sweep car would have seen nothing.' Used so far ahead of the main convoy, it could only be relied upon to describe traffic conditions. As an integral part of the convoy, it could not offer useful forewarning of an attack. It could be used as a ramming vehicle in the event of a kidnappers' road block, 'if the aim of the terrorists is to kidnap rather than kill'.

The report went into some detail to describe how the Red Army Faction obtained illegal registration plates for their vehicles. First, they observed a vehicle which met their needs, 'a van, a motor bike or maybe a BMW for fast getaway'. The owner or driver was placed under surveillance so as to obtain a lot of personal information about him. False documents were then applied for, including registration book, insurance papers, driving licence and identity card. Copies of the car's registration plates were then made. 'Finally they steal an exactly similar model to the original. In this way they can create a replica of a legal car and driver which will satisfy any police computer check . . .'

The use of several vehicles in each operation suggested that a rash of thefts of cars and motorcycles might precede an attack. 'This was certainly the case before the attacks on General Haig, General Kroesen, the Ramstein AFB, Dr Hans-Martin Schleyer and others . . .'

Many Red Army Faction attacks occurred early in the morning during the target's journey to work, and early in the week. This suggested that the terrorists liked to set up an attack during the weekend and make final preparations overnight. 'These preparations are always exhaustive and the firing position may well be occupied for several days before the attack.'

The report concluded that the fact that the RPG-7 was abandoned after both the Kroesen attack and a rocket attack at Orly airport some time before, pointed to a reliable source of supply. 'It is believed that in the case of the Red Army Faction the suppliers are either the People's Front for the Liberation of Palestine or the Libyan government. If this is the case it is also believed that the suppliers have a say in selecting the targets to be hit. The terrorists know how to use them. It is believed that the Red Army terrorists have undergone training in the Lebanon and in Czechoslovakia.

'If an RPG-7 can stop a tank it can stop a Mercedes, or

a Daimler or any other limousine whether it is armoured or not! Because a hit from an RPG-7 is almost certain to destroy its target, the need to identify potential firing points and to ensure that the principal's car is not forced to stop in a possible killing zone is vital.'

The report also examined the responses of those in charge of Kroesen's security:

'The General's driver switched off the ignition as soon as the car was hit. He should have left the killing zone immediately. The back-up crew dismounted from their vehicle as soon as the General's car was hit. They should have pulled up alongside the car to block the terrorists' line of fire. Having dismounted from the back-up vehicle, the crew should have returned fire, even though they were armed only with handguns and even though the terrorists were starting to bug out already.'

The other failure identified by Kroesen's close protection team was to spot the presence of the ambush in the first place. As the debrief points out, the German civil police threat assessment of 14 June, two months before the attack, was excellent. 'Even though the police had not got the information as to the precise time and place of the attack, the CP team should have worked on the assessment to deduce the most likely possibilities. Had they done so, they could not possibly have overlooked the ideal ambush position at the Karlstor.'

Finally, there was a lack of alertness about the reality of the threat. 'When a predicted attack fails to materialise immediately, complacency becomes a real enemy ... because a false sense of security arises from increased security measures. The police knew of the plans for the Ramstein Air Force Base attack and the assassination a full year before they took place. This was a year for the terrorists to perfect their plans and a year for the security forces to become complacent and relax their vigilance.'

There was no lack of vigilance on the part of the team responsible for safeguarding Kroesen when he was taken back to the United States. One of the officers concerned with the General's security at that time told the author that the close protection team had armed mobile security teams with the heavy M-60 machine gun in order to cover the General while he played golf on a civilian course in Georgia.

But the real threat, of course, was in Europe and the Middle East. Just three months after the attack on Kroesen, another US Army general, Dozier, then deputy chief of staff at Nato's southern headquarters at Verona, Italy, was kidnapped in Rome and held in a 'People's Prison', an apartment in Padua, by Red Brigade terrorists. He was rescued after forty-two days by Italian police. Others were less fortunate.

In Paris in January 1982 Lieutenant Colonel Charles Ray, US Military Attaché, was assassinated by the Lebanese Armed Revolutionary Faction. The same group combined with the Red Brigades to murder Lemoyne Hunt, US commander of the UN Sinai desert multinational force, in Rome in February 1984. The leaders of FARL, Maronite 'Christian' Marxists, were also responsible for a series of other outrages including an indiscriminate bombing campaign in Paris in September 1986.

By then, a gathering of 'Euroterrorists' in the Basque region of Spain had brought together terrorists from France, West Germany, Belgium, Italy and Spain to prepare what their communiqué described as 'a guerrilla war in Western Europe'. In France alone (in spite of its indulgence to terrorists) the number of potential victims listed by an official threat analysis totalled 452. They included politicians, judges and industrialists.

Elsewhere, Nato diplomats and military commanders were at risk from individual terrorism as never before. In March 1987 an Italian aerospace expert, General Licio

Giorgieri, was assassinated in Rome. The Interior Minister, Oscar Scalfaro, made no secret of his belief that the killing had been ordered from abroad. It was the result of an alliance of Action Directe in France, West Germany's Red Army Faction and a new offshoot of Italy's own Red Brigades, the Armed Communist Fighters. The primary targets were Nato personnel. As Scalfaro put it: 'Everything about this murder points to a killing decided beyond Italy. It has the stamp of European terrorism.'

Not even the drab bureaucrats of the European Economic Community could rest easy in their beds. In December 1986 the Commission advertised for potential bodyguards to protect all seventeen of its members and their staff. The desired qualifications were that the candidates must have specialist training in firearms and fast-driving techniques, be aged between eighteen and thirty-six, familiar with one language other than English and prepared to work any-where in Europe.

The bodyguards required to protect the seventeen inter-national civil servants, including Lord Cockfield and Stan-ley Clinton-Davis, from Belgium's Communist CCC movement among others, had to be capable of 'physical exertion and long, irregular hours of work'. The salaries on offer were a meagre £15,000 per annum, or about the same as for a competent, 9-to-5 secretary employed by the same organisation.

As the great diplomatic quadrille in search of failsafe security moved into a more anxious and breathless rhythm, only one expert source seemed prepared to analyse the problem afresh, from first principles. Everyone who thought about the problem agreed that diplomatists generally, but particularly US representatives, were at risk as never before. Robert Kupperman, a specialist in the study of terrorism at Georgetown University's Center for Strategic and Inter-national Studies, proposed in 1985 that instead of isolating expatriate American officials in high-security fortresses, they should 'try to blend in more with the local population to avoid being obvious targets'. In parallel, Western intelligence should make the penetration of various terrorist organisations a top priority task.

The second proposal, as we have seen, would fall foul of President Ford's executive order of 1975. The first – adoption of a modest lifestyle – is not practicable. Most diplomats are constantly trying to beat the clock to the next official engagement. If they have to disguise themselves as members of the alternative society, in jeans, trainers, sweat shirts and beards, and drive ageing Italian motor scooters, they might stay alive longer (though not in their own embassy compounds) but they would lose much credibility as diplomats. In diplomacy, as in other areas of political life in the 1980s, the role of the bodyguard seems destined to become so important as to be a political bargaining chip in its own right.

For as Tim Zimmerman observed in his paper 'The American bombing of Libya': 'Between 1979 and 1983 the number of international terrorist incidents averaged 500 per year. In 1984 the number of incidents increased to approximately 600 and resulted in 1,279 casualties (312 dead). In 1985 the number jumped to more than 800, with 2,177 casualties (877 dead). During this same period, Americans and American interests became increasingly frequent targets of terrorism. The most significant attacks were the 1983 bombings of the US Embassy and Marine barracks in Beirut, in which 295 lives were lost . . . Altogether Middle East-related terrorism accounted for more than 50 per cent of the worldwide total in 1985.'

As a consequence, the demands of security on diplomatic budgets is soaring. In 1987 Canada played host to the Commonwealth Conference at Vancouver, dedicating almost half the £8.8 million conference budget to convert the venue into an armed camp protected by more than 2,000 Mounties supported by troops and other police. Two leaders most at risk were Rajiv Gandhi, whose hotel was an official secret, and Mrs Thatcher. Journalists covering the conference noted that 'more relaxed arrangements' were made for the Queen's visit to the same summit and subsequent Canadian tour than were required for the British Prime Minister.

The Manila conference of the Association of South-East Asian Nations ('ASEAN') a few months later was also like some weapons convention. The meeting was cut from three days to two for reasons of security. (Some heads of state would tolerate only one night in Manila in spite of the presence of three navies, fleets of armoured limousines and helicopter gunships.) Nervousness in spite of that degree of protection can only result from doubts about the likely behaviour of the security forces themselves. In a world notionally dedicated to the idea of government by consent, it is the stuff of satire.

PART IV
A Very Private Industry

CHAPTER 12

Muscle, Money,
No Questions Asked

The services of a professional bodyguard armed with the most deadly weapons available as well as the best intelligence of danger that government can afford, have always been the prerogative of a ruling élite. Indeed it is part of the mystique of government that this should be so. If every Tom, Dick and Harry were permitted by law to defend himself with, say, a swordstick then the political implications for established government might be perilous.

But for those who are prepared to break the law in the quest for protection quite a lot can be done. As the biggest prisoner in Bedford (or probably any other) Prison told a journalist in 1986:

'When I was young it was my ambition to go to Broadmoor but I've got an IQ of 151 so there was no chance. I've been in fifty-seven different prisons in my time. I've earned my dough being physical. I crushed Bradford and Hull. I minded clubs and pubs. There are always people afraid of other people.'

Until recently, the world of the non-governmental bodyguard was that of such criminal fraternities as the Kray twins and the Richardsons, Capone and the Mob. In 1964 John Dickson was a young Glaswegian who got caught up in this world after honourable service with 45 Royal Marine Commando in Malaya and Korea. His knowledge of firearms was less important than the fact that he could drive (though he did take delivery, at one unusually tense moment, of a consignment of Bren machine guns). Few gangsters of his generation obtained legal licences because most of them were incapable of passing a driving test.

One night Dickson drove Ronnie Kray to the Blind Beggar pub in London's Whitechapel Road where Kray, accompanied by another of his 'heavies', walked into the bar and shot dead his rival George Cornell. Cornell's offence was to describe the homosexual twin Ronnie as a 'fat poof'. It is thought that Kray, who did not conceal his homosexuality, resented the word 'fat'.

Although the bar was crowded, no one 'saw' the murder. When, much later, the Krays were sentenced to life imprisonment, Dickson received only six months and lived long enough to write his memoir *Murder Without Conviction*.

It was a dreary, restricted life in which 'protection' meant the funds fearful club owners had to hand over to Kray's mobsters. Not only was the bodyguard now a figure of threat: the buzz words associated with security had also undergone a change of meaning which inverted them. By far the most effective protection described in Dickson's account, in fact, is the care taken by Scotland Yard to ensure that witnesses prepared to give evidence against the gang were not intimidated during the nine-month trial. Both witnesses and jury were afforded twenty-four-hour guards of both sexes, and official safe houses.

'The witnesses never appeared on the stand together. They were brought in one by one by detectives. Out of court too they were kept in separate rooms and away from the photographers and journalists. After they had given their evidence for the prosecution, they were taken away from the Old Bailey. None of them was recalled, but they were protected till the end of the trial.'

In retrospect, it is hard to see what attracted an adventurous young Scot to the narrow, obsessive world of the Krays, full of its nursery-like passions and fears. Dickson provides a few clues, however. Accompanying an actor/mobster in London, he writes, 'I was lucky enough to be asked to go to various London pubs with George Raft and Ronnie

[Kray] in the limousine driven by George Raft's chauffeur. Ronnie wanted to show him off. At times I felt like a film actor just walking around with him.' Elsewhere he observes, 'I got the feeling that I was an extra on a film set making a gangster movie,' though Ronnie Kray had spelled out the difference between Raft and himself with the comment, 'He's only a gangster in his films. I'm one for real!'

Kray received a thirty-year sentence, which he serves in Broadmoor Hospital.

Another ecological niche in which people tend to be afraid of other people is on the fringes of professional boxing and other sports which attract gamblers' gold. When casino gaming is illegal, as it is in all of the United States except Nevada and (since 1976) Atlantic City, then the little formality of ensuring that an American's gambling debts – his 'markers' in the language of Sky Masterson – are honoured, is a task sometimes delegated to organised crime, even if the wager was made and lost in a London casino.

The linkage between that sort of sport and the underworld is very intimate indeed. Often, the bodyguard of one or other of the parties involved is a former professional fighter himself. The author's father, as it happens, was an ex-prize-fighter and soldier who became, for a time, a bookies' 'minder' at Doncaster and other racecourses.

The tradition continues. When the world heavyweight boxing champion Tim Witherspoon came to Britain in 1986 to fight Frank Bruno, his sparring partners doubled as bodyguards. His manager, Carl King, explained that he was anxious to keep his boy 'away from the drug-pushers and foxy ladies'.

Unlike such American agencies as Pinkerton's – which always operated in a culture sympathetic to the gun, which the British still like to regard as alien – reputable British companies such as Securicor concentrated their efforts on

guarding property, particularly cash in transit. Tom Clayton's history of the private security industry, *The Protectors*,
does not even discuss personal protection though it does
disclose that twenty bank guards were authorised at that
time – the mid-sixties – to carry guns. He also quotes
Scotland Yard's policy: 'Every application for a firearms
certificate is considered on its merits. Weapons are hardly
ever considered necessary for personal protection services.
Certificates are, however, occasionally granted to employees of companies engaged in the transport of certain
valuable consignments.'

In the absence of a firearm or even an up-to-date threat
evaluation, the 'bodyguard' of the private sector has depended upon sheer bulk to ward off danger, lending an
added gravitas to the word 'heavy'. He often doubles as
the chauffeur, although knowing nothing of evasive driving
or how to spot bombs attached to his vehicle. By contrast,
the modern executive chauffeur will know as much about
Improvised Explosive Devices, including the distinctive
odour of gelignite, as he does about gearboxes. Certainly
the unofficial bodyguard had, and probably has, no knowledge of resuscitation or even first aid should the worst befall
his client. Even his bulk might have come courtesy of
anabolic steroids, making him prey to catastrophic liver
failure.

Some of his potential clients have recognised that a guard
dog might be as reliable, but even here, nothing is guaranteed. Some well meaning but undiscriminating animals bite
the sinned-against rather than the sinner, or, when excited,
whoever is nearest. The most ambitious effort to perfect
this sort of four-footed personal protection was undertaken
by a French boxer who thrived briefly during the 1920s
under the name 'Battling Black Siki'. He alarmed friends
and enemies alike by leading a young lion on a chain around
the streets of Manhattan. It did not change anything, how-

ever, and Siki was soon discovered dead in the gutter, a bullet through his head.

The tradition of the 'heavy' is alive and usually to be found justifying its fees these days putting the boot into journalists, particularly the paparazzi photographers for whom this sort of thing is an occupational hazard of tabloid voyeurism. To paraphrase Oscar Wilde, it is the inarticulate in pursuit of the insensitive. It is all a long way from real close protection but because this sort of 'bodyguard' has become part of the publicity hype surrounding many otherwise non-events, the phenomenon of the heavy is worth some scrutiny.

At the bottom of the heap are the doorstep bouncers, but even bouncers, like the rest of us, cherish a few pretensions. When Bournville College, Birmingham, started a training course for 'The Gentle Art of Bouncing' (leading, perhaps, to a Bachelor of Biceps?) in an effort to upholster the knuckleduster with decent Dralon, the organisers must have needed their own doormen to contain the rush. At least a hundred candidates presented themselves for grooming in such social skills as the management of argumentative drunks. The course also endeavoured to teach body language more subtle than arm locks and hip throws.

But the cultural tide was not flowing with them. As the boss of a security company which provided doormen for more than forty pubs and clubs in the Midlands observed, 'It's got much harder because the troublemakers – a small percentage – have no respect for parents, teachers or police. So how're they going to have respect for us when they come to the door and we ask them not to come in?'

Soon afterwards, in another part of the forest known as London, a typical troublemaker made his lack of respect vividly clear by biting off a bouncer's nipple. More than youthful exuberance led to the shotgun murder of a doorman at a Brixton drinking club in 1986. The killing was part of a gang war for control of the cocaine market. One of the factions, known as 'Yardies', sprang from a ruthless bodyguard team which had once surrounded a Caribbean president.

In this part of the jungle the security guard and the criminal might well be the same person, equally unsuccessful in both occupations. Paunchy Tony Ashe, aged forty-nine, was dismissed from his job as a guard at the Frog and Nightgown pub in London's Elephant and Castle district. A year later, he was also saddled with debt and worried about not being able to fill his children's Christmas stockings. A more intelligent man might have combed the charity shops. Ashe (who, like others of his kind, got a thrill from rubbing shoulders with celebrities, particularly in sight of a camera) 'solved' his cash-flow problem by taking part in an armed robbery. He was the one who was shot dead by police officers. This time the press photographs were of an anonymous corpse, the face covered by a coat.

If the bouncers are mere 'soldiers', equivalent to the outer defence perimeter round an embassy or a royal palace, then the close bodyguard is of greater importance to his showbiz principal than is, say, Superintendent Beaton in relation to the Queen. The difference is important. The worthy Beaton, even with a George Cross to his name, cannot enhance the monarch's status. On the contrary, she enhances his. His public role, much of the time, still appears to the television viewer to be as an opener of royal limousine doors. By contrast, the showbiz personality accompanied by a bodyguard has acquired status as well as additional muscle. The subliminal signal promoted here is that anyone who needs a bodyguard to keep at arm's length an excited hoard of fans, agents and journalists must be very special indeed.

The result of this hype is usually lots of publicity. This is not always of the kindest. Most publicity junkies are not deterred by that, but it sometimes happens that the heavies steal the show. One such event was the wedding of a Nobel Peace Prize nominee whose forty bodyguards generated such headlines as 'Bob Geldof's heavies "beat up my husband".'

The day did not start well for spectators. As the *Daily Mail* reported: 'The bruisers pushed and shoved the crowd in the streets as stars arrived and swore at teenage girls. One even told photographers to "f—— off" in front of the vicar.'

The wedding feast, at Faversham in Kent, was attended by entertainers such as David Bowie and Simon Le Bon and, almost, by Richard McCann. Mr McCann later told the *Daily Mirror*:

'I know I was wrong to gatecrash the party, but Bob has done so much good we wanted to wish him all the best. I climbed the wall and all of a sudden this bloke shone a torch in my face and said, "Who are you?" I said, "All right, you've caught me. I'm a gatecrasher. I'll go quietly."

'There were five of them, all big blokes. I said, "I'll walk out the front gate, no problem!" They said, "You've come in over the wall and you'll bloody well go out over the wall."

'One grabbed my arm. They threw me on the floor and I put my hands over my head. One of them stood on my foot to stop me moving, and the rest laid in with the boot. After what seemed an age, they picked me up and threw me back over the wall.'

Mr McCann's wife, Janet, also failed to attend the party. 'Four of them hustled me out and demanded to know where I lived, but I refused to tell them,' she said.

The bride wore red. The security around her groom generated that rare distinction, a cartoon in a national newspaper, in monochrome. Griffin's Eye, in the *Daily Mirror*, depicted a bridegroom waiting at the church, surrounded by bodyguards, one of whom says earnestly, 'Still no sign of the bride yet, Sir Bob. Only some weird-looking blonde in a red dress – we slung her out.'

Making the same point, though in a more serious vein, Chief Inspector Stuart Donaldson of Kent Constabulary observed after the Geldof party:

'We are very concerned at the way they operated today. If there had been greater co-operation from them and the people inside, then there wouldn't have been any problems. No one informed the police that this ceremony was taking place ... All police leave was cancelled when we heard about this major event but the security people have tried to run their own show. They certainly had no right to push people around or swear at them. Their only jurisdiction was within the church and Mr Geldof's grounds.'

The same security team protected the singer Madonna during one of her British tours. On that occasion, a photographer was hit by the entertainer's Mercedes, though it is unclear who was driving the vehicle. A subsequent visit revealed both police anxiety and the publicity value of PR violence. A Scotland Yard spokesman was quoted as saying, 'Our experience tells us that there is a great danger of trouble from the people who are supposedly there to protect Madonna. They have a habit of taking the law into their own hands, but they must leave the policing to the police ... or else we will deal with them.'

For a subsequent tour, in 1987, Madonna sometimes required the combined services of the regular uniformed police as well as her private minders. For a concert at Roundhay Park, Leeds, the crowd of between 80,000 and 100,000 spectators generated a respectable profit. Ratepayers in West Yorkshire police district did not fare so well. According to the Police Federation, 'The West Yorkshire Police deployed 350 officers on controlling this event. The organisers paid £14,000 to "hire" the seventy police inside the arena and they voluntarily agreed to pay a further

£16,000 towards the total police costs of £90,000. On learning this, the police committee decided to . . . press for more realistic payments towards police costs by promoters of large-scale private events. It is estimated, for example, that although League [football] clubs baulk at the costs charged to them for policing inside grounds, the true contribution they make is only 16 per cent of total police costs . . . Meanwhile, Madonna and Co. go home with a fortune.'

(A detailed study by the *Independent* newspaper the following year revealed that the cost of policing Football League matches on one typical Saturday was £450,000 or about £1 for every spectator at the forty-one matches played.)

The Faversham Forty were criticised not only by Fleet Street but also by another professional bodyguard, Peter Gauchi, whose clients have included Brooke Shields and Diana Ross. Gauchi is a former captain of the Welsh judo team. He takes his profession seriously enough to have studied first aid and defensive driving. He told the *Daily Mirror*'s Alastair Campbell, 'There are only a handful of good, properly trained bodyguards in the pop business. In recent years all kinds of firms have sprung up. But most of them are "cowboys". A good bodyguard is a diplomat as much as anything else. Anyone can set himself up as a minder. You don't need any real credentials.'

Gauchi believes that the government should subject personal security firms to a system of vetting and licensing to 'weed out the thugs'. So far, as will be seen, the government has taken this step in only one part of the realm. Meanwhile, for the rest, the rewards vary. Gauchi's estimate of the pay-off for the Faversham team was no more than £40 a day. Among the favoured, truly expert minority, the stakes are higher. David Bowie is said to spend up to £10,000 a week for personal security, with individuals earning up to £500 daily to care for such entertainers.

The cost can be burdensome – to put it mildly – for punters who hire protection for pop stars even when the stars give their services for nothing. In 1986 between 100,000 and 250,000 young people swamped London's Clapham Common with bikini-clad posteriors to join a rally combining anti-apartheid protest with a pop music concert. Performers freely donating their talents included Sting, Boy George, Sade and Billy Bragg. Organisers, including Mr Richard Caborn MP, had every reason to believe that they would raise a lot of money. Instead, says Mr Caborn, 'We actually lost money. We had a voluntary collection which did not work effectively in raising money because of the heavy security. The cost of hiring teams from three security companies also siphoned off a large proportion of the funds.'

By contrast, the hod-carriers of the security trade 'risk life and limb every day for Dickensian pay', according to their union organiser David Plant. He asserted that one of his 30,000 members was injured every day, normally while guarding or transporting cash. The men's pay for taking this risk might be as meagre as £1.10 an hour before tax. The reality behind the showbusiness hype was also, sometimes, an anti-climax. Reporter Jonathan Margolis, encountering the pop idol Michael Jackson – by coincidence, while they both waited by the baggage carousel at Tokyo Airport – asked:

'Where were the funky, threatening black men who are supposed to surround the living god? There was just one black bodyguard, seven feet tall and wearing a top hat, and several charming, middle-aged white American attendants about as funky as Ena Sharples ... The Michael Jackson you read about is largely imagined by those who have never seen him. It is a tribute to showmanship that he and his team have made a few eccentricities go such a long way.'

There is, of course, a case to be made for the showbiz

bodyguard since such megastars as Elizabeth Taylor are unable to move far in public without recognition and pursuit by cameras dedicated exclusively to that task. Her efforts to mourn decently the death of her erstwhile husband, the actor Richard Burton, at dawn at an isolated cemetery in Switzerland were dogged by paparazzi who had about as deep a regard for her private grief as would a blowfly which chanced upon the corpse itself. But Elizabeth Taylor, among others, takes care to employ a security organisation which aims to protect her rather than to manufacture headlines in a showbiz variant of the propaganda of the deed. It is a question of style. In this as in other areas of close protection, the style of the bodyguard is ultimately set by the person who is being protected.

Here, for example, is the style of screen idol Sylvester Stallone (aka Rocky, aka Rambo) as described by the veteran showbiz writer Victor Davis in the *Mail on Sunday*:

'Today Sly Stallone moves in a miasma of fear and paranoia. Eight bodyguards, at least one of them packing a pistol, are always at hand. Their behaviour is appalling, but it raises no demur from their charge. Last week I saw Sly's thugs manhandling aside middle-aged female fans who wanted only to cheer their idol. On the set even the extras get an elbow if they wander too close to the great man . . .'

Another *Mail* writer, Lesley-Ann Jones, observed the use to which some performers will put their heavies in the cause of Preserving the Image. She had, it seemed, written something to offend the business interests built around an American pop entertainer – a 23-year-old woman with 'fabulous legs, great teeth, body, really nice hair style' but 'a so-so voice' – just before the entertainer, Whitney Houston, was to appear at London's Wembley Stadium. Lesley-Ann Jones reported: 'I received disturbing phone calls from her representatives suggesting that I would not be welcome to take up my review seat for her show at

Wembley Arena . . . Sorry chaps, but I am not that easily deterred. When I arrived I discovered that I was seated right in the middle of the Whitney Houston entourage, among a group of heavyweight men who kept giving me menacing looks. Every time I tried to write a note, it appeared that a hundred cigarettes lit up around me, the smoke wafting over my face and causing my eyes to smart. Was this a silly attempt to prevent me from taking notes for my review?' The review which followed burned as effectively as any cigarette, but it did not glow.

In the matter of real risk to life, limb and human happiness some entertainers are more equal than others. The worst that most might expect is a swift grope from the crowding fans. Male pop singers know the hazard well enough and some have considered using a cricketer's 'box' to avoid becoming inadvertent castrati. The life of an untrained voice, it must be admitted, is already hard enough. The removal of a personal decoration such as a cufflink – later to be hoarded in some soul-less suburban bedsit – is also well within the norms of adulation. Some entertainers provoke a more sinister response.

Elizabeth Taylor's fund-raising efforts to promote AIDS research led to death threats from those seers among us who believe that the disease is God's work. Personal obsessions of the sort targeted at Princess Anne in Britain are directed, often dangerously, towards television actresses in the US. Someone called Daniel Vega believed that his lover was a 42-year-old blonde soap opera queen named Donna Mills. Since he was serving a triple life sentence, his *idée fixe* did not matter until he escaped and got a gun. He was killed during an exchange of fire with the police when, they believed, he was trying to reach the lady.

Victoria Principal, one of the constellation of 'Dallas' stars, declared herself 'paranoid about my safety' after three attacks upon her, two of them sexual assaults. These and many similar episodes occurred in and around Hollywood, where anything can happen, though it is not always clear why. (It is entirely unclear why Sarah Douglas, a British actress in Hollywood's *Falcon Crest* series, failed to acquire an answering machine and a whistle with which to attack a threat-caller's ear drum. Instead, according to one report, she bought a gun and an Alsatian guard dog, and continued to answer the telephone in person, in the middle of the night.)

But it was not the obsessives of the kookie West Coast who finally drove America's theatricals into the arms of the security industry. The murder of John Lennon, the Beatle consort of Yoko Ono, occurred 3,000 miles away, right outside their Manhattan apartment.

The American belief in every man's right to carry and bear arms goes some way towards explaining the continuing fear and loathing in Los Angeles and New York as well as Las Vegas. British entertainers, in general, live with a slightly lower level of personal protection, pop music figures aside. Denholm Elliot, one of the UK's most durable and successful actors, arrives at his city centre gymnasium from his Kew home by motor-cycle, looking less glamorous than the average insurance agent. (For some years, the author used the same gym.) Politically committed actresses such as Glenda Jackson and Vanessa Redgrave regularly appear on public platforms without so much as a Boy Scout to protect them. But then, although their pronouncements sometimes outrage a right-wing press, they do live outside the hall of mirrors of their profession, some of the time. They have also learned, somewhere along the line, one of the great maxims of real close protection: 'Exercise common sense in evaluating the risk and respond appropriately. Don't go over the top.' Most bodyguards outside government service lack the intelligence – in both senses of the word – to gauge their response correctly. By definition, they are certain to over-react unless they have years of experience, and the humility to learn from it.

If there is one group of bodyguards more dangerous than the blind but vigorous heavies of Tin Pan Alley, it is those who surrender their critical intelligence in search of a new way of life, in the service of a guru. A surprising number of the new Messiahs living in the new age of superstition seem to require protection of an earthly kind from the heavenly love they inspire in their followers. The final trick – witness the Jonestown massacre or the Manson murders – may even be a ritualised slaughter which solves everyone's protection problems for good. At Jonestown, the fatal doses of Kool Aid, laced with cyanide, were administered to the doomed disciples by Jim Jones's bodyguard, his 'Angels', before they also drank it.

Cultural isolation combined with dogma plays a strong part in the process, but the guru – having aroused the dangerous emotion of adoration – cannot consistently deliver the bliss his followers expect to receive as reward for their devotion. It is a transference of identity, and responsibility, from individual to group familiar to other élite teams including the Foreign Legion.

This seems to have been the pattern followed by disciples of an Indian mystic known as Bhagwan Shree Rajneesh who briefly attracted such famous pilgrims as Bernard Levin. Rajneesh was the darling of a prosperous family. Since boyhood he had exhibited a taste for the macabre (he loved deathbeds and funerals) and a talent for hypnotism. As a spiritual guide he offered enlightenment through self-indulgence of every kind.

The 'Me-generation' of the sixties deserted their encounter groups in London and California to obtain further enlightenment in the endless, sterile sexual exchanges of Tantric mysticism. In their search for truth-through-orgasm they contrived to ignore the grievous poverty around them. They also dressed in the sub-continent's sacerdotal garb of orange robes, but in a way which emphasised sensuality rather than sacrifice. In all the circumstances it was as tasteless as Marie-Antoinette dressed as a mock shepherdess on her toy 'farm' near Versailles among real peasants suffering real hunger ... or the 'musical appreciation' ostentatiously shared by some of those in charge of Nazi concentration camps.

A bodyguard was finally deemed necessary when one of the inner circle of priestesses was bitten on the nose in a street near the Rajneesh temple or 'ashram' at Poona. Since the guru's audiences often included a variety of hysterics – whose behaviour was often encouraged by Rajneesh himself – the risk of assault was potentially as great within the ashram, from one of the faithful, as from without. At times when no audience was taking place, often in the middle of the night, it was not unusual for a disciple to sense (wrongly) that he or she had been 'called' by the man who claimed the title 'Bhagwan', or god. It was a unique security problem.

The person selected for the role of bodyguard was a Scottish osteopath, Hugh Milne, who, after devoting ten years to the unpaid service of his god, discovered that he had made a mistake shortly before the movement disintegrated under an avalanche of criminal and civil charges. His account of those years is one of the most original contributions to the collective bodyguard experience.

Long exposure to metaphysics combined with a suggestible nature – the essential qualities of the loyal disciple – are required for anyone purporting to 'protect' a god who believes in his regular reincarnation as well as in non-violence; but a god, nevertheless, who does not disdain an armoured Rolls-Royce. Milne writes:

'I made a makeshift weapon – a short club out of the shaft of a pickaxe – and kept it in a potted plant just out of Bhagwan's sight, just in case somebody did come over the fence. It was the primitive start of a security system that ten years later culminated in hundreds of highly trained guards carrying sub-machine guns.'

The club was spotted and banned because its police overtones offended well-heeled young Americans. In time, the weapon was replaced by training in martial arts. By the late 1970s, as thousands of disciples arrived at Poona to hear Rajneesh speak, Milne's team increased to twenty-five including eight male black belts and one female. Armed with short swords and increased again to fifty, the team became known as 'The Samurai Department'.

There was one concerted attack on the Bhagwan Rajneesh. Milne records:

> Twenty minutes into the lecture . . . I was handed a note with the terse words: 'Police inspector warns you attack expected today.' I flashed the 'extreme danger' sign to the twenty guards in the hall. Within seconds a robust-looking Indian man stood up about sixty feet from the stage, on Bhagwan's right. He shouted in Hindi, 'You are insulting our religion,' then started to walk towards Bhagwan with a very determined look in his eyes. Five or six guards had already responded to my signal. A large Canadian sannyasi [disciple], Yogi, grabbed the man firmly and three more guards quickly joined him. A second Indian then got up and grappled with the guards . . . Bhagwan, who had continued speaking until this point, now stopped talking and turned in the direction of the disturbance. 'Be gentle with him . . .' he indicated as the Indian was carried out.

One of the samurai was a German cousin of the Prince of Wales, Guelf of Hanover, who collapsed during a martial arts training session and died in the commune in 1981. According to Milne, Prince Charles met his cousin in Bombay shortly before Guelf died. Referring to the death of Lord Mountbatten, Charles confided: 'You know, since

Uncle Louis was killed I have had nobody to turn to for real advice, no one. You are so lucky that you have your guru. I wish I had your freedom to go and see a man like that . . .'

In 1981 the Bhagwan moved his headquarters to the United States. The samurai travelling with him 'were told that State Department permission would be needed before any foreign national could have a bodyguard. This would entail explaining why such protection was necessary, a difficult step which might prejudice our entry. Therefore Sheela [an executive] informed us that our status was to be that of ordinary tourists . . .'

Later that year the commune moved to a muddy wilderness in Oregon, where Milne, now disillusioned, went his own way. The commune turned in upon itself, seeking heretics within and enemies without. Telephones were tapped and eleven watch-towers built, manned by guards armed with automatic weapons. In an attempt to obtain political control of the local, indigenous township, salmonella was introduced into local restaurants. In 1985 Rajneesh was expelled from the US. A few months later his right-hand woman and the commune's Führerin, Sheela Silverman, was sentenced to up to twenty years' imprisonment for poisoning and attempted murder. A Filipino nurse accused with her and a former housewife from Australia also admitted attempting to murder the guru's personal physician, a British citizen, Dr George Meredith. As they were led away in handcuffs to start their sentences, they smiled like brides.

In spite of its claims to a sort of godliness, the Bhagwan's security system failed to intercept successive plagues which resulted from the extreme promiscuity imposed upon the communards. As a belated response to herpes, AIDS and other sexually-transmitted diseases, a condom and three pairs of rubber gloves were provided for each mating, while oral and anal sex were prohibited. (It is unclear who policed these regulations.) At other times, disciples were expected to wear beads of different colours to indicate whether they were Clean, Unclean or Don't Know.

What the fearful minorities of the communes and the purveyors of protection have in common is a belief in the Threat, the reality of the enemy out there who has to be neutralised. For the high-flying business executive who is a target for criminal kidnap or ideological assassination, the threat is real but the protection available from the state usually short-lived and ineffectual. The business community has therefore discovered a new commodity and a new industry in reliable executive protection. After a bumpy ride and a few moral lapses during the sixties and seventies, the security entrepreneurs have achieved more than respectability. The best of them are virtually indistinguishable from the government agencies for which they once worked.

The pioneer in Britain was Colonel David Stirling, founding father of the Special Air Service Regiment. His Watchguard organisation was set up in Guernsey, Channel Islands, in 1967 at the peak of Britain's post-colonial wars and at the dawn of international political terrorism. Stirling's veterans provided bodyguards and trained others for the rulers of territories ranging from Abu Dhabi to Zambia, by way of Sierra Leone. Among the contracts which he identified but which were then taken over by the regular regiment (and therefore the British government) were the protection of Kenya's President Kenyatta and the Iranian Shah. Stirling also blended straight protection and bodyguard training with more adventurous operations including an attempt to liberate royalist political prisoners from captivity in Gaddafi's Libya.

KMS, as we have seen, was created in 1975 as a tailor-made solution to the otherwise insoluble problem of providing cost-effective personal security for British diplomats in high-risk areas. Others were not slow to jump on the bandwagon. Not all were as fastidious in their choice of clients as Stirling, Johnson, Morrison and other ex-SAS entrepreneurs.

Some were happy to train Gaddafi's bodyguard at a time when the visionary Libyan leader was obliged regularly to put teams of his officers before a firing squad. Among the more elaborate organisations exporting British military expertise was a company called J. Donne Holdings Ltd, which offered to teach the techniques of silent killing, advanced sabotage and lock neutralisation as well as close protection. The VIP Security and Protection Course for twenty students ran for twenty-one weeks. The prospectus promised:

'Students are trained to advanced standard in security intelligence, protective planning, close-quarter marksmanship, unarmed combat, vetting of personnel, vehicle and building searches and protective surveys. In addition, indepth studies of recent assassinations and assassination techniques are conducted. Personnel selected for this course should be thoroughly vetted and should be experienced in security duties.'

Equipment assembled for the course in 1977 included coloured training waistcoats for twenty-eight students, twenty bullet-proof vests, four portable resuscitation appliances and 1,000 paper target facings. The consignment also included ten dummy revolvers.

When Donne Holdings (whose key figures included a former Intelligence Corps Major and a reserve officer of 21 SAS (TAVR)) were selling to Gaddafi, the export of such training and equipment was not a phenomenon unique to close protection isolated from other aspects of trade. With the blessing of successive governments, and aided by such offices as the Defence Sales Organisation and the Export Credits Guarantee Department, sales of British defence equipment of all kinds, with training to match, had been roaring ahead for years and would continue to do so. Britain's top secret Tornado, upon which the country's own air defence depended, was diverted to the Saudi Arabian market in the 1980s.

What differentiated 'low intensity' material and manpower was that it was very much more likely to be used operationally than some of the heavier and more sophisticated weaponry. It is the great paradox of the age that nuclear and advanced non-nuclear weapons, with a few obvious exceptions, have diminished or eliminated general warfare between nation states. The armed conflict has not ceased. It has found surrogate expression in assassination and various forms of terrorism instead. The change is one reason why the bodyguard's political importance has grown so dramatically since the end of the 1960s.

Another is the discovery of the West by Arab rulers who have been riding high on inflated oil revenues since 1973. Although this discovery amounts to a form of reverse colonialism – as some Arabised areas of Britain illustrate – the sheiks have not entirely embraced the philosophy of turning the other cheek, or of resolving quarrels without bloodshed. (It is not part of the culture of Arabia, which must be special in having germinated the greeting to an old friend: 'Long may the neck of thine enemy rest beneath thy foot!') The Arabs' firepower has grown, but not their maturity. So assassination spreads from Mecca to Mayfair and with it, the market for reliable, professional bodyguards. But not even the best-trained bodyguard can do for the Man what the Man rejects in his pursuit of something more amusing than mere 'security'.

In 1977 a six-man training team from KMS was sent to instruct the bodyguard of North Yemen's President Al-Hamdi. The course was completed and the team returned to Britain. Two months later, the President and his brother invited two beautiful French women to the capital, Sana'a, for what was described later as 'a fashion show of leatherwear'. The brothers then dismissed their newly trained bodyguard and drove into the mountains for a weekend of nature study, accompanied by the women. On the return journey they were ambushed and all four killed. The new president paid compensation to the women's families in Europe.

He was soon involved in negotiations with a representative of Communist and republican South Yemen (formerly Aden). The visitor brought with him a gift: a very large suitcase. The President's guards, faithful to their British training, insisted upon opening the suitcase. This embarrassed their head of state, since the case contained a large quantity of US dollar bills. Some time later, the same representative returned with another large case. This time the President and his visitor retired to a private, locked room from which the bodyguard was excluded. They opened the case, entirely unaware that it was a booby trap containing about five pounds of plastic explosive, killing them both and prompting one British expert to comment: 'A superb double bluff!'

Someone who knows KMS well and followed such incidents with impatience at the lack of attention to the SOPs (Standard Operational Procedures) he had advised, observed: 'I am consoled by the knowledge that, in the first instance, the bodyguards had been dismissed and were not responsible for the successful assassinations. The Hamdi brothers must have been consoled that they died after their weekend in the country and not before it.'

For the westernised Arab and his retinue of assorted millionaires, models and stock market analysts moving around the world in a *smala* (or mobile community), the bodyguard represents more than security. At his best he is the quintessential Figaro, the global Mr Fixit. One egregious sheik arrived at the French-Corsican port of Calvi (associated these days with the French Foreign Legion parachutists) with a private yacht and a hundred guests. His KMS bodyguard team leader went ashore with the passports and had some problems convincing the immigration officials that this was a private party and not a cruise ship.

The bodyguard now had to find a sufficient number of taxis to enable the guests to go shopping. The team scoured Calvi but found only three cabs. Glumly they made their way back to the port, past a fairground. Here they spotted a play-train, complete with tassle-fringed canopied carriages and rubber wheels. The driver was persuaded to close for normal business and join the bodyguard. An hour later, Calvi's usually blasé locals watched incredulously as the 'train', full of exotic visitors, emerged from the quayside and turned into the main street, halting at most of the shops, with bodyguards riding on the 'caboose' and cow-catcher.

'One of our finest moments,' sighed a member of the firm later.

CHAPTER 13

Millionaires' Dilemma –
To Be or Pretend Not to Be

If irregular warfare is, as it were, armed conflict on the cheap, it is also accessible to criminals as well as political terrorists. Links between the criminal underworld and political terror have been forged regularly since the birth of political terrorism in the 19th century. And as Laqueur observes, 'In the age of the highly specialised multinational terrorism of the 1970s with so many interested parties and paymasters involved, it is no longer possible to know with any degree of accuracy to what extent these terrorists are still motivated by revolutionary or nationalist fervour or by any "cause" at all. Some undoubtedly are; for others it has simply become a way of life – the only one they know.'

The kidnap industry was a by-product of such forces, but a very profitable one. Brookes McClure, a US authority, argued in a paper entitled 'Hostage Survival' in 1976 that between 1971 and 1975 in Latin America alone kidnappers gained $80 million in ransoms for hostages. Kidnappers in most countries had an 80 per cent chance of escaping capture or death. For the victims the good news was that only about four per cent of them were killed by the terrorists.

The exception to this rule of low-risk/high profit is the hostage taken not for money but for exchange against a terrorist or guerrilla imprisoned by government. Such a hostage is most at risk when the officially detained target for release is in the condemned cell. Among the terrorist movements who have murdered prisoners on a tit-for-tat, death-for-death basis are the Zionist Irgun Zvai Leumi (which hanged two British sergeants in 1947) and the Armée de Libération Nationale, fighting the French in Algeria's War of Independence, which murdered three captive French soldiers held in Tunisia in 1958. More usually, kidnap is about ransom and therefore negotiation between kidnappers and their victims' representatives.

The specialisation within the protection industry known as Kidnap & Ransom – more simply, in the trade, 'K & R' – has become the business of just one or two élite businesses in Britain and a sprinkling of others elsewhere. Such companies tend to operate under a cloak of maximum secrecy and are even criticised on moral grounds by other security organisations on the basis that, by satisfying a market to save some lives, they put other lives at risk.

As Sir Kenneth Newman, then Metropolitan Police Commissioner, observed in 1986, some private security firms were operating 'at the very frontiers' of official tolerance although, 'so far, in my experience, they have kept within them'. He told the *Daily Telegraph*'s Peter Millar that even when insurance companies were prepared to pay ransom money, it was the clear duty of those who had taken out the anti-kidnap policy to co-operate fully with the investigating police.

If the insurers and their risk-taking negotiators were reticent about their activities, there was no secret about the spectacular crimes which had created the hostage market in the first place. The trade in American captives – diplomatic, civil and military – in the late sixties and early seventies reflected the long history of kidnap for profit as a peculiarly American crime, a tradition inherited from its Italian citizens and made notorious by the Lindbergh case in 1932. Kidnaps for profit have occurred at a rate of at least one every month in the US since then. In 1974, the total was almost double that.

As it happened this was the year in which the American heiress Patti Hearst was kidnapped, then converted to terrorism by her captors of the 'Symbionese Liberation Army'. After a period of imprisonment she renounced terrorism, returned home and fell in love with her bodyguard, Bernard Shaw. Patti Hearst met all the desiderata of a contemporary kidnap victim: lots of money, plus the star quality which would prompt an effluent of journalistic clichés. This not only increased pressure upon Hearst's next-of-kin during her SLA period, but it also foreshadowed a series of highly publicised kidnaps elsewhere, starting with the attempted seizure of Princess Anne in London a month later.

It might have been coincidence that the IRA entered the kidnap game the following year by seizing Tiede Herrema, a Dutch executive based in Ireland. Certainly the affair became a test of the technique – then new to Europe – of negotiating a non-violent end to a kidnap once the kidnappers' hideout was revealed. Patti Hearst's comrades had died in a firestorm of flying lead, courtesy of the FBI as they surrounded the SLA's headquarters. But New York's police, faced with similar problems, demonstrated that the choice was not just a surrender to the kidnappers to save life or the use of maximum force, Israeli-style.

Herrema was kidnapped by Eddie Gallagher and Marian Coyle in an effort to spring three IRA prisoners legally detained by the Irish government, one of them Dr Rose Dugdale, an English academic and Gallagher's lover. The kidnap hideaway – a Kildare council house – was discovered and for eighteen days a remorseless process of squeezing the terrorists psychologically went on until the captors came to realise that there was no realistic choice except surrender.

The new science of crisis management combined with applied psychology and hostage negotiation promptly became a discipline in its own right. It was applied with great skill by the Dutch in breaking the resistance of a first wave of Moluccan terrorists whose political demands no government could deliver. Instead, the terrorists were presented with a realisable goal – publicity for their lost cause – and their hostages were released, though not unharmed. They had suffered emotional damage which remained with some of them for years.

In December 1975 the same battery of techniques was applied successfully to the IRA team besieged in Balcombe Street, Mayfair.

The military leaders, and thinkers, in the war against terrorism at this time were the counter-revolutionary warfare experts of the SAS. They were the innovators ('pilgrims' is a word they sometimes use) and they took a keen interest in this refined form of psychological warfare. Indeed it was employed by the SAS commander Lieutenant Colonel Mike Rose to an extent still not generally appreciated to cut short the Falklands conflict. Using the islands' public telephone system, he undermined his opponents' will to resist, employing a technique described by some insiders as 'coercive bargaining'. (A grateful British government recognised the operation with a Mention In Despatches.)

When it works, this technique of coercive bargaining is far and away the most subtle and skilful that any security officer can be called upon to perform in an effort to save life. In the wake of a kidnap, the 'crisis management consultant', as he is becoming known, probably knows little about the person whose life he is working to save. One of the consultant's priorities must be to compile a complete physical and psychological picture of the victim. As one professional puts it, 'I have to "know" the kidnap victim as perfectly as if he were my brother, though we might never meet.' It is as odd a mutation of human relations as anything a turbulent modern world has yet created, its strangeness compounded by the fact that the victim is a prisoner held at an unknown location by unknown people whose motives and temperament are equally opaque. In Europe, the most likely setting for the dangerous poker game which follows is Italy; elsewhere, Colombia.

The game is one in which – just to complete the hall-of-mirrors effect – the consultant is not a player. He is present as an 'adviser' to the company or, more likely, the family of the victim. One veteran of the business puts it like this: 'It would be impractical and potentially dangerous for anyone other than a local person, with total knowledge of the language and culture, to attempt to communicate with the kidnappers. In a highly charged situation, the smallest misunderstanding could prove fatal.'

There are several reasons why the experienced British officer is ideal for such a task. First, he has been trained to impose an orderly framework of analysis upon the apparent chaos of warfare. In dealing with the kidnappers' demands he will employ every military staff technique from log-keeping to the preparation of 'position papers', as well as any intelligence available, to build up a picture of the enemy and the progress of the conflict. Every telephone conversation will be recorded and transcribed; every note subjected to repeated textual analysis.

Second, he will have been exposed to the experience of irregular and often clandestine warfare in Northern Ireland, an experience which has changed the character of the professional British Army since 1969 while leaving other security forces untouched. Third, he will be trained to keep his mind fixed on the agreed objective. This, cut to its essentials, is usually the release of the victim alive and well after a dialogue with the kidnappers which, hopefully, will buy time for the victim to be found and freed by local security forces. A second-best solution is payment of a ransom negotiated down to a realistic minimum, again linked to the safe homecoming of the victim.

The consultant, as a professional, will avoid wasting time or energy in scoring points off the opposition. This is vital in a case which might run for six months or more, in which the emotions of the family being advised will swing from extravagant optimism to deep depression. In both cases, as any professional will confirm, 'We have to absorb their emotions – take on board a lot of unburned adrenalin, as it were – and stay calm as Buddha ourselves. It's a bit like being a human lightning conductor.'

In the developed world, where the problem is more likely to be 'product extortion', such as a threat to poison baby food, the consultant has to be capable of holding his own in the boardroom of a company under attack. In that situation, he might have to determine whether the threat is greater to a company's trading position rather than to a customer's life, and say so.

These truisms cut no ice in Ireland for special, political reasons. Kidnapping has long been a method of fund-raising by the IRA and its splinter groups, and by its 'Loyalist' counterparts. It is one of the activities where the difference between 'freedom fighters' and what residents of the Crumlin Road Prison used to describe as a 'DOC' (for 'decent ordinary criminal') is blurred to extinction. So ransom negotiations between former British intelligence officers of one sort or another and a kidnap team – however deviously conducted and however humane the negotiators' purpose – do not make governments on either side of the Irish Sea swoon with pleasure when they are fighting against the same terror groups.

In 1983 Don Tidey – managing director of a supermarket chain and a man with no political antecedents – was driving his daughter to school, without a bodyguard, in a Dublin street when a man in police uniform stopped them. The 'officer' then put a gun to Tidey's head and led him to another car, and captivity. Tidey was kept in a tent in chains, his head hooded, for twenty-three days, a form of treatment which would provoke howls of complaint by republican prisoners to a European court. He was released by security forces after a confused gun battle in a gloomy Irish forest.

By then, according to a number of credible sources, a British company named Control Risks had started advising the supermarket's holding company, also British, about its negotiating tactics. Control Risks' involvement in the case apparently ended in January 1984 as a result of a difference over policy between the security firm and the holding company responsible for Mr Tidey.

In February 1985, the Irish government identified a Bank of Ireland account holding £2 million as one which might contain the proceeds of 'extortion under threat of kidnap and murder'. But it was November 1987 before the president of Sinn Fein, Gerry Adams, disclosed in a newspaper interview that the IRA had abandoned its policy of kidnap in the Irish Republic. The decision was taken, he said, after the abduction of Don Tidey.

'I would presume,' he went on, 'the experience of the whole Tidey business will have made abductions a very unlikely scenario for Republicans to become engaged in. The IRA said at the time it was a desperate measure and they also said they needed the money.'

As events would demonstrate, republican splinter groups did not feel bound by this self-denying ordinance in Ireland any more than would splinters of the Jihad movement in a Beirut back street.

The civilianised, ex-military kidnap negotiator appeared as a professional in his own right at about the same time as the Herrema and Balcombe Street sieges when, in 1974, Major David Walker, an SAS squadron commander, left the Army to prepare a blueprint for one of the more remarkable British companies of postwar years. This was the firm which would become Control Risks, a subsidiary of the London insurance broker Hogg Robinson. Walker left Control Risks in 1977 to join KMS.

Although there are superficial resemblances still between the two organisations, they have evolved somewhat differently. For example, both provide bodyguards. Those from KMS usually come armed, and they have opened fire more than once. Those from Control Risks usually do not carry weapons. Reflecting the company's evolving style, they more usually act as security co-ordinators for a given contract, somewhat like the Royal Protection team, leaving it to the local security force, in whatever part of the world, to do the job of gun-carrying and bullet-catching.

From the beginning, it was obvious to Walker and his friends at Control Risks that there was a vital difference between the negotiating style available to them as soldiers/ coercive bargainers/psyops warriors working for government, and the more limited scope available to them as civilian advisers to other civilians being held to ransom. As soldiers running a siege they would possess the ultimate sanction of maximum force. As civilian advisers they could rely upon neither that stick nor even the immediate inducement of a 'carrot' in the form of instant ransom money. To advocate such an offer could produce a row with the official police. To negate a ransom already agreed in principle could precipitate the hostage's instant murder. Anyone operating in the morally grey area between these choices is happy to leave moral judgements to journalists and politicians.

People close to the action are unwilling, these days, to explain in detail what mechanisms they can employ to conform with the law and work effectively for a hostage's release. They feel that their operations have been compromised enough already by books about their trade. The fact that Control Risks does continue to pull an apparently impossible trick has everything to do with the weight of experience accrued through 9,000 case-days in twelve years of operations, backed up by the judgement of such senior consultants as Sir Robert Mark, Sir Kenneth Newman, Britain's former NATO Ambassador Sir Clive Rose, and a full-time team drawn from every British security agency including MI6.

As one of them puts it, 'It is a question of knowledge and experience. Our case officer on the ground – the man in the front line – remains in constant contact with the staff back in London. They might well redirect his tactics in the light of what we have on our computer, or in our memories. The accumulated knowledge of Control Risks enables the firm to make some very accurate guesses about a kidnap group and to put it under pressures it did not expect when the operation began.'

The mystique this implies is similar to that cultivated by the SAS Regiment as a means of paralysing opponents in advance of the action, by shrewd psychology. This does not entirely remove the refreshment of surprise from the job. In 1977 two ex-SAS veterans working for Control Risks – Arish Turle and Simon Adams Dale, both former majors – worked in Colombia so as to bring about the release of Gustavo Curtis, a director of the local subsidiary of Beatrice Foods of America. Curtis was released from his clandestine prison after more than seven months' negotiation and after Colombian pesos worth (locally) about £240,000 were handed over in four large suitcases.

Turle (who now works for an American enterprise) and Adams Dale were arrested next day, somewhat to their surprise, and accused of being in cahoots with the kidnappers, in spite of repeated assertions that they had co-operated fully with the local police. After being confined themselves for ten weeks, they were set free and returned home, according to some sources, only after intervention from the presidential office in Bogotá. Subsequently, the judge responsible for their detention was himself charged by the Colombian government with alleged irregularities in the action brought against the two British advisers.

Back in London Control Risks, as usual, said nothing about a specific case in which it might be involved. However, it did not seem plausible, even in the unpoliced wilderness and dense rain-forest that covers much of Colombia, that the foreign advisers should act as bagmen, delivering ransom money. That job is invariably delegated to a friend, a member of the family, a local solicitor, a 'sherpa' from the victim-company's own security department or even an obliging police officer. The role of the adviser at such a tender moment is to minimise the risk that the ransom might be hijacked by someone who falsely claims to have the victim alive and ready for release.

In one lamentable case – the abduction of the Irish racehorse Shergar – a British firm other than Control Risks represented the insurer and advised Shergar's owner. Unfortunately, in a parallel operation, the firm's advice was circumvented and £80,000 taken in the boot of a car to a pub rendezvous as part of a freelance effort to retrieve the horse. There the ransom disappeared. Shergar was never recovered.

Another ploy of which the adviser will be wary is the kidnapper's pursuit of a ransom in exchange for a hostage who has already been murdered. In March 1988 (to quote one typical case) a supermarket manager in Burgoin, France, paid a £35,000 ransom within hours of the disappearance of his son, a student aged nineteen. A day or so later the youth, Hervé Letondu, was found dead.

As the scourge of kidnapping was taken up by terrorist groups in Europe as well as in South America as a method of raising funds, Hogg Robinson did not conceal its satisfaction about the new business it generated. The firm's annual report for 1977 announced: 'Control Risks continues to expand . . . Its kidnap and ransom service is now being used by Lloyd's underwriters as well as by many international companies both within the United Kingdom and around the world.'

The underwriter concerned was Cassidy, Davis Ltd, which had just been created to represent three syndicates. Cassidy, Davis set stringent limits on what the Control Risks teams were at liberty to risk on behalf of a client. As the underwriter's publicity fact-sheet put it in March 1988:

The insurance is designed to be an anti-disruptive package which concentrates on the provision of information and advice as well as possible reimbursement. There are a number of standard conditions which relate to all kidnap and ransom insurance policies:

1. The policy is one of *reimbursement*. No insurer would ever pay or *fund a ransom payment*. Insurers only settle claims once an incident is over.
2. The existence of any insurance policy must *never* be disclosed. If it is disclosed, insurers have the right to void payment of any claim.
3. Co-operation with *law enforcement agencies* is conditional to the contract of the insurance.
4. Underwriters would not reimburse any insured who had committed an illegal act. (As is normal practice in insurance.)
5. The *policy limit* of the insurance is always less than the net worth of the insured.

In 1979, two years after the link between Control Risks and Cassidy, Davis was forged, Control Risks was reputed to have played a decisive role in the release of two British officials of Lloyds Bank International after they had been imprisoned by guerrillas in El Salvador. Other cases attributed to the Control Risks team, but not publicly acknowledged by the company itself, included those of Mrs Jennifer

Guinness, a member of the brewing dynasty, in 1986 and the dentist John O'Grady in 1987, both in Dublin.

Like Bismarck and Geoffrey Jackson, Mrs Guinness had learned from the experience of others before the worst happened to her. In her case, the worst was an eight-day ordeal spent in chains in five different locations. She explained later that she had used conversation to build up a rapport with her kidnappers, from the beginning of her captivity.

'I tried to make some kind of relationship with them. I thought when it did come to the end with the guns, they would have to shoot me standing up, facing them. It would be me they were shooting, not just some woman they had taken . . . I felt any extremes of emotion were a luxury I could not allow myself. I had to channel my mind into keeping myself together and keeping my personal dignity intact. It would have been lovely to cry, to yell, to scream. But I felt in order to survive as a person, I had to talk and keep very calm . . . We talked about all sorts of things, from my love of sailing to religion.'

While this admirable exercise in self-help prompted proper applause, the alleged intervention of Control Risks provoked criticism from the Irish Prime Minister, Charles Haughey, the Irish police, Mrs Thatcher, and the British Labour MP Dale Campbell-Savours. Combined with the company's policy of public silence, such criticism led to predictably hostile journalistic judgements, for nothing enrages print journalists more than a silence that suggests that they don't count for much.

This was not the only source of trouble. The O'Grady kidnap case in 1987 had proved a disaster for the Irish police, the Garda. The principal suspect, Dessie O'Hare (nicknamed 'The Border Fox'), was regularly surrounded and just as regularly escaped, often shooting his way out of entrapment. The presence in Dublin of a Control Risks case officer (identified by the press as David Little, an ex-Scotland Yard detective), combined with the discovery that a local priest was to carry ransom money to the kidnappers' Dublin hideout, generated the belief that the company was fishing in troubled waters. In fact, this time it was the police who finally sanctioned a ransom deal if only as a desperate expedient. As one newspaper report put it:

'Irish police reluctantly agreed to the handing over of the money after the kidnappers chopped off the tops of Mr O'Grady's little fingers. While Father Brian D'Arcy waited with the money, Mr O'Grady was freed in a gun battle between the police and the gang.'

On this foundation was built a suspicion that the London company was negotiating improperly with terrorists (in this case, renegades of the INLA as well as IRA). The public silence of Control Risks made it a useful scapegoat for the numerous twists in the story, each of which, it seemed, collected a new official mishap. Although, in private, a handful of security experts in Whitehall and elsewhere accepted that the company had stayed well the right side of the law, its mere presence made it an alternative target for recrimination. (The kidnapper, O'Hare, was jailed for forty years.)

Another example of the growing misunderstanding between media and Control Risks was the offer made by the company to assist the Anglican Church in its efforts to retrieve its missing envoy, Terry Waite. In January 1988, on the first anniversary of Waite's abduction in Beirut (after Waite had dismissed his British-trained Druze bodyguard and walked into a trap), John Lyttle, chief aide to the Archbishop of Canterbury, confirmed: 'Control Risks approached us offering their services on a contract basis. We consulted various people and carefully considered the matter. We knew all about their expertise in dealing with kidnappers in several parts of the world, but concluded they did not have the expertise for this particular situation.'

The London *Daily Mail* then sought a comment from the chairman of Control Risks, Tim Royle, a brother of Baron Fanshawe of Richmond who, as Anthony Royle, had recruited an SAS bodyguard in a pioneering operation of diplomatic protection in South America. Mr Royle blandly responded that Control Risks never commented about individual cases. The public effect was that the firm appeared to be 'ambulance chasing' in a somewhat heartless search for new business. In fact, since Tim Royle was a member of the Church of England Synod (an ecclesiastical parliament), it would have been eccentric of him not to offer his services. But that important fact went unremarked.

The moral debate about K & R operations was given another outing in 1987 by the authors of *The Kidnap Business*, one of whom, 'Mark Bles', wrote under a penname after SAS service. Bles is a charismatic figure whose former colleagues describe him as an officer with a capacity for lateral thought which verges on the occult in its perception of hidden clues or concealed terrorist weapons. The criminal underworld he and his co-author Robert Low describe is one in which an already-dead kidnap victim is stored in a deep freeze so as to be thawed out for use later in a photograph with an up-to-date newspaper as 'proof' that the victim is still alive and worth bidding for; a culture which bleeds its hostage and sends the bottled blood to the grieving family, or amputates ears and other extremities.

'No doubt kidnap is serious,' Bles observes, 'but humour is not unknown. It is sometimes macabre, like the Guatemalan gang that sent one of its victim's amputated fingers to the parents in a hot-dog roll.'

But what of negotiation, or even advice about negotiating tactics? Bles and Low comment:

'Whether kidnap insurance is right or wrong, companies

with operations in risk areas ought to pay for this insurance. They owe a duty to their employees who work for the good of the company in dangerous areas, and they owe a duty to the shareholders to protect the company's profits which might otherwise go into the pockets of the kidnappers ... Private individuals, with none of the responsibilities of large multi-national companies, may find their money better spent in directly dissuading potential kidnappers with increased personal security.'

This seems to imply that K & R insurance relies more on negotiation after the kidnap than good protection before it. In fact, kidnap-avoidance advice comes with most K & R insurance cover, which is perhaps why, as Bles notes, 'of all the kidnaps that take place every year, fewer than one per cent are insured, so the existence or not of insurance will not make the slightest difference to the kidnappers.'

(That is assuredly true. Experts note that kidnap victims are usually seized as a result of having wealth as popularly perceived by the media. But newspapers sometimes exaggerate, and all that glisters is not gold.)

If Control Risks' corporate style (combined with hasty moral judgement by press and politicians) has generated a mediocre public image, the growth of business behind the scenes has been a steady, modest success. As Cassidy, Davis noted in 1988: 'Kidnap and ransom insurance has been undertaken since 1933. The total volume of the premium income for this class of insurance is currently $70 million worldwide, of which $40 million is underwritten at Lloyd's market per annum ... The volume has remained relatively constant over the last few years. The number of cases has increased but the size of the premium has been reduced, encouraged by the use of prevention services provided by such companies as the Control Risks Group.'

The underwriter noted that between 1975 and 1988 a total of 2,542 kidnaps had been recorded by Control Risks but only ninety-nine of these, or 3.9 per cent of the total, were insured. Of the fourteen highest ransom payments recorded since 1973 – those exceeding $5 million each – only three (21.4 per cent) were insured. Of 115 kidnaps since 1977 in which a ransom exceeding $1 million was paid, only twenty-seven (23.5 per cent) were insured. One implication of these figures was that there was scope for growth in this rarefied and controversial market.

Control Risks' direct involvement in the market up to 1988 was to advise clients in 112 kidnap cases and 118 cases involving other forms of extortion. The experience, as we have seen, amounts to more than 9,000 'case-days'. The firm itself says, somewhat pointedly, that it acts in an advisory role 'and requires clients to keep the authorities informed during the incident'.

Estimates of the cost of premiums for K & R cover vary but such insurance does not come cheap.

Through KMS and Control Risks the psychological weapons of counter-terrorism have been spread, on the whole beneficially, to civilian society as surely as other techniques, such as plastic surgery, which were also the by-product of armed conflict. Control Risks in particular has marketed the fruits of its formidable collective experience through a somewhat special information service. Subscribers paying £3,600 annually are able to obtain an expert, detailed appraisal of security risks of all kinds in ninety countries at any time during the twenty-four hours. As well as his subscription, the client needs a computer, a display unit (screen) and a modem through which he can call up the 'on-line security forecast' via normal telephone lines.

In response to his personal code, punched into the system through his computer keyboard, the system will feed back its own assessment of risk measured as 'red alerts', country by country. At that moment, in the 'red alert' country concerned, all might appear to be normal. Even the local media might hint at no cloud on the horizon larger than a monkey's fist. The Control Risks' report, by contrast, will identify the threat in such detail as to guide the visiting businessman as to his most prudent mode of transport, choice of hotel and 'how to conduct himself'.

The sources upon which such data are based are secret. They are derived from a network of correspondents, most of whom are locals within the country on which they report. Control Risks also has a research team in London, each of whose members studies his own target area from outside. Yet another source is the feedback received by Control Risks from its own clients, some of which are multinational corporations armed with their own formidable information-gathering machinery.

There are also special studies for groups or companies, which commission them privately, and more widely-circulated, off-the-shelf reports about specific threats. Typical of the latter is the 1987 report on 'The Terrorist Threat to Aviation' costing £300. This document analysed 252 'significant incidents' in fifty-nine countries over a period of three years, along with a series of threat-analysis reports covering six parts of the world.

For the regular air traveller, there was a section devoted to mitigating the risk of terrorist attack and 'how best to behave in a hijack situation'. The hijack is not a statistically serious threat, yet. During the period covered by this study, seven hundred civilian deaths were caused by air piracy or terrorism but of those, 329 resulted from the bomb on board a single Air India flight which crashed off Ireland in 1985. In 1987, the journal *Flight International* demonstrated that out of 1,167 people who lost their lives in airliners that year, 833 were accidental and 333 were due to terrorism.

Bombs do not discriminate between the 'innocent' and less innocent, but Control Risks adopts the working assumption that individual terrorists running a hijack do make instant value-judgements about their hostages, which can be fatal for the hostage. A little street wisdom in advance of the event, it is argued, pays off. The firm's guide to hijack survival suggests:

'Your passport should contain only the minimum of anodyne information. If it shows evidence of travel to contentious countries (e.g. Israel, South Africa), get a new one. Documents showing your affiliations with government agencies, companies, political or ex-service associations should be carried in your hold baggage as should most of your credit cards . . . Don't take books or magazines that may be contentious. (Girlie magazines and religious tracts could, for quite different reasons, be equally offensive) . . .'

The three basic guidelines suggested by the report are 'Alertness, Anonymity and Unobtrusiveness'. One press summary said the advice boiled down to remembering to 'dress casually, stay alert, avoid the booze and be prepared to duck'.

Usually, the captives emerge alive from their ordeal and apparently intact. The more serious and frequently reported damage of a siege is in the minds of former hostages, but the professionals of Control Risks have no advice about that, as yet. (Dutch psychiatric teams, by contrast, have done much work on the after-effects of being held hostage. Catharsis by re-enactment of the horror, such as wearing a hood with a rope around the neck, if that happened during captivity, is one way of exorcising the experience.)

Finally, there are the threat evaluation reports prepared by Control Risks in response to a commission from a single, private client. One of these, entitled 'The Anti-Apartheid Movement in Europe: Prospects for Increased Violence', received limited press exposure and probably did not anticipate the assassination of Dulcie September, African National Congress representative, in Paris in March 1988 by opponents of anti-apartheid. Another 'special' by Control Risks' analysts examined the structure of animal rights organisations. The report was commissioned by chemical and food manufacturing companies.

Such activities excite the appetite for conspiracy theory among some journalists, but the firm is careful to disclaim any inside track to official secrets in carrying out this work. In December 1986, Control Risks' spokesman Christopher Grose told one newspaper: 'We do not nor do we wish to receive any intelligence material. It would be unthinkable that anyone would give it to us. We are an information service, not an intelligence agency.'

The point was reinforced by another representative of the company, who told the author, 'We are not an intelligence service, nor a news agency, but a risk-assessment service. The material we produce is not the sort of thing which would be of use, necessarily, to a news service. But some newspapers seem to think they have right of access to any privately commissioned study ... Control Risks is a commercial organisation which stays very much within the law. It would not have the board of directors it has, if it did not stay legitimate.'

Yet another function performed by the firm is its role of international problem-catcher. A response team headed by a retired brigadier will take on, at long distance, almost any problem presented by the cussedness of man and nature. In the early hours of a Sunday morning in 1986, the boss of the response cell received a telephone call from the captain of a tanker in the Gulf. The caller said:

'I have an Exocet missile on my deck. The Dubai port authorities won't allow me in. I have telephoned twelve people worldwide. No one is sympathetic. Help!'

The line was kept open while some short-term technical

advice was traced on another telephone. The job of making the missile safe was finally done by the Greek Navy under the auspices of Control Risks.

In another case an Italian telephoned the company about his son, a solo sailor, missing in mid-Atlantic, somewhere between Iceland and Morocco. He was unable to arrange a co-ordinated search. Control Risks found the wreckage of the small boat on rocks off the Irish coast. The sailor was presumed lost.

Such organisations as KMS and Control Risks were not generally regarded as part of the mainstream of commercial life in Europe until the series of kidnaps of industrial leaders which began with the seizure of Hans-Martin Schleyer in West Germany. Traditionally, private security had been regarded as the preserve of 'plods' capable of guarding property, preferably static property, rather than people. In 1977 Schleyer, then national president of his country's leading industrial 'club', was held by terrorists for forty-three days as a bargaining chip against the release of imprisoned members of the Baader-Meinhof group. When the attempted blackmail failed, Schleyer was murdered. Those responsible were not caught.

The Schleyer case, although it was 'political' rather than criminal, provoked shock waves among the European bourgeoisie similar to the impact upon American high society of Patti Hearst's kidnap and John Lennon's murder. At about the same time, the descent upon London and Paris of wealthy expatriates from Africa and the Middle East, some of whom had good reason not to return home, further boosted the market in close protection. Such clients included, for example, the fugitive Nigerian politician Umaro Dikko, found drugged in a crate at Stansted Airport in 1984 when he was about to be spirited back to Lagos.

During the decade following the Schleyer murder the market burgeoned as European terrorists trained their gunsights increasingly on the softer targets. In Paris they assassinated both ex-military figures (such as General René Audran in 1984) and civilian industrialists including Monsieur Georges Besse, the boss of Renault (1986).

A list of targets compiled by delegates to an international terrorist convention in 1985 itemised 452 names in France alone. In England meanwhile, an anarchist group calling itself 'Hurricane' published a sixty-page booklet detailing the names and private addresses of industrialists, bankers and businessmen. In Italy, criminal kidnap for ransom rather than political abduction amounted to more than 600 cases during the years 1972–87.

In London, targets for assassination ranged from the Marks & Spencer boss Edward Sieff (unsuccessful) to the exiled Seychelles politician Gerard Hoarau (successful). As a West German expert observed after the 1986 assassination there of Dr Gerold von Braunmuhl, the Foreign Ministry's political director and anti-terrorist expert:

'The 1980s terrorists are no longer able or willing to stage spectacular attacks such as the siege of the West German Embassy in Stockholm or the OPEC ministers' conference in Vienna, or long and risky kidnappings such as that of Hans-Martin Schleyer.

'Instead, they prefer to murder selected victims in quick, well-prepared ambushes or else stage bomb attacks against chosen targets ... The murder of Mr Kurt Beckurts, a top Siemens manager, and his chauffeur in July 1986, for instance – their car was blown up by a booby trap bomb – was a strike against the "military-industrial complex".'

Among many target lists now emerging was one itemising those firms and individuals participating in American 'Star Wars' defence programme research, known to the political underworld as 'the Star Wars Mafia'.

In November 1987, in an interesting counter-stroke, what was described as a 'secret society of businessmen' published advertisements in Continental European newspapers offering rewards for information about terrorist attacks in Athens, Frankfurt, Lisbon, Rome and Paris. A total of £400,000 was on offer to informants who were invited to telephone answering services in France, Luxembourg, Holland, Turkey, West Germany and the United States.

The organisation described itself as 'an international consortium composed of private businesses and foundations worried by world terrorism'. The Paris number was traced to an inaccessible apartment in the snobbish 16th *arrondissement*, where the telephone was answered by a woman who spoke English with an American accent.

The exercise prompted one intelligence source to speculate that big business was about to counter-attack, using mercenaries as counter-assassins as well as bodyguards. It was not the only sign of a growing desire for direct action against the terrorist. The normally statesmanlike British newspaper the *Independent* marked the first anniversary of Terry Waite's abduction with a leading article which advocated the forcible rescue of British hostages. 'Such an operation would not be risk-free but, perhaps ideally conducted by surrogates rather than Western commandos, would stand a good chance of success.'

Some of society's richest people eluded the threat under which they lived by simply ceasing to exist, publicly. In Rome and New York, Jewish 'princesses' and other heiresses wore tattered trainers and drove unroadworthy jalopies. But total invisibility was a luxury accessible only to millionaires such as John Paul Getty II, discovered by the *Sunday Express* writer Lynn Barber after a dogged, two-year negotiation in 'a back street in St James's ... in a surprisingly modest looking block of flats with no mention of the name Getty in the porter's lodge: he lives, of course, under a pseudonym'.

Such a lifestyle resembles a painting by one of the surrealists, René Magritte perhaps: the apartment affords a majestic view over Green Park but its owner stares into a blank mirror which reflects no public identity. In Getty's position, the surreal makes sense. In 1973, when he lived in Rome, his sixteen-year-old son Paul Getty III was kidnapped. The ransom was slow in coming, so the kidnappers delivered the boy's ear to a newspaper. They also, it turned out, destroyed the boy psychologically.

Getty fled to London where, in the 1980s, it was not only the top people who were at risk. The effect of revolutionary violence upon some minds was to legitimise all violence against public servants and, by extension, anyone who appeared to be in 'control'. In Britain, public servants who professed to being under threat at work from client violence included 500,000 nurses, many more health service workers, librarians, teachers, magistrates, judges, jurors, secretarial 'temps', social security officials, wardens of refuges for battered wives and the women taking refuge. In such a climate of fear it was hardly surprising that the new, born-again security industry attracted veterans of the Royal Military Police close protection teams as well as former SAS and Parachute Regiment soldiers and ex-Royal Marines. In a society now almost alienated from the random street violence of Victorian times (the cult of football violence apart) such military veterans were the new 'literates' in knowing, from experience, how to apply and avoid the use of force. The number of companies offering them work also mushroomed.

As well as KMS and Control Risks, there was Winguard International, founded by Major Nick Crew, one of the pioneers of RMP bodyguard training and the man responsible for the Queen's security during her 1977 Jubilee Review of BAOR. His firm specialises in 'mobile security', training chauffeurs to keep valuable executives out of harm's way while travelling. There was also DSI, specialising in diplomatic protection and discussed elsewhere; Saladin, Lawnwest, SCI and Cornhill Management Services, all said to have an 'interest' in K & R; Paladin; Argen International Security Consultants; Delta (which seemed to specialise in teaching British housewives to use handguns) and, reflecting a new market, a team of Royal Navy and Royal Marine survivors of the Falklands conflict using that experience of maritime warfare to conduct merchant ships through the hazardous waters of the Gulf. The team operated under the opaque title 'Defence Analysts Ltd'.

The industry was given official public approval when a middle-class housing development in Cheshire recruited forty men to patrol the estate in second-hand police uniforms, sometimes on horseback, and received a £167,000 grant from the Manpower Services Commission for doing so. Military-style guards protecting Sheik Mohamed Al-Fassi's estate at Fulmer, Buckinghamshire, provoked complaints from Fleet Street while the *Observer*'s guru Neal Ascherson thought he detected a socially significant trend. London, he concluded, was becoming a capital city in the mould of eighteenth-century Paris, 'where almost all employment depended on the needs of the Court and the thousands of privileged royal functionaries around it. It means a huge service and craft population, making clothes and cutlery, furniture and designer rugs for the rich, mending their electronics and guarding their homes.'

He had a point. The Ivor Spencer School for Butlers advertised for ex-SAS instructors to groom student butlers in the skills of protection. Jeeves, it seems, now required more than *savoir-faire*. In New York he was also expected to be skilled in martial arts, evasive driving and shooting.

Andrew Nightingale, prior to his death in a high-speed road accident in Oman, was emerging as the prototype for this new model Jeeves. Not only was he required to protect diplomats; but also diplomats' wives and other influential ladies were delighted that their security — or occasional lack of it — presented an excuse to call upon his services as a decorative, good-natured escort. The heiress to a jewellery empire, about to spend a night out at Annabelle's in London, was warned that the gems worth around £5 million which were to dangle from her ear lobes and elsewhere would require a temporary bodyguard. Surveying the talent available from KMS, she pointed unhesitatingly at Nightingale with the comment: 'I'll have that one.'

But the urge for protection did not stop at the decadent gates of Mayfair and Manhattan. In the 'workers' republic' of Liverpool, the City Council's socialist pilgrim Derek Hatton gave his name to a 150-strong, green uniformed security team employed by the council and known as 'Hatton's Army'. Meanwhile in another part of the planet, some of Nightingale's former SAS comrades were also guarding jewels: uncut stones in a dusty diamond mine in Angola where the guards themselves were at risk from political abduction by the South African-backed Unita guerrillas of Dr Jonas Savimbi.

It might seem that the ideal bodyguard would be the potential victim himself, if only the right sort of training and weaponry were available. There, alas, is the rub. In Britain the law permits only the use of minimum force in self-defence, and then only as a last resort. The self-defence philosophy implied by such a doctrine will work in practice only if the victim is not outnumbered and is as strong and bulky as his attacker, with nerves able to withstand the shock of the first assault (for the initiative and the element of surprise are with the assailant). Controlled aggression usually requires superior bodily weight if it is to succeed in practice and remain within the law. The small man or woman who happens also to be a black belt in karate cannot afford to 'pull' his kicks or punches when threatened by a larger opponent. The Catch 22 of his situation, however, is that by using such techniques without inhibition, the victim will cause such injury as to be liable to prosecution for assault himself. The law offers no clearcut way out of this dilemma. Instead, the British Home Office offers dangerously inept suggestions to women at risk concerning the defence potential of their door keys . . . or suggests that they stay off the streets.

In spite of the problems created by a legal counsel of perfection, as Western society has become richer and more envious, the 'self-defence' industry in all its forms has proliferated alongside other types of personal protection. After such preoccupations as self-awareness, aerobics and jogging, the arts of survival have been exploited as the new game in a chic flirtation with violence. Some survival games, in which young stockbrokers hunted one another around countryside estates armed with 'splat' (paint) guns, were – to put it charitably – eccentric. The author declined one insistent invitation to sponsor an 'SAS Survival' game of this sort after the organiser, a Herefordshire landowner, had solemnly explained, 'These young men are earning a hundred grand a year in the City so when they get down here, every one of them has to win a rosette!'

Other experiments were potentially more deadly. In June 1987 London newspapers published a photograph of five grim-looking women armed with pistols. These they held double-handed, in the characteristic forward crouch posture once known to the trade as the 'Grant-Taylor Method' and described by Fleet Street as 'pure Cagney and Lacey'. The women were London housewives and they had paid £150 each to learn marksmanship 'as their best means of self defence'. Their tutor, Mr Peter Eliot, a former Army and police shot, had trained more than five hundred civilians in the preceding three years in the use of firearms for self defence. One of his students, Mrs Louviena Burbage, told a reporter: 'My husband persuaded me to come. He attended one of these courses and we have a gun at home. But if my husband weren't there, I wouldn't know what to do with it. Now I'm learning.'

The Home Office reminded all concerned that anyone holding a firearm required a certificate to do so and that 'self defence is not a reason that can be taken into account when issuing a firearms certificate'. That certainly is the case, as numerous public figures whom the police agree are at risk have discovered when they seek to arm themselves. They are simply not granted the firearms certificate they seek.

Someone, somewhere, had identified a way out of the dilemma, for by 1987, 200,000 firearms certificates had been issued to people in England, Scotland and Wales, and of 60,000 licensed pistols, some 8,000 were held by citizens of London. Only a few months later, after the Hungerford massacre, did it emerge that in some areas of the country, self-styled gun 'collectors' were able to order semi-automatic Kalashnikov rifles by mail order. Until then, the revolution in gun ownership in Britain had been both stealthy and successful.

Another of Mr Eliot's students, Vanessa Walker, a bank worker living in a growingly violent area of South London, explained that she wanted to learn to use her gun in anger because 'I wanted to know how I could cope if, say, some maniac came crashing into my home.' Hungerford, unhappily, demonstrated that some maniacs, disguised as 'collectors', were already in a position to out-gun her with weapons which, like her own, were legally licensed.

The growing danger was not lost upon the Police Federation, whose spokesman Leslie Curtis observed in a speech soon after the massacre:

It is a nonsense that the police can and will refuse to allow a citizen to keep a revolver for home security, but he can go out and buy a shotgun for the same purpose. Only this week, the Chief Constable of Warwickshire announced that ten shotgun thefts had been reported to the police in that county in ten days. Multiply this experience over the country, and bear in mind that unless the weapon is in current use and of value, its theft is unlikely to be reported . . .

What about the increasing sophistication and deadly fire power of so-called shotguns which are being openly sold in gun shops and through mail order? One example is the Franchi STAS 12, which fires eleven shells before reloading, is semi-automatic and can empty its magazine within a dozen seconds . . .

What we may be witnessing is a massive expansion of the gun trade in Britain . . . If something is not done now, we will have to live with the consequences, and some will have to die with the consequences.

There is one weapon which is more readily licensed than a firearm, and which kills seventeen people in Britain every day. This is the automobile. In spite of the fact that successive VIP chauffeurs, from Princess Anne's to General Kroesen's, could have used their limousines as weapons when trapped in a terrorist or kidnap ambush, yet did nothing of the kind, an increasing though still select number of security firms now teach the arts of using your car to stay alive.

A *Guardian* writer, Eithne Power, attended a course in protective driving organised by the Talisman Chauffeur Agency run by one Leslie Cabrera, 'ex-policeman, body-guard and chauffeur' and his ex-service buddy Ralph Lucas. Like others in the same line of business, Talisman trains its people partly at North Weald Airport, whose runways are scorched with the marks of many car tyres as they spin at speed into barely controlled 180-degree turns.

As well as the basic evasive routines such as the handbrake turn, Talisman's two-day, £230 course included noise. As Ms Power described it:

'"Always expect the worst to happen," bawls Leslie Cabrera, leaping towards Yvonne's old banger and proceeding to hammer on the roof with what looks like half a tree trunk. Yvonne goes from bright red to chalky white as she struggles to make a getaway: this isn't easy with the rain of blows on the roof and the terrible face of Ralph suddenly surfacing at the passenger window.

'"Don't flood your engine," bawls Mr Cabrera. "It's conked out," Yvonne bawls back. "Then START it," bellows Mr Cabrera. "Keep calm," he adds, thundering away on the roof.'

The author took part in a slightly longer and more expensive course run by the Royal Military Police bodyguard veterans of Winguard International, run from a suite of nondescript offices in Chiswick. Winguard teaches a whole package of mobile security, which starts sooner than the students, most of them professional chauffeurs, expect. During the first training session, devoted to the art of detecting whether one is under hostile surveillance, they are asked, 'To your knowledge, have you ever been watched or followed?'

The universal answer is 'No.'

Winguard's chief instructor, ex RSM 'Chick' Harding, then passes round photographs of the students themselves, at work the previous week.

'Now, John, here you are at No. 3 Terminal at Heathrow, in your chauffeur's uniform, cap under your arm, waiting for the boss. Only a fairly important traveller would have his own chauffeur waiting for him. And then you drove out along the M4, going west . . .'

Practical lessons in surveillance and counter-surveillance follow in which the student driver delivers a verbal commentary while he is driving on what he sees fore and aft, side-to-side and even above him as potential areas of threat. During a prolonged drive in traffic in and out of London, it becomes apparent that the image of one vehicle recurs in the mirror, however tortuous the route.

'Right, you think you are under surveillance. What are you going to do about it?' asks Harding.

'For a start, a 360-degree turn at the next road island I come to,' the student replies. 'If that vehicle is still behind me after that I reckon he's hostile. I might have to tell the boss to get ready for a bump or two . . . Even tell him to lie down.'

Back in the classroom we study several ways to attach an Improvised Explosive Device to the boss's car. More important, how to detect the presence of a lethal booby trap. Sometimes the most innocuous-seeming object, such as a clothes peg under one of the car wheels, is an explosive initiator, the first contact in a chain of events which leaves the car's occupants dead or maimed for life. Later, as we inspect a lovingly armed limousine at North Weald, Harding – an old hand in the counter-terrorist game – says in passing, 'Don't forget the one under the passenger's head rest. It was a favourite of one of Castro's teams because it decapitated the target.'

At North Weald we change the wheels of an R-registered, two-litre Granada to fit tyres which have seen better days. Like most security lessons, this one starts with a change of perception. It seems that most drivers never test their cars to the full performance 'envelope', well, not deliberately. Even without special anti-roll bars, the average family car can be turned radically, at speed, while remaining approximately horizontal. What happens if this is put to the test in the right environment (i.e. an unused airfield) is that the driver and passengers, including some instructors, are rapidly rendered car-sick.

After throwing up into the weeds at the side of the

runway, everyone resumes a programme of snaky turns through a chicane of obstacles, forwards and backwards. It is the fast reverse, with some evasive turns added to it, which boggles most eyes and churns stomachs.

The 180-degree turns are inaugurated by flicking the steering wheel rapidly after winding up some speed in reverse gear, and then driving off at speed in forward gear without touching the brakes. The hand-brake turn, sometimes known as the 'bootlegger', dispenses with the initial burst in reverse. From a forward speed of around thirty mph, the driver simply hauls vigorously on his hand brake while sweeping the steering wheel in an aggressive right-hand turn. The effect is dramatic. The hand brake locks the rear wheels and the spin of the forward wheels does the rest. All that is now required, if the car is still on the road, is to drop the hand brake and accelerate away. The technique is hard on tyres, and an automatic gear box is recommended for a smooth – well, fairly smooth – transition to the great leap forward that completes the manoeuvre. And, of course, for the driver who sincerely wishes to escape, an in-car sick bag is also recommended.

Winguard rounds off its training with a period of specialised tuition in simulated snow, ice and other skid training by using a mobile platform under the car, capable of tilting one, two or all four wheels off the ground. Its courses are underpinned by the continuous experience gleaned from running a parallel service which provides bodyguards for those who can afford expert protection in Britain and overseas.

Like similar organisations, Winguard has a small nucleus of full-time staffers, most of them ex-RMP soldiers who have served together in uniform for many years, and a computerised list of freelance ex-service people who have almost invariably trained with one of Britain's special force teams, usually the SAS, Paras or Royal Marine Commando.

The best practitioners will admit, however, that the world of private security is not controlled by specific legislation, and this means that anyone, irrespective of his experience, training, psychological condition or criminal record, is at liberty to start his own protection agency. One of the ironies of the situation is that by generating a sufficient degree of violence, the criminal can set in motion a cycle of events in which that violence spawns a demand for heavier protection, which generates more violence to overcome the protection. It is a cycle which the French and German governments have tried to break, with little success so far, by offering amnesty to political terrorists.

The State of Florida, one of the most violent states of the Union, has moved in the other direction by proposing a new package of gun laws permitting virtually anyone to carry a gun openly in the street as a response to violent and armed criminals. For those of more modest lifestyle, it was proposed to issue permits for concealed weapons on payment of $149 and a short training course in weapon handling. As one opponent of this measure, State Congressman Michael Friedman, observed: 'People are wanting to arm themselves, live in big buildings that isolate them from their community, with security guards. You are moving potentially into a period where people [who can afford it] will have personal security guards, roping off "islands", and the rest of us will have to suffer what is left.'

Congressman Friedman might have added that the growing fashion among urban Americans for arming themselves for their own defence exacts a horrifying price. During the 1980s, more than 25 million Americans kept loaded guns at home to deal with intruders, handy, loaded and unlocked. In 1984 more than 1,600 people – 300 of them under the age of fifteen – were accidentally killed by these domestic armouries. Many more were grievously injured. During the 1987 Christmas holiday period in a single suburb of

Houston, Texas, six small boys were shot. Three of them died; one lost his sight.

Among the twelve- to fifteen-year-old group, non-accidental gunshot injuries, including fatalities, totalled 27,000 in 1985. In 1988, *The Economist* was able to report: 'Fists and even knives [among school children] are passé. A judge in Baltimore has found that at one high school in the city, nearly half the boys admit to having carried a gun once . . . sixty per cent know someone who has been shot, intimidated or robbed at gunpoint in school.'

Clearly, the use of firearms – as any good bodyguard knows – is not a business for amateurs and assuredly not for children of any age. What, then, of the 'professional'? In 1984, opening the British Security Industry Association's new headquarters, the Home Secretary, Douglas Hurd, rejected proposals to license security companies in order to 'keep out the cowboys'. True, the American experience has not been replicated so far in Britain and the private security guards allowed to go armed are still, for the most part, licensed to 'carry' only while guarding large quantities of cash. But it should be noted that the plan to license guards as well as firearms came from the chairman and managing director of Group 4 Securitas, Mr Jorge Philip-Sorensen. He reminded the government that even to run an employment agency, he would require official authority.

By 1987 the government had moved towards a system of licensing security guards in just one part of the UK. The exception, as usual, was the province of Northern Ireland, where some security agencies had been set up as front organisations for (mainly republican) paramilitary groups. These 'security guards', operating on building sites as well as offering their own versions of close protection, were in reality bagmen, collecting protection funds for even more suspect groups. The penetration of public housing projects and the siphoning off of tens of thousands of pounds of taxpayers' money had long been a scandal, and this area, at least, could be dealt with by the use of emergency laws of a kind which did not apply to the rest of the United Kingdom. Under the Emergency Provisions Act 1987, anyone offering a private security service was required to apply for a government permit. The effect of the law was dramatic. A majority of the fifty-plus security companies running a legitimate business (most of them guarding property) applied for the necessary permits and got them. A handful of others, whose bagmen were known to the RUC Special Branch, wound up the business and melted away. In becoming suspected fronts for terrorism, this end of the private protection business had come full circle, providing the 'answer' to a threat which it also helped to promote.

PART V
Assassins

CHAPTER 14

John and Yoko and the Lone Crank who Thought He Was John

John Lennon and Yoko Ono got home just before eleven o'clock on a mild December night in 1980. They had been at a recording studio, working on a number written by Yoko. Home was one of several apartments they owned in a guarded luxury block known as the Dakota Building overlooking Manhattan's Central Park from the West Side, downtown from Columbia University and Harlem. Other occupants included Leonard Bernstein and Lauren Bacall.

The building, erected in 1884, expressed solid confidence in spite of the ironic name which implied it was a long way from anywhere fashionable. The couple could have driven their limousine past their friendly gatekeeper, Jay Hastings, and on through the protective iron gates and up the drive to the sanctuary of an echoing courtyard. Instead, they parked on the street knowing that the faithful knot of fans described as 'Dakota Groupies' would be hanging around as usual.

One of these was Mark David Chapman, a fleshy young man in his mid-twenties who had been on the scene for three days with pilgrim piety. A few hours earlier, John Lennon had autographed his album. Chapman continued to wait. While he did so, a down-and-out panhandled him for money. Chapman, to the surprise of gatekeeper Hastings as well as the recipient, handed over ten dollars. Chapman's next gesture would be even more memorable.

As Lennon stepped out of the car holding a tape of Yoko Ono's song, Chapman drew a .38 revolver from his pocket and began shooting. By seven minutes past eleven, Lennon was dead in the local hospital to which he had been taken, bleeding massively from seven wounds, in a police car. When more police arrived, eyes everywhere, hands on holsters, Chapman was still standing outside the Dakota Building. He was rooted to the spot, entirely absorbed in the book he had been carrying for days. This was J. D. Salinger's novel *The Catcher in the Rye*.

Yoko Ono told a friendly journalist in the nightmare days that followed the killing, 'People say there is something wrong with New York, that it's sick. But John loved New York. He'd be the first to say it wasn't New York's fault. There can be one crank anywhere.'

The Lone Crank theory is one to which many people at risk turn as a means of coming to terms with the brutal arbitrariness of sudden, violent death. The political assassin can be – and often is – anticipated and intercepted by security teams who have read the runes correctly before the trigger is squeezed. The criminal contract killer, even in a violent society, is still a very rare beast indeed and, in any case, he will not wish to wait about speculatively on the off-chance that his target will be exposed. As a professional, he will seek to avoid unnecessary exposure himself but, like the political killer, he will probably be obliged to make a reconnaissance which proper counter-surveillance should pick up.

The crank, by contrast, is held to be random, unpredictable and therefore unstoppable. Furthermore, because he is invincible, those close to the victim are not obliged to torture themselves with self-accusatory guilt:

'If only I had/we had done things some other way . . .' There can be one crank anywhere.

This might be so. Yet there are hints, splinters of evidence – no more – to suggest that the 'random' crank is anything but random; that he is highly selective in his choice of victim. When the crank-assassin selects and pursues his quarry and the quarry implicitly courts the pursuit by meeting the assassin half way (as Queen Victoria, among others, did from time to time) then the result will be fatal to the target unless luck, such as a malfunctioning weapon, intervenes. Modern handguns, when properly maintained and loaded with the correct ammunition, tend not to misfire.

The theory that an implicit relationship exists between assassin and victim has been guessed at by rueful body-guards as they observe the behaviour of people in their care, and even written about by some academic experts. Dr David Rothstein, a consultant to the Warren Commission which investigated the killing of President Jack Kennedy, has observed that 'There are notable similarities between leaders and assassins or potential assassins.' One of these is an overwhelming desire to score, to leave a mark on the world.

After examining forty people who had been detained for making threats against an American president, Rothstein concluded that what made the assassin essentially different from the leader/victim was 'an intense need to accomplish success in one drastic step': a single act to set the world to rights rather than a patient, measured pursuit of a goal by stages.

No democracy's self-confidence has been more damaged by assassination than that of the USA. Three rifle bullets one afternoon in Dallas shattered Camelot. So it is not surprising that it is American scientists who have sought a predictive device of some sort to identify the lone assassin as a type. There is no shortage, either, of research material in gun-happy America where the president's bodyguard, the Secret Service, has to check around twenty possible assassins, all legally armed, every day. The phrase 'celebrity killer' is used by American specialists such as Gavin De-becker to describe the 4,000 people 'under assessment' in 1988 as personalities likely to kill a public figure as a means of self-aggrandisement.

Dr Richard M. Restak, a neurologist who studied the problem, acknowledged the practical difficulties of such identification before the deed, not least – as he observed in *Science Digest* in December 1981 – because 'few assassins commit violent acts prior to their assassination attempt'.

In spite of that, efforts by such bodies as the Institute of Medicine of the National Academy of Sciences has produced a composite picture of the American assassin which fits most of those who have killed or tried to kill the country's political leaders. Three characteristics were noted in most of them. They were 'loners', solitary people unable to sustain stable relationships with others. They were also chronic drifters, moving on as compulsively as the Flying Dutchman. And they compensated for their failure to join the human race by what Restak describes as 'a sense of grandiosity'. As John Lennon's murderer, Mark Chapman, put it, 'The Beatles changed the world and I changed them.'

This misplaced sense of destiny – reflecting a belief in their karma, a sense of having been 'chosen' for some special mission in life – was similar to the self-confidence of the public figures who became their targets. It was, Restak asserted, 'combined with a desire for fame, an air of fatalism, a need to play out their personal feelings and motives on a grand public scale in the world and an utter disregard for their own health, safety and comfort.'

In the potential assassin, unlike the public figure who becomes his victim, the sense of identity is incomplete and tends to blend with 'underlying rage at some aspects of the "system"'. The distinguished US psychiatrist Edwin Weinstein observed that potential assassins used the language of politics or other institutions to give them a sense of identity they would not have otherwise.

Lennon's killer, Chapman, matched most of the criteria of lethality defined by American science. Restak comments:

'To such a person, assassination serves as a vehicle for self-definition. Unsure of who he is, the assassin attempts to unite himself with a powerful figure with whom he can identify, at least in fantasy.'

Much of his life, Chapman was hurt by the world's cynicism and wanted to 'do good'. He became a born-again Christian. In a successful artist such as Lennon, the search for identity is called evolution. Lacking talent, as in Chapman's case, the behaviour is said to be unstable.

Chapman went further in his attempts to model himself on Lennon. He played a guitar and married a Japanese-American wife older than himself. She became the bread-winner while he stayed home. He shared Lennon's sense of having been deserted, for both men were the offspring of mothers who left home.

In Chapman's case, his search for purpose led him to conclude that he had to remove the 'phoneys' from the world, including, if need be, himself. He had signed himself 'John Lennon' long before Lennon signed his autograph book. He had also read, apparently, an *Esquire* magazine article of November 1980 whose author had searched for Lennon, 'the conscience of an age', but found only 'a forty-year-old businessman' propelled by lawyers paid to 'squeeze him through tax loopholes'. Lennon, in other words, was a phoney.

Chapman/Lennon, in his self-hating mission to remove the phoney closest to himself, wandered down memory lane from Atlanta to Honolulu and on up to New York with only his gun (the American adult male's substitute for a comfort blanket) and his copy of *The Catcher in the Rye* – an essay about the horrors of adult insincerity and lost childhood innocence – for company. He was a pathetic figure, somewhat like Lennon during the ex-Beatle's eighteen-month drugs binge after the first break-up with Yoko Ono.

'The assassin or would-be assassin,' Dr Rothstein noted, 'unconsciously selects a victim who represents what he himself wants to be but cannot. He wants to be a person who can receive attention and control events – in other words to be like the man he wishes to kill.'

Chapman confided after his arrest that Lennon was a 'phoney' and that he didn't like the way the musician had autographed his record album earlier that day.

'Having done his deed, however, Chapman sat quietly at his arraignment [first legal hearing] reading his favourite book, *The Catcher in the Rye*. Such behaviour is entirely reasonable, according to the logic of the modern-day assassin: rage has been spent, an identity forged, at least temporarily.'

The psychological profile of an assassin selected by government for military operations differs radically from this model. In 1975, the British writer Peter Watson, a psychotherapist as well as a journalist, interviewed for the *Sunday Times* and his own book *War on the Mind*, an American doctor who had been involved in reducing the stress which faced special forces soldiers chosen for assassination missions. The doctor, noted Watson, was referring to 'two types of combat readiness unit: the ordinary commando unit and also to naval men inserted into embassies abroad under cover ready to kill . . . US naval psychologists specially selected men for these commando tasks from submarine crews, paratroops and some were convicted murderers from military prisons.' (Why this should be a Navy operation rather than a Special Forces programme was not explained.)

Selection was based upon those who had good combat records because 'studies of those given awards for valour in battle have shown that the best killers are men with "passive aggressive" personalities. They are people with a lot of drive, though they are well disciplined and do not appear nervous, who periodically experience bursts of explosive energy when they can literally kill without remorse.'

These criteria come interestingly close to the British definition of the ideal military bodyguard as a person capable of 'controlled aggression'.

Watson's source – whose testimony was unconvincingly denied by the Pentagon – said that the potential assassins (the 'right stuff', as it were) were then given further training in reducing the stress of killing. 'The men selected are taken for training to the Navy's hospital in Naples or to the Neuropsychiatric Laboratory in San Diego, California. The men are taught to shoot but also given a special type of "Clockwork Orange" training to quell any qualms they may have had about killing.

'It works like this. The men are shown a series of gruesome films, which get progressively more horrific. The trainee is forced to watch by having his head bolted in a clamp so he cannot turn away, and a special device keeps his eyelids open. One of the first films shows an African youth being crudely circumcised by fellow members of his tribe. No anaesthetic is used and the knife is obviously blunt. When the film is over the trainee is asked irrelevant questions such as "What was the motif on the handle of the knife?" or "How many people were holding the youth down?"'

Assassination is an art which, once taught, is difficult to control even if in time of national peril it is a necessary one. The United States has had a peculiarly extensive experience of losing or nearly losing its political leaders through assassination. The US is an urban, democratic society in which are to be found many lonely, armed people. Yet in many respects it is close to other democratic societies where firearms are less accessible. (The closest European parallel might be Ireland, where tolerance of a gun culture is also traditional.) For all these reasons, and because the assassin is the bodyguard's ultimate *raison d'être*, the American experience deserves some attention in any study of close protection.

Most attempts against US presidents (and at least eleven have come under attack) have been launched by the inadequate personalities described by Restak and others. There is a special reason for this. As a target for an assassin, a US president enjoys, if that is the word, a higher news value than even the Pope. (See, for example, *Violence as Communication* by Alex P. Schmid and Janny de Graaf.)

The following presidents have been targets for lone psychopaths responding to some preordained sense of 'mission', rather than trigger men working objectively for political ends:

Andrew Jackson: seventh president, notoriously liberal in his use of the spittoon, attacked in 1835 by Richard Lawrence, who believed he was King Richard III of England, and that the Bank of the United States owed him a million dollars. Lawrence, with a poor sense of historical identity, armed himself with two cap-and-ball pistols which both misfired, the first from sixteen feet and the second at point-blank range, just before the President battered him unconscious with a walking stick.

James Abram Garfield: shot in the back by Charles Guiteau while waiting for a train in 1881 and *William McKinley*, from the front at a public exhibition in 1901 by Leon F. Czolgosz. Both assassins were religious fanatics who thought they were doing 'God's work'.

Theodore Roosevelt, 1912: the night McKinley died, a man named John Schrank had a dream. He saw McKinley rise from his coffin to accuse Vice-President Roosevelt of engineering the crime. The dream recurred for ten years while Schrank wandered the US until, in 1912, he made his attempt. A fifty-page manuscript in Roosevelt's pocket broke the bullet's impact and he suffered only a broken rib.

Franklin Roosevelt, 1933: as President-elect speaking in Miami where Joseph Zangara fired five shots at him, his aim disturbed by a woman bystander. He killed Anton Cermak, the Mayor of Chicago, instead. An anarchist, Zangara had a mission to wipe out all leaders.

Richard Nixon, 1972: followed down the election trail by Arthur Bremer, who, disheartened by the President's security screen, turned his attention and his gun upon another presidential candidate, Governor George Wallace of Alabama.

Gerald Ford, September 1975: a victim of two separate attempts to shoot him, both by women. The first assailant was Lynette Fromme, a follower of mass murderer and hypnotist Charles Manson (to publicise the Manson credo); the second, Sally Moore, a discarded FBI informant (to 'be taken seriously').

Ronald Reagan, 1981: shot and wounded by John Hinkley to impress a young actress, Jodie Foster. She knew nothing of Hinkley until the shooting, a state of affairs she did not wish to change after the event. A week after Hinkley had wounded Reagan, another young man, seeking attention from the same lady, was intercepted before he could finish what Hinkley had started. Both men were fantasists.

What all the assassins had in common was a more or less publicised intention to kill their quarry, either by making threats or by stalking the target politician. A rational, politically-motivated assassin would not, normally, seek to draw attention to himself. The irrational assassin, by contrast, craves attention.

Sally Moore, one of the women who tried to kill Ford, was recruited by the Federal Bureau of Investigation as an informer on her comrades in radical movements, then changed sides, blew her cover and was trusted by no one. She was now aged forty-five, divorced and a mother of four children. She telephoned the San Francisco police shortly before Ford visited the city, hinting at her intention to 'test the system'. Next morning she was arrested and a .44-calibre revolver was taken from her. She was charged with a misdemeanour, that of carrying a concealed weapon.

A city police lieutenant telephoned the Secret Service to ask if they wanted Moore to be kept in custody. The Secret Service said this would not be necessary. However, one of their men called on her, but set her free without attempting to keep watch on her. Next day she telephoned the three security agencies concerned with the Ford visit – the Secret Service, the FBI and the San Francisco police – but was not particularly coherent. She then drove twenty miles to buy a .38 revolver from a man who had supplied her with firearms before.

An official, confidential report records what happened next.

She returned to San Francisco and by 11.39 hours she was on the street in front of the St Francis Hotel. President Ford had entered the hotel at 11.25 hours. Moore remained on the street until the President came out at 15.29 hours and approached his car.

As the President came out, he acknowledged the clapping and cheers of the people and stopped. Moore, from 23 ft, took her revolver out of her purse, raised it, took careful aim and fired. As she fired, a spectator deflected her arm and the bullet struck the wall about 5½ ft above the ground and some 5 ft to the left of the President. Moore was immediately rushed and taken prisoner.

During the initial interrogation phase she made many irrational and disjointed statements, none of which clearly gave any reason for her attack on President Ford. It is surmised that due to her being rejected by the FBI and radical groups, she was seeking a means of gaining their respect and acceptance. She said, 'I did not want to kill somebody, but there comes a point when the only way you can make a statement is to pick up a gun. I was driven to act.'

Even two of the supposedly rational, politically motivated assassins – John Wilkes Booth and Lee Harvey Oswald – had given some sort of advance warning before one of them murdered Lincoln in 1865 and the other John F. Kennedy in 1963. Such stalkers follow their victims for months or years in advance over thousands of miles. Booth spent much time at Ford's Theatre, where he would kill Lincoln, asking about security and escape routes; Guiteau loitered near the White House. Bremer trailed Nixon to Canada but could not get close enough because of 'damn demonstrators' who provoked a security scare round the President. In Lauran Paine's study, *The Assassins*, the 21-year-old Bremer is quoted:

'Security was beefed up because of these stupid, dirty rats. A woman gave me an anti-war-anti-Nixon leaflet. I gave it back politely. What could I say to her? "You stupid bitch stop this useless accomplish-nothing form of protest, let the security slacken and I'll show you something really effective"?'

Schrank followed Ted Roosevelt for 2,000 miles. Queen Victoria came to know the face in the crowd of her assailant Pate long before he struck. The man who killed Lennon waited for three days, and much of the night, outside Lennon's home. Such people should not pass unnoticed by any normally alert protection officer, but most other people are not on the watch for assassins. The intruder into the Queen's bedroom, Michael Fagan, was able to stroll past domestic staff in the early morning without arousing their suspicion.

There are other clues to the behaviour of the crank killer which a well-tuned psycho-security system might identify. A passion for publicity does not only stimulate the assassin's exhibitionism before the deed. It virtually guarantees that he will perform it in the full glare of publicity. Most of the eleven presidential assassinations and attempted assassinations discussed in this study occurred during high-profile, often ceremonial occasions.

One of these – Lincoln's murder – was actually carried out by an actor, in a crowded theatre. After he had shot the President in a private box he leapt to the stage (breaking a leg on the way) to declaim his carefully rehearsed curtain line, 'Sic semper tyrannus!' ('So die all tyrants!')

The slaughter of a head of state on a public, ceremonial occasion such as a parade also has a ritual quality which invests it with symbolic importance. The assault hijacks the ceremonial lustre of the occasion if not its legitimacy. (Among many such cases, see those of Archduke Ferdinand in a state procession at Sarajevo in 1914 or the murder of President Anwar Sadat of Egypt on his reviewing stand in 1981. Performed publicly as part of a ceremony, such murders are sometimes perceived as an exercise in legitimate tyrannicide rather than straight political murder.)

For the protection team, formal public appearances can be assumed to be times of danger not only because they present an assassin with an opportunity but because they generate an atmosphere which excites the lone psychopath, provoking him to do it. But there are other catalysts, the most potent of which is the urge to copy, or to go one better than the last assassin.

The toxin lies in the publicity. Martin Luther King, the personification of decent Black protest on the civil rights issue, was murdered in Memphis in April 1968. One week later a charismatic leader of student protest in Europe, Rudi Dutschke, was shot in the head by a right-wing fanatic named Erwin Bachman. Bachman admitted that he had been 'inspired' by what happened at Memphis.

Two attempts to kill Ford within seventeen days are held by Schmid and de Graaf (ibid.) to be linked by television coverage. The publicity given to both attempts produced a flood of threats to assassinate Ford, according to the Secret Service. Psychiatrists had even suggested that the presence of television cameras might serve as a stimulus for such deeds.

The copycat effect of television, powerful as it is, can be generated (though only among the literate) by the printed word. Lennon's killer, Chapman, had been reading *Esquire* as well as *The Catcher in the Rye*. Shortly before he shot and wounded President Reagan, John Hinkley was in the crowd that gathered outside the Dakota Building to mourn Lennon and he, too, now carried his copy of *The Catcher in the Rye*. Leon Czolgosz was carrying a Hearst newspaper attacking President McKinley when he was seized. The newspaper observed, 'If bad institutions and bad men can be got rid of only by killing them, the killing must be done.'

For such self-appointed instruments of fate the act bestows not only a glow of moral justification and the power to right a great 'wrong', but also fame at a stroke. 'They can gas me but I am famous,' the Jordanian assassin of JFK's brother, Attorney-General Robert Kennedy, declared after his arrest. 'I have achieved in one day what it took Robert Kennedy all his life to do.'

Thus the voice of the seeker-after-glory who would pretend to switch identities with a more complete human being. In his pocket, completing the predictability, Sirhan Sirhan carried a newspaper article fiercely critical of the Attorney-General. Such cranks can be intercepted and often are. High technology matters less than common sense and a nose on the bodyguard's part for trouble round the next corner. Yet one of the special problems of this age is that the ubiquitous quality of worldwide television means that the next corner approaches at ever increasing speed and frequency. It is an unfortunate and symbolic coincidence, perhaps, that instant live satellite transmission around the globe was an innovation of that deadly year of 1968.

Yet it is still true that timely intervention ultimately depends upon a willingness to act and to risk making mistakes. Edwin Woodhall, when he was personal detective to King George V, observed early in the King's reign that one of his subjects was writing obsessively to the sovereign about a scheme to change the course of the River Thames. The man was watched and seen to join a crowd waiting to see the King and Queen leave London from Victoria Station. Woodhall found his suspect in an ideal position outside the entrance to the station:

> If he was crazed, he could do almost anything . . . With the aid of a uniformed inspector we worked our way, inch by inch, to where he stood, one at each side of the suspect without his being any the wiser . . . and as the royal car was almost abreast of us I grabbed my neighbour's arm. The effect was instantaneous. He whipped round and as he did so, the King went by . . . Later, when the royal train was gone, I explained to the man that we were police detectives and that the reason I had called his attention . . . was because I had seen a man trying to pick his pockets . . . Some few days later, the man went violently insane and ended his life by throwing himself in front of an express train near Croydon Junction.

The art of spotting trouble in a crowded, public situation just before the damage is done is summed up by the bodyguards' catch-phrase, 'Watch the hands!' Statesmen and their bodyguards who have realised too late that one of the hands reaching out of the crowd holds a deadly weapon, are numerous. In 1968, Robert Kennedy was being escorted away from a successful political meeting – a tilt towards the Democratic Party nomination for president – by his personal bodyguard, plus some enthusiastic amateur guardians including an Olympic decathlon champion and a 300-pound footballer. As they took a short cut through the hotel kitchen, one of the guards 'saw a hand sticking out of the crowd between two cameramen, and the hand was holding a gun . . .' (Paine, op. cit.)

The rational assassins – or those, at any rate, who are not certifiably mad – usually operate as part of a conspiracy involving others. The motive might be criminal, as in some of the classic Mafia murders in Italy, or political. The 'control group' of US presidents selected for analysis here includes just two or three attempts out of a total of eleven which seem to be rationally planned and political in origin even if they were clumsy in practice. (Their targets were Abraham Lincoln, Harry Truman and John F. Kennedy.) This means that the rest, the vast majority, were the work of the crank. Such a high proportion of armed and unstable people may reflect the condition of America rather than a worldwide pattern of assassination. The two groups, the 'mad' and the 'sane', also tend to differ in the techniques of murder they employ.

The lone crank, as we have seen, uses almost without exception, a revolver or self-loading ('automatic') pistol. To be effective he must come close to his victim. Political conspirators are more likely to use a rifle, time bomb or other weapon which keeps them at a distance from disclosure and retribution. The two-man Puerto Rican team which in 1950 tried to shoot its way into the Truman residence, past armed guards, carried pistols and so did Lincoln's killer, Booth. But Lee Harvey Oswald, almost certainly acting with others whose identities have not been disclosed, was armed with a rifle to pick off his man from a motorcade

280 feet away moving at more than twenty mph. The man who killed the civil rights spokesman Martin Luther King also used a rifle.

Outside America, where pistolphilia is less pronounced, the style of 'sane' assassination seems to be limited only by human ingenuity, patience and nerve. Charles IX of France, surrounded by guards, was poisoned in 1574 by a fine, gelatinous substance attached to the pages of his favourite book. One of the King's little habits was to wet his fingers with his tongue to make it easier to turn the pages. By poisoning the book, the assassin poisoned the King.

According to an unpublished US government study, 'a group wanted to assassinate the head of government in Bulgaria in 1925. To accomplish this and overcome security, they first assassinated a prominent government official whose death would require a state funeral. The church in which it was to be held was then loaded with explosives and during the funeral service, these were detonated, collapsing the roof on the assembly. In order to kill one man, a total of over 200 people were killed.'

A Californian lawyer who was the target of a dissident political group was killed by a rattlesnake planted in his mail box. When the lawyer returned home and reached into the box for his letters, the snake bit him.

In Sweden, a public official was attacked by a model aircraft loaded with explosives, copying a James Bond idea, while in 1972, King Hassan II of Morocco (like President Diem of South Vietnam in 1962) came near to death after an attack on his palace by his own air force.

Such schemes come close to self-parody and edge towards the world of Woody Allen: 'In 1921, Thomas (The Butcher) Covello and Ciro (The Tailor) Santucci attempted to organise disparate ethnic groups of the underworld and thus take over Chicago. This was foiled when Albert (The Logical Positivist) Corillo assassinated Kid Lipsky by locking him

in a closet and sucking all the air out through a straw . . .'
(*Getting Even*, 1971).

The basic elements of assassination during this century
– one in which the number of political leaders murdered
for political reasons runs into four or five figures – have
not changed much. The killing zone is still what it was,
within fifteen feet of the victim. The weapons most favoured
are still small arms and side arms, bombs, knives, swords
and blunt instruments. The lone assassin still requires a
public, close-quarter killing to ensure he is credited with
his achievement.

The innovations of radio and television have opened up
an opportunity for leaders at risk to communicate from the
safety of an armoured, underground studio. Not for nothing
do such dictators as Chile's President Pinochet describe
home as 'El Bunker'.

What does vary, critically, is the political situation which
creates the momentum for assassination in the first place.
Disintegration of the old regime (France during the Terror
of the 1790s; the Middle East after Britain's withdrawal
from Palestine in 1948; post-colonial Africa in the 1960s)
is usually a signal to the Old Guard that its days are
numbered; a time of harvest for the assassin.

Yet in a democracy, the politician's credibility is seen to
depend upon the personal, public appearance. Even in
Communist states there is unhealthy speculation about any
leader who is not seen in the flesh for a few weeks, however
innocent the reason. As a result, exposure to possibly fatal
risk has given the politician engaged in the small change of
a public appearance a lustre akin to that of the gladiator in
the Colosseum. Implicit in most such appearances, thinly
camouflaged by the prattle and ceremonial, is the nagging
question of whether the chosen one will walk or ride
away intact, or be carried off to the nearest resuscitation
machine.

The role of the bodyguard, when the principal permits this to be discharged, can make a huge difference between life and death. The most spectacular assassinations – i.e. those which do have a material political outcome – seem to be accompanied by startling and often unexplained failures by the protection team. It is a familiar problem. Julius Caesar had a dual bodyguard drawn from two cultures, as well as one which was numerous. (His native Romans, not always to be trusted, were rivalled by his German 'Barbarians'.)

Of the ten attacks on US presidents after Jackson defended himself so robustly in 1835, only three were politically motivated. The first of this series was the tragic but, given his fatalistic determination to shake off the protection he needed desperately in the bitter last days of the Civil War, inevitable death of Abraham Lincoln. The South was all but beaten and an end to legal slavery was in sight but the President's war cabinet, and his generals, knew that he was a marked man. His friend and Marshal of Washington, DC, Ward Hill Lamon, slept outside Lincoln's door with pistols and bowie knives under his blankets when Lincoln was re-elected President towards the end of the war in 1864.

In a biography of the President, Professor S. B. Oates describes how 'Lamon . . . pleaded with [Lincoln] to be careful. "You must understand, Mr President, that You Are In Danger . . . Your life is sought after and will be taken unless you and your friends are cautious; for you have many enemies within our lines."'

Lincoln dismissed Lamon's fears as those of someone who meant well but was 'monomaniac on the subject of my safety'. Lamon was not an old woman. He was a former attorney whose reputation for shrewdness and sense of politics was equalled only by his coarse performances as bar room cheer leader and brawler. It was, on the contrary,

Lincoln who was obsessive in his fatalism and determination to live without close protection.

In 1861, while the war was at its height, 'mounted guards and infantry were detailed to protect the White House' Oates (op. cit.) recounts, but 'Lincoln dismissed them because they made him feel like an emperor . . . He grudgingly consented to the cavalry escort for his carriage rides even though they made such a racket with their jingling spurs and clanging sabers that he and his companions could scarcely hear one another. The story goes that Lincoln liked to prod his coachman to try to outrun the cavalry – the President's carriage careering down dusty roads, the flustered soldiers trying in vain to catch him.'

Whenever the subject of his safety was raised, Lincoln would shrug.

'I long ago made up my mind that if anybody wants to kill me, he will do it. If I wore a shirt of mail and kept myself surrounded by a bodyguard, it would be all the same. There are a thousand ways of getting at a man if it is desired that he should be killed . . . As to crazy folks, I must take my chances.'

In March 1864, after his re-election, Lincoln's inauguration day as President approached and whispers of assassination gusted around Washington. The War Secretary, Edwin Stanton, increased the presidential guard as Lincoln followed the traditional road towards the Capitol, where he would be sworn in. It might have been the setting for another, more antique assassination, described by John Masefield, an English poet not yet born:

> Beware of the Court, of the palace stair,
> Of the downcast friend who speaks so fair,
> Keep from the Senate, for Death is going
> On many men's feet to meet you there.

Watching from a vantage point overlooking the proceedings was an actor and Confederate fanatic, John Wilkes Booth.

During the following days, the rumours did not diminish. As the war drew to its close, the American capital was in a state of unfocused excitement, a place haunted by fugitives of every kind including deserters from both sides. Stanton, observes Oates, 'had done everything he could think of to guard the President; he'd ordered a company of Pennsylvania troops to encamp on the White House lawn . . . The Washington police chief . . . had detailed four plain clothesmen – among them Thomas Pendel and William Crook, both excellent lawmen – to serve as Lincoln's personal bodyguards.' Lincoln was surrounded by detectives at big public events, and escorted by soldiers on his nightly walks to and from the War Department.

During early April the President – though still shrugging off security whenever he could – started to suffer from a long and recurrent nightmare. At the climax of this dream he saw his own corpse stretched on a bier, guarded by soldiers. On 9 April the Confederate Army of Northern Virginia, commanded by General Robert E. Lee, surrendered at Appomattox Courthouse, and the next day Washington shuddered under a celebratory clamour of artillery guns and chanting church bells.

Easter approached. On a freezing, foggy Good Friday evening, 14 April, President Lincoln dismissed his close protection officer Crook and went to Ford's Theatre with his wife. In doing so he ignored the efforts of both Stanton and Crook to persuade him not to offer himself as a target. It was bad luck that the officer allocated to act as Crook's temporary replacement as Lincoln's protection officer was John F. Parker, the least competent member of the local city force. An alcoholic, Parker hurried ahead of the Lincolns to the theatre.

They travelled across town unescorted and arrived after the play had started. When the ovation and the greetings for the President were over, Parker retired to the nearest bar. He apparently did not notice the ragged peephole dug into the door which gave access to the private, presidential box.

Earlier in the day, a local newspaper had published its equivalent of the Court Circular, announcing that the Lincolns would attend the play at Ford's. It would be no great problem for a man of the theatre to discover or guess which part of the house the President would use. But no one seems to have been alerted by Booth's questions to an employee about security there. The play, an 'eccentric English comedy' entitled *Our American Cousin*, got under way again after the brief interruption of the presidential entry. Lincoln's eyes were on the stage, his mind probably turning over matters of state, his back entirely exposed as Booth, a moustached parody of a Victorian villain, gently opened the door giving access to the corridor. Another door, linking the corridor to the main concourse and stairway, was already jammed shut with a wooden wedge.

Booth had armed himself with a stubby, muzzle-loading, cap lock .44 Derringer pistol. It was easily concealed but otherwise an entirely unsuitable instrument of assassination unless the target was unguarded and, hopefully, tethered as well. It fired only one shot. A humane killer would have been hardly less appropriate. Yet Booth was able to point the gun a few inches behind Lincoln's left ear and kill the President with it. The victim twitched upward, scorched by pain, and slumped into a coma from which he would not recover before the last signs of life faded from him nine hours later.

The assassin departed the stage with a Latin line incomprehensible to most of his audience and a shin bone broken as he jumped from the box to the stage. He was on the run for twelve days before a posse of soldiers found him hiding in a barn. It is a moot point whether he then shot himself in the head or whether one of the soldiers did the job for him. Only later did it become apparent that the rumours of an assassination plot were not rumours after all. Booth was not a lone bigot but the leader of a conspiracy of at least nine people, four of whom, including a woman, were later hanged. Three others received life sentences. One conspirator received six years. Many of Lincoln's last hours had been devoted to dispensing pardons to political prisoners, as part of a process of binding national wounds. Lincoln's killers were not amnestied.

Lincoln's assassination did not change the course of history, apart from leading to the creation of the presidential bodyguard, the Secret Service, on 5 July 1865. The service has not always covered itself in glory, old or new, perhaps because the framework within which it is supposed to operate is not the easiest. As Dr Saleen Shah, as chief of the Center for Studies of Crime and Delinquency at the US National Institute of Mental Health, observed, 'Considering the high value placed on freedom in this society and the ease with which firearms can be obtained, it is surprising that there are so *few* assassins.'

What Booth's crime did achieve was to establish that the pen was not mightier than the gun. The mystique that leadership requires for stable government was crippled by the .44 round which ruptured Lincoln's brain. He was the sixteenth president. From now on his successors would come under increasing threat, and while the politics of the smoking gun has not been unknown in democratic Europe – see the rise of Fascism – assassination in Europe lacks the aura of legitimacy that goes with the resolution of argument by gunshot in America.

The death of Lincoln underscored something else about

the emerging United States. It was not only that political murder would become a sort of punctuation mark of American public life at every level. The obfuscation of vital evidence as a follow-through to such murder would become another characteristic American vice. In a society which worships material success beyond most other virtues, crime and politics make natural bedfellows. The life and sudden, brutal death of Huey Long illustrate the point.

During the Depression years of the 1930s in the Southern USA, Huey Long, the Governor (and later Senator) from Louisiana, was a sinister, smiling figure who marked down his enemies and settled scores in unorthodox ways. He had armed bodyguards, of course. One of these, named Battling Bozeman, was approached to assassinate Long's political rival J. Y. Sanders Jnr. When details of the murder plot leaked, there was an outcry and an attempt to impeach Long.

Surprisingly, the Chief Justice required the Louisiana state senators who took part in the impeachment proceedings to vote publicly, one after the other. In such circumstances, there were not enough brave men willing to vote for Long's impeachment and the case died. Long's career blossomed. In some elections he polled 100 per cent of the vote or more. How this happened was related years later by another local politician, Colonel Philemon St Amant:

'The lights would go out at the polling places and when the lights came on again, the ballot boxes had disappeared so they would have to start all over again with new boxes, which already had a number of ballots (votes) in them . . . I'm not charging a particular person with doing it, because I have no personal knowledge, but he [Long] always won the elections.'

Unembarrassed by the latest scandal – the kidnap of someone who had delved into his private life – Long was elected to the national Senate in 1930. Back home, some people talked wistfully of 'killing that sonofabitch' as they aimed their pistols at the after-dinner empties. Louisiana, after all, was the sort of place where even a doctor making his rounds carried a gun as well as a stethoscope. One such was Dr Carl Weiss, aged twenty-nine, an opponent of Long whose wife, Long publicly implied, was of mixed race.

Just after 9 pm on 9 September 1935 Long emerged from a late sitting of the State parliament in New Orleans. From the chamber he went to the governor's office, then re-emerged into a hallway with his usual cohort of ten bodyguards behind him. Dr Weiss appeared on the scene and there was some sort of confrontation and much shooting. Estimates of the number of bullets taken from the body of Dr Weiss vary between sixty-one and seventy-eight.

Long took thirty-six hours to die in a local hospital. There is no agreement about how many rounds had struck him. One was dug out of his body on the undertaker's slab and quietly lost, or so it is said. Other rounds were thought to be calibre .45 – the same as those fired by the bodyguards – rather than the .32 of Weiss's gun.

A full inquest on Long was held only after four adjourned hearings. The delays resulted from the reluctance of the bodyguards to attend. Weiss's funeral, by contrast, was attended by thousands of respectable, grieving citizens who felt that the young doctor had done them even more service as an assassin than as a medical practitioner. Yet the suspicion lingers that he was merely a catalyst for a process of destruction which was really under the control of others. It was the shrewd old Colonel St Amant who observed in a BBC Radio Three documentary ('Realm of the Kingfish', written and produced by Russell Davies in November 1986): 'Now, was there another killer somewhere? No. It was one of the bodyguards . . . I say that if you can hire a man for money to kill another man, someone else can hire him for a little more money to kill you.'

*

In November 1950, while the White House was being renovated, President Harry Truman's official home in Washington was at a smaller building known as Blair House. The end of October had been memorable in Puerto Rico for a short-lived armed rebellion against the local government and in protest against US domination. As the rebels were being put down decisively, two political dreamers decided to strike their blow by killing the US President. Until then, Oscar Collazo, a shop floor trade union bargainer, had worked in a New York factory where he was well regarded. His companion Griselio Torresola was living on public assistance in the same city.

Their style of assassination as well as their timing suggested some affinity with lemmings. They simply tried to shoot their way into Blair House with pistols which had seen better days. Collazo's 9 mm Walther self-loading gun misfired after one shot and jammed. He was rapidly arrested. Torresola blasted on alone, 9 mm Luger in hand. He was fatally wounded in the lobby by some of the twenty-seven rounds fired in the exchange, but so was one of the presidential bodyguards, Leslie Cofelt. Truman, upstairs while the gunfight raged, peeped out of a window but when one of the guards yelled, 'Get back, Mr President!' he did as he was told. Later, Collazo was sentenced to death. It was Truman who commuted the sentence to life imprisonment.

In November 1963, President John Kennedy died, like Lincoln, at a time when the national temperature was stoked up by the excitement of mayhem and sudden death. The abortive attempt to invade Castro-led Cuba at the Bay of Pigs in 1961, together with exotic schemes, separately prepared by the CIA and the Mafia, to assassinate Castro himself, were succeeded in October 1962 by a threat to the whole northern hemisphere. The discovery that Soviet ballistic missiles capable of striking American cities were to be based on Cuban soil plunged the US into a state verging on paranoia. In the perilous confrontation with Russia which followed, Kennedy ordered some military mobilisation.

The Vietnam war had also taken an odd turn on 2 November with the assassination of South Vietnam's President Diem. The US knew a coup was in the offing. It was carefully ignorant of the additional embroidery of an assassination as well as a change of government in Saigon.

Kennedy also had a problem with Texas. The Lone Star State was dogmatically right wing and – of course – well armed. Certainly Dallas in late November 1963 was no safer for a liberal president than Washington had been in 1865. But the Texas state governor, John Connally, assured the White House that Kennedy could expect 'a rousing welcome'.

From the outset, the security surrounding Kennedy's trip to Dallas was pitted with unnecessary gaps. Although the Secret Service conducted one sweep of the area to identify local risks before the visit, it does not seem to have been aware that the Federal Bureau of Investigation – still controlled by the illiberal and sinister J. Edgar Hoover – had identified Lee Harvey Oswald as a potential problem.

Oswald was one of life's misfits. He served with the Marine Corps, where he was a mediocre shot, but in spite of an avowed passion for Communism, he was posted to work as a radar operator in Japan, to liaise with the top secret U2 reconnaissance flights over Russia. He was somewhat accident prone, acquiring both gonorrhoea and a bullet wound – accidental and self inflicted – from a Derringer pistol he should not have had. In 1959 he quit the service, mysteriously acquired funds and defected to Russia. He was even more mysteriously provided with a US government loan enabling him to return to America in 1962 with his wife, one of a well known KGB family. At the time of the Kennedy assassination he was doing a low-grade clerical job for $1.25 an hour in a warehouse which supplied school textbooks.

The FBI checks identified Oswald as an employee of the book warehouse early in November, almost three weeks before the assassination. Oswald's presence on the route appears to have been logged routinely, without provoking any follow-up action. A week before the visit, an official announcement published by the Dallas press revealed that 'a security car will lead the [presidential] motorcade which will travel on Mockingbird Lane, Lemmon Avenue, Turtle Creek Boulevard, Cedar Springs, Harwood, Main and Stemmons Freeway. President and Mrs Kennedy will ride in the second car. Secret Service agents will ride in the next car . . .'

This arrangement overrode a formula often adopted by the Secret Service elsewhere, a convoy in which the President's Lincoln Convertible was the seventh vehicle, preceded by the photojournalists' car to ensure good media coverage. At Dallas the lead vehicle carried the city's police chief, Jesse Curry, a local sheriff, and one White House bodyguard. Photojournalists, whose pictorial record might have been of great value in view of the way things turned out that day, were relegated to seventh place in the convoy.

The degree of exposure to attack, particularly from above, seems to have been measured by the risk of rain rather than a hail of bullets. The presidential limousine had a hardened plastic top which could be removed in fine weather, making Kennedy as vulnerable as those earlier victims of slow-moving, open-topped carriages, the Archduke Franz Ferdinand and Alexander I of Yugoslavia. At Dallas, as it happened, the presidential bodyguard needed all the oxygen it could get. At least nine members of the team had been out on the town until the early hours.

On the day, the sun shone and the hard top was removed.

To complete the exposure of the Kennedys and their fellow passengers, Governor John Connally and his wife, there was only one Secret Service bodyguard in the limousine that day. This was Roy Kellerman, aged forty-eight, sitting alongside a veteran White House chauffeur, Bill Greer, aged fifty-four. Both were in jobs demanding up to eighty hours overtime every month. It was a young man's job, full of stress, and the Kennedys despised their bodyguards as 'Ivy League charlatans' whom the President personally had expelled from their usual perch on the back of the Lincoln four days earlier, in spite of Dallas's reputation for political violence.

On other assignments, prominent on the 'step' at the rear of the presidential limousine as well as on the sides of the vehicle, bodyguards would act as a human shield between the President and any bullet apart from the freakishly lucky ones. At Dallas the Secret Service agent charged with guarding Jacqueline Kennedy could get no closer to her than the running-board of the back-up escort vehicle. This was a Cadillac nicknamed the 'Queen Mary'. It carried a team of ten bodyguards, all heavily armed but about fifteen fatal yards behind those who were ostensibly enjoying their protection. The protection team's view was sometimes obstructed by a posse of police motor-cycle outriders following the Kennedy car.

When the first shot cast its spell around virtually everyone in the strange echo chamber shaped by the Book Depository building and its neighbours, freezing them into immobility, it would be Mrs Kennedy's guardian, Clinton ('Clint') J. Hill, who uniquely exploded into action, hurling himself into pursuit *on foot* of the VIP limousine before the echo of that first shot was overtaken by the crack of the second. Hill said later:

'As we came out of the curve . . . and began to straighten up, I was viewing an area which looked to be a park. There were people scattered throughout the entire park. And I heard a noise from my right ear, which seemed to be made by a firecracker. I immediately looked to my right and, in so doing, my eyes had to cross the Presidential limousine. I saw President Kennedy grab at himself and lurch forward to the left. I jumped from the car, realising something was wrong, ran to the Presidential limousine.

'Just as I reached it, there was another sound, which was different than the first sound. It sounded as though someone was shooting a revolver into a hard object. It seemed to have some kind of an echo.

'I put my right foot ... on the left rear step of the automobile and I had a hold of a handgrip with my hand, when the car lurched forward. I lost my footing and had to run about three or more steps before I could get back up on the car. Mrs Kennedy had jumped up from the seat ... She turned toward me and I grabbed her and put her back in the seat, crawled up on the back of the seat and lay there.'

He heard Jacqueline Kennedy's voice rise in a growing awareness of the horror of what was happening: 'Jack, Jack, what have they done to you? ... My God, they have shot his head off.'

By now large pieces of Kennedy's skull were spread like coconut on the rear seat of the limousine and the road behind them. The dying President was taken directly to the Parkland Hospital, where, notes one author, 'Surrounded by aliens, Kennedy's people ignored the hospital official who said they would break the chain of evidence if they removed the President's body.' The body was now in the jurisdiction of a local JP, who refused to release it, observing, 'It's just another homicide case so far as I'm concerned.'

The entourage surrounding the dying Senator Huey Long had broken into hospital to get their man treated. The Kennedy entourage, faced with a disagreeable legal obstacle to removing their dead leader, broke that down also as a Kennedy aide snapped, 'We're leaving.' An unseemly tug-o'-war followed. The body then departed to Washington and the chain of evidence was broken.

Elaborate efforts were made later by a presidential inquiry – the Warren Commission, headed by Chief Justice Earl Warren – to reconstruct what had happened. Having received testimony which filled twenty-six volumes, it reached a series of conclusions which have been under challenge ever since. Oswald, it concluded, was a lone, deranged individual who had fired all the shots at the President's car.

The rifle used by Oswald and abandoned when he left his sixth-floor sniper's nest was a 6.5 mm clip-fed 1938 Mannlicher-Carcano rifle faithful to a design which had not changed much since the turn of the century. Each bullet could only be fired after the shooter's right hand had worked a bolt back and forward. Even the best shot, with the fiercest grip, could not hold such a rifle firmly on a moving target as he reloaded. It was not capable, like modern assault rifles, of controlled, short bursts of automatic fire merely by squeezing the trigger.

Oswald fired from above and behind the target at a range of 280 feet just after the limousine swung below him in a left-hand turn, round the green triangle formed by three roads. It was moving at about eleven mph. The Commission's conclusion is that the first bullet struck Kennedy's back almost six inches below the collar line, then exited through the throat, taking an upward trajectory. The same bullet then struck Connally in the back near the right armpit (as he sat on a 'jump' seat, facing away from the Kennedys). It still had sufficient velocity to travel through Connally's body, smashing a rib, before plunging through his right wrist and coming to rest, virtually undistorted, in the Governor's left thigh. This round rapidly became inscribed in assassination folklore as 'the magic bullet'.

The second shot clipped the kerb at the feet of a spectator. The third, it is believed, is the one which blew away much of Kennedy's brain.

If there were no professional cameras to record how Kennedy died, there was an amateur 8 mm colour cine film known as the Zapruder film: a unique record, lasting twenty-two seconds and shot by a local dress manufacturer, Abraham Zapruder. This revealed that Kennedy's head was thrust backwards as the third, fatal bullet struck him, though the laws of motion would require that a shot from the back (that is, from Oswald's firing point) would push the head forward.

Even more perplexing is the time element apparently disclosed by the film. The first round, the so-called 'magic' bullet, would have hit Kennedy at 1,775 feet per second. The frames on the film should then reveal a logical sequence in which Connally reacts at an appropriate time to the bullet as it strikes him also. This does not happen. Ten frames elapse between the latest time at which Kennedy would be struck and the time at which Connally was first affected.

The time between the two is five-eighths of a second. Simple arithmetic indicates that a bullet travelling at 1,775 feet per second would in that time cover 1,109 feet. In order to satisfy the Warren Commission conclusion, as others have observed, the magic bullet had to 'hover' after striking Kennedy and before wounding Connally.

Finally, there is the impossibility of finding any marksman, however skilled, capable of replicating the sharpshooting allegedly demonstrated by the mediocre rifleman Oswald that day. Between the first and last of the three shots, as the film confirms, 5.6 seconds elapsed. The FBI's best shots could not fire the rifle, unaimed, and reload to fire a second time in less than 2.3 seconds. They needed 4.6 seconds to fire three unaimed shots. It stretches common sense to accept that Oswald – a man who could not be left safely in charge of a tiny Derringer – fired three rifle shots at an acute angle, at a moving target, and scored two hits in an overall time one second longer than the FBI's best unaimed time.

The Commission found that after the deed, Oswald pushed the rifle among empty cartons in a crude effort at concealment before leaving the scene. The rifle bore no fingerprints: only a badly defined palm print which was not proved to be Oswald's. As he scurried out of the book depository, a police officer rushing towards it in response to the shots challenged him. Oswald was cleared to go when he was identified as a regular employee of the warehouse. (Interestingly, he could have learned from no public source, when he took a job there shortly before, that the warehouse would provide a bird's eye view over the President's motor-cade.)

Oswald was arrested seventy-five minutes later, hiding in a cinema, after he had used a revolver to murder a police patrolman, J. D. Tippit. Two days afterwards, as Oswald was being taken by Dallas police to the county gaol, he was loosely escorted through a basement area full of journalists, television camera crews and Sunday morning strollers. There was no effort to control the crowd and certainly no search for firearms. In spite of that, the local police appeared surprised when an assassin stepped out of the crowd and slaughtered Oswald while the television cameras rolled. The only intervention appeared to be a token gesture by a man whose other hand held a cigar to his lips.

Speculation about the Kennedy killing continues. Such a formidable authority as William Manchester, in *The Death of a President*, goes almost all the way with the Warren Commission. For others, it defies common sense not to accept that more than one gun was shooting at Kennedy's car that day in Dallas. The issue of whose conspiracy this

was remains entirely open. Was there, for example, a plot
to fabricate evidence against Oswald? The day Kennedy
was murdered, a mixed security team searched Oswald's
rented room and found two snapshots of him standing in
the back yard, armed with a long rifle fitted with a telescopic
sniper's sight. The photographs became Warren Commission exhibits. Experts have since challenged the authen-
ticity of one of the pictures, arguing that the 'Oswald'
on one photograph is about twelve inches taller than the
'Oswald' on the other.

The Warren Commission was succeeded by the House
of Representatives Select Committee on Assassinations in
1978. One of those who appeared before this inquiry was
a Cuban woman named Marita Lorenz. She testified that
in November 1963 she was one of a group of Cubans who
drove Lee Harvey Oswald from Miami to a motel room in
Dallas where they were met by Jack Ruby. She remembered
seeing rifles and scopes in the room. The Select Committee,
however, 'found no evidence to support Lorenz's allegations'. (See *Miami* by Joan Didion.)

Kennedy was succeeded for an interim period by his
Vice-President, Lyndon B. Johnson. The next presidential
campaign, in 1968, was one whose three principal candidates were to become assassination targets. They were JFK's
brother Robert, his Republican opponent Richard Nixon,
and Governor George Wallace of Alabama. Robert Kennedy, as Attorney-General, was murdered by an Arab immigrant, Sirhan Sirhan. Nixon was shadowed by a
psychologically tortured loner, Arthur Bremer, until 1972
when Bremer, deterred by Nixon's tight security, turned his
gun on Wallace instead. In all the circumstances the fatalism
of Yoko Ono's opinion – 'There can be one crank anywhere'
– was understandable even if it is misplaced.

CHAPTER 15

Assassins Get Results, Sometimes

There is another fallacy about assassination. This is that it does *not* change the course of history. Disraeli and others were convinced of this. Like the theory of 'one crank anywhere', it serves the therapeutic purpose of reassuring us that crime does not pay. The alternative conclusion – that brute force *is* sometimes victorious over human intelligence – denies the experience of human civilisation.

Politically 'significant' assassinations and attempted assassinations during this century are summarised below. They are the author's subjective choice. The list is far from exhaustive, for the actual number of such murders since 1900 probably runs to tens of thousands. This list has been compiled – or so the author would claim – because it contains elements of disaster which tend to recur in one case after another. History, as someone said, might not always repeat itself but it does tend to rhyme occasionally.

The index illustrates first, that the course of history *is* sometimes altered by a political assassination if this is carried out at the right moment, with appropriate publicity. Second, it demonstrates that too many bodyguards have acted as assassins, or have played a strangely ambiguous role in defending the person they were hired to protect. Third, it reveals that the victims had received the most vivid early warning possible: an attack on them which failed, usually no more than six months before a second, successful assassination attempt. Fourth, it is a reminder that public figures who shrug off warnings of impending danger often contribute needlessly to their own destruction. Finally it illustrates, time and again, the hard truth that the peacemaker might be blessed, but he is often also dead sooner than the combatants. The survivors work at survival. They learn to step carefully, to talk of peace but to carry a big stick or its equivalent.

As well as the famous, the list includes people who became public figures only as a result of their deaths, and the manner of them. Such people are the two British sergeants murdered in Palestine in 1947 and the three Scottish soldiers murdered in Northern Ireland in 1971. Their deaths polarised opinion and had an impact on events (as the assassins intended) no less weighty than the killing of the more eminent.

Where appropriate, the bodyguard's role is described in the cases listed here. Collectively, they make the point that the absence of sound protection sometimes has its price In the first case listed the price was so high that Europe must still count the cost, more than seventy years later.

1914: Archduke Franz Ferdinand, heir to the emperor of the Austro-Hungarian Habsburg empire.

Both he and his assassin, a Serbo-Croat nationalist named Gavrilo Princip, aged nineteen, were victims of a plot engineered by the man responsible for Ferdinand's security when the Archduke made his fatal visit to Sarajevo (then part of Bosnia, now Yugoslavia). Under the code-name 'Apis' the orchestrator of the conspiracy ran both Serbian Army Intelligence *and* the underground Black Hand terrorist organisation. His real name was Colonel Dragutin Dimitrijevic. He had already contrived the murders of King Alexander and Queen Draga of Serbia in 1903.

In 1914, Apis armed and incited the young Princip and his fellow Serbian conspirators to attack the Archduke's open-topped limousine during a public visit to Sarajevo. To start the proceedings, Princip's comrade, Nedeljko Cabrinovic, lobbed a grenade at the car, having first asked a police officer to identify the vehicle for him. The grenade bounced off the target before exploding under the car following it. In spite of this the procession continued but the lead driver took a wrong turning, halting opposite Princip. There was a vivid absence of outriders or other close protection officers as Princip started shooting into the vehicle with a Browning revolver.

The first round fatally wounded the Duchess Sophia and the second her husband. The Archduke cried to her, 'Live, for my children.' Both were dead within thirty minutes. The assassination is widely regarded as the catalyst which set in motion the deadly quadrille which became the First World War. In 1934 the chief of German military intelligence, Admiral Wilhelm Canaris (executed ten years later for his part in the plot to kill Hitler), revealed that Apis had been a German agent. The Sarajevo assassination provided a pretext for German expansion in Central Europe which the Allies then met by force. Serbian independence – the theoretical reason for the assassination – is still unfulfilled.

1924: Giacomo Matteotti, secretary of the Italian Socialist Party.

Matteotti was snatched off a Rome street while on his way to parliament by a gang of Mussolini's friends, including Il Duce's press officer, Cesare Rossi; he was abducted in a car, stabbed to death almost immediately and buried in a shallow grave near Quarterella, where his body was discovered two months later.

Matteotti, who did not believe in bodyguards, had predicted his own death but had done nothing about his security. A spectator noted the number of the abductors' car. It belonged to a member of Mussolini's inner circle. A popular outcry rocked the government and a lukewarm investigation resulted. Some of the principals were imprisoned but most were promoted to high political or even military posts on their release from gaol.

The Socialists missed their chance to destroy Mussolini politically by using the investigation of Matteotti's murder as a springboard. Instead, some of Mussolini's opponents joined the many schemes to assassinate him. A British Foreign Secretary's bodyguard (see Part II) learned much about personal security from Mussolini's protection team.

1932: Tsuyoshi Inukai Ki, Japanese Prime Minister.
Unguarded when nine officers arrived at his residence, the Prime Minister lit a cigarette and suggested they should discuss their grievances with him. The visitors' leader, Lieutenant Yamagishi, replied, 'No use talking.' He then pointed his pistol at the Prime Minister and shouted 'Fire!' Everyone joined in the killing.

Inukai Ki's fatal error was to be a civilian and to entertain pretensions to government of a military caste. Between 1912 and 1945 at least six Japanese prime ministers, as well as a dozen other cabinet ministers, were murdered by various right wing death cults. In 1923 even Emperor Hirohito had been a target. The assassins' favoured weapons were the sword (for ritual killings) or the Thomson sub-machine gun when productivity had to be increased. The day Inukai Ki was slaughtered, the other nominated victim was his visitor, the British comedian Charles Chaplin (as a symbol of American capitalism). Chaplin luckily did not arrive to take tea with the Prime Minister that day.

The assassination was of political significance because of the popular support received by the killers: a perfunctory trial was followed by terms of imprisonment which the men never served. They were lauded as heroes. The affair gave the green light to the expansion of Japanese militarism.

1934: Engelbert Dollfuss, Chancellor of Austria; Fascist (but anti-Nazi) ruler.

On orders from Hitler, the assassination of Dollfuss was to signal a carefully planned *coup d'état* followed immediately by the 'Anschluss', i.e. the absorption of Austria into the Third Reich. The assassins' leader, Otto Planetta, an ex-sergeant, was aided by the order given to guards inside the Austrian Chancellery that they would carry rifles but no ammunition. Such a precaution is a symptom of mistrust between the ruler and his guardians. Dollfuss possibly had in mind an attempt on his life a year before in which he was wounded.

Dollfuss had ignored a chance to flee from the second attack. As other members of his Cabinet ran, ducked and weaved, Dollfuss – just 4 ft 11 ins tall – stood his ground. He punched his hands in front of his face as Planetta fired two bullets, which paralysed him. He received no medical aid as he lay dying for several hours.

The plotters seized the radio station to announce the takeover, unaware that their link to the state transmitter had been cut off, while an alternative studio, which was on air, rallied the Home Guard. Hitler promptly denied any link with the plot, whose failure delayed but did not prevent the Anschluss. The affair was also a reminder to Hitler's opponents that the use of selective assassination was a weapon he did employ, particularly against opponents outside Germany.

Winston Churchill took note and armed an unofficial personal bodyguard in 1939. Legally, as a backbench MP, the future war leader was sailing close to the wind. At the relevant time the bodyguard – the retired Special Branch Detective Inspector Thompson – remained within the grounds of Chartwell Manor, Churchill's home in Kent. He carried a loaded Colt pistol not registered on his firearms licence (even if he still had one) but on Churchill's. ('He gave me his Colt automatic to use – and I may say with pride that I am the only man Mr Churchill has allowed to handle his guns. He is a first-class shot and takes a jealous pride in the care of his personal armoury' – Thompson, op. cit.) In his memoirs, Thompson acknowledged that his role as 'an armed, *unofficial* bodyguard . . . ready to pounce upon a would-be Nazi murderer' was a strange one. Only when he was recalled to the police reserve for wartime emergency duties was his position regularised.

1934: King Alexander I of Yugoslavia and Louis Barthou, French Foreign Minister.

In 1928, after a number of Croat MPs were assassinated in parliament by their Serbian opponents, the King dissolved the institution and took full executive power. He was the first monarch to succeed in unifying the uneasy federation. Croats in exile determined to kill the King to focus attention on their cause.

The plot coincided with an official visit made to France by the King in 1934. The assassin hired for the job was a professional bodyguard of Bulgarian descent, Vlada Chernozamsky, who was first employed as protection officer for the leading conspirator, Ante Pavelic. At least five others took part in the conspiracy, one of them a woman who smuggled the ammunition into France.

Chernozamsky chose his moment, then rushed from the crowd and leapt on to the running-board of the King's open-topped limousine as it drove ceremonially through Marseilles. At close quarters he fired two shots into Alexander, one into Barthou's arm and four into their escort/companion, General Alfonse Georges. Only then was he struck down by an outrider, Colonel Fiollet, with a sabre.

The assassin was lynched and shot in the head instead of escaping, as intended, during confusion provoked by a diversionary explosion. The bomber, a fellow conspirator, had lost his nerve and fled. Alexander died almost instantly. Barthou, surprisingly, was allowed to bleed to death. General Georges survived.

The political effect of the crime was the ultimate disintegration of Yugoslavia, making it ripe for invasion by Hitler, and the replacement as French Foreign Minister of the anti-Nazi Barthou with a future Nazi collaborator, Pierre Laval. Some writers link the plot directly to German plans to invade Czechoslovakia (with French complicity) as well as Yugoslavia. Certainly the leader of the plot, Ante Pavelic, was appointed governor of 'Free Croatia' – a puppet state manufactured after the Nazi occupation – just as Laval was enabled to run Vichy France as an unoccupied zone after 1940.

The immediate effect of the assassination of King Alexander was a demand to the League of Nations to establish an international court to try terrorists. The idea has been discussed since by the UN but there has been insufficient agreement about how to define a terrorist. The 'Free Croats' still practise occasional terrorism.

1934: Sergei Kirov, boss of the Leningrad Communist Party and the man tipped to succeed Josef Stalin.

When the assassin arrived, Kirov was in his office – from which Lenin had launched his takeover – in what had once been a girls' school in Leningrad. The building was now called the Smolny Institute and it was heavily guarded. On the orders of the secret police, however, Kirov's personal bodyguard had been removed. The assassin, Leonid Nikolaev, passed unchallenged through the entrance and shot Kirov several times.

Stalin, apparently upset, descended from Moscow, beat up the local police chief, Medved, and led his own investigation into the killing. Nikolaev, on his knees before Stalin, pointed to the secret police present and screamed, 'They made me do it!' Nikolaev was tortured and shot. Medved was murdered three years later. Borisov, the man in charge of Kirov's bodyguard, was beaten to death.

This was the beginning of Stalin's first great purge of everybody in the Communist Party whose experience matched his own. Thousands, if not tens of thousands, would be despatched for no greater fault than that they were efficient. Some students of Soviet history believe that Kirov's murder was engineered by Stalin; more, that he was inspired by Hitler's example in purging the Nazi élite a few months earlier. The difference was that Hitler did not need to disguise responsibility for the murders of former colleagues, such as the Brownshirt leader, Ernst Roehm, in 1934, through the unattributable, deniable device of assassination. Hitler usually disposed of his Nazi rivals publicly, in daylight, with a bullet from the front. But like Stalin, he also resorted to assassination to dispose of opponents abroad.

1939: Pope Pius XI.

The 81-year-old Pope, born Achille Ratti, was about to denounce Fascism to a convocation of Italian prelates. He requested a chemical stimulant to give him the strength to carry out this task. The stimulant was administered as an injection by Dr Francesco Petucci, the senior Vatican physician. A few hours afterwards, the Pope died without delivering his address. There has been conflicting testimony ever since about whether this was homicide or not. (See, for example, *Assassination Theory and Practice* by Richard Camellion.) Since the days of the Borgias, the use of poison has been a specifically Italian skill and that tradition continues. (In March 1986 Michele Sidona – a member of the P2 conspiracy thought to have engineered the banker Roberto Calvi's death by hanging under Blackfriars Bridge, London, in 1982 – was held in a high-security Italian prison.

He was under continuous surveillance in a wing observed by six closed-circuit television cameras. His food came in sealed containers from the prison officers' mess and was opened only when it reached him. Yet a dose of potassium cyanide found its way into his morning coffee. He died murmuring, 'They've poisoned me.') Those who studied the circumstances surrounding the end of Pius XI observed that his physician's daughter, Claretta Petucci, was Mussolini's mistress. She was executed with Il Duce in April 1944.

The most impressive political result was the succession of Pius XII, a Pope suspected of anti-Semitism and of being soft on Fascism. For both Hitler and Mussolini, the death of Pius XI had almost the same utility as those of Dollfuss, Alexander I, Barthou and Matteotti. It is also possible that this pattern is no more than coincidence. However, Mussolini's words on assassination might also be relevant: 'Terror? Never. It simply is social hygiene, taking those individuals out of circulation like a doctor would take out a bacillus.' (Cited by Laqueur, op. cit.)

1940: Leon Trotsky aka Lev Davidovich Bronstein.
While living in guarded seclusion in Mexico in an effort to elude Stalin's agents, Trotsky was killed by a man wielding an ice axe which he drove through Trotsky's skull with savage force. The assassin, Jacques Mornard, aka Frank Jackson or Jacson, Ramon Mercador or Turkov van den Dresch, spent two years ingratiating himself with members of Trotsky's circle in Paris and elsewhere before he was himself admitted to Trotsky's guarded villa as a trusted visitor.

It is possible that Mornard's operation was initially regarded by the Soviets as a second option if the first, more sure method, did not do the trick. This first attempt was made on the night of 24 May 1940. Trotsky's principal bodyguard, Robert Sheldon Harte from New York, opened the gate guarding the compound around Trotsky's villa. Around thirty men in Army uniform entered and opened fire on the building with machine guns. The Trotskys dived for cover beneath their beds and survived. It was close. Many bullets had torn through the pillow where Trotsky's head should have rested. The raiders – later identified as members of the Mexican Communist Party – withdrew and with them went Harte. A month later, his body was found in a grave some miles away, covered by quicklime. He was the eighth associate of Trotsky to disappear or die violently. Trotsky prophetically commented, 'What distinguishes a revolutionary is not so much his capacity to kill as his willingness to die.' Individual terrorism, he observed after the assassination of his comrade, Kirov, in 1934, was 'bureaucracy turned inside out'.

Three months after the machine-gun attack, Mornard arrived by appointment to discuss with Trotsky the draft of an article he had written. Although Trotsky was beginning to express doubts about Mornard, no particular precautions were taken when Mornard arrived on a fine day, carrying a raincoat over his arm. Three bodyguards did not search the visitor in spite of recent events. To put it another way, Trotsky's bodyguards admitted two consecutive assassins.

Soon afterwards the guards heard a piercing scream as Mornard bludgeoned Trotsky with the sharp, pointed end of his climber's axe. The wound should have been instantly deadly but Trotsky fought his attacker before collapsing. He struggled for life for another twenty-six hours. Mornard, seized by the bodyguard, protested that his mother was in prison and that her captors had made him kill Trotsky. He was tried for murder and sentenced to twenty years' imprisonment in 1943. His true identity was never established. He served his time and, an hour after his release in 1963, was flown by way of Cuba to Czechoslovakia.

The impact of this murder was to enrich the mythology surrounding Trotsky the man and politician, and to demonstrate that it is possible to kill the man but not the idea. It also had the effect of making East European exiles even more paranoid about Stalin's assassination machine. When the Polish wartime leader, General Sikorsky, died in an RAF crash at Gibraltar, many Free Poles blamed (and still blame, though wrongly) a British plot, sanctioned by Churchill, to oblige Stalin, then a comrade-in-arms of the Western allies.

1942: Lieutenant-General Reinhard Heydrich, Nazi governor of Czechoslovakia and former Naval officer turned Nazi genocide specialist.

Heydrich was one of the key planners of the Holocaust. He was ambushed by four members of the Czech underground on a road in Prague. When one of the assassins broke cover and pointed a Sten sub-machine gun at Heydrich's Mercedes, the gun jammed. Instead of driving on, Heydrich's chauffeur – a captain – halted just as the assassins tossed a hand grenade at them. Heydrich got out of the car and drew his Walther pistol as the grenade exploded nearby. He died in hospital a week later of gangrene from apparently minor wounds. As a reprisal the SS and Gestapo annihilated Lidice village and executed another thousand random hostages. When the assassination team was discovered hiding in a Greek Orthodox church in Prague, a gun battle took place inside the building in which nine SS men were shot dead. Some Resistance men also died by their own hand. Others drowned when the fire brigade, under German orders, flooded the crypt. Another 217 Czechs, one of them a former prime minister, were murdered in revenge. Just thirty-three days after Heydrich was assassinated, the Resistance team's radio operator sent a final signal to SOE in London from a hiding place outside

Prague. German direction-finders detected the signal and the radio operator, Emil Potuchek, the last member of the hit team, was killed in the ensuing gun battle.

The result of this sanguinary assassination is not easy to evaluate. British Intelligence, with its own axe to grind, argued that Heydrich was prevented from taking over elements of Nazi intelligence which they obliquely controlled through highly placed double agents such as Admiral Canaris. Other former Allies, including the American OSS, believe that the assassination achieved nothing of lasting value. The German reaction to the affair did not halt the attempts on Hitler's life (see below). It also became part of a heritage which terrorists have used ever since to justify their assassinations. To make that point stick in the postwar world, it is necessary to make an equation between the Nazis and the people they attempted to crush, with – for example – the French in Algeria. The trick does not work because it does not compare like with like.

Occupied Europe between 1939 and 1945 had never been part of a Greater German Empire. Germany itself was not unified until the late 19th century. Algeria, by contrast, had been absorbed, with success, into Metropolitan France from 1831 onwards while retaining its own religions and languages, mainly Berber and Arab but including Saharan cultures such as the Tuareg. The huge French Army of Africa (comprising native regiments) and French language unified the region as the Indian Army and English language still unify the disparate cultures of India. By contrast the Czechs, like the Hungarians, had a German-speaking minority ceded to Germany along with the Sudetenland by the Munich agreement of October 1938. Hitler invaded Bohemian Czechoslovakia five months later.

There is an important difference, as the Romans recognised, between legitimate tyrannicide and indiscriminate terrorism as an act of war against a colonial rule made legitimate by the participation of most of the colonial subjects. The difference is one of consent, or lack of it, which legitimises one administration while making another a proper target for – as a last resort – violent resistance.

1943: Admiral Isoroku Yamamoto, architect of Japanese naval strategy.
On 18 April the Admiral was flying around the occupied Solomon Islands. His schedules, sent ahead of him by radio, were intercepted by American signals intelligence, and the codes, which the Japanese believed invulnerable, were broken. American fighter aircraft picked him off in mid-air (demonstrating the vulnerability of statesmen to attack while airborne) and sent a signal to their commanders, 'Pop goes the weasel!' The event demonstrated that assassination of the opposition's leaders had become Allied as well as Axis policy. The Americans had been shadowing Yamamoto for weeks.

In June of the same year, a British aircraft flying from Lisbon to England was shot down by German interceptors, who believed that Winston Churchill was a passenger. The crash did take with it a VIP: the film actor Leslie Howard.

1944: Adolf Hitler, Nazi dictator of the Third Reich.
A month after D-Day it was clear that the Allied landing on the beaches of Occupied Normandy had blasted a permanent way through Hitler's Atlantic Wall. The German Army was now fighting for survival on three fronts. The hero of Africa, Field-Marshal Erwin Rommel, signalled the Führer: 'The unequal struggle is nearing its end. I must ask you immediately to draw the necessary conclusions . . .'* But Hitler's mind was less susceptible to change than the

---

* Quoted by Hans Spiedel in *Invasion 1944* and cited by Paul Johnson (op. cit.).

concrete overlooking the Channel. He continued to dream his dreams and a longstanding plot to kill him was put into effect. It was the work of the aristocratic old guard of the officer corps, many of whom regarded Hitler as an upstart ex-corporal.

On 20 July, Hitler chaired a meeting of his military staff at Rastenburg. One of those present was Count Claus Schenk Graf von Stauffenberg, whose briefcase contained a bomb made by a sabotage expert, General Freytag von Loringhoven. Stauffenberg slipped the case beneath the conference table, propped it with apparent casualness against a chair leg and rose, murmuring something like, 'Entschuldigen Sie, mein Führer ... Ich kom' gleich zurück . . .' But he was not coming back. He had reached the outer compound when he heard the explosion.

He now made a mistake. Instead of turning back to the wrecked conference room with expressions of concern, he scurried to his aircraft and flew to Berlin to announce Hitler's death. A new military government would now take over. The snag was that Hitler had survived, albeit with perforated ear-drums (which inspired the comment that he had not listened to other people anyway), severe bruising and concussion. Four of those around him were dead or dying. Perhaps he had turned away at the critical moment of detonation. Arguably, the wooden table and floor had absorbed much of the blast: the conference would normally have taken place in a concrete bunker. This would not be the last time that an otherwise deadly explosion would be muffled. Nevertheless, Hitler's survival was remarkable. Later that day he showed guests, including Mussolini, damage created when the walls caught fire and the roof fell in. He boasted, 'I am destined to carry on our great common cause to a happy conclusion.'

Later the same day, as the shock wore off, he exploded in a paroxysm of rage which continued incandescently for half an hour. No one involved in the plot, even women or children, would escape, he screamed. In the purge which followed, more than fifty staff officers were put to death and hundreds more were removed from senior jobs. The Intelligence chief, Admiral Canaris, struggled for life for thirty minutes suspended by an iron collar round his neck. Rommel was sent a revolver and a suicide pill, with the Führer's compliments. The effects of Hitler's unexpected survival were Messianic, accelerating the blind man's march of the Third Reich over the most convenient precipice. It is surprising that the Hitler myth survived, however vestigially.

The lesson for close protection was familiar. Heavily armed security screens are also brittle when penetrated by an insider of senior rank. Hitler's numerous guards were too respectful to examine von Stauffenberg's bag before he entered the presence.

1947: Sergeants Paice and Martin, British prisoners of the Zionist terrorist group, Irgun Zwai Leumi, led by Menachem Begin.

The two soldiers were hanged as a reprisal for the execution of two members of Irgun, and their bodies, booby-trapped to cause further deaths, were left suspended in a eucalyptus grove near Natanya, Palestine.

Taken with the blowing-up of the King David Hotel the year before, these assassinations broke the will of the Labour government in London – some of whose members were overt Zionists – to resist a movement which now had the backing of America's most influential political lobby. Anti-Semitism was made briefly respectable in the UK, with many synagogues attacked. In Palestine, by way of revenge, the departing Tommies discreetly armed the emerging Arab response to Zionism, the Palestine Liberation Organisation. An offshoot of the PLO gave birth in 1968 to the most ruthless forms of international terrorism, forging a tool for disguised, surrogate warfare used against the West by such governments as Libya's ever since.

Paul Johnson (op. cit.) wrote of the Irgun in 1983: 'For the first time modern propaganda was combined with Leninist cell-structure and advanced technology to advance political aims through murder. During the next forty years, the example was to be followed all over the world . . .'

January 1948: Mahatma Gandhi.

Gandhi was shot at close range by a fanatical Hindu newspaper editor, Nathuram Vinayak Godse, as he prepared to conduct an open prayer meeting in his garden at Delhi. Godse and his co-conspirators blamed Gandhi for partition at the time of British withdrawal from India, and regarded him – because of his success in preaching tolerance of Islam – as a traitor to his religion and race. Only ten days before, an earlier attempt to kill Gandhi in the same garden had failed when one of the assassins set off an explosion there. The suspicion has lingered ever since that some police officers had knowledge that another attempt would be made. The man responsible for the explosion was in custody when Gandhi was murdered. Both assassins were hanged and five conspirators given life sentences. The assassination demonstrated that although moral persuasion – the use of non-violence – was effective when applied against a colonial power, such as Britain, with its own ethical beliefs (a Labour government had granted India self-government in 1947), Gandhi's moral force was not so persuasive among his own countrymen.

In the years which followed independence, assassination continued to be a feature of the political landscape. The victims included (see below) Mrs Indira Gandhi (1984); General Arun Vaidya, the former army chief who led the assault on the Sikhs' Golden Temple at Amritsar (1986);

and Prime Minister Rajiv Gandhi (a mismanaged shooting which he survived) (1986).

1948: Arthur Walker, British rubber planter.
Walker was shot dead on Elphil Estate, Perak, Malaya, by three young Chinese assassins of the Lie Ton Ten arm of the Communist Secret Army. The death squad, travelling by bicycle, had been armed by the British to fight a guerrilla war against the occupying Japanese. Like many such irregular forces, this one turned against its colonial creator. A few miles away from the scene of Walker's death, planter Ian Christian and his manager, Mr J. Alison, were bound to chairs and murdered. Christian had armed himself the previous day with an old Luger pistol.

Some Malayan workers had already been assassinated by the Red Chinese teams, one of whose leaders later ritually murdered a pregnant woman with a knife before an audience of horrified fellow villagers. But it required the deaths of Europeans to provoke the declaration of a legal state of emergency in Malaya. By March 1950, a total of 863 civilians, 323 police officers and 154 soldiers had been killed by the Communist Terrorists. One prominent victim of assassination – in a carefully prepared ambush as he drove through the jungle – was the UK High Commissioner, Sir Henry Gurney. The effects of Walker's assassination and those which followed included a jungle war which the Communists lost, costing thousands of lives over a decade, and the creation of 22 Special Air Service Regiment as a full-time special force of the regular British Army.

September 1948: Count Folke Bernadotte, Swedish nobleman, nephew of the King and United Nations mediator supervising the UN takeover of the British Mandate in Palestine that inaugurated Israel.
Bernadotte was shot dead at an Israeli-manned checkpoint

by Stern Gang Hazit Hamoledeth terrorists in army uniform. With Bernadotte were his chief of staff, General Aage Landstrom, and a French officer, Colonel Serot. Their progress was systematically signalled by unnecessary halts at Israeli checkpoints. Landstrom later wrote: 'In the Qatamon Quarter [of Jerusalem] we were held up by a Jewish Army-type jeep, placed in a road block and filled with men in Jewish Army uniform. At the same time I saw a man running from the jeep. I took little notice of this because I merely thought that it was another checkpoint. However, he put a tommy-gun through the open window on my side of the car and fired point-blank at Count Bernadotte and Colonel Serot. I also heard shots fired from other points and there was considerable confusion . . .'

Bernadotte had come to Israel, 'the child of the UN' as the writer David Hirst puts it in *The Gun and the Olive Branch*, full of warmth for the Zionist ideal, possibly because he had been instrumental in saving 30,000 Jews from concentration camps. But the Zionists, pleased with their victory in the 'Ten Day War', did not welcome his efforts to mediate between the two communities in Palestine. Hints that he should go away were followed by heavy-handed threats. A broadcast 'reported' his assassination before it happened. When General Lindstrom suggested they take a low-profile route into Jerusalem, Bernadotte refused. 'I have to take the same risks as my observers,' he said. 'Moreover I think no one has the right to refuse me permission to pass through the line.' As they made their return journey, the assassins were waiting. Bernadotte had no trained protection team with him. He had not learned from earlier Zionist assassinations, including that of Lord Moyne, British Resident in the Middle East. Worse, he worked secretly with Britain to revise UN partition proposals. Zionists saw him as a British puppet, but his assassination provided further legitimacy for Arab fanaticism.

August 1949: Husni Za'im, President of Syria.
Za'im was shot dead by a lieutenant in his own army in
revenge for his deportation to Lebanon of a Syrian extremist
wanted there. It was an early example, encouraging to
Israel, of the Arab habit of wiping out one another as part
of their internecine struggles. Most Arab rulers observed a
need for foreign bodyguards. Engineers of this coup bribed
the commander of Za'im's Circassian guard to be absent
when the death squad arrived with armoured cars. The
other guards surrendered and Za'im was taken away in his
pyjamas. Those who congratulated the plotters included
King Abdullah of Jordan (assassinated in 1951) and Iraq's
leader, Nuri as-Said (murdered in 1958).

July 1951: King Abdullah of Jordan.
In 1948, shortly before the first war between the new state
of Israel and her Arab neighbours, King Abdullah was
warned by a Zionist friend, Ezra Danin, 'Your Majesty,
beware when you go to the Mosque to worship and let
people rush up to kiss your robe. Some day a man will
shoot you like that.'

Abdullah (see *O Jerusalem* by Larry Collins and Dominique Lapierre) replied: 'My dear friend, I was born a free
man, a Bedouin. I cannot leave the ways of my father to
become a prisoner of my guards.'

On Friday 19 July the King went to the Mosque of Omar
in Jerusalem to mingle on equal terms with his 'brothers'
in Islam, as the sabbath law requires, and was shot dead as
he entered the place. He knew his time had come and had
just nominated his Sandhurst-trained grandson, Hussein,
to succeed him. Hussein (like President de Gaulle) survived
an estimated thirty attempts to assassinate him. With American aid, he overturned revolutionary elements in his own
country and established an authoritarian rule based on the
army and the Bedouin tribal organisation opposed to the

Palestinians, who created armed camps in his country. In the 1970s he defeated a Palestinian attempt to take over Jordan, using tanks to do so. He has remained a friend of the West (one of the few in the region) and become one of the world's most elusive statesmen in his determination not to repeat the error of Abdullah by becoming an easy target.

1954: Guy Monnerot, French schoolteacher on an aid programme in an impoverished part of Algeria.
With his French wife and a local 'caid' (a French-appointed official) Monnerot, a young idealist, was on a bus in the Aures mountains when it was halted by an armed gang. The three were taken off the bus, while local Berbers and Arabs were left unmolested, and shot in cold blood. The caid's body was put back on the bus and the vehicle continued its journey. Monnerot died slowly, leaning against a milestone on a cold mountain pass, his wife, also wounded, beside him. Algeria's war of 'liberation' had begun. No bodyguard accompanied the French couple but the bus driver, responsible for his passengers' safety, did not need to stop when signalled, or drive away leaving Monnerot to die. It is thought that the driver was intimidated in advance by the terrorists. The war which followed claimed 400,000 lives and provoked a mutiny against the decision of President de Gaulle to withdraw from Algeria. The mutiny was led by the French Foreign Legion's élite 1st Parachute Regiment, which was promptly disbanded.

1956: President Gamal Abdel Nasser of Egypt.
Nasser, an advocate of assassination whose proposed targets included King Hussein of Jordan, was the target of a British Secret Service (MI6) plot during the Suez crisis. British Premier Eden characteristically changed his mind about the scheme when it seemed that collusion with France and Israel would bring down the Egyptian leader without

the coarseness of assassination. But later, when American opposition halted orthodox military operations, British intelligence cobbled together a new plot against Nasser. Nasser, although a loud-mouth, had an intelligence network more effective than that of his successor Sadat (see below). When it became clear that several whistles were being blown in Cairo, Eden again backed off and the plan was ditched. The effect was to reinforce even further Egypt's repudiation of the West. For a long time thereafter, Egypt became a Soviet satellite.

1956: Nikita Khrushchev.

At the Soviet Communist Party's 20th Congress in Moscow, Stalin's successor Khrushchev publicly denounced the country's godfather for his years of terror and execution. In 1988, in the dawn of *perestroika*, Khrushchev's former speech-writer, Fyodor Burlatsky, revealed: 'The 1956 speech was one of those rare occasions in history when a political leader risked his own power and even his life in the name of the greater public good.'

Writing in the weekly *Literary Gazette*, Burlatsky (now a prominent member of the reforming Gorbachev administration) described the dangerous power game in the Kremlin following Stalin's death. As reported by Robert Evans of Reuters, Burlatsky quoted Khrushchev's version of 'the plotting that went into the arrest and execution of Stalin's secret police chief and potential successor, Lavrenty Beria. This included the famous scene, never before publicly recounted in Moscow, of how Beria was thought to have been about to draw a gun at the Politburo meeting when his dismissal was voted.

'Politburo members froze in fear when Beria went for the gun hidden in his briefcase, but Khrushchev, also armed, slapped the briefcase down and held it while pushing a secret button to summon an arrest team. "Seize this serpent

. . . and take him away," he snapped as Beria collapsed on the floor, mumbling incoherently.'

Khrushchev was eventually ousted from power, though peacefully, and died in political obscurity in 1971. In Gorbachev the ghost of moderation has come back to haunt the Stalinists, who are still numerous. It may be supposed, if he follows Khrushchev's example, that Gorbachev himself will also go armed at meetings they attend.

1958: King Faisal of Iraq and Prime Minister Nuri as-Said.

Faisal's death during a military coup ended a short-lived royal dynasty created by the British. A hard-line socialist and republican regime succeeded. The country's former prime minister, Nuri as-Said, regarded as Britain's front man in the Middle East, was captured while trying to escape from Baghdad disguised as a woman. He was murdered on the spot and his body dragged through the streets behind a jeep.

1960 onwards: Fidel Castro, President of Cuba.

By his own account, this Communist leader has been the target of twenty-four CIA-sponsored assassination attempts. American insiders claim that the plots of which he knew were *not* the work of the CIA, but that there were others which the 'Company' did engineer. These showed a taste for the exotic which broke the basic rule for successful assassination, 'Keep It Simple'. The methods proposed included sniper rifles; poison pens and pills; exploding cigars and bacteria. The day President Kennedy was murdered, a CIA case officer handed a poison pen to a Cuban assassin for use against Castro. Many of these schemes later came to light before the Senate Select Committee to Study Government Operations with Respect to Intelligence Activities. In agency eyes, Soviet development of Cuba as a base so close to the US mainland was more than a provocation.

It was a 'clear and present danger' tantamount to an act of war. When this was combined with the aid Castro provided other revolutionaries in the Americas (as does Gaddafi in Europe) to attempt to kill Castro became seen as legitimate self-defence in the eyes of a liberal American government as well as the CIA.

The assassination plots were most intense at a special time and for a peculiar reason. In May 1960, a US spy plane was shot down over the Soviet Union, and with it, Washington's intelligence about Soviet missile progress. Until the first American photo-reconnaissance satellite was launched in late 1962, the West had no accurate information about the 'missile gap' thought to be developing in Russia's favour between the super-powers. In this vulnerable period, Castro's flirtation with Moscow, culminating in the acceptance of intermediate range missiles on Cuban soil, made him a priority target. Castro's international charisma derives as much from his reputation as the man the CIA (and the Mafia) could not kill as from his image as a bearded jungle warrior.

1961: Rafael Trujillo, 'El Benefactor', Dictator of Dominican Republic.
After a run of thirty-one years, Trujillo was assassinated with CIA complicity. By then he had conjured enemies from every group between the Roman Catholic Church and the White House. Trujillo had arranged the deaths and disappearances of many political opponents and/or their closest kin. In a variant of the medieval murder by defenestration, he fixed mysterious road crashes over the edges of cliffs fronting the island's precipitate coast. He signed his own death warrant by promoting a scheme to assassinate President Romulo Betancourt of Venezuela in June 1961. The Senate Select Committee on Intelligence found that the CIA worked indirectly but lethally to remove Trujillo. A

despot with many enemies, he was vulnerable to any who could lay their hands on the weapons to do the job. Sandy Lesberg writes in *Assassination in Our Time*: 'No disclosure was made outside the CIA except to the State Department representative in the Dominican Republic, of the fact that the weapons had been sent to the Dominican Republic via the diplomatic pouch.' Soon afterwards the Kennedy administration had sought to withdraw its support for assassination but it was too late.

Trujillo depended for his security (like more successful heads of state including King Hassan of Morocco) upon continuous unannounced movement rather than round-the-clock bodyguards. At any one of twelve homes, his dinner would be prepared without it being known to his domestic staff where he would dine, or sleep. For close protection he relied upon his chauffeur and his own revolver. His movements were betrayed by some of his inner circle, one of whom, Lieutenant Amado Garcia, joined the shooting party. Trujillo's unescorted vehicle was ambushed by three others just outside the capital and more than fifty rounds fired into it. The chauffeur survived and identified Garcia. Trujillo did not survive. His dynasty stayed in power long enough to avenge itself on most of the assassins. The political results were to underscore the message in the Americas (see Chile; Grenada *et al.*) that political power in the Caribbean and overtures to the Communist world were incompatible.

1963: President Ngo Dinh Diem of South Vietnam and his brother Nhu.

Both men were assassinated by a major in their own army during a coup launched with the foreknowledge of the US government. Washington was concerned that the Diem regime was alienating its own support to a point of jeopardising the war against the Communist North (which finally won the war to create the existing Republic of Vietnam). After the coup, Diem and Nhu were captives, hands bound behind their backs, in an armoured vehicle. Their escorting major stabbed Nhu with his bayonet, then shot both men with his revolver, allegedly to settle a personal score.

Diem and Nhu had created the most operatic defence ever to an impending coup. They persuaded themselves that they could stage a pseudo-coup, pre-empting opposition to themselves. They were to 'escape' to a hideout away from the capital, Saigon, while (in the words of an official US study later published unexpectedly as *The Pentagon Papers*) there were 'several days of hooliganism including the murder of several prominent Vietnamese and some Americans'. Troops loyal to themselves would then assault the capital, defeat the pseudo-enemy in a rigged contest and permit Diem and Nhu to return as heroes.

When the real coup happened, they believed it was a benign event. It was not. Further, at the rebel headquarters was a CIA representative. Diem, as the truth dawned, telephoned the US Ambassador, Henry Cabot Lodge. The official record reveals that Lodge was 'not well enough informed' to brief Diem on America's attitude to the rebellion, adding, 'As I told you only this morning [just before the revolt began] I admire your courage and your great contribution to your country . . . Now I am worried about your physical safety. I have a report that those in charge of the current activity offer you and your brother safe conduct out of the country if you resign. Had you heard this?'

Diem: No. (And then after a pause) You have my telephone number.

Lodge: Yes. If I can do anything for your physical safety, please call me.

Diem: I am trying to re-establish order.

A palace guard and a tank unit alone remained loyal and

prepared to fight to the last, believing that the brothers were with them. They were not. They sneaked out through the sewers to another refuge. Some hours later a three-hour battle for the palace involved an artillery and aerial bombardment. Then, using a communications link prepared for such an eventuality, Diem was able to order the cease-fire to the men who thought he was sharing the battle with them.

When the brothers' hideaway was traced they fled to a Catholic church. There they were captured, put into the armoured personnel carrier, and murdered. Three months before, the State Department had secretly signalled Ambassador Lodge, 'The US government will support a coup which has a good chance of succeeding but plans no direct involvement of US armed forces.' The Ambassador even proposed that the CIA representative should assure the coup leader that the US would not thwart his plans and 'offer to review his plans, other than assassination plans'. Washington, it would seem, was indifferent on the assassination issue this time.

The coup's success increased US confidence in victory in Vietnam and led to a vast increase in the number of GIs committed to the war. The effects of that are still felt throughout the Western world.

The lesson for future besieged leaders was that survival plans on which everything depends should not include a double-bluff such as a pseudo-coup which defeats its own ends.

1963: Hugh Gaitskell, Leader of the Opposition.

Gaitskell's sudden death from the rare disease lupus disseminata provoked suspicion within MI5 that he was yet another victim of KGB Department XIII, responsible for political assassination. (Earlier victims were usually defectors such as the renegade intelligence chief Walter Krivitsky in Washington, February 1941, or other native-born enemies such as Trotsky.) In 1988 it emerged that Gaitskell's opponent, the Conservative Prime Minister Harold Macmillan, had opened a file in 1957, a year after the Suez adventure, on 'Leader of the Opposition'. Unlike many other papers of that year, this file was not released for publication under the thirty-year rule but is the subject of a seventy-five-year embargo. The file's contents will not be known until AD 2032. Meanwhile, MPs and historians continue to ask why there should be such a mystery about Gaitskell's last six years, and why the allegations of assassination go unanswered.

January 1965: Hassan Ali Mansour, Prime Minister of Iran. Shot dead by Islamic fundamentalists.

February 1965: Malcolm X aka Malcolm Little.
Back street hustler and convict turned Black Muslim turned apostle of racial tolerance, Malcolm X was shot dead while addressing a meeting in a New York ballroom. His case is of interest to this study not because of his political status – as a civil rights leader he was not in the same league as Martin Luther King. But the tactics used to kill X have been noted with interest by specialists in close protection. The victim, like many other targets for assassination, had received warnings of trouble ahead. A week before he was slain an attempt was made to burn his house down. It was uncertain whether that crime was the work of some of the Black Muslims' wilder spirits, who regarded him as a heretic, or whether this was an attempt to inspire by example. Malcolm X had bodyguards who on the day of the killing were apparently lured away from his immediate presence by a diversionary smoke bomb at the rear of the hall. Amid much confusion a man armed with a sawn-off shotgun then blasted Malcolm X in the chest at short range.

Two others were seen to shoot at him. All escaped, eluding the bodyguards. Three men (two of them Black Muslims) were later imprisoned for the crime but the surrounding circumstances generated a widespread belief that the godfathers who planned the murder were never brought to book.

January 1966: Abubakar Tafawa Balewa, Federal Prime Minister of Nigeria.

Killed during a military coup, ending one of emergent, post-colonial Africa's few trials of civilian government.

September 1966: Hendrik Verwoerd, Prime Minister of South Africa.

As the architect of the apartheid code, Verwoerd knew how much he was at risk in April 1960, when he was shot twice in the head as he addressed a public meeting. He unexpectedly survived. Six years later, as he sat on the front bench of an adjourned House of Assembly in Cape Town, he was approached by a parliamentary messenger, smartly turned out in the green-and-black livery of the place. He hardly glanced up as the man stood over him, raised his arm, and then plunged a dagger into him, three times.

In fact, this was not a political assassination, but an act of madness by a notorious schizophrenic, Demitrio Tsafendas, the Mozambique-born offspring of a Cretan father and a mother of mixed blood. He fulfilled all the American criteria of the lone, psychopathic killer: a man who made no lasting human relationships, and a compulsive drifter. His journeys – sometimes as a merchant seaman – took him to North America, Europe and the Middle East. He believed that his body, and sometimes his mind also, had been taken over by an enormous tapeworm which lived inside him. His recruitment as a parliamentary messenger added very little to the reputation of the South African security services. Politically, the murder was a non-event. It demonstrated the truism that people can be killed, but ideas cannot.

April 1968: Martin Luther King, disciple of Mahatma Gandhi; black civil rights leader.

King was a worldwide symbol of non-violent protest against racial injustice and a Nobel Peace Prize winner in 1964. His hypnotic oratory, based upon such Biblical texts as 'The Eagle Stirreth Her Nest', was still powerful when he arrived at Memphis to win rights for the city's sewage and garbage workers. His enemies ranged from the Ku Klux Klan to the FBI boss J. Edgar Hoover, whose agents secretly tape-recorded King's sexual frolics in hotels around the country, then invited him to commit suicide before the transcripts were published. Newspaper editors – even white supremacists – declined to use the FBI material. What British intelligence had done to Roger Casement after his execution, the FBI failed to achieve, in King's case, before the event. King would not be silenced or blackmailed although by 1968 the FBI had logged fifty threats to assassinate him. This figure was probably an underestimate. He received up to forty threatening letters each day and more than twenty telephone calls uttering telephone threats against himself, his wife Coretta, and their daughter. He was also worn down by the 'freezing and paralysing effect' of fear. (See for example, *Let The Trumpet Sound* by Stephen B. Oates.) In 1956, his house was bombed. He tolerated armed guards for a time but then ordered them away. Like many others, he would place himself in God's hands. In Nashville, a police officer threatened to kill him if he returned. Southern businessmen offered up to $50,000 for his head. In his last great speech – the 'Mountaintop' address – Luther King recalled how he had been stabbed in New York ten years before, when the blade was so close to his aorta that he would have died if he had sneezed. He recalled a threat of a bomb on his aircraft that morning. He rejected the hatred with the words: 'With this faith I will go out and carve a tunnel of hope from a mountain of despair.' Those close to him sensed a premonition.

The following evening, as he emerged on to the second-floor balcony of the Lorraine Motel on the fringe of Memphis's black ghetto, a rifle shot cracked and the bullet smashed into the right side of his jaw, shattering his spine. A white man was seen to flee from the area, in a white car. Within ten minutes, a .30-06 rifle fitted with a sniperscope was found near the scene. It bore the fingerprints of a veteran gaolbird, James Earl Ray. Nevertheless, Ray was able to pick up false identity papers from an unknown source and travel to Europe before being arrested two months later at Heathrow Airport, London. He confessed to the killing but after receiving a 99-year sentence, retracted the confession, claiming that he merely bought the weapon and drove the getaway car. The assassin was someone he knew only as 'Raoul'. Ray had a backer, or backers, to provide him with funds and documents, but who they were remains a mystery.

The impact on the US was considerable. King's non-violent search for civil rights was discredited as Stokely Carmichael declared, 'When White America killed Dr King, she declared war on us. Get your gun.' Many did. In riots across 110 cities, almost thirty-nine people (most of them black) were killed. But 75,000 military reservists and regular soldiers were needed to keep order.

It was a white Attorney-General, Robert Kennedy, who arranged for King's body to be flown in a chartered jet, to his Atlanta home. Two months later, Robert Kennedy was also a victim of assassination.

1969: Tom Mboya, Kenyan politician, likely successor to founding father Jomo Kenyatta.

As Mboya walked from a shop in the centre of Nairobi accompanied by his bodyguard, a car glided into the kerb and a gunman stepped out, killing Mboya with a single carefully aimed shot to the chest before being driven away. Mboya's bodyguard stood and wept. The killing had the hallmarks of a professional assassination. Later a bodyguard for other political figures, Nahashon Isaac Njenga Njoroye, was hanged for the crime. As in many such cases, the plotters who inspired the murder were not brought to justice. Eighteen months before his death Mboya was the target for a first, unsuccessful attempt on his life when an army sentry guarding his home started shooting at him. The incident was attributed to madness on the guard's part. The effect of the killing, when it did occur, was to rob Kenya and Africa of one of its few talented moderates, capable of rising above the deadly call of tribal loyalty: Mboya was born into the minority Luo tribe. It is even possible that Mboya's death was provoked by that breadth of mind, as in the case of Mahatma Gandhi and others. His murder was also one of the first of many killings of a rising African politician by fellow Africans in post-colonial Africa for reasons unconnected with the East-West struggle.

1971: Dougald McCaughey, John McCaig, Joseph McCaig, 1st Battalion, Royal Highland Fusiliers.

The men were 'walking out' (off duty) in a Belfast bar, unarmed and in civilian clothes. John McCaig was aged eighteen and his brother Joseph, seventeen. The three were 'befriended' by young people of their own age who led them to a Provisional IRA team. The assassins also simulated an old-fashioned Irish welcome. That night, having been plied with alcohol, the soldiers were taken to lonely Squire's Hill near Divis Mountain. There each was shot in the back of the head by three separate assassins, one of whom put a bullet into all three victims. Only eighteen months earlier the Catholic community of Belfast had welcomed the soldiers as saviours from Protestant intimidation.

These cold-blooded killings envenomed (as the terrorists intended) efforts to establish political stability and brought down the Unionist government of James Chichester-Clark. Angry Protestants demonstrated for and got internment of IRA suspects without trial. The brutality which that caused – old scores were settled but the wrong people paid – alienated most Catholics so completely that it took another sixteen years and the atrocity of the Enniskillen cenotaph bombing of 1987 before perceptions changed to any degree.

The 1971 killings were a successful exercise in the use of political murder to polarise opinion. Within a year of the triple assassination Britain was obliged to impose direct rule on Northern Ireland from London. The cenotaph bomb fifteen years after that was one of a series of sectarian attacks on Protestants probably aimed at the ultimate de-stabilisation: a religious war engulfing both communities on a scale seen so far only in Beirut.

November 1971: Wasfi al-Tal, Jordanian Prime Minister. King Hussein's iron man in the drive against an attempted Palestinian takeover of Jordan was shot down on the steps of Cairo's Sheraton Hotel by four freelance members of the Black September movement. The writer and Arabist David Hirst believes that al-Tal was the first victim of 'a whole new phase of Palestinian violence – pure, unbridled terrorism' in a backlash of Arab v. Arab which followed the Palestinian expulsion from Jordan backed by the King's Bedouin-manned tanks. The four assassins were charged in Cairo but released as a result of popular pressure. Other Jordanian spokesmen who became targets were the London Ambassador, Zaid al-Rifai (wounded by forty sub-machine-gun rounds while driving to the Embassy on 15 December 1971), and Ambassador Ibrahim Zreikat in Geneva, the target of a parcel bomb which injured two Swiss police officers. A confidential study of the al-Tal murder comments: 'Tal had some Jordanian security people with him but had also refused full security measures and as a result they were not providing him with any sort of moving escort.'

The assassination team sat drinking coffee in the hotel lobby for almost three hours as they awaited their victim. Though they created a commotion at one point, they were not checked by security staff.

1973: Salvador Allende, President of Chile.

Allende was shot dead during a gun battle with his own army during a military coup. It was probably not an assassination as such (one version of the story is that the death was suicide). (But see the case of Orlando Letelier, Pinochet *et al.* under 1976 below.)

December 1973: Carrero Blanco, Prime Minister of Spain.

Blown up by Basque ETA terrorists (see Part II).

1973: Teddy Sieff, a prominent British Zionist, President of Marks & Spencer.

This was one act of terror by Carlos Marighella ('The Jackal') which did not accomplish its aim. When he attacked Sieff on New Year's Eve in London, Marighella's gun jammed and he had to abandon the attempt. It demonstrated that even experts sometimes have technical problems.

1975: Ross McWhirter, publisher.

McWhirter was shot dead on the doorstep of his house in the Home Counties after publicly offering a reward leading to the arrest of an IRA murder squad operating in England. As Walter Laqueur (op. cit.) has noted, 'the most dangerous threat to terrorists is the promise of a reward for information leading to their capture'. Gladstone used the device after the Phoenix Park murders of 1882. In the 1970s and 80s, after McWhirter's murder, there was no one bold enough to step into his shoes.

1975: King Faisal of Saudi Arabia.

The King was shot dead by his nephew, Prince Faisal, while receiving formal homage from visitors including the assassin. Prince Faisal was an unstable wanderer who had passed years in the US brooding over the fact that he was a prince, drinking and gambling ... and then brooding over the death of his brother Prince Khalid, an Islamic fundamentalist. In 1966 Khalid led a mob attacking a new Saudi television station, reasoning that it was a defiance of Koranic law. All Arab monarchs have learned to beware of falling foul of Islam's 'hedge priests', purists claiming to have a hot line to the Prophet. This is particularly true of the Saudis, whose kingdom encompasses the shrine of Mecca. So Khalid was engaged in a particularly dangerous form of subversion, in Saudi eyes, when a policeman stopped his protest with a bullet. His brother, Prince Faisal, one of thousands of princes descended from the Ibn Saud stud, all enjoying a superior status over other citizens, demanded that the police officer should be put to death. The King refused.

After a nine-year ride through the adventure playground of the US during which he was arrested for possessing drugs, Prince Faisal returned home to make the great moral gesture he believed his brother's death required. As a member of the family he was able to walk past armed guards unimpeded. As the King waited to greet him, Prince Faisal stood over him, drew a revolver from his robes and fired three shots, shouting, 'Now my brother is avenged!' He was arrested and beheaded publicly soon afterwards. King Faisal was succeeded by his half-brother Khalid. If the assassination affected Saudi policies at all, it was to make the ruling family even more sceptical of the benefits offered by the fundamentalists, particularly those who sought to export their revolution to Saudi Arabia from Iran via the pilgrimage to Mecca. In 1987 an Iranian-led assault on police in the holy city replicated Prince Khalid's offence on a large scale and again the police opened fire, killing about two hundred demonstrators.

1975: President Ngarta Tombalbaye, Ruler of Chad.
Killed during army coup.

1975: Sheik Mujibur Rahman, President of Bangladesh.
Killed during army coup.

1976: General Murtala Muhammad, head of state of Nigeria.
Shot dead during attempted military coup.

These three cases (among many) are illustrative of the growing disorder in former colonies, a generation after independence. See also Uganda.

1976: Orlando Letelier, former minister in Allende's socialist government and leader of Chilean exile resistance in the US.
After the Pinochet military coup of September 1973 which overthrew the democratically elected President Salvador Allende, Letelier was imprisoned without trial with thousands of others, then released and told to stay out of politics. From Washington, Letelier developed close links with Castro's Communist Cuba but shrugged off as paranoia

warnings that he was a target of the Chilean Secret Police, DINA. While his car was parked, unguarded, on his front drive an agent of DINA – Michael Vernon Townley, a native of Iowa aka Juan Andres Wilson or Kenneth Enyard or Jan Williams Rose or Hans Petersen Silva – crept under the vehicle and taped to the bodywork beneath the driver's seat a high-explosive bomb he had constructed several hours before in a motel. Two Cuban exile opponents of Castro then trailed Letelier's car and detonated the bomb using an adapted radio-paging device as the initiator. The device killed Letelier and an American woman sympathiser, Ronni Karpen Moffitt, who had married a fellow American only a few months before.

Townley escaped to Chile but the regime of President Carter was determined to identify the source of political assassination in the heart of its own capital. After a diplomatic tug-o'-war Townley was extradited to the US where his plea bargain with the US government resulted in May 1979 in an admission of conspiracy to murder Letelier and a ten-year sentence with parole eligibility after three years and four months. He was rapidly given a new identity by the FBI and released. The Letelier murder did not dampen the enthusiasm of Pinochet's opponents or reduce his need of bodyguards.

In September 1986 a team of thirty guerrillas armed with rockets and machine guns fired on Pinochet's convoy, which included four escort vehicles, on a road near his weekend home ('El Bunker') at Santiago. Three cars including one of the two presidential vehicles were destroyed and five bodyguards killed outright, with up to twenty more injured. Pinochet's life was probably saved by his chauffeur, one of the few ambushed security drivers in such episodes who has had the wit to reverse out, swing round and double back to safety. Pinochet suffered a wound in one hand. He imposed a state of siege on the country and said, 'My first instinct was to get out of the car but then I remembered that my grandson was with me so I covered his body with mine.' If Pinochet had got out of the car, he would probably have followed the examples of Heydrich and others, into the grave. In February 1987, the FBI spirited another of the Letelier assassination team – Armando Fernandez – out of Chile and into protective custody under armed guard. He also pleaded guilty as part of a process of judicial bargaining.

1976: President Jorge Rafael Videla of Argentina.
Escaped when a bomb in a parade ground blew up the reviewing stand moments after he left a closely-guarded military zone. This was a sign of continuing instability following the Peron years and the military coup led by Videla against Isabel Peron. The same instability led to counter-assassination and abduction by government agents and finally – in a desperate attempt to unify the nation against the collective enemy abroad – invasion of the Falklands in 1982.

October 1977: Hans-Martin Schleyer, murdered after forty-three days as terrorist captive.
Schleyer, the figurehead of West German industry, was a marked man and already under guard when his kidnappers struck on the street near his Cologne home. He was chauffeured by a police officer with an escort of three armed police officers in a back-up Mercedes. A yellow Mercedes moved into the clear path between them and a woman pushed a perambulator into the remaining area of open road. Schleyer's driver was unwilling to run over a baby and halted. The pram was part of the trap and a ruse. Six terrorists emerged from the yellow Mercedes and a Volkswagen bus parked nearby and used automatic weapons to kill the four policemen.

The operation demonstrated the professional training received by the new generation of European terrorists – the Red Army Faction – and seemed to offer advantages over assassination and hijacking, including concealment of the terrorists while they played cat-and-mouse with the authorities and the victim. But the ultimate murder of Schleyer (his body had three bullet wounds in the head when found in a car boot at Mulhouse, in France) added nothing to the credibility of the 'people's' justice. Soon afterwards, the terrorists Andreas Baader, Gudrun Ensslin and Jan-Carl Raspe, who had expected to gain their freedom through the blackmail of Schleyer's kidnap (combined with the Mogadishu hijack), were found dead in their cells at Stammheim prison, presumed to be suicides. British bodyguards, studying the case, have since been heard to swear that any attempt to force their car to halt by the sudden appearance of a perambulator will be doomed to failure. One of them told the author: 'If it happens in Ireland I will drive right on. The Irish can make another baby if I have made a mistake. I cannot replace a good General Officer commanding the area.'

January 1978: Said Hammami, Palestine Liberation Organisation London representative.
Hammami was shot dead in his London office. A moderate in the world of rabid Arab politics, Hammami was thought to be negotiating with the Israelis on behalf of PLO leader Yasser Arafat for an end to the Middle East's oldest conflict, combined with recognition for the PLO. Left-wing Palestinians of the PFLP or a similar group were suspected of engineering this assassination. The conflict had made little progress ten years later, when Arafat's military commander, Abu Jihad (real name, Khalil al-Wazir), was assassinated with military precision at his villa near Tunis, probably by agents of Israel's secret service, Mossad. Wazir's killing was

preceded by the deaths of his bodyguard and gardener, with silenced weapons. The telephones were jammed electronically and the killing filmed by a woman member of the assassination squad, which abandoned its three vehicles on a beach thirty miles away. A senior PLO official, Ahmed Abdel Rahman, observed acidly that assassination was becoming 'an ordinary thing'. He added: 'Our central committee used to have fifteen members. Now it is down to ten.'

The Israelis, in reply, reminded the world of the murder of its eleven Olympic athletes at Munich in 1972 and later operations for which it blamed Abu Jihad, notably the seizure of a bus on the coast road between Tel Aviv and Haifa in 1978 in which thirty-three Israelis were killed. In 1973, an Israeli revenge squad, 'Wrath of God', bombed and shot its way across Europe, killing one enemy in Paris with a bomb triggered by a phone call to his home.

At the bottom line, the lesson for the PLO leadership was stark: assassination by its own wilder elements if it tried to make peace with Israel; assassination by Mossad if it did not.

May 1978: Aldo Moro, Italian elder statesman, murdered in captivity by Red Brigades.

In an operation similar to the Schleyer killing, Moro's car with its escorts was boxed in by superior numbers (possibly thirty terrorists or more) and hit by superior firepower. All five bodyguards (three in a back-up car) were shot dead during the initial kidnap in March 1978. By 1987 the Italian government was permitting some of the assassins holiday breaks from long terms of imprisonment. In the *Daily Mail*, Ronald Singleton wrote on New Year's Day: 'Adriana Faranda, a beautiful 37-year-old, was driven from a top security prison to her parents' home in Rome's classy Monte Mario quarter. She let in the New Year with champagne, traditional chicken, cake ... and hugged and kissed her daughter Sandra, aged 15.'

Asked if she had regrets she said: 'Yes, for all the life I have not lived. For not being with my daughter. For errors which led me to contribute towards a terrorist war machine.'

The holiday shocked the Moro family and the widows and children of the dead bodyguards.

1978: Georgi Markov.

Markov, a Bulgarian defector and the author of hostile broadcasts from the West to Bulgaria, was stabbed in the buttock by an agent using an umbrella tipped with a poisoned dart. The attack might have come from a fictional spy thriller. Markov was injected as he waited for a bus home from the headquarters of the BBC External Service, Bush House, in the heart of London. While he was dying, he had the additional nightmare of trying to persuade the authorities that he had been injected in this way. An autopsy revealed that a fragment of the dart, one-twelfth of an inch long, was still lodged in his body. The poison employed was said to be 'twice as deadly as cobra venom'. Markov was not the only expatriate enemy of the Bulgarian regime to be murdered in this fashion. Another case in Paris soon after demonstrated that Smersh, or its equivalent, was not just a figment of Ian Fleming's imagination.

1979: President Park Chung Hee of South Korea.

Shot dead during a political rally, after a series of attempts on his life launched from North Korea. The first of these was on 21 January 1968 when a North Korean commando team was wiped out by armed guards as it crept towards President Park's official residence. In August 1974, President Park was making a Liberation Day speech at an auditorium in Seoul when Mun Se Kwang, a Japanese-

Korean aged twenty-two, ran down an aisle and started
shooting at him. Park was saved on that occasion by a
quarter-inch-thick bullet-proof steel screen around his lec-
tern. Kwang had penetrated the security cordon by arriving
in a hired limousine. Security guards, assuming that he was
a VIP, waved him through their cordon. A confidential
US analysis of this attack observed that the President's
Protective Force had 'lots of fancy equipment and many
men on hand . . . but they did not react instantaneously
. . . All lights were focused on the stage, so guards were
blinded and unable to aim accurately . . .'

In 1983 an attempt by North Korean agents to kill
President Park's successor, President Chun Doo Hwan, was
launched on Burmese territory. A bomb in Rangoon killed
seventeen members of a visiting South Korean delegation,
but President Chun Doo Hwan survived by arriving late.

The North Korean attempts to destabilise South Korea
also included a bomb planted on board a KAL Boeing
airliner in 1987, killing 115 passengers. Officials in South
Korea added it to their register of 4,000 'provocations'
logged since the official end of the Korean war in 1953.

1979: Earl Mountbatten *et al.*

At mid-morning on 27 August Mountbatten sailed out of
the holiday fishing village of Mullaghmore on the coast of
Sligo in his 29-foot motor cruiser to lift lobster pots 200
yards offshore. With him were five members of his family.
They were his daughter Lady Patricia Brabourne; her husband Lord John Brabourne; Lord John's mother, the
Dowager Lady Doreen Brabourne, aged eighty-three; and
Mountbatten's twin grandsons, Timothy and Nicholas Brabourne, aged fourteen. As crew, the Earl had a fifteen-year-old
boy named Paul Maxwell, from Enniskillen, across the border.

An Irish police bodyguard of two men was left ashore to
watch them through binoculars from a car on the adjoining

coast road. As Mountbatten stopped the boat to lift the lobster pots an explosion caused by about five pounds of gelignite erupted almost under his feet. Mountbatten had recently asked for security around him to be reduced. As a result a twenty-four-hour guard had been removed from the boat, making it a soft target. The bomb, concealed somewhere between cockpit and engine, was detonated by a line-of-sight radio command sent from a device designed to control model aircraft in flight.

Everyone on board was blown high into the air, the blast tearing the clothes from their bodies. The dead were Mountbatten, Paul Maxwell and Nicholas Brabourne. The Dowager died soon afterwards. Lord and Lady Brabourne and their son Timothy survived in spite of serious injuries.

Lord Mountbatten was the first of a series of public figures to be attacked by death squads within a period of months. On 16 January 1981, a Republican socialist, Mrs Bernadette McAliskey (formerly Bernadette Devlin MP), was resuscitated by British troops after being shot at her home. Only five days passed before the Stormont Speaker, Sir Norman Strong, was gunned down in the library of his home. His son was murdered with him. On 15 November, the Rev. Robert Bradford MP (Unionist, S. Belfast) was murdered and his RUC bodyguard wounded.

The Mountbatten murder should have swept away any doubt that for the present generation of Irish Republicans, as for the Fenians a century earlier, members of the British royal family were now in the front line.

1981: Pope John Paul II.

In St Peter's Square, Rome, the Pope mingled with a crowd of well wishers among whom was a convicted Turkish murderer, Mehmet Ali Agca. Agca produced a Browning self-loading pistol and fired over several heads to hit the Pope. The first person to react was a nun, Suora Letizia, who snatched at the gunman's arm and hung on tenaciously as he shouted 'Not me!' He was arrested, tried and imprisoned. Rumours of a Bulgarian-inspired plot to murder the Pope because of the inspiration he gives to his fellow Poles and other East European Catholics have circulated ever since. In March 1986 three Bulgarians and three Turks were acquitted in Rome of conspiracy to kill the Pope on the grounds that 'there was not enough evidence to convict'.

The Pope, as God's representative for millions of Roman Catholics, is the most difficult man to persuade of the value of close protection. To make matters worse, he is an enthusiastic skier. A Pole who skis and happens to be Pope is not likely to heed warnings for his safety, even if they come from such a reliable source as the French intelligence organisation, SDECE. There is good reason to believe that the SDECE sent two representatives to the Vatican two weeks before Agca struck, to give warning of an impending attack. The Pope took it seriously but fatalistically. Conducting Mass a week before the incident he told his Swiss Guard, 'Let us pray that the Lord will keep violence and fanaticism far from the Vatican's walls.' There was nothing the guards could do when their man was exposed at close quarters to a throng of thousands of people, even a comparatively static and obedient throng. They must have felt that only luck, or providence, remained when, a year after Agca's attempt, a Spanish priest lunged at the still convalescent John Paul with a sixteen-inch bayonet. So in 1986, when a third attempt was made, the would-be assassin was not given the benefit of the doubt. Roberto Porfiri drove to the Pope's summer palace at Castel Gandolfo at 4 am and threw a parcel (later found to contain rubbish) at the gates with the cry, 'This present is for you and the Pope.' A police motor-cycle patrol chased his car twelve miles, and cornered him near Rome. Porfiri stepped out, brandishing an axe, and was shot dead by the police motor cyclists.

In 1987 yet another potential Papal assassin – a Turk named Samet Aslan – committed suicide in prison in the Eastern Turkish city of Agri. Aslan had been arrested on firearms charges during John Paul's visit to the Netherlands in 1985.

March 1981: President Ronald Reagan.

The President was shot at by John Hinkley as Reagan left a reception at the Washington Hilton hotel, and wounded in the shoulder by a ricochet from the armour-plating of the presidential limousine. His senior bodyguard, Special Agent-in-Charge Jerry Parr, noted droplets of blood near the President's mouth and in spite of the pandemonium around him instantly recognised it as bright, newly-oxygenated blood which might indicate lung damage. He promptly pushed Reagan into the limousine and rushed him to hospital, alerting a medical team by radio.

Parr's swift action arguably saved Reagan's life but because it was not publicly obvious – in contrast to Hinkley's attack – the Presidential Detail was criticised for failing to cope with the assassination attempt. In the confusion that followed, a less disciplined team might have shot innocent spectators. Instead they flattened the culprit and brought him to trial, causing no other casualties. A Secret Service agent later told the author: 'For perfect security we would like to keep the President in a totally sterile environment, away from the public. But the American people would not stand for that and nor would the President. We just do our best.'

Hinkley was tried and successfully pleaded – with the backing of expert psychiatric testimony – that he was not guilty by reason of insanity. In a case which bore similarities to those involving attempts against the life of Queen Victoria, the jury accepted Hinkley's plea. Five years later, Hinckley campaigned for his freedom, claiming he was now sane. A court rejected this but a year later, in 1987, psychiatrists at St Elizabeth's Mental Hospital, Virginia, gave him a twelve-hour leave pass. He drove with his parents to Fellowship House, a Christian mission for released prisoners, to eat chicken cordon bleu. Outside, a team of Secret Service agents waited grimly for him to eat up and return to hospital.

Elsewhere, political life continued as usual. On 19 May 1986, the President signed legislation to weaken the 1968 Gun Control Act by relaxing federal controls and allowing gun dealers to sell rifles and shotguns by mail order. The 1968 Act was passed after the murders that year of Martin Luther King and Senator Robert F. Kennedy. The new legislation was justified by the White House spokesman, Larry Speakes. He said that Mr Reagan believed that the new Bill stressed the necessity of protecting law-abiding citizens 'without diminishing the effectiveness of criminal law enforcement'. In 1988 Mr Speakes publicly confessed that he had manufactured certain quotations about other issues attributed by him to President Reagan.

1981: Iranian President Muhammed Ali Rajai and Prime Minister Muhammad Javad Bahonar.

Killed in Teheran bomb blast. This car bomb was attributed by the Iranian government to agents of the CIA. One unconfirmed newspaper report implied that it was set up in Saudi Arabia with the help of a British freelance. It is equally likely that the exiled Iranian Communist (Tudeh) movement, or even a faction of the Iranian National Guard, was responsible.

1981: President Anwar Sadat of Egypt.

Sadat once told his wife, 'No one will kill me, Jehan, unless it is the fundamentalists.' He had not expected to discover them in the army, which he had purged a month before.

He had too many enemies, after seeking an honourable peace with Israel. It was another case of 'Blessed – but dead – are the peacemakers . . .' When some of those enemies left military vehicles parading before him and hurled themselves at the lines of VIPs sitting in a vulnerable, ground-level reviewing stand there were no armed bodyguards to intervene and no screens to deflect the bullets. After the screams, 'Get down!' and the groans of the wounded, the President's wife was airlifted by helicopter to safety. She survived because her place, as a wife in Islam, was several rows back and twenty-five yards away from the target area. She remade her life in the United States, in a well protected house at Great Falls, Virginia, behind the security of chain fences and the presence of an Egyptian brigadier-general who acts as her bodyguard.

She is wise. The three sources of violent conflict in the Middle East – the war with Israel, Islamic fundamentalism and Arab rivalry for leadership in the region – have continued to claim prominent victims. These have included Bashir Gemayal, president-elect of Lebanon (killed by assassin's bomb, September 1982); former President Camille Chamoun (wounded by a car bomb, Beirut, January 1987); Lebanese Prime Minister Rashid Karami (killed by a helicopter bomb explosion in June 1987). A former aircraft mechanic was later arrested and detained in Sweden as a suspect in that death.

11 November 1982: Gervaise McKerr, Eugene Toman, Sean Burns.

All three were acknowledged IRA men. They were shot dead in a hailstorm of RUC gunfire after a car chase near Lurgan in Northern Ireland. The three were unarmed. The three police officers who shot them were charged with murder and acquitted. The dead men were linked, apparently on the word of an informer, with the landmine murder two weeks earlier of three other RUC officers. The killing of McKerr and his companions was later perceived by many people as the first clear use of an officially-sanctioned counter-assassination policy of 'shoot-to-kill'. Two weeks after the McKerr deaths seventeen-year-old Michael Tighe (a youth with no known political links) was shot dead in an isolated hayshed near Lurgan by another RUC team. With him was Martin McCauley, aged twenty-one, who was seriously wounded. Three antique Mauser rifles were also in the shed. McCauley was later convicted of possessing these weapons. On 12 December, two members of the left-wing republican INLA, Seamus Grew and Roddy Carroll, were shot dead by an RUC officer as they walked home. They, too, were unarmed.

In 1984, the deputy chief constable of Manchester, John Stalker, was asked to investigate fictitious cover stories about the killings fabricated by Special Branch officers. A year later, after he had filed an interim report to the Director of Public Prosecutions, Stalker was removed to face disciplinary charges which later proved groundless.

In January 1988, the Attorney-General, Sir Patrick Mayhew, confirmed that there was evidence that police officers had tried to pervert the course of justice, perjured themselves and obstructed other police inquiries into the six republican deaths, but he added that there would be no prosecutions in the interests of national security.

The impact of the affair was to give back to the IRA the credibility it had lost in the Enniskillen cenotaph massacre of November 1987. An immediate armed bodyguard was ordered to surround Sir Patrick Mayhew twenty-four hours a day.

1983: **Benigno Aquino**, leader of Philippine political opposition.

Aquino was shot in the head as he stepped on to Manila

airport from the aircraft which had brought him from exile in the US. The assassination triggered the overthrow of President Ferdinand Marcos and swept Aquino's widow to power in 1986. Officers loyal to Marcos claim that Aquino was murdered by a Communist assassin, Rolando Galman, whom soldiers shot dead immediately after Aquino's death. But five years later, it was the soldiers responsible for Aquino's security who were on trial for his murder.

1984: Mrs Indira Gandhi, Prime Minister of India.

Mrs Gandhi was assassinated by two Sikh bodyguards, both police officers. Her security was the responsibility of the Indian intelligence service but it is believed that she over-rode advice to replace 'her' Sikhs (see Part I). In the autumn of 1986, another Sikh opened fire on Mrs Gandhi's son and successor as Prime Minister, Rajiv Gandhi, as he arrived at an open-air prayer meeting. He was unhurt although six people nearby were wounded. The attacker used a worn-out revolver and a mix of incompatible ammunition. The first shot, fired as the Prime Minister arrived, went wide. The second, a misfire, struck a British cartridge without detonating it. The chamber revolved and the attacker pulled the trigger yet again, striking a shotgun-type cartridge containing pellets. This wounded six people.

The Indians looked again at their leader's close protection. Reforms had been made after Mrs Gandhi's death. Following the style increasingly adopted elsewhere, three layers of protection were created: the outer cordon, manned by local police; an inner line held by the Central Reserve police force, and a close protection team operating up to 100 yards from the Prime Minister. This group, officially known as the Special Protection Group, was nicknamed the 'Black Cats' after the dark jumpsuits worn by the men on duty. The Cats were under Defence Ministry control. It was expected that they would be taken over by the Prime

Minister's office. As an additional precaution, Rajiv Gandhi was advised not to announce his movements in advance and to continue to wear a bullet-proof waistcoat on public occasions (like so many American leaders). One eventuality not covered by India's threat evaluators was that any member of a guard of honour might try to club him with an unloaded, ceremonial rifle ... until this happened as he inspected Sri Lankan sailors in 1987. He was again lucky to escape without serious injury. His luck, if not his bodyguard, was catlike.

The effects of Sikh extremism were felt wherever there were Sikh communities, from Vancouver to Southall. In the UK, seven Sikh leaders were shot or stabbed to death between 1984 and 1987 in the struggle for mastery of Britain's 300,000 Sikhs. Such violence had immediately followed a Sikh rebellion against the Delhi government, provoking Indian forces into storming the Sikh Golden Temple in Amritsar, an operation planned by the Indian chief of staff, General Arun Vaidya. Mrs Gandhi was murdered in reprisal and in November 1986, General Vaidya was assassinated by four gunmen riding two motor-cycles. They overtook his car, shot him dead and sped off before Vaidya's own bodyguard, travelling in the back of his car, could draw his gun.

In Britain, meanwhile, police suspected that the deadly internecine rivalry was as much concerned with the vast funds flowing through 130 Sikh temples in the United Kingdom, as with doctrinal matters in the Punjab, 4,000 miles away.

1984: Mrs Margaret Thatcher, British Prime Minister, and other members of her government.
They were targets of an IRA bomb which destroyed the hotel in which members of the government were staying during the Conservative Party conference at Brighton (see

Part II). She survived in part because she was not in bed when the bomb exploded in the early hours as she had been sitting up late, putting the final touches to her big speech for later that day. After the shock of Mrs Gandhi's assassination and her own near-miss, Mrs Thatcher became even more wary. Security around her built up to a point not previously needed by a British Prime Minister, except in front line positions in time of war. Although (unlike Churchill) she did not carry her own gun, she was now accompanied by – among others – an armed woman officer of the Special Branch protection team. Mrs Thatcher still took calculated risks when this seemed necessary. In November 1987 she flew by helicopter to Enniskillen, Fermanagh, for the second cenotaph remembrance ceremony at which victims of the recent massacre were commemorated as well as war veterans. There had been no preliminary announcement of her visit. At any other time, use of a helicopter would have been prudent. But – following an intercepted arms shipment from Libya – it was now thought possible that the IRA might possess surface-to-air missiles capable of hitting a low-flying aircraft. Why none of these weapons had been used already was a mystery.

Threats to Mrs Thatcher had been growing sharply since the IRA hunger strike deaths of 1981, which she dismissed as the IRA's 'last card'. The first overt move was made that year by an 'A' level sociology student, Nigel Eastwood, aged eighteen. Armed with a twelve-inch knife, he eluded security staff at the Houses of Parliament and attacked a worker before he was overpowered. He was imprisoned for three years for trespass with intent to inflict grievous bodily harm on Mrs Thatcher, but acquitted of threatening to kill her.

1985: Gerard Hoarau, exiled Seychellois political leader. Hoarau was hit by automatic fire outside his home at Hornsey, North London, in an apparently professional assassination. It followed numerous threats and an earlier attempt to kill him. Hoarau had allegedly been plotting a coup to remove the Marxist President Albert René in 1982. A denial was made on René's behalf in 1987 that he had imported a team of Soviet bodyguards.

September 1985: Hugo Spadafora, opposition leader in Panama.

Reputedly murdered on the orders of General Manuel Noriega: tortured, sodomised and finally beheaded. This was one of several political murders in the Western hemisphere which are said to link unauthorised CIA operations in the Caribbean, and Central and South America with the drugs trade in exchange for political influence to suppress Communism in the region. A similar interface was traced by a British reporter, Susie Morgan, after she and others were blown up at a jungle press conference in Nicaragua on 30 May 1984. Three journalists died and seventeen were wounded, but the main target, the dissident Contra leader Eden Pastora, was unhurt. In 1988, the Reagan administration repudiated Noriega because of his alleged links with a powerful Colombian cocaine cartel.

January 1986: Politbureau chieftains of the People's Democracy of South Yemen (formerly Aden).

They were murdered by an armed gang representing President Ali Nasser Muhammed who charged into their meeting with guns blazing intent upon a massacre. The dead included the Vice-President, Ali Antar; the Defence Minister, Saleh Musleh Qassem and the former Interior Minister, Ali Shayi Hadi. In the resulting two-week civil war, 12,000 people died and Ali Nasser went into exile. A year later the Marxist state celebrated twenty years of 'freedom' from British rule, and tried to forget its own more recent history.

1986: Antonio da Empoli, Finance Minister of Italy.

Empoli dived for cover in time to save his life when the assassins came for him. He had stepped out of his car in Rome to buy a newspaper when the shooting started. His bodyguard, sitting at the driving wheel, drew a self-loading pistol. The assassin, a 28-year-old blonde named Vilma Monaco, ran up a grassy bank towards her getaway vehicle, a motor scooter. She tripped and fell and was an easy target for the bodyguard, who killed her without getting out of his car. Two men and another woman terrorist escaped by other means. All were part of a splinter group of the Red Brigades. In the war against terrorism it was one of the few successes by bodyguards achieved after the shooting started. It was also a reminder that radical, left-wing terrorism was still stalking the unwary in Europe.

1986: Olof Palme, Prime Minister of Sweden.

Palme was enjoying a night on the town with his wife, Lisbet, when he was shot dead by a single assassin as he crossed a street in central Stockholm. The assassin had shadowed the couple for more than four hours as they dined and strolled unaccompanied by a bodyguard. Palme was a marked man and he knew it. Swedish intelligence had warned him to take care after a series of assassinations in Sweden by fanatics belonging to a militant immigrant movement combining Turkish and Iraqi Kurds, known as the PKK. Palme's government had just refused an entry permit to one of the PKK's leaders. Inquiries into the murder rapidly led to conflict among competing security agencies. Twelve senior detectives – members of Stockholm's CID – resigned when they were ordered to limit or halt inquiries directed at Palme's extra-marital affairs. But there were as many theories and suspects as resignations from the police force. One of these linked the Chilean secret police, DINA (see Orlando Letelier, 1976 above), with Palme's death, asserting that the Pinochet government was angry about a diplomatic snub administered in 1980 by President Marcos of the Philippines but prompted by Olof Palme. Almost two years after Palme's assassination there was no convincing sign that the Swedish investigation was getting anywhere.

1987: Rudolf Hess.
Found dead at Spandau Prison, Berlin, where he was the sole prisoner. Initially it was believed that at the age of ninety-three Hitler's former deputy had strangled himself with a wire flex. Dr Hugh Thomas, a British Army surgeon who examined the body, was not convinced and in *Hess, A Tale Of Two Murders*, published in 1988, deployed (in the words of his publisher) 'extraordinary new evidence . . . that Hess did not commit suicide but was brutally murdered'.

If this were to prove the case, the event would provide a focal point for the small but influential and emergent generation of neo-Nazis in West Germany and elsewhere. Most causes benefit from a martyr and Hess's obstinate refusal to die in captivity had created its own legend before he expired, naturally or otherwise. The West German authorities took the murder allegation seriously and began a formal homicide investigation.

1987: Ali-Adhami, Arab expatriate cartoonist.
He was shot dead with one round by a Palestine Liberation Organisation assassin in Ives Street, Chelsea, London. Adhami had ignored PLO threats and published a cartoon identifying the alleged mistress of Yasser Arafat. In the ensuing police investigation an agent of the Israeli Secret Service, Mossad, who had penetrated a ring of PLO terrorists in London, was arrested and his cover inadvertently blown. The lesson was that Mossad probably knew more about this type of terrorism in London than the British Security Services. It was also a reminder that members of

Arafat's bodyguard, Force 17 (including an Englishman, Ian Davidson, now imprisoned in Cyprus for murder), were ready to double as assassins when called upon. Those who thought Britain's links with the grief of Palestine ended with British withdrawal in 1948 were obliged to reflect that the problem had followed them home to London after four decades.

1987: Captain Thomas Sankara, President of Burkino Faso (formerly Upper Volta).
Killed by allies of his boyhood friend and successor, Captain Blaise Compaore, in the fifth coup since the territory gained independence from France in 1960. Sankara gave the territory its new name, which means 'Land of the Dignified'. His bodyguard died with him.

November 1987: George Seawright, Loyalist extremist from Glasgow.
Expelled from Ian Paisley's Democratic Unionist Party for advising Belfast council to acquire an incinerator in which to burn Catholics and their priests, Seawright was shot and paralysed in Belfast by INLA, now renamed the Irish People's Liberation Organisation. It was one of a sharpening pattern of sectarian republican attacks, the ugliest of which was the murder of Protestant worshippers at the Enniskillen Cenotaph Remembrance Day service. During the year a total of eighty-seven lives were taken by sectarian killings in Northern Ireland.

December 1987: John McMichael, Second-in-Command, Ulster Defence Association (largest Loyalist paramilitary group in Northern Ireland).
He was blown up by a booby-trap bomb apparently linked to his car's ignition system outside his home at Lisburn, Northern Ireland, in December. McMichael was fanatically

cautious about his security, changing his car every two weeks and usually accompanied by a bodyguard. He was suspected of inspiring sectarian attacks on Catholics in Northern Ireland. Ironically, he was murdered soon after it seemed he was changing course politically, negotiating with Catholic leaders and advocating power-sharing. When the murder did not provoke a Protestant backlash, some security sources suggested that some of his own team might have colluded in his death. Belfast folk myth provides at least one precedent: Lennie Murphy, the Shankill Butcher, a psychopathic mass murderer who ran out of all political control and was set up for assassination by the Ulster Volunteer Force by the IRA in November 1982.

January 1988: Duchess of York.
In New York to see *The Phantom of the Opera*, she was the target for an attack by Michael Shanley, an IRA supporter demonstrating outside the hotel where the Duchess was staying. Shanley was armed with a six-foot wooden flag-pole. He was brought down by State Department body-guards before he could strike. A British official dismissed the incident as minor. Possibly he was unaware that Queen Victoria, during seven assassination attempts against her, suffered serious injury in only one case, in which the weapon used to batter her head was a cane. Before the attack, newspapers were speculating that the Duchess was pregnant for the first time. A few days after it, her condition was officially confirmed.

March 1988: Mairead Farrell; Daniel McCann; Sean Savage.
The three were members of an acknowledged IRA 'Active Service Unit' on a reconnaissance/bombing mission to Gibraltar, a British colony, when they were shot dead by an SAS team. The three were not carrying firearms. An initial

official claim that they had just left a car bomb near Gibraltar's public area, in anticipation of a ceremonial changing of the guard two days later, proved unfounded. A car had been left but it contained no bomb. A real car bomb was discovered later, parked in Spain where the local police, having noted that the three were using false passports, had tracked them for four months. To some people on both sides of the Irish Sea the deaths looked like another pre-emptive, officially approved counter-assassination.

The bodies were flown from Gibraltar to Dublin and driven ceremonially to Belfast. The RUC sent a message to the next-of-kin: 'We wish you to bury your dead in peace.' A new, low-profile policy of policing such funerals removed the RUC presence from Milltown Cemetery where many IRA dead are buried. On 16 March, as the Gibraltar Three were about to be interred, a lone assassin appeared among the mourners hurling hand grenades before he retreated, firing a pistol. Three people were killed in this incident and sixty injured. One of the dead, Kevin Brady, belonged to the IRA. The alleged assassin was said to be a maverick Catholic supporter of extreme Loyalists, who disowned him. He was beaten up by mourners before being arrested by the RUC and charged with murder.

Three days later, on 19 March, another unpoliced funeral cortège moved from Andersonstown towards Milltown Cemetery with the body of Brady. It was a more than usually tense occasion in view of the grenade attack which had killed Brady. When a civilian car carrying two men in civilian clothes approached the cortège at speed, the crowd sensed another impending attack. The car was stopped and two men inside rapidly identified as British soldiers, not paramilitary irregulars. The two – Royal Signals Corporals Derek Wood and David Howes – were lynched and assassinated with their own pistols. Their restraint in not driving their vehicle indiscriminately through the cortège,

or shooting recklessly into the crowd around them, contrib-
uted as much to their own deaths as did their original error
in driving into the area. The lynching, if not the murders,
was recorded by television cameras and transmitted live to
horrify a world which had thought itself hardened to Irish
brutality.

The soldiers' deaths (which among the Irish, had the
victims been Irish, would qualify as 'martyrdom') did much
to restore the political and diplomatic relationship between
London and Dublin which had been badly damaged by the
Stalker affair. Proposals to invest heavily in Republican West
Belfast, supported by Dublin but not much to the liking of
the Northern Ireland Office in London, suddenly enjoyed
British support. The new mood was one in which there was
recognition that something had to be done to reduce the
deprivation and isolation of the IRA's principal ghetto.

29 March 1988: Dulcie September, African National Congress representative, Paris.
Ms September, aged forty-five, was shot dead at point-blank
range as she arrived at the office of the ANC on the fourth
floor of a building near the Gare de l'Est. Six .22 cartridges
were lying on the landing. Her key was still in the door and
she was still holding the morning post. Police described the
killing as the work of a professional who had waited for
her to arrive.

According to her friends she had asked for police protection after receiving threats but was told by the French
government to stop her political activities first. In Britain a
Labour MP, David Winnick, suggested that a South African
murder squad might be responsible for the assassination.
South Africa's Foreign Minister, R. F. Botha, denied this.
He hinted that 'serious differences' within the ANC were
the cause. While unconfirmed French reports alleged that
an assassination team known as the 'Z Squad' had done

the job before fleeing to London, Scotland Yard warned ANC representatives in London that they, too, might be targets. The practical effect of that advice was not immediately clear.

CONCLUSION

1688 And All That –
A Licence to Kill?

It is fashionable in 1988 to defend NATO's nuclear deterrent in Europe by reminding critics of that strategy that there has been no war in Europe for forty-three years. That is true, but only up to a point. One of the lessons of this book is that while officially-declared warfare might be held in check by the fear of Armageddon, armed conflict of another sort continues.

There is an obvious explanation of this apparent paradox. When Armageddon happens everyone dies, from ageing heads of state to their unborn great-grandchildren. There are no winners. But irregular warfare ('low-intensity conflict' in military jargon) permits the participant to nourish the hope that he or she will survive to see it all on television in domestic comfort.

In the years since the Second World War ended terrorism has become a routine form of conflict in which there is no Geneva Convention to limit the cruelty and in which there is little to distinguish warrior from criminal. To begin with, however, this conflict appeared to be something else. The university sit-ins and street demos of the 1960s seemed to be nothing more sinister than intellectual horseplay in a good cause, such as an end to the Vietnamese war or to housing and job discrimination in Ulster.

The year in which the horseplay took a sinister turn was 1968. In Berlin, Paris, Belfast and Derry middle-class students professing universal love and non-violence took their firebomb recipes from the *Anarchists' Cook Book* and laced their petrol bombs with detergent to create a sticky, napalm effect. In Newry one day, by way of a change, student members of the People's Democracy movement rolled blazing buses down the hill towards a cordon of policemen who were not, that day, looking for trouble.

The first British soldier to be murdered was Gunner Robert Curtis, aged twenty, on the night of 6 February 1971. By then, the Baader-Meinhof Group in West Germany, the Weathermen in the USA, the Japanese Red Army and the Angry Brigade in Britain were all flexing their muscles. All, as Wilkinson (op. cit.) has noted, were 'the spoilt children of affluence' rather than victims of deprivation.

There seemed to be a lot of spoilt children at large and they were, in a sense, born at the wrong time. In the northern hemisphere, after the defeat of German and Japanese Fascism, there seemed to be no great causes to die for and even war itself was off-limits. Instead there was nothing but dreary old social democracy in which discussion and voting and other sedentary, middle-aged practices counted for more than the youthful, martial virtues of the 1940s and 50s.

What the leaders of the spoilt generation could not improve upon or rival by their own creativity, they would seek to destroy. What else was there to do with all that youthful energy? And anyway, one got noticed. Most people in the media (including the author, then Chief Reporter of the *Sunday Times*) were, it must be confessed, too indulgent of their tantrums, too ready to be seduced by the glamour of these pretty young animals, whether in the Paris Sorbonne or Queen's University, Belfast, to observe their true nature. This was an instinct to reject existing culture in favour of barbarism, but a barbarism made comfortable by the automobile, the microwave oven, the vibro-massager and any other consumer goodies that organised society had to offer.

Through the 1970s, terrorism grew into an internationally-financed industry in which careers were to be made, largely financed by funds from the Middle East, using weapons from Eastern Europe. Soon the paymasters of terrorism were not content to leave the public play to middle-class Westerners. They sent their own 'soldiers' to Europe and America to demonstrate that the sword is mightier than the pen.

Democratic governments evolved their own special forces to meet the threat (forces such as the SAS counter-terrorist team) whose legitimacy was promptly challenged by the defenders of democracy in the media. The democracies even banded together – as in the Anglo-German assault on a hijacked Lufthansa aircraft at Mogadishu in 1977 – to fight this new, bewildering form of warfare without frontiers. It is easily forgotten now that one of the architects of that policy was James (later Lord) Callaghan in his days as Prime Minister.

From the big, set-piece spectacles of theatrical terror such as the Munich Olympics massacre of 1972 and the OPEC conference hijack of 1975 (which commanded television audiences running into hundreds of millions of people but were also counter-productive in winning sympathy for the cause), the revolutionaries turned – or, rather, groping for a new strategy, discovered – kidnap. When it became clear in the 1980s that this strategy had also failed to destabilise society they chose the weapon of assassination. The clock had now turned back a century to the heyday of political murder as practised by anarchists and nihilists, with the difference that the Habsburgs and the Romanoffs were no longer available as targets, having long since been removed.

In Ireland, a similar tactical change could be observed.

The great street battles of the 1970s were replaced in the 1980s by selective assassination plus occasional sectarian atrocities such as the Enniskillen cenotaph bomb of 1987, whose only purpose must have been to precipitate the long-threatened 'Protestant backlash' and a Beirut-style civil war.

Democratic government was somewhat slow to react but the response – led by the bodyguard skilled in every aspect of security and armed with every weapon of psychology and electronics, as well as his own intelligence and courage – is gaining momentum. Until 1958, as the *Guardian*'s writer Richard Norton-Taylor recently pointed out, Special Branch was run exclusively by the Metropolitan Police in London. Now all provincial forces have their own Branch units and at least 1,800 Special Branch officers are based outside the capital. Many of these are concerned, one way or another, with keeping legitimate politicians alive. Provincial forces have also (as in Wiltshire) trained their own specialists to guard political VIPs living or speaking in their parishes.

This process is not without its growing pains. At the operational end, not all new bodyguards are able to cope with the combination of stress and boredom that makes the job uniquely difficult. In Wiltshire in 1987 two officers belonging to the close protection team of the Ulster Secretary, Tom King, were returned to uniformed duties when they were found to be five miles away from their post at Mr King's country home. (One of the officers was visiting a lady friend while his partner waited in their unmarked car nearby.)

A more spectacular failure, in 1986, turned an experienced detective-sergeant into a criminal. Graham Sayer, a member of the Thames Valley police, was tasked with 'minding' Roger Dennhart, a professional armed robber turned police informer. Sayer later told a jury at his own trial: 'I felt my life was not my own and my private life was crumbling.'

There are many bodyguards including those on royal or political duty who will say 'Amen' to that. But Sayer did not choose a sound solution to his problem. Having discovered that his criminal companion was not a reformed character after all, he remarkably agreed to join the robber Dennhart in his next great adventure, a £307,000 shotgun robbery at a Mansfield post office. Dennhart and the money then disappeared and Sayer, the police bodyguard, went to prison.

We shall be hearing more of such problems in future but they are essentially domestic, if newsworthy. Certainly they are of less public significance than the impact of armed close protection on the way democratic society is governed and runs its daily affairs. The United States, a gun-loving society, pays the price of familiarity with the process. It has to live with an enormous number of firearms casualties each year, thousands of which are accidental and self-inflicted. (There were 1,600 deaths from this source in the US in 1984.) In Britain, the phenomenon is likely to grow as more guns come into circulation domestically and politically. In 1988, Marion Montgomery, an American singer living in England, was fined for possession of an unlicensed revolver. The fact that she had the gun came to light when her domestic help's boy friend discovered the gun and – without the owner's knowledge – played Russian roulette with it, killing himself.

In another accident, soon afterwards, a police marksman on a roof at Leeds-Bradford Airport inadvertently fired his rifle as the Prime Minister's jet was taking off for London. Episodes of this sort and the casualties which sometimes result are as obvious as a bloodstain and just as easy to comprehend. They will increase. What is less evident is the damage done to the fabric of a democratic society by the need for more firepower, and what that need implies. In Britain, where there is no traditional right to carry and bear arms freely, the acceptance of the armed official bodyguard comes less easily than in the US or, for that matter, Ireland.

Resistance to the trend will come, as it always did, from the royal family. The attitude of Queen Victoria (that dissuasion of a potential assassin by deterrent law was better than expecting the monarch to hide like a fugitive in Buckingham Palace) may be discovered, for example, in the last days of her grandson, Earl Mountbatten. He put his Garda protection team ashore with the comment, 'Whoever would want to murder an old man like me?', ignoring warnings from friends on both sides of the Irish Sea about the risk he was taking. Instead, he made preparations, in consultation with the Queen, for a funeral – his own – at which 'everyone should be jolly'.

Politicians, as we have observed, do not have to stay behind a protective screen like exotic zoo animals as a way of life from cradle to grave, as do monarchs and those close to them. They enter the cage voluntarily, for a limited time. Mrs Thatcher – witness the comments of Roger Stott MP, quoted in Chapter 6 – took vigorous steps to improve her personal security from the moment she was elected Prime Minister in 1979. This was five years before the IRA attempt to kill her at Brighton but only a few months after her personal aide, Airey Neave MP, had been blown up within the Palace of Westminster.

One of the consistent lessons of this history is that those VIPs who shrug off attempts to protect them from an assassin are virtual accomplices in their own murders. Fatalism is a narcotic, not a prophylactic. The problem facing British democracy, after twenty years of modern terrorism and almost a decade of Thatcherism, is how to protect the constitutional leader without causing real, if unseen, damage to the constitution.

As it happens, 1988 is the tercentenary of that Glorious Revolution which made the royal prerogative subject to parliamentary control, underpinning all the freedoms obtained since the Magna Carta. An increasing number of legal and academic authorities are now calling into question the extent to which the unwritten rights of the British Constitution still hold good and function dynamically within a system of checks and balances between one centre of power and another.

One of these critics is Lord Scarman, who wants a Bill of Rights. Another is Patrick McAuslan, Professor of Public Law at the London School of Economics. He makes a direct link between the arbitrary use of the royal prerogative (by Downing Street, not the Palace, which is a servant of elected government) to enhance security while undermining the constitution. In an article in the *Independent* in January 1988, McAuslan drew attention to an 'unusual use of prerogative powers . . . sanctioned by the courts'.

In 1986, McAuslan recalled, the Home Secretary had invited chief constables to 'go behind the backs of their police authorities and obtain the support of HM Inspector of Constabulary to try and bounce the authorities into agreeing to the chief constables' stocking supplies of plastic bullets and CS gas'. If any authority was unwilling to allow such stocks to be held, the Home Office would supply them all the same.

When one authority – Northumbria – challenged the lawfulness of this circular, both the Divisional Court and the Court of Appeal found it to be within the law. 'The proposed action was justified as being an exercise of power under the royal prerogative: the prerogative of the maintenance of peace within the kingdom.'

As Professor McAuslan's expert eye read this judgement, it could be a licence to kill. As he puts it: 'Officers of the security services could even be empowered to kill their fellow citizens, for one aspect of the royal prerogative is the defence of the realm ... If there were any doubt, it should have been dispelled by the decision ... not to prosecute police officers who covered up unlawful killings in Northern Ireland. National security considerations were cited by the Attorney General as one reason for this.'

Such a state of affairs, he concluded, was not consistent 'with any notion of constitutional democracy under the rule of law ... It is indeed alarming that exactly 300 years after the Glorious Revolution, the executive is reviving the use of the prerogative to extend its power over the citizenry.'

Most dictators depend upon cohorts of bodyguards. So, at times of great and unusual peril, do some democratically elected leaders. But the greatly increased use of armed bodyguards in British public life, as described in this history, can only be made respectable in the long run if the constitution itself is seen to be above suspicion, particularly where matters of national security are concerned. Otherwise an increasing number of authoritative voices will be heard questioning the sincerity of British democracy as it has evolved in recent years, and terrorism will have scored the great psychological victory it has sought over government by consent for the last century. Terrorists have a vested interest in proving that democracy and the rule of law are fraudulent. If armed guards are necessary in a free society (and they are in response to terrorism) then the justification of their firepower must rest upon more than an arbitrary power such as a prerogative, royal or otherwise.

BIBLIOGRAPHY

Allason, Rupert: *The Branch* (Secker and Warburg, 1983)

Allen, Woody: *Getting Even* (Random House, 1971)

Bles, Mark and Low, Robert: *The Kidnap Business* (Pelham, 1987)

Brust, Harold: *In Plain Clothes: Further Memories of a Political Police Officer* (Stanley Paul, 1937)

Bunyan, Tony: *The Political Police in Britain* (Julian Friedmann, 1976)

Camellion, Richard: *Assassination Theory and Practice* (Paladin, 1977)

Cassar, George H.: *Kitchener: Architect of Victory* (William Kimber, 1977)

Churchill, Winston S.: *The Gathering Storm* (Cassell, 1948)

Clayton, Tim: *The Protectors* (Oldbourne, 1967)

Collins, Larry and Lapierre, Dominique: *O Jerusalem* (Granada, 1972)

Coogan, Tim Pat: *The IRA* (Pall Mall, 1970)

Courtney, Nicholas: *Princess Anne* (Weidenfeld, 1986)

Dickson, John: *Murder Without Conviction* (Sidgwick and Jackson, 1986)

Didion, Joan: *Miami* (Weidenfeld, 1988)

Dillon, Martin and Lehane, Denis: *Political Murder in Northern Ireland* (Penguin, 1973)

Ewart-Biggs, Jane: *Pay, Pack and Follow* (Weidenfeld, 1984)

Frazer, J. G.: *The Golden Bough* (Macmillan, 1900)

Fulford, Roger: *Votes for Women* (Faber, 1956)

Gay, John: *The Beggar's Opera*

Geraghty, Tony: *Who Dares Wins: History of the Special Air Service* (Arms and Armour Press, 1980; Fontana, 1983)

Gould, Robert and Waldren, Michael: *London's Armed Police* (Arms and Armour Press, 1986) de Graaf, Janny and Schmid, Alex P.: *Violence as Communication* (SAGE Publications, 1982)

Gravel, Senator M. and Others: *The Pentagon Papers* (Beacon Press, Boston, 1971)

Hirst, David: *The Gun and the Olive Branch* (Faber, 1977)

Home, William Douglas (ed): *The Prime Ministers* (W. H. Allen, 1987)

Hough, Richard: *Mountbatten: Hero of Our Time* (Weidenfeld, 1980)

Hurt, Henry: *Reasonable Doubt – An Investigation into the Assassination of John F. Kennedy* (Sidgwick & Jackson, 1985)

Jackson, Geoffrey: *People's Prison* (Faber, 1973)

Jennings, Ivor: *The Sedition Bill Explained* (1934) (Quoted in Bunyan, op. cit.)

Johnson, Paul: *A History of the Modern World* (Weidenfeld, 1983)

Landstrom, Aage: *Death of a Mediator* (Institute for Palestine Studies, Beirut, 1968)

Laqueur, Walter: *Terrorism* (Weidenfeld, 1977)

Lesberg, Sandy: *Assassination in Our Time* (Peebles Press International, London, New York, 1976)

Longford, Elizabeth: *Victoria RI* (Weidenfeld, 1964)

Magnus, P.: *King Edward the Seventh* (John Murray, London, 1964)

Manchester, William: *The Death of a President* (Michael Joseph, 1967)

Marshal, Dorothy: *The Life and Times of Victoria* (Weidenfeld, 1972)

Martin, Theodore: *Life of the Prince Consort* (Smith and Elder, 1882)

Masefield, John: *The Rider At The Gate*, Collected Poems (Heinemann, 1946)

Milne, Hugh: *Bhagwan, The God that Failed* (Caliban, 1986)

Oates, Stephen B.: *Let the Trumpet Sound* (Search Press, 1982)

Oates, Stephen B.: *With Malice Toward None* (Allen and Unwin, 1977)

Paine, Lauran: *The Assassins* (Hale, 1975)

Pankhurst, Sylvia: *The Suffragette Movement* (Virago, 1977)

Patrick, Derrick: *Fetch Felix – The Fight Against Ulster Bombers, 1976–77* (Hamish Hamilton, 1981)

Restak, Richard M.: article in *Science Digest*, December 1981

Royal Archives

Speidel, Hans: *Invasion 1944* (Tubingen, 1961)

Taylor, A. J. P.: *English History 1914–45* (O.U.P., 1965)

Thomas, Dr Hugh: *Hess – A Tale of Two Murders* (Hodder, 1988)

Thompson, Leroy: *Dead Clients Don't Pay: The Bodyguard's Manual* (Paladin, 1984)

Thompson, W. H.: *I Was Churchill's Shadow* (Christopher Johnson, 1951)

Trevor-Roper, H. R.: *The Last Days of Hitler* (Macmillan, 1947)

Queen Victoria's Journal

Watson, Peter: *War on the Mind* (Hutchinson, 1978)

Wilkinson, George: *Special Branch Officer* (Odhams, 1956)

Wilkinson, Paul: *Terrorism and the Liberal State* (Macmillan, 1986)

HRH Duke of Windsor: *A King's Story* (Cassell, 1951)

Woodhall, Edwin T.: *Guardians of the Great* (Blandford, 1934)

Zimmerman, Tim: 'The American Bombing of Libya – A success for coercive diplomacy?' (International Institute for Strategic Studies, *Survival*, May/June 1987)

INDEX